THE
BOOK OF DANIEL

the Smart Guide to the Bible™ series

BE SMART · BE INSPIRED

Daymond Duck

Larry Richards, General Editor

Published by
THOMAS NELSON™
Since 1798

www.thomasnelson.com

The Book of Daniel
The Smart Guide to the Bible™ Series
Copyright © 2007 by GRQ, Inc.

Published in Nashville, TN by Thomas Nelson. Thomas Nelson is a trademark of Thomas Nelson, Inc.

Thomas Nelson, Inc. titles may be purchased in bulk for educational, business, fundraising, or sales promotional use. For information, please email SpecialMarkets@ThomasNelson.com.

Originally published by Starburst Publishers under the title *Daniel: God's Word for the Biblically-Inept*. Now revised and updated.

Scripture quotations are taken from The New King James Version® (NKJV), copyright 1979, 1980, 1982, 1992 Thomas Nelson, Inc., Publishers.

To the best of its ability, GRQ, Inc. has strived to find the source of all material. If there has been an oversight, please contact us, and we will make any correction deemed necessary in future printings. We also declare that to the best of our knowledge all material (quoted or not) contained herein is accurate, and we shall not be held liable for the same.

General Editor: Larry Richards
Managing Editor: Lila Empson
Associate Editor: W. Mark Whitlock
Scripture Editor: Deborah Wiseman
Assistant Editor: Amy Clark
Design: Diane Whisner

ISBN-10: 1-4185-0998-1
ISBN-13: 978-1-4185-0998-9

Printed in the United States of America
HB 01.13.2020

Introduction

Welcome to *The Book of Daniel—The Smart Guide to the Bible™*, which presents the Scriptures in a new, easy-to-follow format. Understanding Bible prophecy is often very difficult. The same can be said about understanding what the Old Testament writers said, especially the one called Daniel. What they are saying is not always clear. So we have created this new series because we want to present the latest and most accurate scholarship in a style that is true to the text but fun to read.

To Gain Your Confidence

The Book of Daniel—The Smart Guide to the Bible™ is for those who are not interested in all that complicated stuff. You can be sure that I have tried to take an educational approach, but much effort has gone into keeping things simple.

In Revelation, Jesus promised a blessing to all those who read, hear, and keep those things written (Revelation 1:3). He also promised a curse on all those who add to or take away from it (Revelation 22:18–19). I am sure that God also intended this same blessing and curse for the book of Daniel, so I take them seriously and have undertaken this project with great care. To help explain things in the book of Daniel I will use the age-old Golden Rule of Interpretation that states: When the plain sense of Scripture makes common sense, seek no other sense. . . . The Bible explains itself. You don't need to go anywhere else. That is why I have included other verses of Scripture from the Bible to explain difficult areas of the book of Daniel.

A Word About the Bible

The Bible is divided into two major sections called the "Old" Testament and the "New" Testament. The word *Testament* means "covenant." The Old Testament deals with the "old covenant" that God had with his Hebrew people, the Jews. The New Testament deals with the "new covenant" that God has with all people.

The Old Testament is the first, oldest, and longest section of the Bible. It contains 39 books that were written over a period of about 1,500 years. The New Testament is the second, newest, and shortest section of the Bible. It contains 27 books that were written over a period of fewer than 100 years. All the books in the Bible were written by men, but the source of their writings was God. Men wrote what God inspired them to write—nothing more and nothing less. For this reason the entire Bible is called the Word of God.

Why Study Daniel?

The book of Daniel is the only apocalyptic book in the Old Testament. The word *apocalyptic* comes from the Greek word *apocalypse*, which means "revelation" or "uncovering of something hidden." Daniel is the book of revelation in the Old Testament (Revelation is the only apocalyptic book in the New Testament), and it may well be the greatest "prophetic" (what will happen in the future) book in the entire Bible.

More and more it seems like we are living in perilous times. The revelations found in the book of Daniel are of particular interest today because they prophesy world events that are now coming to pass, and world events that will signal the Tribulation Period, the Second Coming of Christ, and the arrival of God's Millennium.

There is much to learn from the life of Daniel. Daniel had to endure trials just like all of us, but he knew his God was always in control. In him alone Daniel put his trust, and because of his faithfulness he prospered. He was a man of faith and prayer; a man of intelligence and wisdom; a man of courage and humility, and a man we can learn much from. Here are six good reasons to study the book of Daniel:

1. It is part of the Word of God (the Bible).

2. It teaches us many things about God, politics, and faith.

3. Jesus said Daniel was a prophet (Matthew 24:15), and we are to listen to God's prophets.

4. It accurately revealed many things about the past, present, and future.

5. Because so much of the book of Daniel has accurately been fulfilled, we can logically expect the rest to be fulfilled.

6. It gives us details not found in any other book of the Bible.

How to Study Daniel

As you study the book of Daniel, keep in mind it has two main sections:

Chapters 1–6 (Part One) are *historic* in nature and are called "Events in the Lives of Daniel and His Friends." These chapters show how Daniel and his friends survived in a pagan society by trusting in their God. The message for all of us is that we can do the same. It is more important to obey God than it is to obey man.

Chapters 7–12 (Part Two) are *prophetic* in nature and are called "Daniel's Prophecies." These chapters cover some very interesting things about the future, and we see some of these future events coming on the scene today.

Also Keep in Mind Four Other Main Points:

1. The theme of the book of Daniel is the sovereignty of God. No matter who rules on earth, God has the final say.

2. Some things in the book of Daniel are sealed (hidden away). The book is protected by God and not everything in it will be fully understood until the End of the Age (the Tribulation Period). Remember, "the main things are the plain things, and the plain things are the main things."

3. Daniel's main focus is the Jews. He ignores the Church (the followers of Jesus Christ).

4. What Daniel prophesies about the end times is often explained by other books in the Bible, particularly Revelation.

Which Book Should I Study?

You need to study both Revelation and the book of Daniel to have a good understanding of Bible prophecy. They are like Siamese twins; joined together, but different. Their subjects are similar, but each book contains details not found in the other book. They are the two most important prophetic books in the Bible and together they reveal more information about the closing scenes of this age than any other portion of the Bible. Here are just a few reasons why this is true:

1. The book of Daniel accurately reveals the First Coming of Jesus, his death, and the destruction of Israel, Jerusalem, and the Temple. Revelation begins with events that will take place after these.

2. The book of Daniel gives an outline of world history from King Nebuchadnezzar to the First Coming of Jesus not found in Revelation. But Revelation gives an outline of what will happen after the Second Coming of Jesus not found in the book of Daniel.

3. The book of Daniel will be helpful to those who miss the Rapture to know how to identify the beginning of the Tribulation Period, what group of nations will rule the world, and who will be their last leader.

4. The book of Daniel gives us a clearer understanding of God's ability to protect the Jews than any other book in the Bible.

5. The book of Daniel gives us information about the influence of evil spirits on nations and their leaders.

6. The book of Daniel gives us the skeleton of the end times (an outline). Revelation gives us the flesh (many of the details). They combine to give us a more complete picture.

The books of Daniel and Revelation enhance each other. They are like the bookends of prophecy. Each book will help you understand the other, as well as all the other prophetic books in the Bible. How amazing to have two different books, written by two different authors hundreds of years apart, that are in complete agreement with each other.

Who Wrote Daniel?

Prophecy experts do not believe it was a fictitious Daniel as many critics claim. We still think the entire book of Daniel was written by the real Daniel who lived about 600 years before the birth of Christ. He was a member of the royal family of Israel and was captured by King Nebuchadnezzar as a teenager, carried off to Babylon, and trained to serve in the king's palace. He was a brilliant and godly man who, because of his faithfulness, was given special insight and visions by God.

Symbols, Symbols, and More Symbols

The book of Daniel is filled with symbols because Daniel had several visions of the future. Depending upon the Bible translation we use, the singular word *vision* occurs about twenty-two times and the plural word *visions* occurs about ten times. King Nebuchadnezzar's dreams and Daniel's visions were pictures or symbols of things to come. God chose to do it this way so Nebuchadnezzar would have to rely upon Daniel for help, and to keep many future events sealed up until the End of the Age. As you read this book you will find that the unsealing has begun. We do not fully understand all of the symbols, but we now know what most of them mean.

So Many Critics and Different Viewpoints

Critics have spent an incredible amount of energy questioning the authenticity and historicity of the book of Daniel. According to some, the miracles in the book of Daniel, such as the deliverance of Shadrach, Meshach, and Abed-Nego from the fiery furnace, could not have happened; prophesying the future is impossible; and there is no evidence that many of the events found in the book of Daniel ever occurred. But these same critics have not been able to prove their claims, and their efforts to discredit the book of Daniel have only resulted in embarrassment to themselves and their faulty brand of reasoning. The surprising thing is not that some keep trying to destroy this book, but rather that their record of failure is so long. Let's study the book of Daniel with confidence and leave the critics to face the God who revealed it.

A Word About Dates

Many experts have differing opinions about dates in the book of Daniel. Variations of one to two years in some cases are not uncommon. But archaeologists keep making new discoveries so that many of the dates are now known and thought to be accurate. Where discrepancies occur the most commonly recognized date is given.

About the Author

Daymond is the best-selling author of *On the Brink, An Easy-to-Understand End-Time Bible Prophecy, The Book of Revelation—The Smart Guide to the Bible™ series, The Book of Daniel—The Smart Guide to the Bible™ series,* and *Prophecies of the Bible—The Smart Guide to the Bible™ series.* He is the coauthor of *The End-Times Survival Handbook.* And he is a contributing author to *Forewarning—The Approaching Battle Between Good and Evil; Foreshadows of Wrath and Redemption; Piercing the Future—Prophecy and the New Millennium;* and *Prophecy at Ground Zero.*

Daymond worked his way through college and graduated from the University of Tennessee with a B.S. in agricultural engineering. In 1979, at the age of forty, he entered the ministry and became a bi-vocational pastor. He completed the five-year Course-of-Study Program at Emory University for United Methodist Pastors. He has twice served as honorary state chaplain for the Tennessee Rural Carriers, is a prophecy conference speaker, and is a member of the Pre-Trib Study Group in Arlington, Texas. Daymond and his wife, Rachel, make their home in Dyer, Tennessee. They have three children and five grandchildren.

About the General Editor

Dr. Larry Richards is a native of Michigan who now lives in Raleigh, North Carolina. He was converted while in the Navy in the 1950s. Larry has taught and written Sunday school curriculum for every age-group, from nursery through adult. He has published more than two hundred books that have been translated into twenty-six languages. His wife, Sue, is also an author. They both enjoy teaching Bible studies as well as fishing and playing golf.

Understanding the Bible Is Easy with These Tools

To understand God's Word you need easy-to-use study tools right where you need them—at your fingertips. The *Smart Guide to the Bible*™ series puts valuable resources adjacent to the text to save you both time and effort.

Every page features handy sidebars filled with icons and helpful information: cross references for additional insights, definitions of key words and concepts, brief commentaries from experts on the topic, points to ponder, evidence of God at work, the big picture of how passages fit into the context of the entire Bible, practical tips for applying biblical truths to every area of your life, and plenty of maps, charts, and illustrations. A wrap-up of each passage, combined with study questions, concludes each chapter.

These helpful tools show you what to watch for. Look them over to become familiar with them, and then turn to Chapter 1 with complete confidence: You are about to increase your knowledge of God's Word!

Study Helps

The thought-bubble icon alerts you to commentary you might find particularly thought-provoking, challenging, or encouraging. You'll want to take a moment to reflect on it and consider the implications for your life.

Don't miss this point! The exclamation-point icon draws your attention to a key point in the text and emphasizes important biblical truths and facts.

death on the cross
Colossians 1:21, 22

Many see Boaz as a type of Jesus Christ. To win back what we human beings lost through sin and spiritual death, Jesus had to become human (i.e., he had to become a true kinsman), and he had to be willing to pay the penalty for our sins. With his <u>death on the cross</u>, Jesus paid the penalty and won freedom and eternal life for us.

The additional Bible verses add scriptural support for the passage you just read and help you better understand the <u>underlined text</u>. (Think of it as an instant reference resource!)

How does what you just read apply to your life? The heart icon indicates that you're about to find out! These practical tips speak to your mind, heart, body, and soul, and offer clear guidelines for living a righteous and joy-filled life, establishing priorities, maintaining healthy relationships, persevering through challenges, and more.

This icon reveals how God is truly all-knowing and all-powerful. The hourglass icon points to a specific example of the prediction of an event or the fulfillment of a prediction. See how some of what God has said would come to pass already has!

What are some of the great things God has done? The traffic-sign icon shows you how God has used miracles, special acts, promises, and covenants throughout history to draw people to him.

Does the story or event you just read about appear elsewhere in the Gospels? The cross icon points you to those instances where the same story appears in other Gospel locations—further proof of the accuracy and truth of Jesus' life, death, and resurrection.

Since God created marriage, there's no better person to turn to for advice. The double-ring icon points out biblical insights and tips for strengthening your marriage.

The Bible is filled with wisdom about raising a godly family and enjoying your spiritual family in Christ. The family icon gives you ideas for building up your home and helping your family grow close and strong.

Isle of Patmos
a small island in the
Mediterranean Sea

something significant had occurred, he wrote down the substance of what he saw. This is the practice John followed when he recorded Revelation on the **Isle of Patmos.**

What does that word really mean, especially as it relates to this passage? Important, misunderstood, or infrequently used words are set in **bold type** in your text so you can immediately glance at the margin for definition. This valuable feature lets you better understand the meaning of the entire passage without having to stop to check other references.

the big picture

Joshua
Led by Joshua, the Israelites crossed the Jordan River and invaded Canaan (see Illustration #8). In a series of military campaigns the Israelites defeated several coalition armies raised by the inhabitants of Canaan. With organized resistance put down, Joshua divided the land among the twelve Israelite

How does what you read fit in with the greater biblical story? The highlighted big picture summarizes the passage under discussion.

what others say

David Breese
Nothing is clearer in the Word of God than the fact that God wants us to understand himself and his working in the lives of men.[5]

It can be helpful to know what others say on the topic, and the highlighted quotation introduces another voice in the discussion. This resource enables you to read other opinions and perspectives.

Maps, charts, and illustrations pictorially represent ancient artifacts and show where and how stories and events took place. They enable you to better understand important empires, learn your way around villages and temples, see where major battles occurred, and follow the journeys of God's people. You'll find these graphics let you do more than study God's Word—they let you *experience* it.

Chapters at a Glance

INTRODUCTION iii

PART ONE: Events in the Lives of Daniel and His Friends

CHAPTER 1: DANIEL 1—DANIEL AS A TEENAGE CAPTIVE 3
His Characteristics 4
His Capture 10
His Commitment 14

CHAPTER 2: DANIEL 2—NEBUCHADNEZZAR'S
DISTURBING DREAM 25
His Request 28
His Temper 30
Daniel's Request 35
Daniel's Interpretation 44

CHAPTER 3: Daniel 3—DANIEL'S FRIENDS AND THE
FIERY FURNACE 63
The Image of Gold 64
The Three Jews and the Fiery Furnace 80

CHAPTER 4: DANIEL 4—NEBUCHADNEZZAR'S
WRITTEN TESTIMONY 91
The King's Dream 95
Daniel's Interpretation 108
The Dream Fulfilled 115
The Result 121

CHAPTER 5: DANIEL 5—THE KING WHO DEFIED GOD 125
The Big Party 127
The Hand of God 130
Daniel Rebukes the King 136
Daniel Interprets the Message 142

CHAPTER 6: DANIEL 6—THE CONSPIRACY AGAINST DANIEL **149**

The Political Structure of the New Empire 149

The Plot Against Daniel 151

Daniel Prays 156

Daniel Thrown into the Lions' Den 160

The Deliverance of Daniel 165

The Destruction of Daniel's Enemies 166

PART TWO: Daniel's Prophecies

CHAPTER 7: DANIEL 7—DANIEL'S VISION OF THINGS TO COME **173**

The Four Beasts 179

The Heavenly Court 189

The Heavenly Being 192

The Interpretation 198

The End of Things 205

CHAPTER 8: DANIEL 8—THREE END-OF-THE-AGE POWERS **207**

A Very Powerful Ram 209

A Very Fast Goat 210

A Very Small Horn 214

A Very Helpful Angel 218

A Very Sick Prophet 228

CHAPTER 9: DANIEL 9—A FANTASTIC PRAYER— A FANTASTIC ANSWER **231**

Jeremiah's Prophecy 233

Daniel's Prayer 234

Gabriel's Visit 248

God's Plan 250

CHAPTER 10: DANIEL 10—DEMONIC WARFARE **265**

The Message Daniel Received 265

The Man Daniel Saw 267

The Men with Daniel 269

The Man Who Touched Daniel 270

The Many Different Angels 274

CHAPTER 11: DANIEL 11—PAST PICTURES OF FUTURE EVENTS **279**
    Four Kings of Persia 281
    Fighting Between North and South 282
    A Fake King Appears 296
    A Future Fake 309

CHAPTER 12: DANIEL 12—FINAL REMARKS **323**
    A Time of Distress 324
    A Time to Awake 327
    A Time to Be Wise 329
    A Time of the End 329
    A Thousand Two Hundred and Ninety Days 334
    A Time of Blessing 335

APPENDIX A—TIME LINES **341**

APPENDIX B—THE ANSWERS **345**

ENDNOTES **349**

INDEX **357**

Part One

EVENTS IN THE LIVES OF DANIEL AND HIS FRIENDS

Daniel 1 Daniel as a Teenage Captive

Chapter Highlights:
• Babylon's Attack
• Daniel's Qualifications
• Daniel's Great Decision
• A Ten-Day Test
• God Rewards the Faithful

Let's Get Started

When <u>Moses led</u> the Hebrews (the Jews) out of Egypt God made a special **covenant** with them. He promised to be their God and to bless them, but there was a condition. They would have to obey him by keeping his laws, offering sacrifices, and letting the <u>land</u> rest every seventh year. The Hebrews agreed to do this, but they soon forgot their promise and slowly abandoned their God. Over the years they turned toward a life of wickedness, so that by Daniel's time only a few people were keeping God's commandments.

God's **prophets** warned the people of Judah (see Illustration #4) that he was growing weary of their wickedness. These prophets admonished the people to repent of their sins or <u>Judah would be destroyed by Babylon</u>. But the people's ears were tickled by the sweet-sounding words of many **false prophets**, and they refused to heed the dire warnings of his <u>true prophets</u>.

The Hebrew word for *prophet* means "one who is inspired by God." The Greek word means "one who foretells future events." Prophets are also called "seers" and "men of God" in the Scriptures. They were divinely inspired men who were commissioned by God to speak and/or record his messages. They often revealed his will on moral issues, exhorted people to be faithful to him, warned people of the consequences of sin, and called on people to repent. True prophets were expected to have a 100 percent success rate when foretelling future events. False prophets made mistakes. Some of what they said might be true, but not all of it.

The book of Daniel opens around the year 605 BC (see Time Line 1, Appendix A). It begins by telling us about <u>Judah's wickedness</u> and how Daniel <u>wound up in Babylon</u>. It tells us about a crisis that came into Daniel's life, how he handled it, and his resultant rise to power and prominence in Babylon.

Moses led
Exodus 6–14

covenant
Exodus 19:5–8

land
Leviticus 25–26

Judah would be destroyed by Babylon
Jeremiah 25:8–11

false prophets
Jeremiah 14:14;
Matthew 7:15

true prophets
2 Chronicles 36:16

Judah's wickedness
Jeremiah 36:30–31

wound up in Babylon
Habakkuk 1:1–6

covenant
agreement between
two or more parties

prophet
one who is inspired
by God

false prophets
those who claim to
speak for God but
actually spread false
teachings

Who Was Daniel?

Noah
Genesis 8:18;
10:1–8

began with the cities of Babel . . .
Genesis 10:10

Daniel was a Hebrew and a member of the royal family of Judah. We do not know the exact place or year of his birth, but he was probably born in Jerusalem around the year 620 BC. He was about thirteen or fourteen years old when King Nebuchadnezzar captured him at Jerusalem (a city in Judah), along with the other Israelites (the people of Israel and Judah), and carried them off to Babylon (around 605 BC). Even though Daniel was already well-educated, he was selected for additional training in the language and literature of the Babylonians. His name, Daniel, which means "God is my judge," was changed to Belteshazzar, which means "whom **Bel** favors" or "keeper of the treasures of the prince of Bel." Daniel quickly distinguished himself because of his determination to be faithful to God. He gained the blessings of God and reaped the confidence and favor of those around him. When he interpreted a troubling dream for the hot-tempered Nebuchadnezzar he was promoted to a position of authority over all the wise men of Babylon. He spent the rest of his life as one of the most powerful men in the world, faithfully served several world leaders, and is widely recognized as one of the greatest men of all time.

Bel
the chief god of the Chaldeans

Some Background on Babylon

When <u>Noah</u>, his three sons, and their wives came out of the ark they began to multiply and migrate. Noah's son Ham bore a son named Cush. Cush bore a son named Nimrod who settled in a flat, fertile plain between the Tigris and Euphrates rivers called the Land of Shinar (later called Mesopotamia or Chaldea) and also affectionately called "the cradle of civilization" (see Illustration #2). This is the same area where the Garden of Eden was located.

Nimrod established a great kingdom that the Bible says <u>began with the cities of Babel</u>, Erech, Accad, and Calneh. He is even credited with establishing several great cities in Assyria. He was astute, powerful, and wicked. His city of Babylon is mentioned more than three hundred times in the Bible. Because of all the evil in Babylon, some Bible experts have started referring to it as the "City of Satan" as opposed to the "City of God" (Jerusalem).

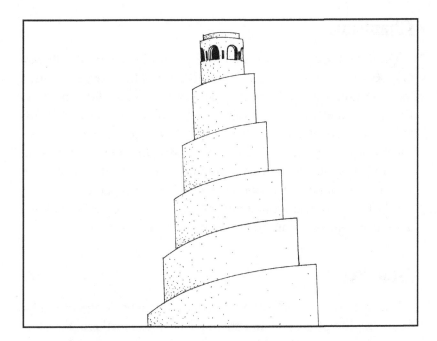

Illustration #1
Babylonian Ziggurat—This is how the Tower of Babel might have looked.

Tower of Babel
Genesis 11:1–9

Nimrod built several towers in the area. The most famous one, called the <u>Tower of Babel</u> (see Illustration #1), was built at Babylon. He made it the focus of his rebellion against God. He welcomed pagan religions, catered to the occult (satanic practices), and promoted sexual gratification and prostitution. He merged his city-states, put them all under his control and took over their education systems. Because of the religious harlotry (unfaithful practices) he began at Babylon, the city is called the "Mother of Harlots." And because of the love for big government he began at Babylon, the city is recognized as the beginning of world government.

what others say

Jack W. Hayford

Daniel found himself as a teenager far from home and in negative circumstances. He had been abducted from his homeland and taken to the conquering country of Babylon, where he was selected to become a trainee in the king's court. There his personal character and religious convictions were immediately tested. His personal integrity sustained him and secured a position in the king's palace and a place of prominence through the parade of two world powers and four kings.[1]

Daniel
Daniel 7:1; 8:1; 9:2;
10:1

Ezekiel
Ezekiel 14:14, 20;
28:3

**Abomination of
Desolation**
Matthew 24:15

Septuagint
Greek translation of
the Bible written in
3rd century BC

Dead Sea Scrolls
a large library of
scrolls found in a
cave near the
Dead Sea

**Alexander the
Great**
head of the Greek
Empire

Ezekiel
Jewish prophet who
wrote the book of
Ezekiel and was also
a captive in Babylon

**Abomination of
Desolation**
statue or **Image of
the Beast**

Image of the Beast
a statue or image of
the Antichrist

Chaldeans

The Chaldeans were Semitic nomads who lived near the Persian Gulf in what is now Kuwait and southeastern Iraq (see Illustration #2). Starting around 1100 BC, there were several different tribes that were wandering in and out of Babylon at will, but by 875 BC some had permanently settled in Babylon. During the 700s BC, some Chaldean leaders ruled as kings of Babylon. One of their leaders, a man named Nabopolassar, united all the Chaldean tribes and was crowned king of Babylon in 626 BC. He was succeeded by his son Nebuchadnezzar around 605 BC. Today, the terms "Chaldean" and "Babylonian" mean essentially the same thing.

Israelites

The nation of Israel divided into a Northern Kingdom and a Southern Kingdom (see Illustration #4). The Northern Kingdom retained the name "Israel" and was taken captive by the Assyrians. The Southern Kingdom was called "Judah" and was taken captive by the Babylonians. The people in both kingdoms were called Israelites.

The author identifies himself as Daniel more than a dozen times. But in spite of this, many critics vehemently deny Daniel's authorship. Why? Because they do not believe in the supernatural, and the prophecies that have already been fulfilled are so accurate they have no other explanation. So they declare the book of Daniel is a forgery. But modern Bible-believing experts are not fooled by the critics. We know that the book of Daniel was included in the **Septuagint**, that a good copy was found with the **Dead Sea Scrolls** in 1947, and that Josephus, a Jewish historian, mentions that **Alexander the Great** (356–323 BC) read it. We know that the prophet **Ezekiel** lived at the same time as Daniel and he wrote about Daniel. Even the reference of Jesus to the **Abomination of Desolation** spoken of through the prophet Daniel implies that Daniel is the author. So there is little doubt that Daniel is the author and the last recorded event was probably written before 530 BC when, if he was alive, Daniel would have been almost ninety years old.

Off They Went

DANIEL 1:1 *In the third year of the reign of Jehoiakim king of Judah, Nebuchadnezzar king of Babylon came to Jerusalem and besieged it.* (NKJV)

Daniel's initial words identify several historical facts about Babylon's first attack on Jerusalem: (1) It was in the third year of Jehoiakim's reign, (2) Jehoiakim was king of Judah, (3) Nebuchadnezzar was king of Babylon, and (4) Nebuchadnezzar attacked Jerusalem. Based on these facts, most experts date the first strike against Jerusalem as beginning in 606 BC and ending in 605 BC.

A Babylonian tablet found by archaeologists states that Nebuchadnezzar's father was king of Babylon (see Illustration #2) in 605 BC, but the king died in August of that year. Nebuchadnezzar had not completed the attack, but he broke off and returned home to be crowned king.

what others say

Uriah Smith

Jeremiah places this captivity in the fourth year of Jehoiakim, Daniel in the third. This seeming discrepancy is explained by the fact that Nebuchadnezzar set out on his expedition near the close of the third year of Jehoiakim, from which point Daniel reckons. But he did not accomplish the **subjugation** of Jerusalem till about the ninth month of the year following; and from this year Jeremiah reckons.

Many claim God's statue in Chapter 3 never existed. Then archaeologists uncovered the base of the statue. They said nothing has ever been found in secular history about Belshazzar which means he was a fictitious person who never existed. Then archaeologists found the **Nabonidus cylinder**, proving the book of Daniel right and the critics wrong. The critics also said Daniel was written in the 2nd century BC not the 6th century BC. Then a scroll of Daniel was found with the Dead Sea Scrolls which contained a style and phrasing of words that is much older than the 2nd century BC.[2]

Jeremiah
a Jewish prophet who predicted the fall of Judah

subjugation
process of conquering, subduing, and bringing under complete control

Nabonidus cylinder
one of several cuneiform cylinders unearthed in Babylon

cuneiform
the symbols used in the writings of ancient Babylon, Assyria, and Persia

Illustration #2
Babylon—Modern-day map of the Middle East showing the location of ancient cities.

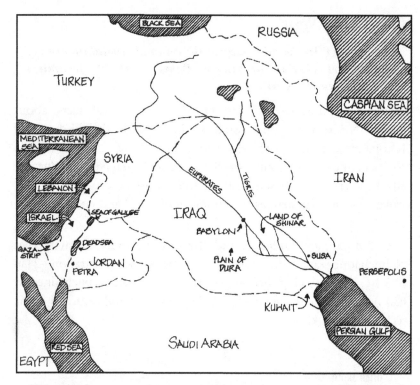

The Jews have gone into captivity several times. The different captivities and their approximate dates are shown in the following chart.

Major Jewish Captivities

Event	Approximate Date
Egyptian Captivity	1875–1445 BC
Assyrian Captivity of Northern Kingdom (Israel)	722 BC
1st Babylonian Captivity—Jerusalem (Daniel and Friends)	605 BC
2nd Babylonian Captivity—Ten Thousand Jews	597 BC
3rd Babylonian Captivity—Southern Kingdom (Judah) First destruction of Jerusalem	586 BC

Jews from Judah returned in three phases:
    1st Return
    2nd Return
    3rd Return
	
	536 BC
	458 BC
	445 BC

Domination by Greece	331–63 BC
Domination by Rome	63 BC–AD 500
Second destruction of Jerusalem by the Romans	AD 70

A Broken Covenant

DANIEL 1:2 *And the Lord gave Jehoiakim king of Judah into his hand, with some of the articles of the house of God, which he carried into the land of Shinar to the house of his god; and he brought the articles into the treasure house of his god.* *(NKJV)*

This was a dark day in Judah's history. It was a day when our loving God showed his great displeasure with the Jews for constantly breaking his covenant. He had been patient with them for 490 years, but he refused to be patient or protect them any longer. He **delivered** them into the hands of Nebuchadnezzar and Babylon. He used a **pagan king** to defeat his own nation.

But that is not all. God added insult to injury. He showed the Jews that by breaking the covenant they had also set aside his promise to be their God. He allowed the **Temple** (see Illustration #17) to be plundered and some of the **Temple treasures** to be taken back to Babylon and placed in the house of Nebuchadnezzar's god. Nebuchadnezzar worshiped many gods, but his chief god was Bel, who was sometimes called Baal, Marduk, or Merodach (see Illustration #3).

what others say

Kay Arthur

God rules. He is sovereign. He is the One who changes the times and the epochs, who removes and establishes kings. Because He is Alpha and Omega, the beginning and the end,

go to

Israelites did disobey God
2 Chronicles
36:11–21

eunuchs
men who have parts
of their genitals
removed

He knows the beginning from the end; therefore, if you want to know what the future holds, you need to seek the wisdom of the One who holds the future in His hands.[3]

Merrill F. Unger

The early capture of Jerusalem by "King" Nebuchadnezzar was not authenticated till very recent times, and it has been commonly denied and cited by some modern critics as the first in a list of alleged "historical errors" in the book. However, within the past several decades ancient documents have come to light that indicate Nebuchadnezzar's presence in Judah at that time.[4]

Bring Me the Best

DANIEL 1:3 *Then the king instructed Ashpenaz, the master of his eunuchs, to bring some of the children of Israel and some of the king's descendants and some of the nobles,* (NKJV)

At the same time Nebuchadnezzar captured King Jehoiakim, he also captured several members of the royal family. He ordered the prince of his **eunuchs**, a man named Ashpenaz, to take them back to Babylon. Although it is not stated, it appears that they were also made eunuchs and placed under Ashpenaz's supervision.

what others say

Hal Lindsey

It was a common practice of the kings of that day to take parts of the royal family back to their capital in order to hold as hostages so they could keep the king they left in place in check.[5]

Peter and Paul Lalonde

The Israelites did disobey God, and true to his word, he allowed them to be taken captive into Babylon. Ever since the Babylonian captivity, about 2,500 years ago, the Jews have been scattered about in nations all around the world. Still, in all of that time, the Jews have never lost their identity and we all know that today the phrase, "the wandering Jew" has even become a cliché.[6]

Teach Them Our Ways

DANIEL 1:4 *young men in whom there was no blemish, but good-looking, gifted in all wisdom, possessing knowledge and quick to understand, who had ability to serve in the king's palace, and whom they might teach the language and literature of the Chaldeans. (NKJV)*

This reveals the kind of people Nebuchadnezzar wanted Ashpenaz to take back to Babylon. It also tells us about the qualifications of Daniel and his friends. Nebuchadnezzar wanted young males who were perfect physical specimens, sharp intellectuals, and had already been taught a wide variety of subjects. They needed to meet the high requirements for service in his palace. He did not want these young men to be used for low or base things. He wanted them to be educated in the language and literature of Babylon. It included astronomy, **astrology**, **black magic**, the interpretation of dreams, history, medicine, **omens**, and philosophy. This was a rigid job description with very high qualifications, and many authorities think Daniel was only about thirteen or fourteen years old at this time.

what others say

David Jeremiah with C. C. Carlson

Mind control begins with the young. By destroying their beliefs and **indoctrinating** them into a **counterculture**, the ruling forces of evil can capture a generation for their purposes. Today our children are being **subverted** in a more subtle fashion than the Hitler Youth, but the **web of control** is just as strong.[7]

World Book Encyclopedia

Hitler also set up organizations for young people between the ages of 6 and 18. These groups included the Hitler Youth for boys 14 years and older and the Society of German Maidens for girls 14 years and older. The organizations were designed to condition German children to military discipline and to win their loyalty to the Nazi government. All German children were required to join such groups from the age of 10. They wore uniforms, marched, exercised, and learned Nazi beliefs. The Nazis taught children to spy on their own families and report anti-Nazi criticism they might hear.[8]

Give Them the Best

DANIEL 1:5 *And the king appointed for them a daily provision of the king's delicacies and of the wine which he drank, and three years of training for them, so that at the end of that time they might serve before the king. (NKJV)*

captives
Colossians 2:6–8

oblation
an offering or sacrifice that has been presented to God or a god

inner self
the mental and spiritual part of a person

Most captives would be glad to receive just a little to eat, and they would not expect a high quality of food. However, these captives were to receive food and drink from Nebuchadnezzar's own table, and, as was the regular practice, it was probably food and drink that had been offered as an **oblation** to the Babylonian gods.

Most <u>captives</u> would not expect to receive an education. But Nebuchadnezzar commanded that these captives be trained for three years. He wanted them to receive the best education money could buy in those days, and after three years, these highly educated sixteen- and seventeen-year-old captives were to be given good jobs. They were to be given positions of honor and trust in the Babylonian kingdom.

what others say

Grant R. Jeffrey

Archaeologists recently discovered, next to the ruined palace in Babylon, the elaborate ruins of the special schools for training the "wise men."[9]

Jack Van Impe

There's a virtual "culture war" against the values of the Bible in the United States. While Christians are not yet being locked up for their beliefs in our country, they are being broadly discriminated against in the public square. Is it so difficult to imagine what the next phase might be?[10]

John Hagee

Parents of America believe their children go to school to be educated in the disciplines of reading, writing, and arithmetic. Not so! Other countries are teaching their children this core curriculum; in America our children are being taught how to get in touch with their **inner selves** and to become subservient pawns of a global society.[11]

Four Hebrew Boys

DANIEL 1:6 *Now from among those of the sons of Judah were Daniel, Hananiah, Mishael, and Azariah. (NKJV)*

This verse reveals the Hebrew names of four members of King Jehoiakim's family who were taken captive by King Nebuchadnezzar and placed under the supervision of Ashpenaz. Four members of the royal family that were taken to Babylon during the first attack and the Hebrew meanings of their names are listed in the following chart.

Hebrew Names and Their Meanings

Hebrew Name	Hebrew Meaning
Daniel	God is my Judge
Hananiah	God is gracious; God is gift
Mishael	Who is like God? God is great
Azariah	God is my helper

what others say

J. Vernon McGee

These four young men from Judah are singled out and identified to us, and the reason is that they are going to take a stand for God.[12]

New Names

DANIEL 1:7 *To them the chief of the eunuchs gave names: he gave Daniel the name Belteshazzar; to Hananiah, Shadrach; to Mishael, Meshach; and to Azariah, Abed-Nego. (NKJV)*

The Hebrew names of these four young men identified some of the characteristics of their God. As long as they went by those names they would remember him, which is exactly what Ashpenaz didn't want. He wanted to switch their allegiance from the true God to the Babylonian gods, so he changed their names.

According to Babylonian custom, people received a new name when their careers changed. As indicated in the following chart, the names given to Daniel and his friends were intended to show they were servants of Babylonian gods.

Babylonian Names and Their Meanings

Hebrew Name	Babylonian Name	Babylonian Meaning
Daniel	Belteshazzar	whom Bel favors; keeper of the treasures of the prince of Bel
Hananiah	Shadrach	illumined by Shad (a sun god)
Mishael	Meshach	who is like Shach (a love goddess)
Azariah	Abed-Nego	the servant of Nego (a fire god)

monotheism
the belief in one
God

polytheism
the belief in more
than one god

These names are important. The Hebrew names reveal the judgment of God, the grace of God, the greatness of God, and the provision of God. The Babylonian names reveal Satanism and goddess worship. The Hebrew names reveal **monotheism**, and the Babylonian names reveal **polytheism**.

what others say

Arno Froese

Daniel, the Jewish captive in the land of Babylon, is an image of the One who was to come: the greatest Jew of all time, the Lord Jesus Christ. We read the Father's testimonial words on earth: "This is my beloved Son, in whom I am well pleased" (Matthew 3:17). Hebrews 10:7 explains why the Father was pleased: "Then said I, Lo, I come (in the volume of the book it is written of me,) to do thy will, O God."[13]

Jay Alan Sekulow

In 1990 the outrage case that stood out involved students who were suspended for "possession" of Christian literature on campus. In 1991 it was Luanne Fulbright who was told that her report on baby Jesus violated the "Separation of Church and State" and could not be displayed in the classroom.

1992 saw an outrage which took us to the Supreme Court when a church was denied access to school facilities in the evening because it wanted to show a film on family issues from a Christian perspective. . . . Adam Villa in 1993 caused a stir when he wanted to sing the Christian song, *Shepherd Boy*, in a school talent show. School officials said "no" until our legal teams intervened. In 1994 it was Emily Hsu, a high school student from New York who wanted to make sure her Christian Bible Club was led by Christians. School officials said "no," and we [the American Center for Law and Justice] are still in court.[14]

Not Me!

DANIEL 1:8 *But Daniel purposed in his heart that he would not defile himself with the portion of the king's delicacies, nor with the wine which he drank; therefore he requested of the chief of the eunuchs that he might not defile himself. (NKJV)*

Changing Daniel's name did not change his character nor did it make him forget what he had learned from the Scriptures. He knew that partaking of these royal delicacies would ceremonially defile him according to the **Law of God**, so he determined in his heart that he would not eat them. Then he respectfully asked Ashpenaz for permission to remain true to his God. It's hard to believe that Daniel had such integrity and steadfastness at the age of thirteen or fourteen.

go to

Law of God
Leviticus 7:19–27

forbid
Leviticus 11

God worked on his behalf
Romans 8:31

Law of God
the rules God gave to Moses

holiness
sincere conformity to the nature and will of God

separation
withdrawal from worldly things

what others say

John Phillips

The temptation that Eve faced in Eden was based on food. The first temptation that Jesus faced in the wilderness was based on food. The temptation that Daniel and his friends faced was based on food. To eat or not to eat, that was the question. And, as the balance came down, two worlds were at stake—this one or the world to come.[15]

Theodore H. Epp

The step Daniel took was one of courage, and the courage came from his walking and talking with God.[16]

Daniel was willing to live in a foreign land, serve a pagan king, and change his name, so why was he unwilling to eat the king's food? The answer may lie in the fact that the Scriptures did not forbid these activities, but they did <u>forbid</u> him from eating certain foods. These Scriptures teach **holiness** and **separation**; some things are wholesome and some things defile; we should make healthy choices, right decisions, and avoid carelessness. When confronted with a tough decision about the king's food, Daniel decided that obeying God was more important than obeying man.

Daniel and God Together

> DANIEL 1:9 *Now God had brought Daniel into the favor and goodwill of the chief of the eunuchs. (NKJV)*

Daniel had the right stuff and the God who was really in charge on his side. When he determined to be faithful, <u>God worked on his behalf</u> by giving Ashpenaz an understanding and sympathetic heart.

what others say

John R. Rice

It is wonderful to have the blessing of God! You can't have the blessing of everybody else, but wouldn't you rather have the blessing of God? That will turn out better, eternally better.[17]

go to

determined not to defile himself
John 14:15

offer himself
Romans 12:1–2

He'll Have My Head

DANIEL 1:10 *And the chief of the eunuchs said to Daniel, "I fear my lord the king, who has appointed your food and drink. For why should he see your faces looking worse than the young men who are your age? Then you would endanger my head before the king."* (NKJV)

Ashpenaz was on the spot. He reminded Daniel that it was Nebuchadnezzar who had commanded the young captives to eat and drink from the king's table. He let Daniel know that he was afraid of Nebuchadnezzar and believed he would be risking his life by granting the request. Ashpenaz speculated that Nebuchadnezzar would see Daniel looking more pale and haggard than the other captives, hold him personally responsible, and have him killed. If that happened, it would be Daniel's fault.

Why Not Do This

DANIEL 1:11 *So Daniel said to the steward whom the chief of the eunuchs had set over Daniel, Hananiah, Mishael, and Azariah,* (NKJV)

Daniel did not want to be responsible for the death of Ashpenaz. However, he loved God and was <u>determined not to defile himself</u>, so he made a suggestion to the guard Ashpenaz had appointed to watch over him and his friends.

A Vegetarian? I Don't Think So

DANIEL 1:12 *"Please test your servants for ten days, and let them give us vegetables to eat and water to drink.* (NKJV)

Daniel wanted to <u>offer himself</u> to God by doing God's will and, by faith, he was expecting God to help him. So, he wisely proposed a test: he and his friends would eat nothing but vegetables and water for ten days.

what others say

Charles Stanley

A value is something that's important to you. That's not a complicated concept. Values—or what's important to people—

determine what they ought and ought not to do . . . Christians, as well as non-Christians, share in the struggle that what we want to do doesn't always match what we should do.[18]

Stephen R. Miller

Daniel's diet was similar to many so-called health food diets today. By this request Daniel was not suggesting that eating meat was wrong, for a meat diet was permitted and in some instances even commanded in the law (e.g., in the case of the Passover lamb and other sacrifices).[19]

go to

Smyrna
Revelation 2:8

parable of the ten pounds
Luke 19:12–27

parable
a story about familiar things that teaches or illustrates unfamiliar things

A Ten-Day Test

DANIEL 1:13 *Then let our appearance be examined before you, and the appearance of the young men who eat the portion of the king's delicacies; and as you see fit, so deal with your servants."* (NKJV)

After ten days, Daniel and his three friends wanted to be compared to those who ate the king's choice food. They wanted Ashpenaz to base his decision on the outcome of that comparison. They believed better health would be the end result of keeping the diet God wanted them to observe.

So Be It

DANIEL 1:14 *So he consented with them in this matter, and tested them ten days.* (NKJV)

Ashpenaz was still laying his life on the line, but he liked Daniel so he consented to the ten-day test. He must have been a true friend. Nebuchadnezzar was a hothead. If the king thought he was being trifled with or crossed, the outcome would be terrible.

what others say

Charles Halff

"Ten" in the Bible is symbolic of testing. The ten commandments were the special test that God gave to Israel. God told the church at Smyrna that they would be tested for ten days with severe persecution. The **parable** of the ten pounds illustrates how the Lord will test our service when he returns.[20]

Now Look at Us

DANIEL 1:15 *And at the end of ten days their features appeared better and fatter in flesh than all the young men who ate the portion of the king's delicacies. (NKJV)*

Here we have the outcome of the test. The ten days passed and now Daniel and his friends stand before Ashpenaz. They are examined and found to look healthier and better fed than any of those who had eaten the king's food, which was the best in the land.

All the Vegetables You Want

DANIEL 1:16 *Thus the steward took away their portion of delicacies and the wine that they were to drink, and gave them vegetables. (NKJV)*

Because Daniel and his friends passed the test, Ashpenaz felt safe in letting them refuse the king's food and drink. They would not be forced to defile themselves. The guard was instructed to stop giving them the royal delicacies and to provide them with vegetables instead.

Knowledge Beyond Human Understanding

DANIEL 1:17 *As for these four young men, God gave them knowledge and skill in all literature and wisdom; and Daniel had understanding in all visions and dreams. (NKJV)*

God rewarded the faithfulness of these four teenagers by giving them special knowledge and understanding in the literature and languages of the various nations comprising the Babylonian Empire. It was not self-attained but a gift from God. It was not ordinary knowledge and understanding but superior knowledge and understanding. Daniel and his friends had wisdom and knowledge beyond the sharpest minds in Babylon.

Some mainline denominations highly emphasize education, but there continues to be a divergence between the education they offer and what the Bible teaches. Education is good if it is the right kind of education and it is accompanied by wisdom, but it is bad if it is the wrong kind of education or it stands alone without wisdom. The priests and rabbis in Jesus' day, and the time of the early Church, had a highly touted education, but they were lost because they didn't know who Jesus was. They marveled at the wisdom of Jesus and his unlearned disciples. If religion is going to be worth anything, it must be based upon a true interpretation of the Scriptures, and the educated must have a stronger relationship with the Lord than they have with the system.

Still, Daniel received an even greater gift: the ability to understand **visions** and **dreams**. Explaining visions was a science in Babylon to which much importance and esteem was attached. Yet God knew Daniel would soon have need of such a gift, so he supplied it beforehand.

In the future, Daniel would interpret dreams, and have dreams and visions. The Holy Spirit is here revealing that this was a God-given gift. The following chart shows the important role it played in Daniel's life.

visions
dreams, trances, and/or pictorial revelations that stimulate the mind and are regarded as omens of future events

dream
in the Old Testament a vision of spiritual or prophetic significance

Dreams and Visions in Daniel's Life

Dream or Vision	Scripture
Nebuchadnezzar's First Dream	Daniel 2
Nebuchadnezzar's Second Dream	Daniel 4
Daniel's Dreams and Visions of Four Beasts	Daniel 7
Daniel's Vision of the Ram and Male Goat	Daniel 8
Daniel's Vision of a Certain Man	Daniel 10

what others say

Tremper Longman III

This section anticipates the next chapter, where the plot revolves around God's granting wisdom to Daniel through revelation (cf. 2:22). After all, they had grown physically robust not because of their Babylonian diet but because of the grace of God, that is, in spite of their diet of vegetables. The effect of the theme of "God's giving" throughout the chapter is to press home who is really in control of the events of Daniel's life, not to speak of fate of the people of God in general.[21]

Alexander Maclaren

Fill the present with quiet faith, with patient waiting, with honest work, with wise reading of God's lessons of nature, of providence, and of grace, all of which say to us, Live in God's

go to

Satan
Deuteronomy
13:1–4

Christians
believers in Jesus
Christ

future, that the present may be bright; and work in the present, that the future may be certain![22]

Rick Joyner

Visions can come on the impression level also. They are gentle and must be seen with "the eyes of our heart." These, too, can be very specific and accurate, especially when received and/or interpreted by those who are experienced. The more the "eyes of our hearts" are opened, as Paul prayed in Ephesians 1:18, the more powerful and useful these can be.[23]

Visions and dreams do not belong to any particular age or group of people. The Bible records Jews, Egyptian pharaohs, Babylonian kings, **Christians**, and others who had them in Old and New Testament times. The world has always had people who claimed to have them, whether true or counterfeit. God said the visions and dreams of those who are true will always be right, but the visions and dreams of counterfeiters will sometimes be right and sometimes wrong. So how do we recognize counterfeiters? God says we are not to believe them if they do or say things that deny the truths of the Bible. God does not send dreams or visions to people who contradict his Word, but <u>Satan</u> does.

The Bible contains dozens of stories about visions and dreams. God often used them to convey his will or a revelation to the recipient. A list of examples follows.

Examples of People Who Had Visions and Dreams

Who?	Where in the Bible?
Abimelech	Genesis 20:3–7
Jacob	Genesis 31:10–13, 24
Joseph	Genesis 37:5–11
Pharaoh	Genesis 41:1–40
Solomon	1 Kings 3:5–15
Joseph	Matthew 1:20–25; 2:13–15, 19–20
Pilate's Wife	Matthew 27:19
Peter	Acts 10:10–16
Paul	Acts 22:17–22

God's ways are perfect, full of mystery, and far-reaching. Some people attribute to him what they consider to be good things, but they refuse to recognize that he may have a role in what they consider to be bad things. The truth is, people rarely understand the full extent of what he is doing. Here are three things this chapter says God did:

1. He delivered Jehoiakim into Nebuchadnezzar's hand, which resulted in the destruction of Israel and the death of many Jews (Daniel 1:2).

2. He caused Ashpenaz to show favor and sympathy to Daniel, which allowed him to do God's will (Daniel 1:9).

3. He gave gifts to Daniel and his friends, which helped propel them to the top levels of the Babylonian government (Daniel 1:17).

Here They Are, My Lord

DANIEL 1:5 *And the king appointed for them a daily provision of the king's delicacies and of the wine which he drank, and three years of training for them, so that at the end of that time they might serve before the king. (NKJV)*

DANIEL 1:18 *Now at the end of the days, when the king had said that they should be brought in, the chief of the eunuchs brought them in before Nebuchadnezzar. (NKJV)*

When the three years of schooling ordered by Nebuchadnezzar were completed, it was the responsibility of Ashpenaz to take Daniel and his friends before the king. This implies that the king took a personal interest in his captives and that he was careful to see his orders were carried out. Also, it is not too hard to speculate that it was an anxious moment for these youngsters. After all, how often does one stand before the most powerful man in the world?

The Wisest in the Land

DANIEL 1:19 *Then the king interviewed them, and among them all none was found like Daniel, Hananiah, Mishael, and Azariah; therefore they served before the king. (NKJV)*

King Nebuchadnezzar wanted to make his own determination of the condition and learning of these teenagers, so he personally interviewed them. Following the examination, it was his finding that these four were superior to everyone else, and that they would be of great value to his government.

Ten Times Wiser

> DANIEL 1:20 *And in all matters of wisdom and understanding about which the king examined them, he found them ten times better than all the magicians and astrologers who were in all his realm. (NKJV)*

God had exceedingly blessed them. <u>Whatever the king asked they knew</u>. And he found them not just a little better than all of his so-called wise men, but *ten times better*. God was involving himself so he could give them a voice in the government and use them to protect all the other Jewish captives.

Ninety Years

> DANIEL 1:21 *Thus Daniel continued until the first year of King Cyrus. (NKJV)*

Couple this with Daniel 1:1 and we gain insight into the approximate length of Daniel's life—about ninety years. We can also determine several other things: (1) that he served four major kings: Nebuchadnezzar, Belshazzar, Darius, and <u>Cyrus</u> (see Time Line #1, Appendix A); (2) that he held his position in government at least until the first year of King Cyrus; (3) that he was alive at least two years after he vacated his office.

go to

whatever the king asked they knew
Psalm 119:97–100

Cyrus
Daniel 10:1

Chapter Wrap-Up

- Babylon attacked Jerusalem, captured the royal family, and seized the Temple treasures. (Daniel 1:1–2)

- Daniel was a perfect physical specimen, healthy, good-looking, intelligent, and well-informed. (Daniel 1:4)

- Daniel resolved not to defile himself with the king's food. (Daniel 1:8)

- Daniel suggested that he and his friends be given nothing but vegetables and water for ten days—then be compared to those who ate the king's food. Daniel and his friends were found to be ten times better. (Daniel 1:12–15)

- God rewarded Daniel and his friends with unusual knowledge and understanding. He also gave Daniel the ability to understand visions and dreams. (Daniel 1:17)

Study Questions

1. Who caused Jerusalem to be captured and what did he use?

2. How did Nebuchadnezzar change Daniel's life and what was he unable to change?

3. Daniel 1:9 says Daniel found favor with Ashpenaz, so why didn't Ashpenaz want Daniel to change his diet?

4. Other than not defiling himself with the king's food, what evidence do we have that Daniel trusted God?

5. What changes occurred as a result of Daniel's (and his friends') faithfulness to God?

Daniel 2 Nebuchadnezzar's Disturbing Dream

Chapter Highlights:
- A Disturbing Dream
- A Deadly Command
- Daniel Prays
- His Prayer Answered
- A Destroying Rock

Let's Get Started

God made a covenant with <u>Abraham</u>, <u>Isaac</u>, <u>Jacob</u>, <u>David</u>, and <u>many of the prophets</u> to establish a kingdom that will never end. Many people call that kingdom Israel, "God's covenant nation." Following the <u>death of King Solomon</u>, ten of the twelve tribes of Israel seceded (broke away) and formed the Northern Kingdom called Israel. The other two tribes formed the Southern Kingdom called Judah.

Both kingdoms failed to keep the covenant and continued to sin. First, the Northern Kingdom was taken captive by Assyria, then the Southern Kingdom was taken captive by Babylon. According to Scripture, these captivities were temporary. God's covenant had not been abolished; it had only been set aside for a period of time.

When Babylon captured Judah the world began a temporary period of time known in the Bible as the **Times of the Gentiles** (see Time Line #2, Appendix A). Just as the captivities were temporary, so will be this period. It will not last forever. It will end at the **Battle of Armageddon** with the <u>Second Coming</u> of Jesus. God will return Jerusalem to the Jews and establish the kingdom of his covenant. The modern restoration of Israel as a nation in 1948, the rebuilding of Jerusalem as a city, the current Arab/Israeli conflict over Jerusalem, the restoration of Europe as a Gentile world power, and many other signs indicate that the Times of the Gentiles is about over. It seems that the world is now in a transition period—between the Times of the Gentiles and the Second Coming of Jesus. This chapter will detail the first dream of King Nebuchadnezzar, and provide some amazing and important information about how God will establish his kingdom on earth.

go to

Abraham
Genesis 12:1–3

Isaac
Genesis 26:1–5

Jacob
Genesis 28:1–22

David
2 Samuel 7:8–16

many of the prophets
Deuteronomy 30:1–10;
Jeremiah 31:31–40

death of King Solomon
1 Kings 11:41–43

Times of the Gentiles
Luke 21:24

Armageddon
Revelation 16:12–16

Second Coming
Revelation 22:6–7

Times of the Gentiles
the period Gentiles exercise some control over Jerusalem from the Babylonian captivity to the Second Coming of Jesus

Battle of Armageddon
a great battle on earth during the Tribulation Period

Illustration #4
Jewish Kingdoms—
The Northern
Kingdom was called
Israel and the
Southern Kingdom
was called Judah.

go to

**promise he made to
Solomon's father,
King David**
1 Kings 11:29–34

Rehoboam
1 Kings 12:1–9

Jeroboam
1 Kings 11:29–33

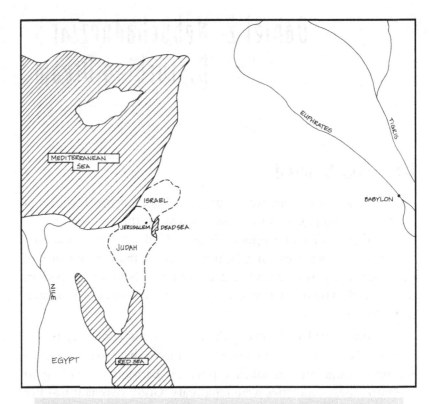

what others say

Tim LaHaye

Nebuchadnezzar's vision was from God and constitutes, when interpreted by the prophet of God, the most important single prophecy in the Bible concerning gentile nations. As such, it proves the supernatural ability of God to reveal history in advance.[1]

King Solomon

King Solomon was a failure in many ways: he had hundreds of wives and concubines, got involved in false religions, and greatly increased taxes to fund his large building projects. His failures angered God and provoked him to declare that the kingdom would be divided. But God waited until after Solomon died because of a promise he made to Solomon's father, King David. When Solomon died, Rehoboam (Solomon's son) took the throne. It wasn't long until Jeroboam (a high-ranking official to Solomon) visited Rehoboam with a delegation to ask for lower taxes. Rehoboam's advisers suggested he lower them, but instead he raised taxes. This angered the people and caused a rebellion that divided the nation in which Jeroboam left with ten of the twelve tribes to form Israel, the Northern Kingdom.

Twelve Tribes

Israel originally was made up of twelve tribes. It was sometimes called the United Kingdom and Jerusalem was its capital. Then Israel divided. The ten tribes in the north were called the Northern Kingdom, or Israel. The two tribes in the south were called the Southern Kingdom, or Judah. Jerusalem was in the Southern Kingdom. In fact, it was the capital of the Southern Kingdom. A small minority of people disagree, but modern-day Israel is made up of all twelve tribes. This has been proven with DNA and the use of computers to compile genealogies.

People do not talk about it, but the nation is again a United Kingdom. It is a problem for the nations of the world, because Israel calls the rebuilt Jerusalem their capital, and the Palestinians are trying to also claim it as their capital.

The First Dream

> **DANIEL 2:1** *Now in the second year of Nebuchadnezzar's reign, Nebuchadnezzar had dreams; and his spirit was so troubled that his sleep left him.* (NKJV)

Nebuchadnezzar had not reigned very long and Daniel was still a teenager when the king began to have disturbing dreams (see Time Line #1, Appendix A).

what others say

Tremper Longman III

Nebuchadnezzar had a dream that disturbed him greatly, so he called his professionals—not psychologists, of course, but the ancient equivalents, "the magicians, enchanters, sorcerers and astrologers." These professionals had dream interpretation on their list of responsibilities. Indeed, these people were the political consultants, trend spotters, and religious gurus of the day.[2]

magicians
Isaiah 48:1–15

magic
Revelation 9:21

In spite of the fact that this verse tells us this dream occurred in the second year of king Nebuchadnezzar's reign, some debate exists among Bible experts about the exact time of this event. Most experts believe Daniel and his friends were actually captured before Nebuchadnezzar became the official king of Babylon. After Nebuchadnezzar's father died, he was recognized as the "acting king," but he was not officially crowned until later. If Nebuchadnezzar was officially king when Daniel and his friends began their three years of schooling, as some experts believe, then this event occurred before they graduated. But, on the other hand, if he was only the "recognized king," and had not been officially crowned, this event occurred after they graduated.

Bring in My Wise Men

DANIEL 2:2 *Then the king gave the command to call the magicians, the astrologers, the sorcerers, and the Chaldeans to tell the king his dreams. So they came and stood before the king.* (NKJV)

The troubled king called in several of his special advisers. He summoned: (1) magicians who were skillful in tricks and illusions (sleight of hand), and understood mysteries and black magic (using secret charms and spirits to make unnatural things happen); (2) enchanters who were chanters of evil spells and incantations (sets of words spoken as a magic charm); (3) sorcerers who talked to the dead and practiced magic with the aid of evil spirits; and (4) astrologers who read horoscopes and studied the stars and other heavenly bodies to foretell the future. When they arrived they stood before the powerful Nebuchadnezzar.

> **what others say**
>
> **John Phillips**
>
> These were the powerful leaders of the Babylonian religion whom Nebuchadnezzar had summoned. They were the professionals. Their specialty was the world of the unknown. Nowadays we would call them "psychics." The king was not at all convinced of the integrity of this ragtag-and-bobtail collection of notables.[3]

A Troubling Dream

DANIEL 2:3 *And the king said to them, "I have had a dream, and my spirit is anxious to know the dream." (NKJV)*

abomination
Deuteronomy 4:19;
17:2–5

Nebuchadnezzar told his special advisers that he had a troubling dream, and he wanted to know what it meant. There is nothing wrong with this. Daniel will soon tell us he dreamed about the future. Every king should be interested in what will happen to his people in the future.

zodiac
the 12 imaginary
signs in heaven

Tell Us Your Dream

DANIEL 2:4 *Then the Chaldeans spoke to the king in Aramaic, "O king, live forever! Tell your servants the dream, and we will give the interpretation." (NKJV)*

The astrologers' statement indicates that they thought this would be a simple matter. All they wanted to know was the dream. Once that was revealed they would give the interpretation.

Today many writers say prophetic dreams are the product of one's imagination, indigestion, or some other problem. They delight in saying the Bible is the full revelation of God and so dreams are no longer needed. But on the first Pentecost following the resurrection of Jesus, Peter clearly pointed out that the prophet Joel said young men will have visions and old men will dream dreams in the last days (Acts 2:17). Any dream or vision that contradicts the Bible is not of God, but that does not exclude the fact that God may use dreams or visions to enforce, explain, or remind people of what the Bible says.

The Zodiac

The ancient occultic practice of astrology is still popular today. Astrologers relate the time of one's birth to one of the twelve signs of the **zodiac**. Then, based upon the position of celestial objects, they profess to predict people's futures. They have had thousands of years to prove their theories scientifically valid but have never managed to do so. If this pagan practice was an abomination to God in ancient times and something he condemned, is it not still an <u>abomination</u> and something that we should condemn today?

Which Language Is It?

Daniel's native tongue was Hebrew, but the commercial language of his day was Aramaic. The astrologers were not Jews. They stood before the Babylonian king, and they spoke Aramaic. Up to Daniel 2:4, Daniel wrote in Hebrew, but beginning with this verse he wrote in Aramaic. He switched back to Hebrew at Daniel 8:1.

The use of the **horoscope** is one of the most common occultic practices of our time. Even though most scientists tell us there is no scientific basis for believing in them, multitudes still use horoscopes to determine things about their character and future. Some even use them to make important decisions. The idea that the positions of the sun, moon, and planets influence one's character, fortune, future, and personality was an abomination unto God during Old Testament times, and nothing has changed. God wants us to commit our life to him, to give him charge of our character and future, and to pray for guidance before making important decisions. Instead of reading the horoscope published in the newspaper he would have us read the Bible. Those who use horoscopes are making the terrible mistake of ignoring the will of God.

I'll Cut You into Little Pieces

> **DANIEL 2:5** *The king answered and said to the Chaldeans, "My decision is firm: if you do not make known the dream to me, and its interpretation, you shall be cut in pieces, and your houses shall be made an ash heap. (NKJV)*

What a scene this must have been. We talk about lowering the boom, but this must have filled the wicked hearts of the king's advisers with terror. On the throne was a powerful world ruler not used to being denied or refused anything; in front of him was a cowering bunch of **frauds** who knew they were being asked to do the impossible. The angry king issued a decree; a decree that he would not, and could not, go back on. By law what he said could not be reversed. These advisers would have to tell him his dream and interpret it, or their heads would roll and their houses would be leveled.

Destroying houses has never gone out of style. When Israel captures a terrorist today, one of the first pieces of information sought is the location of the terrorist's residence. If Israel has access to that place, there is a good chance the army will be sent in to demolish the building the terrorist lived in. The Jews receive much criticism because of this policy, but they claim it is very effective.

Riches to the One Who Knows

> DANIEL 2:6 *However, if you tell the dream and its interpretation, you shall receive from me gifts, rewards, and great honor. Therefore tell me the dream and its interpretation."* (NKJV)

Nebuchadnezzar really wanted to know the dream, have it interpreted, and be sure he had been told the truth. So this is the carrot: he would give gifts, rewards, and honor to his advisers if they did what he asked. He also wanted them to believe that he did not want to kill them, so he encouraged them to reveal the dream and its interpretation.

what others say

Rodney Stortz

But the wise men of Babylon did not have the Spirit of God living in them; so they could not know the dream or the interpretation. They were weak and powerless to do what only God can do.[4]

A Second Request

> DANIEL 2:7 *They answered again and said, "Let the king tell his servants the dream, and we will give its interpretation."* (NKJV)

A second time Nebuchadnezzar's special advisers courteously asked him to tell them the dream, and they promised to interpret it.

Everyone dreams, but some people never recall dreaming. Others remember only a little about a dream they had just before awakening and nothing about earlier dreams. No one recalls every dream and, in general, dreams are very easily forgotten.

I Warn You!

> DANIEL 2:8 *The king answered and said, "I know for certain that you would gain time, because you see that my decision is firm:* (NKJV)

This dream was becoming a nightmare for Nebuchadnezzar's advisers. He was accusing them of trying to buy time because they knew he would carry out his decree and have them killed and their houses leveled.

The possibility also remains that Nebuchadnezzar believed this dream signified that he would be overthrown. He could have been accusing his advisers of treason or trying to stall until a successor took over.

Another Threat

DANIEL 2:9 *if you do not make known the dream to me, there is only one decree for you! For you have agreed to speak lying and corrupt words before me till the time has changed. Therefore tell me the dream, and I shall know that you can give me its interpretation." (NKJV)*

It was time to "put up or shut up." Nebuchadnezzar gave these advisers a choice: tell him his dream or die. He would not accept any excuses. However, he explained that if they would tell him the dream, he would also believe their interpretation. But, he implied that if they did not, he would consider them fakes.

what others say

The Nelson Study Bible

Nebuchadnezzar reasoned that if the wise men could supernaturally interpret his dream, they should first be able to tell him the content of it.[5]

No One Can Do What You Ask

DANIEL 2:10 *The Chaldeans answered the king, and said, "There is not a man on earth who can tell the king's matter; therefore no king, lord, or ruler has ever asked such things of any magician, astrologer, or Chaldean. (NKJV)*

These trapped men were desperately struggling to preserve their lives. This was a veiled admission that they were imposters and could not do what the king asked. They were saying the king's demand was impossible and implying that he was being unreasonable.

Only the Gods Could Possibly Know

DANIEL 2:11 *It is a difficult thing that the king requests, and there is no other who can tell it to the king except the gods, whose dwelling is not with flesh." (NKJV)*

Nebuchadnezzar's advisers were nervously restating their defense: the king's request was impossible. They were also admitting that they were out of touch with the <u>gods</u> and they added something today's **New Agers** would very much disagree with: the gods do not live among men.

gods
1 Corinthians 8:5–6

New Agers
followers of a false religious movement interested in astrology, fortune-telling, metaphysics, occultism, reincarnation, witchcraft, and so forth

> what others say
>
> ### The Pulpit Commentary
>
> This excuse of the wise men is a preparation for Daniel's claim to reveal the secret of the king by the power of a higher God than any that communicated with the Babylonian soothsayers.[6]

It is not their intent to get involved with dangerous cults, but a lot of good people are doing so by taking up New Age beliefs. They do not seek to be involved in sin, but without realizing it they are being enticed by people holding doctrines as dangerous as Satan himself. One such doctrine is the New Age idea that we are all gods. Unfortunately, one's New Age trek toward godhood always winds up hurting that individual because it winds up being a walk away from the one true God. Thinking they are gods they trust in themselves instead of the God who can make them better and secure their future. Millions now claim that they are gods, but there is no evidence that the world is getting better.

Off with Their Heads

DANIEL 2:12 *For this reason the king was angry and very furious, and gave the command to destroy all the wise men of Babylon. (NKJV)*

The edgy king probably decided that his advisers really were traitors or, at least, imposters. Either way, he was so upset he ordered they be put to death. Unfortunately, this wide-ranging order included Daniel and his friends, Hananiah (Shadrach), Mishael (Meshach), and Azariah (Abed-Nego).

Those who served as advisers to a king often had many advantages and perks, but there were times when serving the king was risky business. Some monarchs pretended they wanted to know the truth when in fact they wanted to have their thoughts, policies, or actions reinforced. Crossing them could bring imprisonment, torture, or death. It wasn't unusual for advisers to face fierce opposition and harsh criticism. Before he died Daniel faced jealousy, false accusations, anti-Semitism, and attempts on his life. Shadrach, Meshach, and Abed-Nego experienced some of the same problems. These so-called wise men were up against a king who wanted his way no matter what, and it didn't matter if innocent people got hurt in the process.

what others say

Leon Wood

The number of all the wise men would have been large, but all were to be killed. Apparently, the king reasoned—with what reason remained to him in his fury—that if these men could not do their job, they might as well be done away with.[7]

Search Them Out

DANIEL 2:13 *So the decree went out, and they began killing the wise men; and they sought Daniel and his companions, to kill them.* (NKJV)

The command was given to execute the wise men. And from this verse we learn that Daniel and his friends were included in that group. They were innocent victims in this sordid affair, but trifles like this did not matter to the fiery Nebuchadnezzar.

A Word of Wisdom

DANIEL 2:14 *Then with counsel and wisdom Daniel answered Arioch, the captain of the king's guard, who had gone out to kill the wise men of Babylon;* (NKJV)

The commander of the king's guard took his troops and went forth to round up the wise men for execution. It wasn't long before he located Daniel, who was just a teenager, but he already possessed a godly character beyond his young years. He did not act like an unjustly condemned man by arguing or protesting, but instead used his head, was composed, and had good manners.

pray
James 5:16

What Is the Problem?

> DANIEL 2:15 *he answered and said to Arioch the king's captain, "Why is the decree from the king so urgent?" Then Arioch made the decision known to Daniel. (NKJV)*

Daniel was unaware of what had transpired until Arioch arrived with the arrest warrant. One thing Daniel wanted to know was why Nebuchadnezzar had issued such a cruel command. Arioch, being commander of the king's guard, had probably witnessed the entire matter, so he took the time to explain everything to Daniel.

Take Me to Your Leader

> DANIEL 2:16 *So Daniel went in and asked the king to give him time, that he might tell the king the interpretation. (NKJV)*

Daniel's *first step* was to obtain permission to speak to Nebuchadnezzar. Then his *second step* was to ask him for time. He was not stalling out of a desire for the king to be overthrown or change his mind, but because he was acting on his unshakable faith in God. He obviously believed that he could reveal the dream if he had time to <u>pray</u>.

This is really an incredible thing. One would expect Daniel, being the teenager that he was, to be susceptible to fear, weakness, inexperience, confusion, needing counsel, and more. One would not expect him to act with the faith that he did. God does not always deliver his people. John the Baptist was beheaded, Stephen was stoned to death, and Jesus was crucified, but Daniel boldly proclaimed by faith that he would come up with the dream and its interpretation if he could have the time. How much time he asked for or was given is not revealed, but the text shows that he only needed one

go to

friends
Matthew 18:20

Jews, followers of Jehovah
Isaiah 10:20–22

prayer
Matthew 18:20

God of heaven
Jehovah God of Israel. He created the heavens.

night. It also shows that he did not know the answer and could not come up with it on his own. It was only revealed after he and others talked to God.

Listen to Me, My Friends

DANIEL 2:17 *Then Daniel went to his house, and made the decision known to Hananiah, Mishael, and Azariah, his companions,* (NKJV)

Daniel's *third step* was to go home and tell his friends what had happened. They are identified here by their Hebrew names, which is a reminder that they were still Jews, followers of Jehovah.

Pray!

DANIEL 2:18 *that they might seek mercies from the God of heaven concerning this secret, so that Daniel and his companions might not perish with the rest of the wise men of Babylon.* (NKJV)

Daniel's *fourth step* was to ask his friends to join him in prayer. The *fifth step* was for them to actually pray. They prayed to the **"God of heaven"** and specifically asked him for mercy concerning this dream. If he granted it, they would live. If he did not, they would die.

The Bible uses many names for God, all of which have great significance. In this case, Daniel was using a name first used by Abraham (see Genesis 24:7). When used by Daniel, who had been sent to Nebuchadnezzar's brainwashing school, it meant that he was going to rely on the God of his fathers instead of on Babylonian deities, astrology, horoscopes, and worthless things like that. They were subordinate to the God of Israel, who has dominion over the entire creation. They have no control over the future, but the God of heaven knows and controls all things.

So That's It

DANIEL 2:19 *Then the secret was revealed to Daniel in a night vision. So Daniel blessed the God of heaven.* (NKJV)

Daniel and his friends prayed and went to bed. It is impossible to say exactly what happened, but the dream was probably <u>revealed</u> as Daniel dreamed the same dream Nebuchadnezzar dreamed. Then he woke up and his *sixth step* was to praise the same God he and his friends had prayed to: the God of heaven.

Daniel was one of the greatest men who ever lived. No doubt his two greatest strengths were his commitment to God and his prayer life. The following chart shows his approach to this problem—pleading, prayer, and praise—and the role prayer played in resolving it.

go to

revealed
Amos 3:7

source of wisdom
James 1:5

authority
Matthew 28:18

omniscient
God knows everything

omnipotent
God has power over everything

Prayer Changes Things

Number	Step	Approach
1	Daniel obtained permission to speak to the king.	
2	Daniel asked for time.	Pleading
3	Daniel went home and told his friends.	
4	Daniel asked his friends to join him in prayer.	
5	Daniel and his friends prayed.	Prayer
6	Daniel and his friends praised God.	Praise

Wisdom and Power

DANIEL 2:20 *Daniel answered and said:*
"Blessed be the name of God forever and ever,
For wisdom and might are His. (NKJV)

This is Daniel's first reaction in response to God answering his prayer. It is a prayer of praise and thanksgiving. Daniel called for the name of his God to be praised forever and ever, and he acknowledged that wisdom and power are Divine qualities of his God. His God's great name should be praised because he is the sole <u>source of wisdom</u> and strength. He has all <u>authority</u> because he is both **omniscient** and **omnipotent**. The God of heaven is the Supreme Being in the universe and the One whom man should reverence more than anyone or anything else. Three reasons why are shown in the following chart.

Attributes of God

Omniscient (all-knowing)	
1 John 3:20	God knows everything
Psalm 147:5	God's understanding has no limit

go to

bring them down
Psalm 75:7

knowledge
Proverbs 1:7

Attributes of God (cont'd)

Omnipotent (all-powerful)	
Job 42:1–2	The Lord can do all things
Matthew 19:26	With God all things are possible
Omnipresent (everywhere)	
Psalm 139:7–10	You are there
Jeremiah 23:24	I fill heaven and earth

what others say

Theodore H. Epp

Daniel's prayer at this time gives us an insight into his heart attitude toward God. The first thing he asked for was for the mercies of God. He came as a suppliant before his God and not as a haughty member of the king's cabinet. His prayer was also very definite, for he laid before the Lord the problem that faced him and asked God to reveal to him the dream Nebuchadnezzar had dreamed and then had forgotten. Daniel also added praise to his prayer. He thanked God for what He was going to do. God gave him just what he asked for.[9]

He Can Give and He Can Take

DANIEL 2:21
And He changes the times and the seasons;
He removes kings and raises up kings;
He gives wisdom to the wise
And knowledge to those who have understanding. (NKJV)

Daniel praised God because God is in control.

1. God controls times and seasons—he can end one age and begin another.

2. God controls kings and rulers—he can raise them up or <u>bring them down.</u>

3. God controls wisdom—he can give people the ability to rightly use their knowledge.

4. God controls <u>knowledge</u>—he can impart information and the ability to learn.

go to

knowledge and understanding
Daniel 1:17

hidden
Hebrews 4:13

light was found in God
1 John 1:5

Oliver B. Greene

Times and seasons are not under the control of chance, but are regulated by established laws; yet God, who appointed these laws, has power to change them, and all the changes which occur under these laws are produced under his power and control.[10]

Remember, God is in control of everything!

To these four young men God gave <u>knowledge and understanding</u> of all kinds of literature and learning. **Discernment** comes from God alone, not from astrologers, psychics, or sorcerers.

discernment
the act of showing good judgment

revelation
the act of making known

enlightenment
imparted information, instruction, understanding, or perception

Nothing Is Hidden from God

DANIEL 2:22
He reveals deep and secret things;
He knows what is in the darkness,
And light dwells with Him. (NKJV)

Daniel praised his God because:

1. God reveals deep and complex secrets.

2. God reveals <u>hidden</u> things that no one else knows.

3. God is the source of **revelation** and **enlightenment.**

Daniel knew that it was his God who revealed to him Nebuchadnezzar's dream that was hidden from everyone else. All of Nebuchadnezzar's wise men were in darkness, but <u>light was found</u> in God.

We, Not Me

DANIEL 2:23
I thank You and praise You,
O God of my fathers;
You have given me wisdom and might,
And have now made known to me what we asked of You,
For You have made known to us the king's demand." (NKJV)

fathers
Deuteronomy 6:10

death
Ezekiel 33:11

Daniel gave his God thanks and praise for answering prayer. It is the God of his <u>fathers</u>, Jehovah God of Israel, the God of Abraham, Isaac and Jacob, who gave him wisdom and power. And notice that Daniel did not take all the credit for gaining God's favor. He thanked God and praised him for what we asked, and for making known to us the king's demand. He knew that God's answer was in response, not only to his prayer, but to that of his companions as well.

Too many people are distracted or in a hurry when they pray. Quite often their prayers consist of nothing more than a list of requests. But one should never be so distracted or in such a hurry that they don't have time for praise and adoration, and every prayer should be accompanied by thanksgiving. Paul even said prayer requests should be accompanied by thanksgiving (see Philippians 4:6). Make your prayers a three-fold ART (Adoration, Requests and Thanksgiving).

Spare Them

> **DANIEL 2:24** *Therefore Daniel went to Arioch, whom the king had appointed to destroy the wise men of Babylon. He went and said thus to him: "Do not destroy the wise men of Babylon; take me before the king, and I will tell the king the interpretation."* (NKJV)

After taking time to give thanks and praise to God, Daniel went to Arioch, the commander of the king's guard. He told Arioch to stop putting the wise men to <u>death</u>, because he could interpret the king's dream if Arioch would take him to the king.

Daniel was a stickler for obeying God. The first great commandment is to love God, but the second is to love others. Here Daniel interceded for the other wise men of Babylon. He literally saved their lives, but they would eventually forget it and try to have him killed (see Daniel 6:1–27).

Pride and Humility

> **DANIEL 2:25** *Then Arioch quickly brought Daniel before the king, and said thus to him, "I have found a man of the captives of Judah, who will make known to the king the interpretation."* (NKJV)

There seems to be a contrast here between the humble Daniel and the proud Arioch. When God revealed Nebuchadnezzar's dream to Daniel, he did not claim all the credit. Instead Daniel included his companions when he thanked and praised God for giving what we asked for. But the warrior Arioch was made from a different mold. He had done nothing, but yet he rushed Daniel to the king and said, "I have found a man of the **captives** of <u>Judah</u>, who will make known to the king the interpretation." God revealed the dream to Daniel, but Arioch tried to make it look like he should get all the credit.

captives
Nehemiah 7:6

Judah
1 Chronicles 9:1

possible
Matthew 19:26

wise men
1 Corinthians 1:20

captives of Judah
Jews taken from
Jerusalem

Let Me Have It

> DANIEL 2:26 *The king answered and said to Daniel, whose name was Belteshazzar, "Are you able to make known to me the dream which I have seen, and its interpretation?" (NKJV)*

Apparently Nebuchadnezzar did not think this was <u>possible</u>. He was somewhat skeptical of either Arioch's claim or Daniel's ability to do what Arioch said. He surely remembered Daniel coming before him on the previous day to ask for time, but he probably thought, *That teenager can't do what all the wise men of Babylon couldn't do.* He probably thought, *We destroyed his kingdom and know his God can't do what the Babylonian gods couldn't do.* So he was asking, "Are you able?"

No Man Knows the Answer

> DANIEL 2:27 *Daniel answered in the presence of the king, and said, "The secret which the king has demanded, the wise men, the astrologers, the magicians, and the soothsayers cannot declare to the king. (NKJV)*

Daniel made no boasts about his ability or that of his friends. He began by politely letting the hotheaded king know that he was asking the impossible of his <u>wise men</u>. This answer could even be considered a mild rebuke to the fiery Nebuchadnezzar. "The Chaldeans answered the king, and said, 'There is not a man on earth who can tell the king's matter'" (Daniel 2:10 NKJV).

A Prophecy of Things to Come

> DANIEL 2:28 *But there is a God in heaven who reveals secrets, and He has made known to King Nebuchadnezzar what will be in the latter days. Your dream, and the visions of your head upon your bed, were these: (NKJV)*

This tells us both the source and purpose of Nebuchadnezzar's dream. Daniel let the king know that the source of this dream was the God in heaven—a reference to Daniel's God, the God of Israel. He also let the king know that the purpose of this dream was God's desire to reveal the future.

At this particular time, Daniel used the term *latter days*. It is synonymous with the term *last days*. Basically both terms mean "what will happen before the end of the age." God was starting with Nebuchadnezzar and showing him what will happen before Jesus returns or before the end of the times of the Gentiles. Do not confuse this with the end of the world or the end of time or anything like that. It's a time line of events leading up to, and cutting off with, the Second Coming of Jesus. Other events (millennium, eternity, and so forth) will follow in the age to come.

The Revealer of Mysteries

> DANIEL 2:29 *As for you, O king, thoughts came to your mind while on your bed, about what would come to pass after this; and He who reveals secrets has made known to you what will be. (NKJV)*

Daniel began by reminding Nebuchadnezzar that the king was lying in bed thinking about the future. It is reasonable to assume he went to bed speculating about what kind of king he would be, how he would be remembered, what kind of decisions he should make, and who his successor might be. With the future on his mind the king fell asleep, and God, who "reveals secrets," gave him a revelation about the future.

Many people want to know what the future holds. Almost all the Old Testament prophets talked about it. The disciples even asked Jesus, "What will be the sign of your coming, and of the end of the age?" And Jesus talked about it. Daniel's answer reveals that this age or current history is moving toward the Second Coming of Christ.

People need to study the remainder of this chapter over and over again, because the Second Coming (the Rapture is a different event that will take place before the Second Coming) won't take place until we have one final Gentile world government that is divided into ten regions.

David
1 Kings 14:7–11

house of David
family, lineage, or descendants of King David

scepter
a special rod that kings held to signify their authority or sovereignty

> **what others say**
>
> ### C. I. Scofield
>
> The vision prophetically portrays the course of world empire and its destruction by Christ, who called this period "the times of the Gentiles" (Luke 21:24).[11]

So That You May Know

> **DANIEL 2:30** *But as for me, this secret has not been revealed to me because I have more wisdom than anyone living, but for our sakes who make known the interpretation to the king, and that you may know the thoughts of your heart. (NKJV)*

Daniel's thoughts turned from the king's dream to himself. He was humbly saying something like this, "This mystery has been revealed to me not because of my ability, my greatness, my understanding, or my wisdom, but because God wants you to know what went through your mind and what it means."

Witnessing to others is often difficult. Many people don't have time, are not interested, or are preoccupied. Witnessing to Nebuchadnezzar would be about the same thing. Before Daniel came along, it's doubtful that he had given an audience to even one teenager, let alone a teenage Jewish captive. Now the captive Daniel has a captive audience. He has the king's undivided attention. Getting to this point had been an ordeal for the monarch. So while the king was listening intently for what he desperately wanted to know, Daniel was saying, "It's not me. It's God. Get to know him."

> **what others say**
>
> ### J. Vernon McGee
>
> Because of the failure of the **house of David**, God is now taking the **scepter** of this universe out from the hands of the line of David [the Jews], and he is putting it into the hands of the gentiles. It will be there until Jesus Christ comes again to this earth.[12]

God's Statue

prophet
Matthew 24:15

DANIEL 2:31 *"You, O king, were watching; and behold, a great image! This great image, whose splendor was excellent, stood before you; and its form was awesome. (NKJV)*

As Daniel began to tell what the dream was, he reminded Nebuchadnezzar that he was looking into the future when he saw a great statue (see Illustration #5) standing before him. It was an enormous, dazzling statue, awesome in appearance; as we shall soon see, it was an unusual statue of a man.

Jesus called Daniel the <u>prophet</u>, and this great statue of a man is a prophecy that represents several phases or stages of Gentile world government, which will dominate Israel during the times of the Gentiles. Daniel's description of the statue started at the top of its head and moved down to the tip of its toes—from Nebuchadnezzar and Babylon to the Second Coming of Jesus. God revealed this to Nebuchadnezzar, but he also revealed it to Daniel for the apparent purpose of giving the Jews hope while they were being dominated by Gentiles, and also for the apparent purpose of showing the world he has a plan that includes a kingdom ruled by his Son.

Gold, Silver, and Bronze

DANIEL 2:32 *This image's head was of fine gold, its chest and arms of silver, its belly and thighs of bronze, (NKJV)*

The head of the statue was made of pure gold, the most precious of metals. Its chest and arms were made of silver, a significantly less precious metal. Its belly and thighs were made of bronze, a metal less expensive than silver but still precious in Nebuchadnezzar's lifetime.

Iron and Baked Clay

DANIEL 2:33 *its legs of iron, its feet partly of iron and partly of clay. (NKJV)*

The legs of the statue were made of iron, a metal less expensive than bronze but still valuable 2,600 years ago. Its feet were made of a mixture of iron and clay, a crude conglomeration that would be brittle and easy to shatter and the least expensive of all the materials. Thus we see that each segment of the statue decreased in value.

Illustration #5
God's Statue—The statue from Nebuchadnezzar's first dream. Each metal represents a world power during the Times of the Gentiles.

Another interesting point is the fact that the metals decrease in weight starting with the head and going down to the feet. Gold is heavier than silver. Silver is heavier than bronze. Bronze is heavier than iron. Iron is heavier than a mixture of iron and clay. This means the statue was top-heavy, unstable, and poorly constructed.

Notice, too, that the metals in the statue, starting with its head and going down to its feet, increased in hardness. Gold is not as hard as silver. Silver is not as hard as bronze. Bronze is not as hard as iron.

The decreasing value and weight of the materials indicate the Gentile world governments will deteriorate in some ways. And the increasing hardness of the materials indicates the Gentile world governments will strengthen in some ways. It's just speculation, but based on history this seems to mean Gentile world governments will grow worse and worse, not better and better. They will grow more immoral, not more godly. And they will develop stronger weapons and become more destructive. The course of Gentile world government is in the direction of bad, not good; in the direction of being worthless, not valuable; in the direction of being less and less able to

world gentile rule
the period of time when Gentile nations have some authority or control over the nation of Israel (the Times of the Gentiles)

cudgels
clubs used for weapons

thermonuclear devices
atomic bombs

supernaturally
It did not come into being in a normal way.

solve the world's problems and more and more likely to face confrontation. God will ultimately replace Gentile world government with his own kingdom.

Some expositors see the bodily proportions of this statue as an indication of the duration of these empires. The head, Babylon, would be the shortest (612–539 BC). The chest and arms, Medes and Persians (538–331 BC), would be close to the length of the belly and thighs (330–63 BC). The legs, Rome, would be the longest (63 BC–AD 476 for the western empire and to AD 1453 for the eastern empire). And the feet and toes will not last as long as the head.

what others say

Grant R. Jeffrey

The metals symbolized the course of **world gentile rule** [see Time Line #2, Appendix A] for the next two-and-a-half thousand years. The progression from gold to silver to bronze to iron indicated that each of the following empires would be progressively stronger in military power but of lesser value as they degenerated from a monarchy to military rule and finally ended with democracy and dictatorship.[13]

John Hagee

You'll notice that as Daniel's eye traveled down the image, the strength of the metals progressed from soft (gold) to very hard (iron). This is a prophetic picture of the military strength of nations that would develop in years to come. Mankind has progressed from relatively weak weapons such as spears and **cudgels** to smart bombs, scud missiles, and **thermonuclear devices** that could leave earth a spinning graveyard in space.[14]

Watch Out for That Rock

DANIEL 2:34 *You watched while a stone was cut out without hands, which struck the image on its feet of iron and clay, and broke them in pieces. (NKJV)*

As Nebuchadnezzar was looking at the statue in his dream, a rock was **supernaturally** cut out without the help of human beings. It streaked like a missile at the brittle feet of the statue and shattered them.

This is such an awesome picture it's difficult to imagine how Nebuchadnezzar could not remember it. One can almost visualize that rock exploding all over the feet of that great statue and blowing it to bits. But the fact is, God's revelations come primarily through believers rather than unbelievers, and underneath it all was God's plan to elevate Daniel in the kingdom as a reward for his faithfulness and to accomplish his other purposes.

Timber!

DANIEL 2:35 *Then the iron, the clay, the bronze, the silver, and the gold were crushed together, and became like **chaff** from the summer **threshing floors**; the wind carried them away so that no trace of them was found. And the stone that struck the image became a great mountain and filled the whole earth. (NKJV)*

When the feet shattered the entire statue broke into chunks of iron, clay, bronze, silver, and gold. Then the chunks broke into smaller particles of the same materials, and the smaller particles were pulverized into powder. A wind came up and blew all the powder away, but the rock began to grow. It grew into the size of a boulder, then into the size of a mountain, and it continued to grow until it covered the whole earth.

A rock is a Bible symbol of Jesus (Matthew 21:44), and a mountain is a common metaphor for a kingdom (Psalm 48:2; Isaiah 2:2; Jeremiah 51:25; Ezekiel 20:40; Zechariah 8:3). This Rock (Jesus) will establish his mountain (kingdom). Some say Jesus will establish a spiritual kingdom, but this is the destruction of earthly kingdoms to be replaced by a literal earthly kingdom.

This is a picture of a sudden and total destruction. Even the dust was done away with. Later, it will become obvious that this last Gentile world government will be the one ruled by the Antichrist. God will be so greatly displeased with this world government he will destroy every aspect of it in the blink of an eye, and there will be no evidence that it ever existed.

Some teach that the First Coming of Jesus fulfilled this. But he came during the legs of iron and not during the feet of iron mixed with clay. And he didn't establish a world government. The world government that existed in his day killed him. Also, that world government wasn't destroyed suddenly. It divided into two legs, which collapsed at different times over a period of hundreds of years.

go to

chaff
Psalm 1:4

threshing floors
Jeremiah 51:33

chaff
bits of straw and grain husk that are removed by threshing

threshing floors
stomping floors used to separate grain from the chaff

go to

God of heaven
Genesis 1:1; 14:22

exist with his permission
Daniel 5:21

Furthermore, some teach that the Church will convert the world, but the kingdom established by this rock doesn't appear gradually over a period of thousands of years. It will appear like the flashing of lightning from the east to the west. Additionally, the coming kingdom won't coexist with these Gentile empires. It will destroy and replace them.

"We" Will Tell You What It Means

> DANIEL 2:36 *"This is the dream. Now we will tell the interpretation of it before the king. (NKJV)*

This was Nebuchadnezzar's dream, but Daniel did not wait for him to acknowledge it. He immediately said, We will interpret it to the king. Not "I," but "we." Daniel included his prayer partners: Shadrach, Meshach, and Abed-Nego. But, most of all, he included God.

Dominion and Power from God

> DANIEL 2:37 *You, O king, are a king of kings. For the God of heaven has given you a kingdom, power, strength, and glory; (NKJV)*

Daniel began interpreting the dream by reminding Nebuchadnezzar where the king got his kingdom and who put him on the throne. Daniel told the king the God of heaven did these things. There are no kings or kingdoms except those God allows. There is no dominion, power, might, or glory except that which God permits. All of them exist with his permission, or they do not exist at all.

The First Kingdom

> DANIEL 2:38 *and wherever the children of men dwell, or the beasts of the field and the birds of the heaven, He has given them into your hand, and has made you ruler over them all—you are this head of gold. (NKJV)*

This reveals just how extensive Nebuchadnezzar's kingdom (see Illustration #6) was. God had given all men, all wild animals, and all the birds of the air into his hands. God had made Nebuchadnezzar ruler over all he had made. He had given Nebuchadnezzar a world-wide government—a government that included every living creature.

Daniel used "king" and "kingdom" interchangeably. He informed Nebuchadnezzar that he (and his kingdom) was the statue's head of gold.

God placed the whole world in Nebuchadnezzar's hands. He was the most influential and powerful man on earth, but he never controlled all of the earth. He could have. He just didn't do it. It's like the land God gave to Israel. He gave them much more than they ever controlled. They could have taken it, but they didn't. In the future, power will be given to the Antichrist over all kindreds, and tongues, and nations (Revelation 13:7). He will have the power, but he will never fully realize a universal kingdom. There will be only one, and that is the one Jesus will rule over.

Times of the Gentiles
Luke 21:24

what others say

C. I. Scofield

"The times of the Gentiles" (Luke 21:24) is that long period that began with the Babylonian captivity of Judah, under Nebuchadnezzar, and is to be brought to an end by the destruction of Gentile world power by the "stone cut out without hands" (Daniel 2:34–35, 44), i.e. the coming of the Lord in glory (Revelation 19:11, 21). Until then Jerusalem will be, as Christ said, "trodden down by the Gentiles" (Luke 21:24).[15]

The Times of the Gentiles (see Time Line #2, Appendix A) is that period of time when the city of Jerusalem is under the control of Gentile governments. Not everyone agrees, but it is generally recognized to be that period of time that runs between Babylon's capture of Jerusalem and the Second Coming of Christ at the end of the Tribulation Period.

Some would argue that Jerusalem is not under the control of Gentile governments today, but the Palestinians claim East Jerusalem as the capital of their hoped-for future Palestinian state. Israel claims all of Jerusalem as the undivided capital of the Jewish nation, but the United Nations, the EU, and all others refuse to recognize Israel's claim. And Gentiles will trod it down during the Tribulation Period *until* Jesus returns. "Until" means Gentile influence will come to an end.

go to

Medes and Persians
Daniel 5:28;
Daniel 8:1–21

Illustration #6
Babylonian
Empire—The head
of gold in God's
Statue.

The Second and Third Kingdoms

DANIEL 2:39 *But after you shall arise another kingdom inferior to yours; then another, a third kingdom of bronze, which shall rule over all the earth.* (NKJV)

After Nebuchadnezzar and his world kingdom, there would be a second world kingdom (see Illustration #7) inferior to Babylon. Then there would be a third world kingdom (see Illustration #8), a kingdom of bronze, that would rule the whole earth.

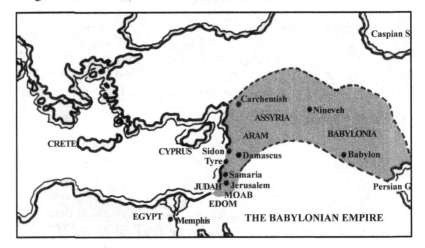

Daniel did not identify these world kingdoms, but we do not have to speculate about who they are. The Bible and history make clear that the second world kingdom was the silver empire led by the <u>Medes and Persians</u>. And the third world kingdom was the brass empire led by the nation of Greece under Alexander the Great.

The second Gentile world government had two arms and was divided into two main divisions: the Medes and the Persians. The fourth Gentile world government had two legs of iron and was divided into two main divisions: Eastern Roman Empire and Western Roman Empire. The last Gentile world government will have two feet and ten toes, which probably signifies a world government with two main divisions and ten subdivisions.

A Fourth Kingdom

DANIEL 2:40 *And the fourth kingdom shall be as strong as iron, inasmuch as iron breaks in pieces and shatters everything; and like iron that crushes, that kingdom will break in pieces and crush all the others.* (NKJV)

There was a fourth world kingdom (see Illustration #9) in Nebuchadnezzar's dream. Daniel did not identify it, but there is general agreement that the iron kingdom was the Old Roman Empire. That empire replaced the Greeks. The Romans literally crushed all their enemies. They graphically demonstrated the prophesied increase in the hardness and destructiveness of the Gentile world governments. They were the major power on earth when Jesus first came, and his brutal death is a good example of how they dealt with people.

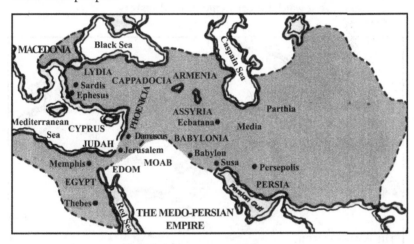

Illustration #7
Medo-Persian Empire—The chest and arms of silver in God's Statue.

Illustration #8
Greek Empire—The belly and thighs of bronze in God's Statue.

scenario
overall outline

consummation of history
the End of the Age (the End of the Times of the Gentiles)

Illustration #9
Old Roman Empire—The legs of iron in God's Statue.

what others say

Mark Hitchcock

Amazingly, there have been four—and only four—world empires. As much as others have tried since the fall of the Roman Empire, they have always failed in their lust to rule the world. God's Word stands as the anvil of truth.[16]

David Breese

He [Daniel] gives us the **scenario** of history in a few short verses and reminds us of the triumph of God over it all. Because of the emphasis given on this fourth kingdom, we need to think further about Rome and the role it will play as we move toward the **consummation of history**.[27]

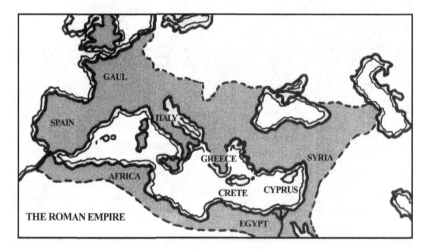

GAUL

SPAIN

ITALY

GREECE

SYRIA

AFRICA

CRETE

CYPRUS

THE ROMAN EMPIRE

EGYPT

A Fifth Kingdom

DANIEL 2:41 *Whereas you saw the feet and toes, partly of potter's clay and partly of iron, the kingdom shall be divided; yet the strength of the iron shall be in it, just as you saw the iron mixed with ceramic clay. (NKJV)*

Up to this point in Nebuchadnezzar's dream we have been looking at events that are history to us—events that, although they were future to Daniel, are past to us because they have now been fulfilled. In the remainder of Chapter 2 we are going to be looking at a prophecy about the future—events that are now coming on the scene; they have yet to arrive, but we can see them approaching.

Daniel's interpretation moved from an explanation of the legs of iron down to an explanation of the feet and toes made from a mixture of iron and potter's clay. This will be a fifth Gentile world kingdom. It will be the last Gentile world kingdom, and shortly after it comes to power it will be destroyed by the <u>Second Coming</u> of Christ.

Daniel revealed that the last Gentile world kingdom will be a divided world kingdom. Based upon what we have already learned, it is reasonable to assume this fifth kingdom will organize into two main divisions at first corresponding to the two feet of the statue. Later on, it will subdivide into <u>ten minor divisions</u> corresponding to the ten toes of the statue.

Daniel also told us it will be a mixture of iron and potter's clay. It is difficult to say exactly what he meant, but it seems it will be a mixture of iron nations coming out of the **Old Roman Empire** and non-iron (potter's clay) nations that existed apart from the Old Roman Empire. Those non-iron nations could include countries from Central Europe. It is even possible that the mixture of iron and baked clay could be the United Nations.

The fact that this fifth Gentile world kingdom will have some of the strength of the iron in it means that much of its power will come from the iron nations that were in the Old Roman Empire. They will give the fifth world kingdom power by transferring their weapons, resources, and military to it.

This needs to be emphasized and closely studied. Many expositors refer to this last Gentile world government as the Revived Roman Empire, reconstituted Europe, Rome II, contaminated Europe, and so forth. It is not Europe alone (not Iron alone). It is Europe plus others (Iron plus potter's clay). The ten toes are not ten toes of iron (ten divisions in Europe). They are ten toes of iron plus potter's clay (ten divisions in a new Gentile world government more than Europe, but dominated by Europe). The potter's clay indicates the involvement of nations that were not formerly part of the old Roman Empire (nations that were not iron). They are non–Roman empire nations (clay) that join with the old Roman Empire nations (iron) to make up the New World Order (iron plus clay). Europe is not the last Gentile world government. It's the strength of the last Gentile world government. It joins its political, economic, and military clout with others to form one last Gentile world government. And one should not automatically assume that this last Gentile world government will be composed of ten nations, because it may be composed

Second Coming
Revelation 19:11–21

ten minor divisions
Revelation 13:1;
17:12

Old Roman Empire
that part of the world controlled by Rome at the time of Christ

of ten groups of nations. If it is ten groups of nations, the EU will probably be just one group out of ten. Nevertheless, it will be the most powerful group. Clay may be a contaminant, but the EU and its Antichrist will be the primary source of corruption in this group.

what others say

Peter and Paul Lalonde

Today, a world which feared communism sweeping westward is finding that instead, democracy ("of the people, by the people, for the people") is sweeping eastward. As the two systems adapt to embrace each other, as is the case in Eastern Europe, we may be beginning to see the formative stages of one empire made "partly of iron and partly of clay."[18]

The next, and final, Gentile world government that will be in place when Jesus comes back is depicted by the chart below. This Gentile world government will probably be an EU-led restructured United Nations with two main divisions and ten subdivisions. It's sometimes called the New World Order.

Gentile Kingdoms (Daniel 2)

Kingdoms	Ten Divisions
1. Babylonian (gold)	
2. Medo-Persian (silver)	
3. Greek (bronze)	
4. Rome (iron)	
5. United Nations (iron + clay)	2 feet with 10 toes

2 feet with 10 toes

1	6
2	7
3	8
4	9
5	10

The iron + clay will be the EU + others who will unite in a restructured United Nations Gentile world government.

The 2 feet with 10 toes will be 2 divisions with 5 subdivisions in each.

The Antichrist will subdue 3 of the 10 subdivisions (Daniel 7:24). Then all 10 will submit to him (Revelation 17:13).

Strong but Brittle

DANIEL 2:42 *And as the toes of the feet were partly of iron and partly of clay, so the kingdom shall be partly strong and partly fragile. (NKJV)*

The fifth and final Gentile world kingdom will lack uniformity. It will be "partly strong and partly fragile," signifying a precarious mixture of strong Old Roman Empire nations and weaker non–Roman Empire nations. They will be brought together by treaties and agreements that will have the outward appearance of unity, but these treaties and agreements will fail to tightly bind the nations together.

Discussions about a New World Order are actually discussions about a one-world government. Many people say *globalism* means global corporations, global standards, global trade, and things like that. They are right, but that is just part of the story. *Globalism* also means global cooperation to deal with hunger and poverty, to protect the environment, to protect natural resources, and to settle disputes. *Globalism* is a system of global rules and regulations, and that is one-world government.

World leaders have already created a World Bank, a World Health Organization, a World Trade Organization, two world courts (The International Criminal Court and the International Court of Justice), and an International Monetary Fund. The United Nations is already asking for a World Constitution, a World Currency, a World Income Tax, a World Military, a Global Identification Number (Mark), and a Global Ethic (religion). World leaders are already in a vital debate about restructuring the United Nations, with one of the main proposals being to increase the number of permanent members of the Security Council to ten (toes, horns, kings representing ten groups of nations or ten divisions of the world).

Some world leaders are already calling for "global management," and "the rule of world law." Australia wants "collective sovereignty that supercedes national sovereignty." France wants "collective security" run by the United Nations Security Council with all nations ceding their power to the United Nations. *Global management, the rule of world law, collective sovereignty, global sovereignty,* and *collective security* are buzz words for one-world government. God is the only One who knows the future, but after all this gets ironed out and the last Gentile world government comes on the scene, the Antichrist will take over.

military juggernaut
a powerful military

factionalism
internal differences
and dissension

what others say

David Reagan

In subsequent dreams and visions, the Lord revealed to Daniel that this kingdom of iron mixed with clay would be a loose confederation of ten nations (Daniel 7:24). This confederation would arise out of the territory of the empire of iron—the Roman Empire (Daniel 7:7–8). Daniel was also shown that this revived European confederation would serve as the base for the construction of the last great Gentile world empire—namely, the empire of the Antichrist (Daniel 7:8, 24–26; 8:19–27).[19]

United We Fall

DANIEL 2:43 *As you saw iron mixed with ceramic clay, they will mingle with the seed of men; but they will not adhere to one another, just as iron does not mix with clay. (NKJV)*

The people in the last Gentile world government will be just like the unstable mixture of iron and baked clay. They will be forced into a one-world government, but they will not stay united.

The reason for this is uncertain and one that stirs much debate. Some speculate that this instability will have something to do with the difficulty of blending cultures in the last Gentile world government. Others say it will be the problem of trying to mix democracy with communism. But a few say the mention of the "seed of men" is an indication that the instability will be the result of fallen angels or demonic activity (Genesis 3:15; 6:1–7). The Bible does teach that demonic activity will be a major problem at the end of the age (1 Timothy 4:1). Satan worship will play a big role in the government of Antichrist (Revelation 13).

what others say

Charles H. Dyer

The Achilles' heel of this **military juggernaut** will be its **factionalism**.[20]

A Sixth and Final Kingdom

DANIEL 2:44 *And in the days of these kings the God of heaven will set up a kingdom which shall never be destroyed; and the kingdom shall not be left to other people; it shall break in pieces and consume all these kingdoms, and it shall stand forever.* (NKJV)

Here is an important clue concerning the Second Coming of Christ and his subsequent reign here on earth. He will return to establish his own kingdom on earth while the one-world government is organized into ten subdivisions under the leadership of <u>ten kings</u>. And his world kingdom will be different from the Gentile world kingdoms in two ways: (1) it will never be destroyed, and (2) it will never be taken over by anyone else.

The kingdom that is to be established by Jesus will bring an end to all rebellion against God. It will bring an end to all sin. All kings will <u>fall down</u> before him, and his kingdom will endure forever.

go to

ten kings
Revelation 17:12

fall down
Psalm 72:11

Antichrist
1 John 2:18, 22; 4:3; 2 John 1:7

Antichrist
an enemy of Christ who will come during the Tribulation Period

Beast
person who is full of evil (i.e., the Antichrist)

Messiah
the Christ; Jesus

what others say

Grant R. Jeffrey

The Club of Rome, the Trilateral Commission, and the Council on Foreign Relations each use a "ten kingdom" administrative model in their plans for the coming world government. In the book of Revelation the prophet John revealed that the **Antichrist**, the **Beast** (the first beast of Revelation), and his ten-nation confederacy will rule the world for seven years during the coming Tribulation Period until the **Messiah** returns to establish the Kingdom of God on earth.[21]

Richard Booker

Many people think the world is going to end when Messiah Jesus comes. But the world is not going to end. What is going to end is the present age in which we live. But first, this present world order must come to an end. It must come to an end because it is an anti-God system. The Tribulation Period will bring it to an end. Then Messiah Jesus will come and establish a new world order based on justice and righteousness.[22]

C. I. Scofield

This passage fixes, in relation to other predicted events, the time when the millennial kingdom will be established. It will be "in the days of these kings," i.e. the days of the ten kings (compare 7:24–27) symbolized by the toes of the image.[23]

The Rock

DANIEL 2:45 *Inasmuch as you saw that the stone was cut out of the mountain without hands, and that it broke in pieces the*

rock
Deuteronomy
32:3–4, 15

offering and
incense
honor, worship, and
the burning of
sweet-smelling
perfume

iron, the bronze, the clay, the silver, and the gold—the great God has made known to the king what will come to pass after this. The dream is certain, and its interpretation is sure." (NKJV)

Here is some important information concerning the <u>rock</u>. "Cut out of the mountain without hands" means the rock will be the work of God. As a world kingdom, it will not come into being.

It is again stated that the rock will break the other world kingdoms. It is added that God himself revealed these things to the king; that absolutely nothing can change them, and that they will definitely be fulfilled. This is demonstrated in the story about Shadrach, Meshach, and Abed-Nego in chapter 3. Nebuchadnezzar built a statue that denied this dream, but he wasted his time and money. When God says something will come to pass, it's a done deal. Because he said the final Gentile world government will be destroyed by the Second Coming of Jesus, historians can write it down because nothing can keep it from happening.

Many Scriptures in both the Old and New Testaments teach that this "Smiting Stone" is Jesus. Three New Testament verses are shown in the following chart.

The Smiting Stone

Stone Reference	Scripture
Jesus is the rock that Moses struck.	1 Corinthians 10:4
Jesus is a stone of stumbling and a rock of offense to unbelievers.	1 Peter 2:8
Jesus is the chief cornerstone of the Church.	Ephesians 2:20

Flat on His Face

DANIEL 2:46 *Then King Nebuchadnezzar fell on his face, prostrate before Daniel, and commanded that they should present an offering and incense to him. (NKJV)*

An extraordinary thing happened when Daniel finished revealing the dream and its interpretation. The arrogant and powerful Nebuchadnezzar fell down on his face before Daniel and worshiped him. When he got up he commanded that an **offering and incense** be given to Daniel.

Father, Son, and Holy Spirit

> **DANIEL 2:47** *The king answered Daniel, and said, "Truly your God is the God of gods, the Lord of kings, and a revealer of secrets, since you could reveal this secret."* (NKJV)

This does not appear to be a **confession of faith** on the part of Nebuchadnezzar. Notice that he spoke of Daniel's God as "your God" and not "my God." But it does appear to be an unwitting acknowledgment of the **Trinity**. The *God of gods* is Jehovah God or God the Father. The *Lord of kings* is the King of kings and Lord of lords or God the Son. The *revealer of secrets* is the one who <u>searches all things</u> or God the Holy Spirit. Nebuchadnezzar also acknowledged that Daniel had succeeded in revealing the secret.

Power and Riches I Give to You

> **DANIEL 2:48** *Then the king promoted Daniel and gave him many great gifts; and he made him ruler over the whole province of Babylon, and chief administrator over all the wise men of Babylon.* (NKJV)

Nebuchadnezzar rewarded Daniel by giving him the two things in life that most of society thinks will make a man great: power and riches. When a man has both he is respected, whether he deserves it or not. Daniel was made ruler over the entire province of Babylon; he was put in charge of all the so-called wise men, and he was lavished with many gifts. That would swell the heads of many people, but as we continue we will see that it did not affect the **God-fearing** Daniel.

Remember My Friends

> **DANIEL 2:49** *Also Daniel petitioned the king, and he set Shadrach, Meshach, and Abed-Nego over the affairs of the province of Babylon; but Daniel sat in the gate of the king.* (NKJV)

As soon as Daniel was rewarded, he began to reward his friends. One of his first acts was to request some changes. He wanted new appointments for Shadrach, Meshach, and Abed-Nego, who had been his prayer partners in this whole matter. They were made

go to

accepts God and his Son, Jesus
John 3:16

searches all things
1 Corinthians 2:10–11

confession of faith
a public acknowledgment that a person <u>accepts God and his Son, Jesus</u>

Trinity
a word not found in the Bible, but it refers to the idea that God exists in three ways: as God the Father, as God the Son, and as God the Holy Spirit

God-fearing
submitting to the power and authority of God

administrators over the province of Babylon, so Daniel could remain at the royal court.

Daniel 2 reveals that there will be five Gentile world governments before Jesus returns. He will not return before then. The Rapture could have taken place any time in the last 1,900 years, but the Second Coming cannot happen until the fifth Gentile world government is in existence and divided into ten regions with a ruler over each one of them. But know this: if the last Gentile world government is close, the Rapture is even closer. The chart below is an outline of Gentile world governments leading up to the Second Coming of Jesus.

Four Down and One to God

Body Parts of God's Statue	Metal	Gentile Kingdom Represented
Head	Gold	Babylonian
Chest and Arms	Silver	Medo-Persian
Belly and Thighs	Bronze	Greek
Legs	Iron	Old Roman Empire
Feet	Iron and Clay	United Nations

Before we leave this chapter, it seems important to ask, "Where is modern society on this statue?" The Times of the Gentiles started at the top of the statue's head 2,600 years ago. A vast majority of the most prominent pre-Tribulation scholars in America agree that the statue's feet are now forming. Astute students know the Second Coming will take place after the toes are formed. But one has to back up from the toes to allow for a seven-year Tribulation Period. And back up a little farther to allow for the Rapture.

Chapter Wrap-Up

- Nebuchadnezzar dreamed a disturbing dream that troubled him and interfered with his sleep. (Daniel 2:1)
- Nebuchadnezzar summoned his wise men to reveal the dream and its meaning. In spite of offers of rewards, the wise men were unable to reveal the dream and its meaning. Consequently, Nebuchadnezzar ordered the wise men to be executed. (Daniel 2:2–12)
- When Daniel heard of the king's decree he asked for time, so that he might interpret the dream. Then he went to his friends and urged them to pray for God's mercy. (Daniel 2:13–18)
- God revealed the king's dream and its interpretation to Daniel. It concerned a great statue with a head of gold, chest and arms of silver, belly and thighs of bronze, legs of iron, and feet of part iron and part clay. Each part of the statue represented a different Gentile world kingdom. (Daniel 2:19–43)
- A great rock smashed the statue. The rock (Jesus) grew and filled the earth (representative of the kingdom of God on earth). (Daniel 2:34–35, 44–45)

Study Questions

1. Why did Nebuchadnezzar decree that the astrologers tell him both what the dream was and what it meant?

2. Why were the magicians, enchanters, and astrologers unable to tell Nebuchadnezzar his dream and interpret it for him?

3. What six steps did Daniel go through to get an interpretation for Nebuchadnezzar's dream?

4. Who will set up the only kingdom that will never be destroyed?

5. Did Nebuchadnezzar become a believer as a result of Daniel's amazing feat?

Chapter Highlights:
- Statue of Gold
- One-World Worship Service
- Three Faithful Jews
- Our God Is Able
- A Fourth Man

Daniel 3 Daniel's Friends and the Fiery Furnace

Let's Get Started

The Bible does not say when the fiery furnace occurred, but according to the Septuagint it took place somewhere between sixteen and twenty years after the events described in chapter 2. Chapter 1 opens around 605 BC when Daniel and his friends were about thirteen or fourteen years old. Chapter 2 probably took place after the young Jews had completed a few years of schooling; when they were about seventeen or eighteen years old. All this leads us to believe the events of chapter 3 occurred around the year 585 BC, when Shadrach, Meshach, and Abed-Nego were in their early thirties (see Time Line #1, Appendix A).

Not much else had changed. Nebuchadnezzar is still the king and just as arrogant, demanding, and dangerous as ever. The so-called wise men are still serving under Daniel and his friends. They, of course, have forgotten that Daniel knew and interpreted Nebuchadnezzar's dream when they could not. Now they are stewing with jealousy and hurt pride.

Most expositors say this chapter is entirely historical with no prophetic revelations. Some agree with the historical aspect, but they also say the chapter is filled with types of things to come. They observe that many of the characteristics of Nebuchadnezzar are similar to those of the Antichrist. His great statue is comparable to the one the Antichrist and his False Prophet will set up during the Tribulation Period. His worship service represents an attempt to establish a one-world religion. Shadrach, Meshach, and Abed-Nego in the fiery furnace represent Israel in the Tribulation Period. The attempt on their lives represents the attempt to exterminate the Jews. Their deliverance from the fiery furnace represents the remnant that will flee into the wilderness and be saved at the end. And Daniel's absence in this chapter represents the absence of the raptured church.

troubling dream
Daniel 2

go to

Hal Lindsey

I believe the Holy Spirit has selected these true historical incidences out of all of those years that they [the Jews] were under Babylonian captivity, and one incident is under Medo-Persian captivity, to show how God would protect the Jew in the midst of the time when gentiles would be in power over the whole world. It also shows by application how God will preserve those who believe in him in the midst of the most desperate situation caused by an alien government that is against the true faith.[1]

A Tall Golden Statue (Nebuchadnezzar's Statue)

DANIEL 3:1 *Nebuchadnezzar the king made an image of gold, whose height was sixty cubits and its width six cubits. He set it up in the plain of Dura, in the province of Babylon.* (NKJV)

Sixteen to twenty years had passed, but Nebuchadnezzar still had that <u>troubling dream</u> on his mind. It seems that he was obsessed with it, and I'm sure he did not want his kingdom to come to an end. He obviously liked Daniel, but Nebuchadnezzar probably hoped Daniel was wrong. He wanted Babylon to be the kingdom that would never be destroyed.

So Nebuchadnezzar decided to make a great statue of his own (see Illustration #10). He could have the statue like the one in his dream—a statue of gold, silver, bronze, iron, and clay. But he did not want that. He did not want the kingdom of Babylon to be overthrown. He did not want those other Gentile world kingdoms to appear. He did not want the Times of the Gentiles to come to an end or Jesus to come and set up his own kingdom.

Gold represented the kingdom of Babylon in the king's dream so he made this statue entirely of gold. Obviously Nebuchadnezzar refused to believe his kingdom would be overthrown. He made a statue to contradict his dream, a statue to signify that his kingdom would last forever, a statue to signify that the prophecies of God would not come to pass.

The statue was about ninety feet ("sixty cubits") high and about nine feet ("six cubits") wide. Something that tall could easily be seen from a great distance, especially something placed in a wide-open space and made of glistening gold. It would also be disproportionate, very tall and very thin.

It was set up in the Plain of Dura (see Illustration #2). *Smith's Bible Dictionary* tells us an archaeologist named Oppert found the site almost a century ago. It is southeast of Babylon and at a place now called Duair.

It's an extensive, almost-level area that would allow a great number of people to view and worship the statue and its maker, the king.

Some writers are intrigued by the fact that the number of man is six (man was created on the sixth day, he works six days and rests on seventh, and so forth), and this statue of a man was sixty cubits high and six cubits wide. Astute students of the Word know that the False Prophet will set up a statue and command people to worship it, and that the number of the Antichrist is 666 (Revelation 13:14–18).

Illustration #10
Nebuchadnezzar's Statue— Nebuchadnezzar's attempt at immortality.

go to

image
Exodus 20:4–6

satrap
an office just below
the king (similar to a
prince or vice
president)

All Must Come

DANIEL 3:2 *And King Nebuchadnezzar sent word to gather together the **satraps**, the administrators, the governors, the counselors, the treasurers, the judges, the magistrates, and all the officials of the provinces, to come to the dedication of the image which King Nebuchadnezzar had set up.* (NKJV)

Nebuchadnezzar called on the government leaders in the top seven levels (or offices) of his world kingdom plus many more to attend a dedication service for the image. It would be the greatest gathering of politicians and bureaucrats the world had ever seen.

what others say

H. A. Ironside

This event, though actual history, is a typical scene picturing the trial and deliverance of a faithful remnant of Daniel's people that is to take place in the time of the end. There will come a day when (like the great image set up by Nebuchadnezzar) what the Lord Jesus calls "the abomination of desolation, spoken of by Daniel the prophet" (Matt. 24:15), is going to be set up in Jerusalem by the Antichrist of the future.[2]

A. Edwin Wilson

Today, there is a centralized trend in government, religious totalitarianism, and the attempt of the National Council of Churches to curtail all freedoms of non-conformist churches and Christians.[3]

Not everyone agrees on what these government offices actually were, but there is little question that they were the top offices in Babylon's world government.

A One-World Worship Service

DANIEL 3:3 *So the satraps, the administrators, the governors, the counselors, the treasurers, the judges, the magistrates, and all the officials of the provinces gathered together for the dedication of the image that King Nebuchadnezzar had set up; and they stood before the image that Nebuchadnezzar had set up.* (NKJV)

We can logically assume that the city of Babylon began to bustle as the great dedication day approached. With important dignitaries arriving from all over the world the level of excitement probably reached a new high. Then the well-planned-for dedication arrived and a great crowd moved to the Plain of Dura. They stood before the image like the multitudes who stand before our flag at a baseball game.

go to

great-grandson of Noah
Genesis 10:1–10

Some scholars note that these dignitaries are listed in descending order of rank with titles that were common in Babylon six hundred years before Jesus. At least three of the musical instruments in verse 5 have Greek names, which causes a few skeptics to say the book of Daniel was written by a different Daniel who lived in Greece about four hundred years later. It seems more likely that these instruments were manufactured in Greece and sold in Babylon. Researchers have found plenty of evidence that the two were trading with each other at that time. If the book of Daniel was written in Greece it would probably have more Greek words in it. It doesn't, but one major section was written in Aramaic, which was the language of Babylon. This is the kind of information that is sometimes used to establish when something was written. In plain English, the book of Daniel was written about five hundred to six hundred years before Jesus came along.

what others say

Kenneth O. Gangel

Some scholars have noted that the very titles used favor the early dating of Daniel in the sixth century. We cannot be sure of the specific duties of these various officials, nor would that knowledge enhance our understanding of the chapter. In wording this kind of edict today, we might say, "Everyone on the federal payroll must show up."[4]

The Bible does not say whether or not Daniel was present during this worship service, but many Bible experts hold the position that he wasn't. Their reasoning being that if Daniel had been present he would have refused to bow and also been thrown into the fiery furnace. Since that did not happen most experts contend he was away tending to the king's business.

something to ponder

Nimrod was the great-grandson of Noah. He lived after the flood and was a lawless person who tried to establish a world religion and a world government. He is credited with founding several new cities including Babylon, and as the head of the first great anti-God civi-

Nimrod
Genesis 10:8–10;
11:1–9

**people from all
the earth**
Revelation 13:7–8

lization, he is a forerunner of the Antichrist. Babylon is sometimes called the city of Satan, and it's interesting that <u>Nimrod</u> tried to establish a one-world religion and government there, Nebuchadnezzar followed in his footsteps and tried to do the same thing, and the Antichrist will finally come along and do it. But God scattered everyone at the tower of Babel, he brought about the defeat of Babylon, and Jesus will return and cast the Antichrist into the Lake of Fire.

The First Decree

herald
messenger similar to
a master of cere-
monies

horn
probably a coronet
or trumpet

flute
long slender wind
instrument

harp
large stringed instru-
ment

lyre
ancient hand-held
instrument similar to
a small harp

psaltery
stringed flat box,
similar to a zither

> DANIEL 3:4 *Then a herald cried aloud: "To you it is commanded, O peoples, nations, and languages,* (NKJV)

One of Nebuchadnezzar's **heralds** made an announcement. It was a loud command that <u>people from all the earth</u> had to follow.

what others say

Arno Froese

The golden image Nebuchadnezzar had built in the Babylonian province was created to unify all religions. All people had to become equal; therefore only one god and one type of worship was accepted. We have to keep this fact in mind because Babylon is the first Gentile superpower and the last Gentile superpower is called "Mystery Babylon, the great, the mother of harlots and abominations of the earth" (Revelation 17:5).[6]

The Pulpit Commentary

True religion is nothing less than the purest love of the human heart pouring itself out, in service or in speech, unto the living God; and if love, must ever be spontaneous and free, in order to be love at all, so must be the piety of the human soul. Spontaneity is a necessity in religion. If compulsion be employed, its essence evaporates, its spirit disappears.[6]

All Must Bow

> DANIEL 3:5 *that at the time you hear the sound of the **horn**, **flute**, **harp**, **lyre**, and **psaltery**, in symphony with all kinds of music, you shall fall down and worship the gold image that King Nebuchadnezzar has set up;* (NKJV)

The herald told everyone that at the sound of music they were commanded to fall down and worship the golden <u>image</u>. With the music coming from many different kinds of instruments (see Illustration #11) being played at the same time, it appears that the musicians were acting similar to a band or orchestra in a modern church service. But this was no church service, and there may have been many who wished they didn't have to be there.

go to

image
Revelation 13:8

worship
Revelation 13:15

evil men
2 Timothy 3:12–17

angel
heavenly being who serves God; usually a messenger

what others say

John C. Whitcomb

We know from Scripture that the Babylonians greatly loved beautiful and exotic music. God had said of Babylon: "Your pomp and the music of your harps have been brought down to Sheol" (Isaiah 14:11).[7]

David Jeremiah with C. C. Carlson

Almost every major cult and -ism, every false religion, has found some way to use music for its perverted purposes. It's a type of mind control. I believe with all of my heart that music belongs to God. It belongs to the **angels**. It belongs to God's people. The world will take what belongs to God and prostitute it for its own purposes.[8]

Not everyone agrees on what these instruments were, but there is little question that music was an important part of this worship service.

Oops! A Little Too Hot for Me

DANIEL 3:6 *and whoever does not fall down and worship shall be cast immediately into the midst of a burning fiery furnace."* (NKJV)

Everything was fast and furious. Freedom of religion and <u>worship</u> was suspended. An <u>evil man</u> commanded that all who did not immediately fall down and worship the image would die. There would be no delay. A giant furnace was set to swiftly carry out the sentence. In essence the command was "bow or burn." What a choice! Many would rather bow and try to justify what they did at a later time.

Illustration #11
Ancient
Instruments—Today
archaeologists have
uncovered many
instruments similar
to these.

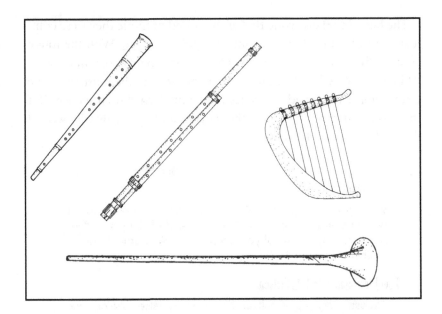

what others say

David Breese

The Scripture specifically predicts the coming of the anti-Christ and warns us that he will invent a global religion where everyone will be forced to worship. . . . The religion of the anti-Christ will be:

Satanic—People will worship the dragon [Satan] which is another name in Scripture for the devil.

Humanistic—They will worship the beast [Antichrist] who is the anti-Christ himself.

Universal—All the world will be involved.

Ecumenical—Every religion in the world, except Christianity will be involved.

Phenomenalistic—The anti-Christ will work miracles and even call down fire from heaven.

Pagan—The world will worship the Image of the Beast.

Cruel—All who do not worship will be killed.[9]

Forcing people to worship this image is similar to what the spiritual leader called the **False Prophet** will do during the Tribulation Period. As the head of the one-world religion during that time he will force people to worship the Image of the Beast and give all allegiance to the Antichrist (the one-world political leader). All who refuse will be killed.

False Prophet
the spiritual leader
of the one-world
religion

So Much Music

> **DANIEL 3:7** *So at that time, when all the people heard the sound of the horn, flute, harp, and lyre, in symphony with all kinds of music, all the people, nations, and languages fell down and worshiped the gold image which King Nebuchadnezzar had set up. (NKJV)*

What an event. Most people knew what they were going to do in this worship service. There was very little hesitation or reluctance, if any. As soon as the music started people from all over the world hit the ground and the prayers to this idol started to flow. But this was just a <u>form of godliness</u>. It was not true worship and about the only positive thing it accomplished was the appeasement of Satan and Nebuchadnezzar.

The scene is awesome with foreboding implications for the future. It shows how easy it is to get large numbers of people to bow down to an idol when they fear their lives are on the line. The unlearned and unsaved will bow with little or no hesitation. Satan's Antichrist and False Prophet will threaten the lives of people during the Tribulation Period to force them to bow, and multitudes will drop to their knees as if their feet were suddenly kicked out from under them.

Down with the Jews

> **DANIEL 3:8** *Therefore at that time certain Chaldeans came forward and accused the Jews. (NKJV)*

This may have been an act of jealousy, a power grab, an effort to stamp out religious competition or just plain old **anti-Semitism**. Some of the Chaldeans were acting as spies at this event. Their <u>lives had been spared</u> about sixteen years earlier when Daniel and his three friends prayed to their God and received the revelation of Nebuchadnezzar's dream. Whatever the reason, the Chaldeans ignored what the Jews had done for them and reported the Jews for disobeying this new command.

Scholars say the word translated *accused* means "devoured piecemeal" or "swallowed them up piece by piece." This is an example of state-monitored or state-controlled worship with brutal character assassination. The astrologers knew these young men would not bow

form of godliness
2 Timothy 3:1–5

lives had been spared
Daniel 2:24

anti-Semitism
prejudice or hostility
against Jews

adoration
admiration, love, or
worship

dispatches
letters, messages,
official communications

to an idol, so they prepared a list of accusations to take them apart
or discredit them before the whole world. It's a picture of the future
persecution of Christians and Jews, except that during the Tribulation
Period the dismemberment will be literal. It will be done in the name
of religion, but it will be false religion that is intolerant of true godliness. It's a reminder of what Paul said about the perilous times of the
last days, that "men will be lovers of themselves, lovers of money,
boasters, proud, blasphemers, disobedient to parents, unthankful,
unholy, unloving, unforgiving, slanderers, without self-control, brutal,
despisers of good" (2 Timothy 3:1–3 NKJV).

what others say

Henry M. Morris

One of the most amazing aspects of religious history is the
hatred of other religions against Christ and His followers.
Wherever Christianity has gone, preaching the gospel of the
love of Christ and salvation by God's grace, it has been resisted. Perhaps more often than not, it has been resisted by
bitter persecution, at least for a time.[10]

Daniel said, "Do not destroy the wise men of Babylon; take me
before the king, and I will tell the king the interpretation" (Daniel
2:24 NKJV). "Then the king promoted Daniel and gave him many
great gifts; and he made him ruler over the whole province of
Babylon, and chief administrator over all the wise men of Babylon.
Also Daniel petitioned the king, and he set Shadrach, Meshach, and
Abed-Nego over the affairs of the province of Babylon; but Daniel
sat in the gate of the king" (Danniel 2:48–49 NKJV).

O King, You're the Best!

DANIEL 3:9 *They spoke and said to King Nebuchadnezzar, "O
king, live forever!"* (NKJV)

The Chaldeans approached the haughty Nebuchadnezzar with an
expression of **adoration** that was often used to flatter rulers in
ancient times. It was also sometimes used in **dispatches** like the
modern-day "Dear Sir." But the fact is that it was pretty ridiculous
and something everyone knew to be untrue. In essence they were
saying, "O king, you are so great, and we love you so much, we hope
you will live forever."

This flattery was nothing more than a tool of the astrologers who sought to gain the king's favor and induce him to pursue their evil self-serving interests. Through the cloak of flattery they were setting a trap for Shadrach, Meshach, and Abed-Nego. The followers of Antichrist, too, will do this, asking, "Who is like the beast? Who is able to make war with him?" (Revelation 13:4 NKJV). The words of honey were designed to overthrow righteousness.

weapon
Isaiah 54:17

satanic
inspired by Satan

Remember Your Word

DANIEL 3:10 *You, O king, have made a decree that everyone who hears the sound of the horn, flute, harp, lyre, and psaltery, in symphony with all kinds of music, shall fall down and worship the gold image; (NKJV)*

The Chaldeans reminded Nebuchadnezzar of his decree. It was not that they thought that he was getting senile. No, it was that they wanted him to be embarrassed and angered at what appeared to be an element of disrespect, ingratitude, and outright rebellion. The astrologers wanted to make sure that a confrontation took place and that Nebuchadnezzar was sufficiently stirred up when it happened. In this case, we see that they were using the hotheaded king to their own advantage. He was their <u>weapon</u> against any Jews who would not bow with Shadrach, Meshach, and Abed-Nego among them.

what others say

Kay Arthur

The God who rules over kingdoms and their kings, who sets kings up and removes them, tells us we are to worship Him and Him alone. We are to have no other god! And we are to obey Him no matter the cost, no matter the raving and threats of the world.[11]

Into the Fire They Must Go

DANIEL 3:11 *and whoever does not fall down and worship shall be cast into the midst of a burning fiery furnace. (NKJV)*

This is a reminder of Nebuchadnezzar's **satanic** decree. The Chaldeans were making sure that he remembered what he said the penalty for disobedience would be. They did not want any mistakes. They wanted to see their immediate rulers (Shadrach, Meshach, and Abed-Nego) dead.

go to

obedience
Acts 5:27–29

the Bible says
2 Timothy 3:1–4

last days
the last days of the
Times of the
Gentiles

Three Faithful Jews

DANIEL 3:12 *There are certain Jews whom you have set over the affairs of the province of Babylon: Shadrach, Meshach, and Abed-Nego; these men, O king, have not paid due regard to you. They do not serve your gods or worship the gold image which you have set up."* (NKJV)

This is a list of accusations and a plain statement of who was being accused. It was alleged that Shadrach, Meshach, and Abed-Nego:

1. did not pay due regard to the king

2. did not serve the king's gods

3. did not worship the gold image which the king had set up

Pay attention to the fact that the Chaldeans mentioned the political position—"you have set over the affairs of the province of Babylon"—of Shadrach, Meshach, and Abed-Nego. Their point is that, in their opinion, the three Jews, being high officials in Nebuchadnezzar's one-world kingdom, should have been examples of <u>obedience</u>.

<u>The Bible says</u> in the **last days** terrible times will come because people will be abusive, slanderous, and treacherous [characteristics of the astrologers], rash, and without self-control [characteristics of Nebuchadnezzar]. How bad do you think it will get for Christians and Jews trying to live in a world like that, a world that embraces a one-world religion and a one-world dictator?

what others say

King James Bible Commentary

What courage must have been in the hearts of these Hebrew lads. Instead of rationalizing their way into compromise and sin, they literally stood fast for the Lord. They disobeyed a civil law because God had clearly instructed them to do otherwise in His written Word. Acts 5:29 states, ". . . We ought to obey God rather than men."[12]

Come to Me at Once

DANIEL 3:13 *Then Nebuchadnezzar, in rage and fury, gave the command to bring Shadrach, Meshach, and Abed-Nego. So they brought these men before the king.* (NKJV)

Nebuchadnezzar was like a stick of dynamite with a short fuse. He had a real anger problem, was easily upset, and quick to fly into a rage. It was during one of these rages that he summoned Shadrach, Meshach, and Abed-Nego.

Say It Isn't So

DANIEL 3:14 *Nebuchadnezzar spoke, saying to them, "Is it true, Shadrach, Meshach, and Abed-Nego, that you do not serve my gods or worship the gold image which I have set up? (NKJV)*

Here we learn what Nebuchadnezzar thought about the character of the Chaldeans versus the character of Shadrach, Meshach, and Abed-Nego. It shows that he did not wholeheartedly believe his astrologers, and he was willing to give Daniel's three friends the benefit of the doubt.

Merging religion and government is always dangerous. Government controls the military and soon tires of religion not doing what it says. Then it goes on the attack. In Nebuchadnezzar's case, his religion wasn't based on the Bible, it didn't come from God, and his effort to force it upon the Jews and spread it worldwide was satanic. He went on the attack, but it was an attack upon those who were truly committed to God.

This is the problem with Islam. Fundamentalist clerics believe non-Muslims are infidels who must submit to them. They use their religion to gain political power. Then they use the financial and military resources of their government to destroy other religions and spread theirs. One of their three main goals is the destruction of Israel.

Nebuchadnezzar's one-world religion didn't work, Islam's one-world religion won't work, and the one-world religion of the Antichrist won't work because they are rooted in paganism and based upon false doctrines that are anti-God and anti-Christ. Inclusiveness sounds good, but it is a never-ending slide toward unbelief, it applauds too many things that are an abomination to God, and it comes down too hard on God's true people. It's a situation he won't accept.

Come On, Just One Little Bow

> DANIEL 3:15 *Now if you are ready at the time you hear the sound of the horn, flute, harp, lyre, and psaltery, in symphony with all kinds of music, and you fall down and worship the image which I have made, good! But if you do not worship, you shall be cast immediately into the midst of a burning fiery furnace. And who is the god who will deliver you from my hands?" (NKJV)*

About sixteen to twenty years earlier Daniel interpreted the king's first dream. Nebuchadnezzar fell on his face before Daniel and said, "Truly your God is the God of gods, the Lord of kings, and a revealer of secrets, since you could reveal this secret" (Daniel 2:47 NKJV). He knew the Jewish God then. Now Nebuchadnezzar is pretending he has forgotten him.

what others say

John F. Walvoord

It is an amazing fact that Nebuchadnezzar adds the challenging question, "Who is that God that shall deliver you out of my hands?" He is quite conscious of the demonstration of the superiority of the God of the Hebrews over Babylonian gods in interpreting his dream in chapter 2, but he cannot bring himself to believe that the God of the Jews would be able in these circumstances to deliver these three men from his hand. The fact is that Nebuchadnezzar feels supreme in his power and does not expect any god to interfere.[13]

David Jeremiah with C. C. Carlson

The history of the church has been written in blood. There will always be warfare between the powers of darkness and the powers of light, and there will always be pagan rulers who will cry out in sarcasm, Who is that god?[14]

Answer #1

> DANIEL 3:16 *Shadrach, Meshach, and Abed-Nego answered and said to the king, "O Nebuchadnezzar, we have no need to answer you in this matter." (NKJV)*

This is the first of a threefold response to the fiery king. Their minds were made up. They did not have to think about it. They did not have to pray about it. There was no need to reconsider their actions. They had purposed in their hearts that they would not <u>bow down</u> under any circumstances. Their worship would go to God.

Nebuchadnezzar's confrontation with Shadrach, Meshach, and Abed-Nego continued. He must have loved these three men because he was giving them a second chance to redeem themselves. If they would reconsider and bow down to his image, he would put out the fire. If they would not reconsider, disown their God, and bow down, he would cast them into the fire. He was turning this into a religious competition, a war of the gods so to speak. He believed he and his gods were more powerful than the God of these three Hebrews. Their enemies were probably lurking around in eager anticipation of what they thought was about to happen. They may have smiled and thought promotions were coming because the king would be happy with them.

Do you think it took courage for Shadrach, Meshach, and Abed-Nego to stand up to this violent king? Where do you think their courage came from? If they were afraid of him, nothing is said about it.

go to

bow down
Exodus 20:3–6

God
Matthew 22:21

trust
Isaiah 26:3–4

love
Matthew 22:37–39

forever
Micah 4:5

what others say

John Phillips

Nobody had spoken thus to this pagan king in all of his memory and experience. He was thunderstruck. His personal condescension had been spurned, his new golden god had been scorned, the God of these fanatical Hebrews had been extolled, his proposed global religion had been challenged, and his threat of fire and brimstone had been treated with utter contempt.[16]

Answer #2

DANIEL 3:17 *If that is the case, our God whom we serve is able to deliver us from the burning fiery furnace, and He will deliver us from your hand, O king. (NKJV)*

This is the second part of the threefold response. These men <u>trusted</u> in their God. They knew he could save their lives and actually believed he would. It seems obvious that they <u>loved</u> him very much and were committed to following him <u>forever and ever</u>.

Many people will face a situation like this during the Tribulation Period. They will be told to take the mark of the Beast and bow to the statue of the Antichrist or they will be killed. People will have to

go to

grace of God
Hebrews 4:16

successful
Joshua 1:8–9

grace of God
the undeserved
favor of God

decide whether or not they really believe God. It will take faith to stand firm and believe God will raise them from the dead when people are dying all around them. It will take faith to believe remaining faithful is worth dying for, but it will be because those who take the mark will not be allowed in heaven.

Nebuchadnezzar asked, "Who is the god who will deliver you from my hands?" (Daniel 3:15 NKJV). Shadrach, Meshach, and Abed-Nego responded, "Our God whom we serve is able to deliver us from the burning fiery furnace, and He will deliver us from your hand, O king" (Daniel 3:17 NKJV). Why don't we have this kind of faith?

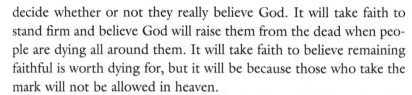

what others say

John Wesley

They that live by faith, walk by faith. But what is implied in this? They regulate all their judgments concerning good and evil, not with reference to visible and temporal things, but things invisible and eternal. They think visible things to be of small value, because they pass away like a dream; but, on the contrary, they account invisible things to be of high value, because they will never pass away.[16]

Answer #3

DANIEL 3:18 *But if not, let it be known to you, O king, that we do not serve your gods, nor will we worship the gold image which you have set up." (NKJV)*

This is the third part of the threefold response. The **grace of God** was upon Shadrach, Meshach, and Abed-Nego. Even if God did not deliver them they would not change their minds; they would not worship any other god or anyone's image.

It is clear that Shadrach, Meshach, and Abed-Nego believed God can do all things, so this was not a case of their questioning his ability to deliver them. This happened so fast they hadn't had time to pray and were simply saying they hadn't yet learned God's will. His will might be to let them die and go to heaven. Whatever he did, it would be the best thing.

Does success by the world's standards ruin people? Some stop serving the Lord when they prosper enough to afford vacations, boats, or a membership in the Country Club. Are they really <u>successful</u>? Did success by the world's standards affect Shadrach,

Meshach, and Abed-Nego? Were they failures? To truly be successful in life, one needs to discover God's will for his life and carry it out. God has a plan for every person who ever came into being. When people stand before the judgment seat of God, their success in life will not be measured by the fortune they amassed, the people they supervised, the problems they overcame, or anything like that. Their success in life will be measured by their response to the things God wanted them to do. Did they say yes when God asked them to accept Jesus? Did they give, serve, love, and set an example for others? These things will determine our success in life.

There is something more important than life—whom we serve.

People often ask God for things they never seem to receive, and they ask him to do things he never seems to do. Many ask why? The following chart lists seven reasons why a persons prayer may not be answered.

Unanswered Prayers

Reasons Why	Scripture
Ignoring the poor or a failure to give	Proverbs 21:13; 19:17; 1 John 3:17
Sin in one's life	Isaiah 59:2; 1:15; Ezekiel 14:3; Psalm 66:18; John 15:7
Unbelief	Matthew 13:58; Hebrews 11:6; James 1:6–7
Asking for the wrong reason	James 4:3
Mistreating a wife	1 Peter 3:7
Asking for things that are contrary to God's will	Luke 22:42
Asking for things that are not good for us	2 Corinthians 12:9

Seven Times Hotter

DANIEL 3:19 *Then Nebuchadnezzar was full of fury, and the expression on his face changed toward Shadrach, Meshach, and Abed-Nego. He spoke and commanded that they heat the furnace seven times more than it was usually heated. (NKJV)*

In modern language, Nebuchadnezzar blew his top. He exploded in anger at Shadrach, Meshach and Abed-Nego. We have already noted that he must have loved them and was giving them a second chance, but his whole attitude toward them changed at this point.

go to

burned up in the fire
Jeremiah 29:22

noticed their faith
Matthew 9:2

He was so angry he ordered the great furnace heated seven times hotter. He was burning with rage and he wanted their bodies to be totally <u>burned up in the fire</u>.

A few scholars question whether the furnace was literally heated seven times hotter, for example from 1,000 degrees to 7,000 degrees. They doubt that this could be done and believe seven times hotter is an expression that means to perfection or completeness. Others believe that Nebuchadnezzar had a furnace especially designed for this and that he probably disposed of several people in it over a period of years. Regardless of who is right, the furnace was more than hot enough to kill these three young men. Nebuchadnezzar was so full of rage and violence that even the expression on his face changed. He is a type of the Antichrist, and this says much about the nature of that evil man.

<u>Into the Fire They Must Go</u>

> DANIEL 3:20 *And he commanded certain mighty men of valor who were in his army to bind Shadrach, Meshach, and Abed-Nego, and cast them into the burning fiery furnace. (NKJV)*

We must wonder if Nebuchadnezzar was afraid of Shadrach, Meshach, and Abed-Nego or if he feared their God. Perhaps he <u>noticed their faith</u> and was afraid their God would help them escape. Whatever the case, it appears he did not want to take any chances, so he issued a command for his strongest men to tie them up and cast them into the blazing furnace.

Illustration #12
Fiery Furnace—
Babylonian furnaces
were used to melt
metal.

The Bible says, "Faith is the substance of things hoped for, the evidence of things not seen" (Hebrews 11:1 NKJV). To further explain, divide this faith into two parts:

1. "The substance of things hoped for"—*substance* is something that is real. *Things hoped for* are such things as going to heaven and having eternal life. So faith in Jesus is how the Christian's hopes in heaven and eternal life become a reality.

2. "The evidence of things not seen"—*evidence* is a clue, sign, or proof of something. *Things not seen* include God, Jesus, and the Holy Spirit. A detective may not see who committed a crime, but he looks for clues that will help him identify the criminal. He tries to find things he can see that will point him to what he cannot see. Faith is the same way because faith in Jesus (which can be seen through changes in people and the production of good works) is the evidence of things not seen (God, Jesus, and the Holy Spirit).

It seems likely that Nebuchadnezzar thought the faith of Shadrach, Meshach, and Abed-Nego could be evidence of the existence or reality of their God. That would explain why he ordered his strongest men to tie them up. He saw their faith and was afraid of what he could not see.

No Time to Change

DANIEL 3:21 *Then these men were bound in their coats, their trousers, their turbans, and their other garments, and were cast into the midst of the burning fiery furnace.* (NKJV)

This was a **royal occasion**, so Shadrach, Meshach, and Abed-Nego were properly dressed in their official attire for such an event. Their formal wear included some expensive trousers, **turbans**, and fancy silk garments. They were not even given time to change out of these outfits or do anything else. Nebuchadnezzar's best men quickly seized them, tied them up, and threw them into the furnace. We can almost visualize it in our mind. When the king gave this terrible command his top soldiers moved with great haste.

Here is more evidence that the book of Daniel was written several hundred years before Jesus. This list of clothing worn by Daniel's three friends is a mystery. The ancient manuscripts are available, but

royal occasion
an event attended by the king

turbans
scarves they wore around their hats or head

the meaning of the words for the items of clothing listed in the text was lost by the time the Jews translated the book of Daniel for the Greek Septuagint (probably around 200–150 BC, but maybe older). If the book of Daniel was written at that time, words would have been used that people understood. Because the meaning of the words was unknown at that time, many scholars believe the book was written several hundred years earlier.

Oops! I Didn't Mean Them, Too

DANIEL 3:22 *Therefore, because the king's command was urgent, and the furnace exceedingly hot, the flame of the fire killed those men who took up Shadrach, Meshach, and Abed-Nego. (NKJV)*

The upset king went overboard with his demands. His command was extreme and insistent. The furnace was roaring, and the flames were so high that his best soldiers died when they took Shadrach, Meshach, and Abed-Nego to the top. They gave their lives for this angry tyrant.

Those who oppose God and his people during the Tribulation Period will not get away with anything either. In Revelation their fiery furnace is called "the lake of fire burning with brimstone." John said, "And I saw the beast [the Antichrist], the kings of the earth, and their armies, gathered together to make war against Him who sat on the horse [Jesus] and against His army [God's people]. Then the beast was captured, and with him the false prophet who worked signs in his presence, by which he deceived those who received the **mark of the beast** and those who worshiped his image. These two were cast alive into the lake of fire burning with brimstone. And the rest [the wicked] were killed with the sword which proceeded from the mouth of Him who sat on the horse. And all the birds were filled with their flesh" (Revelation 19:19–21 NKJV).

In They Went

DANIEL 3:23 *And these three men, Shadrach, Meshach, and Abed-Nego, fell down bound into the midst of the burning fiery furnace. (NKJV)*

The intense heat did not kill Shadrach, Meshach, and Abed-Nego, but they were still tied up when they fell into the furnace. Nothing is said about the great crowd who witnessed all of this, but we can guess that many were stunned. It is likely that some even screamed when this happened. On the surface, it looks like a terrible thing, but <u>good</u> things did come out of it.

good
Romans 8:28

will kill multitudes
Revelation 6:9

> what others say
>
> **John C. Whitcomb**
>
> The superb sense of drama should not be overlooked here. Not only did they fall, but it was into the midst of a furnace of blazing fire. The utter helplessness of these three men could hardly be pictured more vividly. Thus, God's power to deliver is magnified, for with Him all things are possible (compare Jeremiah 32:17, 27).[17]

Standing firm in our faith will not keep Christians out of persecution. Jesus said, "If you were of the world, the world would love its own. Yet because you are not of the world, but I chose you out of the world, therefore the world hates you" (John 15:19 NKJV). The Antichrist and his followers <u>will kill multitudes</u> of Christians during the Tribulation Period because of their strong obedience to the Word of God and their testimony of faith.

What Is Going on Here?

> DANIEL 3:24 *Then King Nebuchadnezzar was astonished; and he rose in haste and spoke, saying to his counselors, "Did we not cast three men bound into the midst of the fire?" They answered and said to the king, "True, O king." (NKJV)*

The furnaces in those days had a large opening in the side so they could be stoked and fueled. Nebuchadnezzar could probably see Shadrach, Meshach, and Abed-Nego through such an opening. As he looked, he was expecting, and hoping, to see his three godly advisers burned to a crisp. That did not happen, and he could not believe his eyes.

A Fourth Man

> DANIEL 3:25 *"Look!" he answered, "I see four men loose, walking in the midst of the fire; and they are not hurt, and the form of the fourth is like the Son of God." (NKJV)*

go to

Jesus was transfigured
Matthew 17:1–13

fire
Isaiah 43:2

God
Romans 8:31

Nebuchadnezzar was counting and what he saw startled him. There were four men walking around in the fire, not three. No one was tied up and no one was harmed, but the Fourth Man looked like a son of the gods. This was a perceptive statement to be coming from a pagan king, and most experts think he was looking at the **pre-incarnate** Christ.

The appearance of the Fourth Man in the furnace is called a **theophany**. Some other theophanies in the Bible are:

1. The appearance of God to Moses as the burning bush (Exodus 3:2).

2. The appearance of God to lead the Jews as a pillar of cloud and a pillar of fire (Exodus 13:21).

3. The appearance of God to Moses and the Jews as thunder, lightning, and smoke on Mount Sinai (Exodus 19:18–20).

4. The appearance of Jesus to Peter, James, and John in dazzling white clothes on the **Mount of Transfiguration** (Mark 9:2–7).

5. The appearance of the Holy Spirit to the 120 believers as wind and tongues of fire on **Pentecost** (Acts 2:2–3).

pre-incarnate
before Jesus was born to Joseph and Mary

theophany
visit from God

Mount of Transfiguration
the mountain where Jesus was transfigured

Pentecost
a holy day celebrated fifty days after Easter

There is wide agreement among Bible experts that the Fourth Man in the fire was Jesus. The Son of God visited earth during this world-wide religious service and took control of the fire. This shows that the supernatural world is real and a power to be reckoned with by everyone.

Dancing Before the Lord

DANIEL 3:26 *Then Nebuchadnezzar went near the mouth of the burning fiery furnace and spoke, saying, "Shadrach, Meshach, and Abed-Nego, servants of the Most High God, come out, and come here." Then Shadrach, Meshach, and Abed-Nego came from the midst of the fire.* (NKJV)

Nebuchadnezzar was probably sweating and nervous as he approached the opening in the side of the blazing furnace. He could see that the ropes used to bind these men had burned away. He could see them walking around in the fire, and it seemed like God was with them. They were, however, in no hurry to get out. This confirmed something Nebuchadnezzar already knew—they were servants of the **Most High God**. He asked them to leave the furnace and come to him.

Most High God
the Supreme God

> what others say
>
> ### Charles R. Swindoll
>
> The fact is, God would still have been in control had He allowed Shadrach, Meshach, and Abed-Nego to die in the flames—as He allowed thousands of martyrs throughout history to die. He may deliver; He may not. Our part is to trust His character and His sovereign plan, whatever it may be, and to obey.[18]

Not Even a Singed Hair

DANIEL 3:27 *And the satraps, administrators, governors, and the king's counselors gathered together, and they saw these men on whose bodies the fire had no power; the hair of their head was not singed nor were their garments affected, and the smell of fire was not on them. (NKJV)*

This startling event had completely changed directions. It was so filled with tension that worship of the great image had long been forgotten. Everyone was crowding around Shadrach, Meshach, and Abed-Nego to inspect them. Fire had killed Nebuchadnezzar's best soldiers, and burned the ropes off the other three men, but fire had not:

1. burned their bodies

2. singed their hair

3. scorched their robes

4. left its smell on them

What a tremendous testimony to the power of God! Nebuchadnezzar had tried to start a one-world religion by giving glory to his statue, but before it was all over, God got all the glory instead.

go to

take his mark
Revelation 13:15–17

guardian angels
angels assigned to
help children and
believers

Many will choose to die during the Tribulation Period rather than
worship the image of the Antichrist, <u>take his mark</u>, his number, or
the number of his name.

Praise Be to God

DANIEL 3:28 *Nebuchadnezzar spoke, saying, "Blessed be the
God of Shadrach, Meshach, and Abed-Nego, who sent His Angel
and delivered His servants who trusted in Him, and they have
frustrated the king's word, and yielded their bodies, that they
should not serve nor worship any god except their own God!*
(NKJV)

This miracle changed things dramatically. Nebuchadnezzar was
the powerful leader of a one-world government, but he quickly
accepted defeat and began to praise God. He was somewhat confused, not knowing the difference between the Most High God, one
like a son of the gods, and his angel, but he knew that he had seen
a heavenly visitor. He acknowledged the great faith and faithfulness
of Shadrach, Meshach, and Abed-Nego, their trust in God, and their
courage to stand firm and be faithful in the face of death.

This shows the importance of taking a stand for God. These young
men went to this dedication service with no idea that they would
have to take a stand for God or be thrown into a fiery furnace. They
didn't have a clue about how many people would learn about this
event over the next 2,500 years. But they were true to God. They
became the center of attention. And what they did has meant the difference between heaven and hell for multitudes.

> **what others say**
>
> **King James Bible Commentary**
> If we would be willing to yield to the same degree as these
> men perhaps our testimonies could be used to change even
> the commandments of kings that are contrary to the gospel.[19]

Do angels watch over us? Jesus was warning us about teaching or
doing things that lead little children astray or into sin when he said,
"Take heed that you do not despise one of these little ones, for I say
to you that in heaven their angels always see the face of My Father
who is in heaven" (Matthew 18:10 NKJV). Many scholars think this
means each one of us has one or more **guardian angels**.

The Second Decree

> DANIEL 3:29 *Therefore I make a decree that any people, nation, or language which speaks anything amiss against the God of Shadrach, Meshach, and Abed-Nego shall be cut in pieces, and their houses shall be made an ash heap; because there is no other God who can deliver like this."* (NKJV)

Nebuchadnezzar issued another decree. If anyone said anything against the God of Shadrach, Meshach, and Abed-Nego:

1. they would be cut into pieces, and

2. their houses would be destroyed.

The reason behind this decree is very important. The most powerful man in the world said, no other god can save in this way. This is an acknowledgment before the world of the omnipotence and superiority of the Jew's God.

God often reveals himself through miracles, wonders, and signs. He used one on this occasion to glorify his name and to honor those three young men for what they did. But if they had not been grounded in the Word of God they could not have taken the strong stand they did. To do something like this a person first needs to be equipped by God. To be equipped by God, a person needs to learn the Scriptures and allow them to grow in his heart.

Nebuchadnezzar's first decree stated, "Everyone who hears the sound of the horn, flute, harp, lyre, and psaltery, in symphony with all kinds of music, shall fall down and worship the gold image; and whoever does not fall down and worship shall be cast into the midst of a burning fiery furnace" (Daniel 3:10–11 NKJV). It was very difficult for a king to change or rescind a decree, but here, Nebuchadnezzar came close to doing that. Here is a small step away from paganism and idolatry and a giant step toward the True and Living God.

Rewards for the Worthy

> DANIEL 3:30 *Then the king promoted Shadrach, Meshach, and Abed-Nego in the province of Babylon.* (NKJV)

God let these three young men endure a terrible test, and because of their faithfulness he let them be rewarded. They received promotions giving them even more power than they had held before. This was a great upset for those who had tried to eliminate Shadrach, Meshach, and Abed-Nego. God's will and purpose for man and this earth cannot be changed by human will or power.

In chapter 2, Nebuchadnezzar was told the dream is certain and its interpretation is sure. In chapter 3, Nebuchadnezzar and all the world were told God is in control and can do anything he wants to do. Notice what God did for Shadrach, Meshach, and Abed-Nego:

1. He removed their bonds.

2. He protected them from the fire.

3. He joined them in the furnace.

4. He got glory for his name.

5. He silenced their enemies.

6. He had them rewarded.

Chapter Wrap-Up

- Nebuchadnezzar was hoping to prove that his disturbing dream in chapter 2 was not true, so he built a great statue. It was gold from head to foot and contradicted Daniel's interpretation of the dream. Nebuchadnezzar was trying to show that his kingdom would last forever. (Daniel 3:1)

- Nebuchadnezzar held a worldwide worship service to dedicate his great statue. The service began with music. People from all nations were present and ordered to bow or suffer a terrible punishment—being thrown into a blazing furnace. (Daniel 3:2–6)

- Nebuchadnezzar was furious when he was told that three Jews did not obey his command. Although he gave them a second chance, they still refused. (Daniel 3:8–18)

- The answer given by the Jews angered the king even more. He had the furnace heated to its maximum capacity, then commanded some of his best men to tie up the Jews and throw them into the fire—but the fire had no effect on them. (Daniel 3:19–21, 27)

- When Nebuchadnezzar saw a Fourth Man in the fire he was amazed. He saw that the fire had no effect on Shadrach, Meshach, and Abed-Nego, so he asked them to come out of the furnace. Then he praised their God and promoted them. (Daniel 3:24–30)

Study Questions

1. What motive did the Chaldeans have for telling the king that Shadrach, Meshach, and Abed-Nego did not obey his decree? Why is that bad, and how does it apply to us?

2. What decree did Nebuchadnezzar issue and what was the penalty for disobedience? If given this choice during the Tribulation Period, what would you do?

3. Do you think the three Jews would have worshiped the golden image if they had believed God would not save them from the fire?

4. What amazing sight did Nebuchadnezzar see in the fire? Why was it amazing and what did he ask the three Jews to do?

5. How did Nebuchadnezzar change his decree? What does it show about free speech and freedom of worship in Babylon?

Daniel 4 Nebuchadnezzar's Written Testimony

Chapter Highlights:
• Written Testimony
• Another Terrible Dream
• Refusal to Repent
• The King Is Humbled
• The King Is Healed

Let's Get Started

Time is passing (see Time Line #1, Appendix A). Daniel has been in Babylon for more than forty years and is now well past fifty years old. Nebuchadnezzar is in his early seventies, nearing the end of his reign, and the end of his life. A big change has come over him, and we are now going to see what caused it.

To better understand this change in the king's life, this chapter is told by the king himself. It is his personal written testimony. Some critics have denounced the book of Daniel on the grounds that the words of a pagan king should not be called Scripture. They seem to overlook the fact that the Bible contains the words of many lost people, the words of a donkey, and even the words of Satan himself, but every jot and tittle of the sixty-six books is referred to as the Word of God. One of the most interesting prophecies in the Bible was made by the high priest Caiaphas, who was instrumental in the crucifixion of Jesus, "You know nothing at all, nor do you consider that it is expedient for us that one man should die for the people, and not that the whole nation should perish" (John 11:49–50 NKJV). Simply put, Nebuchadnezzar and Caiaphas were tools in the hands of God to reveal something he wanted people to know.

saved
Ephesians 2:8–9

saved
to receive forgiveness of sins and eternal life

Hear Me, Hear Me

DANIEL 4:1 *Nebuchadnezzar the king,*
To all peoples, nations, and languages that dwell in all
the earth:
Peace be multiplied to you. (NKJV)

We are beginning to look at one of the most ancient written testimonies known to mankind. It appears to have been written by the great king himself. He presents it as a true historical event. Could this once-violent king have become a **saved** man? At one time he would have been a poor role model as a wild barbarian, but at this time he was setting a good example for everyone to follow. Here he tells the whole world what God did for him.

go to

signs
Genesis 9:12–13

wonders
Exodus 3:20

great
Hebrews 2:3

dominion
Psalm 145:13

eternal
Matthew 25:46;
John 3:16

signs
evidence of things
like miracles and
covenants

wonders
supernatural events

dominion
power and authority

The Most High God

DANIEL 4:2 *I thought it good to declare the signs and wonders that the Most High God has worked for me. (NKJV)*

"I thought it good" indicates he was sharing this testimony out of his own desire to do so. He was not being coerced or forced. It was his genuine desire and a pleasing thing to him to be able to reveal these things to the world. Miraculous **signs** and **wonders** had taken place—amazing things that the Most High God had performed for Nebuchadnezzar personally.

The Most High God is the same God Shadrach, Meshach, and Abed-Nego worshipped. When Nebuchadnezzar approached the opening in the side of the fiery furnace he said, "Shadrach, Meshach, and Abed-Nego, servants of the Most High God, come out, and come here" (Daniel 3:26 NKJV).

Signs and Wonders

DANIEL 4:3
*How great are His signs,
And how mighty His wonders!
His kingdom is an everlasting kingdom,
And His dominion is from generation to generation. (NKJV)*

The evidence of God is revealed through <u>great</u> signs. The amazing miracles of God are mighty wonders. The kingdom of God is a spiritual kingdom, and his **dominion** is <u>eternal</u>. It will take on a physical nature when Jesus returns. Then it will be both spiritual and physical.

The death of Jesus is a great sign of God's love; the miracle of Jesus' resurrection could be called a mighty wonder; and heaven is a part of his spiritual (or eternal) kingdom. These three great signs provide evidence of God.

The Antichrist, the False Prophet, and some of their followers will perform great signs and wonders during the Tribulation Period. Jesus said, "False christs and false prophets will rise and show great signs and wonders to deceive, if possible, even the elect" (Matthew 24:24 NKJV).

A New Man?

DANIEL 4:4 *I, Nebuchadnezzar, was at rest in my house, and flourishing in my palace. (NKJV)*

This is the opening statement in Nebuchadnezzar's testimony. It tells us where he was, and how he perceived himself. He looked at his life and said he was pleased. He was happy and prospering. He had soldiers to guard him, servants to wait on him, and wise men to advise him; he had anything money could buy. He even built one of the seven greatest wonders of the world. Earthly kingdoms and kings are only temporary, but God's kingdom will last forever.

The Seven Wonders of the Ancient World

1. Pyramids of Egypt at Giza

2. Hanging gardens of Babylon

3. Temple of Artemis at Ephesus

4. Statue of Zeus at Olympia, Greece

5. Mausoleum at Halicarnassus in southwestern Turkey

6. Colossus of Rhodes on the island of Rhodes

7. Lighthouse of Alexandria on the island of Pharos near Alexandria, Egypt

what others say

Harper's Bible Dictionary

Reconstructions of Babylon, based on meticulous excavations, help modern Bible students to envision the heavily walled, massively moated city with its twin Citadel and Famous Ishtar Gate (see Illustration #13) adorned with glazed-tile lions and dragons, through which ran a festival avenue or "Procession Street" to the quarter of the city where stood the vast palace of Nebuchadnezzar, with its "hanging gardens" on the roof; the stepped Tower of Babel, supporting a temple associated with the worship of Marduk, chief god of Babylonia.[1]

go to

rich man
Luke 16:19–31

hell
a place of eternal
punishment

Ishtar Gate
the main gate lead-
ing into the city of
Babylon and dedi-
cated to their god-
dess of fertility

Kenneth O. Gangel

One immediately gets the impression that the warrior king has begun to age, most of his enemies have been subdued, and things have calmed down in Babylon. Even the great construction projects and the overall greening of the city had perhaps been completed.[2]

H. A. Ironside

God had spoken once to Nebuchadnezzar in giving him the dream of the great image of the times of the Gentiles. But the heart of the king was willful, and he continued to go on with his own purpose in his pride and folly. God spoke twice by the marvelous vision of the Son of God in the midst of the fiery furnace, keeping His faithful witnesses from all danger and harm. But again the proud king kept on his way, with unsubject heart and unsubdued will. Now God speaks the third time, and this in a most humiliating manner, to this great world ruler, confusion before his princes.[3]

Jesus talked about a rich man who dressed in purple and fine linen and lived in luxury every day. This man had the best the world had to offer, but great riches and fine living are not everything. The rich man died without God. He left all his worldly possessions behind and wound up begging for mercy in **hell**. When death comes the man who has a good relationship with God is rich, but the man who has no relationship with him is a pauper.

**Illustration #13—
Ishtar Gate**
The main entrance to Babylon, which Saddam Hussein has rebuilt. Note the depictions of Babylonian gods like Marduk. The War on Terrorism and America's invasion of Iraq stopped Saddam's construction, but President Bush asked several nations, including the U.N., to contribute large sums to Iraqi building projects once the area is secured.

A Second Dream

DANIEL 4:5 *I saw a dream which made me afraid, and the thoughts on my bed and the visions of my head troubled me.* (*NKJV*)

go to

Peter
Acts 10:1–23

rebellion
Deuteronomy 13:1–5

listen to astrologers
Deuteronomy 18:9–14

listen to his prophet
Deuteronomy 19:15–19

ability to understand
Daniel 1:17

In chapter 5 we will learn that Babylon was an armed fortress with very high and very thick walls, massive gates, soldiers constantly on guard, a deep moat surrounding the city, and drawbridges that could quickly be closed. It would seem that Nebuchadnezzar had nothing to be afraid of, but not so. Something scared him, even terrified him. It was not enemy troops, but **thoughts** and **visions** that passed through his head while he was lying in his bed. It was a nightmarish experience, and he may have sensed that it had something to do with him. The more he thought about it the more uneasy he got.

Nightmares may be the result of something we ate. They may also be the result of physical or emotional problems. In some cases they may be the result of tension or drug or alcohol abuse. Nebuchadnezzar has already said he was at rest and flourishing. This leaves one more thing. This bad dream was a message from God. There was something wrong in his relationship with God, and the Lord was letting him know.

thoughts
here it refers to mental pictures

visions
images that occur while in a trance

trance
a dazed or stunned condition similar to sleep

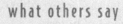

what others say

Rick Joyner

Another higher level prophetic experience is a **trance**, such as Peter had when he was first instructed to go to the house of Cornelius and preach the gospel to the gentiles for the first time, and such as Paul had when he prayed in the Temple in Acts 22.

Trances were a common experience of the Biblical prophets. Trances are like dreaming when you are awake. Instead of just seeing a "screen" like in an open vision, you feel like you are in the movie, that you are actually there in a strange way.[4]

God warned the Jews to beware of people who foretell by dreams and to put them to death if they used dreams to teach <u>rebellion</u> against him. He did not want them to <u>listen to astrologers</u>, diviners, magicians, soothsayers, interpreters of dreams, or those who contact the dead. He instructed them to <u>listen to his prophet</u>. But he gave Daniel the <u>ability to understand</u> visions and dreams. Could it be that

something to ponder

go to

wise men
Daniel 2:2, 12

the elect
true Christians

key point

the interpretations of vision and dreams can be demonic or satanic, and the only safe interpretations are those that come directly from God through his special prophets? If God gives the dream only God can give the interpretation, and he will not give the interpretation to anyone who is not one of his servants.

Jesus was talking about the End of the Age when he said, "False christs and false prophets will rise and show great signs and wonders to deceive, if possible, even **the elect**. See, I have told you beforehand" (Matthew 24:24–25 NKJV). Beware of modern-day "prophets" with ear-tickling "prophecies" and "great signs." Their messages may be partly right, but multitudes will be deceived by that which is wrong. Messages, prophecies, and visions are false if:

1. they contradict anything in the Bible.

2. they approve of anything the Bible calls sin.

3. they speak against Jesus (anything from his virgin birth to his resurrection).

4. they approve or call for harm to those who believe in Jesus.

5. they stress political correctness above biblical correctness.

6. they call for worship of any god, goddess, or being other than the God of heaven.

7. they come from other religions or ignore the Bible.

Not Again!

> **DANIEL 4:6** *Therefore I issued a decree to bring in all the wise men of Babylon before me, that they might make known to me the interpretation of the dream. (NKJV)*

It seems that Nebuchadnezzar had to learn some lessons the hard way—by experience. He should have called for Daniel to come in and interpret the dream, but he did not. He did the same worthless thing he did about forty years earlier. He called for his <u>wise men</u>.

Humanity didn't have the Scriptures in ancient times, so interpreters were needed for some dreams. This may by why Nebuchadnezzar kept this crew on his payroll. He should have fired them, but he probably believed he needed them because it was the custom in those days.

Nebuchadnezzar may have thought he did not need Daniel because this was a different situation. He could not remember the dream he had forty years earlier, but he could remember this one. Perhaps he thought all these great wise men from all over the world could explain at least this dream since they would know what it was.

We Couldn't Do It Then, So How Can We Do It Now?

> DANIEL 4:7 *Then the magicians, the astrologers, the Chaldeans, and the soothsayers came in, and I told them the dream; but they did not make known to me its interpretation. (NKJV)*

Nebuchadnezzar tells us that the result was the same as <u>before</u>. These supposedly gifted people came in, listened to the dream, and still couldn't interpret it.

Acts 16:16–19 tells us about a slave girl who was possessed by an evil spirit. She was very good at telling fortunes and predicting the future. She even earned a lot of money for her owners. But after the **apostle** Paul commanded the evil spirit to come out of her in the name of Jesus Christ, she lost the ability to do these things. Some psychics and fortune-tellers may be successful because they are demon-possessed.

Holy Before the Lord

> DANIEL 4:8 *But at last Daniel came before me (his name is Belteshazzar, according to the name of my god; in him is the Spirit of the Holy God), and I told the dream before him, saying: (NKJV)*

After the wise men failed miserably again there was one last resort—the **true prophet** of God. Daniel went in to see the king and Nebuchadnezzar told him the dream. This was the same Daniel whose name was changed to <u>Belteshazzar</u>. Nebuchadnezzar confirmed that Daniel had a special spirit in him that was holy.

The only spirit in the Bible that is called "holy" is the **Holy Spirit**, the only god that is called "holy" is the God of heaven, and the only person who is called "holy" is the <u>Holy One of God</u>—Jesus.

go to

before
Daniel 2:2–11

Belteshazzar
Daniel 1:7

Holy Spirit
Luke 4:1

Holy One of God
Mark 1:24

apostle
someone commissioned by God to represent Christ

true prophet
one who speaks under the influence of God

Holy Spirit
the Spirit of God or God himself

go to

Old
Psalm 51:11;
Isaiah 63:10

shamanism
a primitive religion
that believes certain
priests can influence
spiritual powers that
control things

Hinduism
the common religion
of India with many
philosophies and
cults

Yoga
a Hindu technique
designed to help a
person reach the
state of union with
the Hindu concept
of God (a.k.a.
enlightenment)

what others say

Ron Carlson and Ed Decker

Historical antecedents [the roots or ancestry] of the New Age
Movement can be found in several major religious groups:

1. witchcraft and **shamanism** (prehistoric)
2. astrology (circa 2000 BC)
3. **Hinduism** and **Yoga** (circa 1800 BC)[5]

Some of the Characteristics of the New Age Movement

Astrology—The study of the stars and planets to determine their supposed influence on persons or events (Deuteronomy 4:19; 17:2–5; Isaiah 47:12–15).

Fortune-telling—The effort to predict events in one's life before they happen (Deuteronomy 18:9–14; Jeremiah 14:14; Acts 13:6–10).

Metaphysics—The study of hard-to-understand metaphors, and fanciful or elaborate images (Genesis 41:8).

Occultism—Belief in satanic or evil powers (Leviticus 20:6–27; Acts 16:16; 19:13–19).

Reincarnation—The passing of a soul into another body (Hebrews 9:27).

Witchcraft—The effort to obtain power to do evil (Deuteronomy 18:9–14; Acts 8:9–24).

Some people think the existence of the Holy Spirit is solely a New Testament concept, but he is mentioned in the <u>Old</u> Testament too. Some Old Testament writers visualized God as an invisible spirit. They could not see him, but they believed he was just as real as the wind or our breath. They even believed he could live in people. Because of the special abilities that Daniel had displayed, Nebuchadnezzar believed that the Holy Spirit lived in him.

Only You Know the Answer

DANIEL 4:9 *"Belteshazzar, chief of the magicians, because I know that the Spirit of the Holy God is in you, and no secret troubles you, explain to me the visions of my dream that I have seen, and its interpretation.* (NKJV)

Nebuchadnezzar told the world that he addressed Daniel as the chief of his wise men and that he complemented Daniel before he told him what he wanted. He expressed his certainty that Daniel had a special spirit of the holy gods in him and praised him on his understanding of mysteries or hidden truths. Then he explained that he had a dream he wanted Daniel to interpret

A Tree in the Middle

DANIEL 4:10
These were the visions of my head while on my bed:
I was looking, and behold,
A tree in the midst of the earth,
And its height was great. (NKJV)

Here we are told what the dream was. Later we will be told its interpretation. But it will be helpful, at this time, to understand that a tree is sometimes used in Scripture as a symbol of something else. For example:

1. A tree can symbolize a man. "He [the man who follows God] shall be like a tree planted by the rivers of water, that brings forth its fruit in its season, whose leaf also shall not wither" (Psalm 1:3 NKJV). "He [the man who trusts God] shall be like a tree planted by the waters, which spreads out its roots by the river" (Jeremiah 17:8 NKJV). The Two Witnesses are represented by olive trees (Revelation 11:3–4).

2. A tree can symbolize a nation. "Indeed Assyria was a cedar in Lebanon, with fine branches that shaded the forest, and of high stature; and its top was among the thick boughs" (Ezekiel 31:3 NKJV). Israel is the Bible Fig Tree (Matthew 24:32–33).

3. A tree can symbolize the false church (Matthew 24:32–33).

It Reaches to the Heavens

greatness
1 Chronicles 29:11

glory
Isaiah 62:3

beasts of the field
Jeremiah 27:6

DANIEL 4:11
The tree grew and became strong;
Its height reached to the heavens,
And it could be seen to the ends of all the earth. (NKJV)

The tree became so large and so strong that its highest branches reached into the heavens, allowing it to be seen all over the world. Never before had there been such a great tree.

Keep in mind the fact that this tree can be a symbol of a man, and if it is, then it is easy to see how this part of the dream refers to a man's accomplishments—his authority, power, and fame. This would be a man whose achievements and notoriety far exceeded those of most men. He would be a man of greatness and glory. A man known to all the world.

A Tree of Protection and Plenty

DANIEL 4:12
Its leaves were lovely,
Its fruit abundant,
And in it was food for all.
The beasts of the field found shade under it,
The birds of the heavens dwelt in its branches,
And all flesh was fed from it. (NKJV)

This tree was covered with beautiful leaves. It was a fruit tree loaded with enough delicious fruit to feed everyone. It was also a shade tree with strong thick branches. Beasts of the field could stand under it for protection from the sun, wind, and rain, and the birds could nest in its branches.

It is obvious that God had blessed this tree. It was flourishing like Nebuchadnezzar in his palace (verse 4). And the reason why God blessed it so much is given: it was so God could provide for his creatures. This is the love of God. He even provides for those who do not know him.

A UFO?

DANIEL 4:13 *"I saw in the visions of my head while on my bed, and there was a watcher, a holy one, coming down from heaven. (NKJV)*

This is a complex verse surrounded in controversy. It is plain that Nebuchadnezzar was lying on his bed and that he saw someone coming down from heaven, but there is much disagreement about who or what that someone was. Some experts believe the watcher and the holy one are two different types of angelic beings. Others think the watcher is a holy one. Here it looks like there is just one "holy watcher," but when we get to Daniel 4:17 we will discover watchers (plural).

Some say this watcher was an angel. They contend that an unbeliever in Babylon would not know much about angels, and, in their opinion, Nebuchadnezzar didn't know what an angel was, so he did the best he could to describe what he saw. It wasn't like the fourth man in the fire, but it was a heavenly being.

Others say Satan and his rulers of darkness in high places are active on earth, and God and his holy angels are involved to counteract them. They believe these watchers are created beings that God has assigned to administer his creation. They say God has his administrators, Satan has his administrators, and this was one of God's administrators (Daniel 10:13; Ephesians 6:12; Hebrews 1:14).

It is a known fact that the angel Gabriel appeared to Daniel more than once (Daniel 8:16; 9:21). He appeared to Zacharias (Luke 1:11–20) and Mary (Luke 1:26). He is one of the archangels. The Bible mentions two. The Apocrypha mentions seven, and some say they are the same seven angels that sound the trumpet judgments and dump the bowls of wrath in the book of Revelation. There is little doubt that this was a messenger sent by God.

The Jewish **Talmud** teaches that God has a council of angels who rule over matters and issue decrees in much the same fashion as the Jewish **Sanhedrin** did during the earthly life of Jesus. There even seems to be a hierarchy of angels who rule over some or all of the nations. Could it be that Nebuchadnezzar saw an <u>angel</u> coming down to earth?

go to

angel
Matthew 1:20;
Luke 1:26

Talmud
a book of Jewish
sacred writings

Sanhedrin
a council of Jews
similar to the U.S.
Supreme Court

something to ponder

Timber!

DANIEL 4:14 *He cried aloud and said thus:*
'Chop down the tree and cut off its branches,
Strip off its leaves and scatter its fruit.
Let the beasts get out from under it,
And the birds from its branches. (NKJV)

go to

cut down
Luke 13:1–9

four horsemen of the Apocalypse
riders of the four horses mentioned in the sixth chapter of Revelation

winds of the earth
air breezes coming from any point on the compass

seal of the living God
a mark or symbol used by God to identify and protect his people

It would be wise to pay attention to the sequence of events here. The watcher said:

1. The tree would be <u>cut down</u>.

2. The branches would be cut off.

3. The leaves would be stripped off.

4. The fruit would be scattered.

5. The animals would flee.

6. The birds would be scattered.

This shows that the tree would go through a great calamity, but it would be worse than that. There would be consequences that would affect every living thing dependent upon it.

Angels, Angels, Angels

Up until just a few years ago, very little was said in our modern society about the ministry of angels. But all of that has changed. In recent years, we have rediscovered the existence and activity of angels. As the morals of our society decline and we approach the coming Tribulation Period, we are becoming more aware of the activity of angelic beings. According to the Bible, angels will be very active during the Tribulation Period. Not all, but most will be involved in carrying out the judgments of God. The following angels are part of the book of Revelation:

- *Four Living Creatures*—restrain and command the **four horsemen of the Apocalypse** and worship God (4:6, 8)

- *Four Angels*—control the **winds of the earth** (7:1)

- *Angel from the East*—carries the **seal of the living God** (7:2)

- *Angel with Trumpet #1*—brings hail, fire, and blood to burn up one-third of the plants (8:7)

- *Angel with Trumpet #2*—throws a huge mountain into the sea to pollute one-third of the sea, kill one-third of the sea creatures, and sink one-third of the ships (8:8–9)

- *Angel with Trumpet #3*—causes a blazing object to fall to earth, causing one-third of the fresh water to be polluted (8:10–11)

- *Angel with Trumpet #4*—causes heavenly bodies to be struck, causing one-third of the sun, moon, and stars to be darkened (8:12)

- *Angel with Trumpet #5*—opens the **bottomless pit,** which releases the demon-possessed locusts (9:1)

- *Angel with Trumpet #6*—causes the four angels to be released at the **Euphrates River**, and one-third of mankind killed (9:14–15)

- *Four Fallen Angels*—four powerful allies of Satan (9:14)

- *Mighty Angel*—claims the earth for his King (10:1)

- *Angel with Trumpet #7*—sounds a heavenly declaration of praise (11:15)

- *Michael*—God's head **archangel** in battle (12:7)

- *Angel #1*—proclaims the eternal Gospel to all people (14:6)

- *Angel #2*—declares the fall of Babylon (14:8)

- *Angel #3*—warns against worshiping the Antichrist or taking the Mark of the Beast (14:9)

- *Angel #4*—takes his sickle and reaps the earth because the harvest is ready (14:15)

- *Angel #5*—brings a second sickle from God (14:17)

- *Angel #6*—tells the fourth angel to take his sharp **sickle** and gather the clusters of grapes (14:18)

- *Angel with Bowl #1*—brings ugly and painful sores (16:2)

- *Angel with Bowl #2*—causes the sea to turn to blood, and everything in it to die (16:3)

- *Angel with Bowl #3*—causes rivers and springs of water to turn to blood (16:4)

- *Angel with Bowl #4*—causes the sun to scorch people with fire (16:8)

- *Angel with Bowl #5*—brings darkness over all the earth (16:10)

- *Angel with Bowl #6*—causes the Euphrates River to dry up (16:12)

- *Angel with Bowl #7*—proclaims "It is done!" (16:17 NKJV)

- *Angel that Illuminates the Earth*—sheds light since he was in the presence of God (18:1)

- *Angel Throwing **Millstone** into Sea*—symbol of Babylon being destroyed forever (18:21)

bottomless pit
a deep pit where demons are kept

Euphrates River
a great river in Iraq known as the dividing line between east and west

archangel
a leader or angel of the highest rank

sickle
an implement for cutting grain

millstone
a large round, flat stone (doughnut-shaped) used for grinding corn, wheat, or other grain

go to

hedge
Job 1:10

• *Angel that is Unnamed*—has the key to open the Abyss and a great chain to bind Satan (20:1)

A Hedge of Protection

DANIEL 4:15
Nevertheless leave the stump and roots in the earth,
Bound with a band of iron and bronze,
In the tender grass of the field.
Let it be wet with the dew of heaven,
And let him graze with the beasts
On the grass of the earth. (NKJV)

Here we have an act of mercy. It shows that the coming calamity would not be permanent. The watcher said:

1. Leave the stump in the ground.

2. Leave the roots in the ground.

3. Bind them with iron and bronze.

4. Do not disturb the grass around them.

5. Let him be watered with the dew of heaven.

6. Let him live.

7. Let him dwell with the animals among the plants of the earth.

In essence, the instruction is to cut the tree down but not to kill it. Surround the stump and its roots with a <u>hedge</u> or fence of iron and bronze, so they cannot be harmed. Preserve and protect the life of the tree. Give him water and let him live. Verse 10 revealed that this tree was in the midst of the earth. Cutting the tree down without removing the stump means the stump would remain on earth. The potential to keep living on earth would still be there.

The last sentence provides an important clue about this verse because it starts referring to the tree as a him. This dream about a tree is actually a dream about a man. Notice the change starting in verse 15. All of a sudden this tree is a him instead of an it. This may be one of the things that terrified Nebuchadnezzar. He must have wondered if he was the *him*.

Frank Ramirez

It's an apt image, since the birds of the air and the beasts of the field are sheltered and nourished by trees. A ruler is also expected to shelter and nourish the people. Though it may seem like rulers did nothing but exploit their subjects, in reality they gained the cooperation of the people by providing protection.[7]

Seven Years

DANIEL 4:16
Let his heart be changed from that of a man,
Let him be given the heart of a beast,
And let seven times pass over him. (NKJV)

The watcher turned his thoughts to the man's mind. He decreed that the man's mind would be changed. It would no longer be the mind of a man but would be transformed into the mind of an animal. This mental affliction would last for seven times.

Oddly enough, there are real life stories of people with mental diseases who claimed to be various kinds of animals. The thought may have originated in Greek mythology with a story about the god Zeus turning a king into a wolf. A man-wolf was called a werewolf. The word for *werewolf* is *Lycanthrope*, and the disease is called Lycanthropy. Most of this is superstition and not to be believed, but history has identified several legitimate cases of people with the illness.

There is a translation problem with the phrase "seven times." It can rightly be translated several ways, but its usage in other verses, for example Daniel 7:25, makes it clear that the period in view is seven years (see chart at Daniel 7:25).

It is very important to remember that seven times means seven years. From that we calculate that "one time" equals one year; also that "one-half time" equals one-half year; also that the "dividing of a time" equals the dividing of a year or one-half year; and last of all, that "times" equals two years. It is important to remember this because it explains other major verses in the Bible. "Then the saints shall be given into his [the Antichrist's] hand for a time [one year] and times [two more years] and half a time [one-half year]," which will be the last 3 1/2 years of the Tribulation Period (Daniel 7:25 NKJV). The woman [Israel] was given the two wings of a great eagle,

so that she might fly to the place prepared for her in the desert (probably Petra), where she would be taken care of for a time [one year], times [two more years], and a half time, out of the serpent's [Satan's] reach, which will be the <u>Tribulation Period</u>.

God, the Decision-Maker

DANIEL 4:17

This decision is by the decree of the watchers,
And the sentence by the word of the holy ones,
In order that the living may know
That the Most High rules in the kingdom of men,
Gives it to whomever He will,
And sets over it the lowest of men.' (NKJV)

Keep in mind the fact that this is Nebuchadnezzar's testimony to the whole world about what a messenger from heaven told him in a dream. Let's break it down because it seems so important. He said:

1. The decision is announced by the watchers, the holy ones declare the verdict. There was a council of angelic beings involved in Nebuchadnezzar's affairs. They had made a decision concerning him and his one-world kingdom. This was the announcement of their decision and we will see that it contains implications for the whole world.

2. "In order that the living may know" gives the purpose of their decision. The council of angels sent a message to Nebuchadnezzar, so every living person can know:

   a. That the <u>Most High</u> rules over the kingdoms of men. God is the ultimate ruler of nations not presidents, kings, or dictators. God's rank and power are paramount and no one can change that.

   b. That God gives them [the nations or control over the nations] to anyone he wishes. God decides who will be in power.

   c. That God sets over them the lowliest of men. God sometimes gives us idiots and fools to rule over us. When we complain about our leaders we should remember that

God gives us what he thinks we deserve. They are a reflection of our relationship with him.

God rules nations and chooses their leaders. Sometimes he chooses weak leaders to teach us to follow him.

angels
Psalm 34:7;
Jude 1:9

what others say

Billy Graham

The Bible teaches that <u>angels</u> intervene in the affairs of nations. God often uses them to execute judgment on nations. They guide, comfort and provide for the people of God in the midst of suffering and persecution. Martin Luther once said . . . , "An angel is a spiritual creature without a body created by God for the service of christendom and the church."[8]

Angels guide, comfort, and provide for the people of God in the midst of suffering and persecution.

what others say

Sinclair B. Ferguson

The purpose of this decree was not left to Nebuchadnezzar's imagination: it was to teach men that God reigns, that He sets up and pulls down kingdoms, that His actions in history focus on the work of humbling men in order that they may dispense with their foolish pride and acknowledge Him as their God.[9]

Now, What Does It Mean?

DANIEL 4:18 *"This dream I, King Nebuchadnezzar, have seen. Now you, Belteshazzar, declare its interpretation, since all the wise men of my kingdom are not able to make known to me the interpretation; but you are able, for the Spirit of the Holy God is in you." (NKJV)*

Nebuchadnezzar has concluded the telling of his dream. Now he appeals to Daniel [Belteshazzar] to solve this mystery. He pointed out to the world a second time the failure of his wise men. And he also repeated to the world why he believed Daniel could interpret this dream: because Daniel had the spirit of the Holy God in him.

Reading this testimony that was sent to the whole world must have struck the wise men like a ton of bricks. When Daniel completed the ten-day test in chapter 1, Nebuchadnezzar found him ten times better than all the wise men in his kingdom. When the wise men couldn't interpret Nebuchadnezzar's dream in chapter 2, Daniel did. When the wise men tried to have Shadrach, Meshach, and Abed-Nego killed in chapter 3, they failed. When they tried to interpret this dream in chapter 4, they failed again. And these men were supposed to be trained in all the **ancient wisdom** of the Chaldeans.

The word *Trinity* is not in the Bible, but the Scriptures speak of the Father, the Son, and the Holy Spirit, and Christians call these three the *Trinity*. Sometimes they call them the *Godhead* or the *Three-in-One*. These words mean that God sometimes chooses to reveal himself as the Father, sometimes as the Son, and sometimes as the Holy Spirit, but that all three are God. They are not three different gods, but one God who reveals himself in three different ways. The chart below demonstrates the existence of the Trinity in Daniel's day.

The Trinity in the Book of Daniel

References to the Trinity	Scripture
When Shadrach, Meshach, and Abed-Nego were thrown into the fiery furnace, Nebuchadnezzar saw one "like the Son of God."	Daniel 3:25
Nebuchadnezzar called the God of Shadrach, Meshach, and Abed-Nego the Most High God (Daniel 3:26; 4:17). He called Daniel's God the God of gods and the Lord of kings.	Daniel 2:47
Nebuchadnezzar said Daniel could interpret his dream because he had the Spirit of the Holy God in him.	Daniel 4:18

Daniel's Interpretation

> DANIEL 4:19 *Then Daniel, whose name was Belteshazzar, was astonished for a time, and his thoughts troubled him. So the king spoke, and said, "Belteshazzar, do not let the dream or its interpretation trouble you." Belteshazzar answered and said, "My lord, may the dream concern those who hate you, and its interpretation concern your enemies! (NKJV)*

When Daniel heard the dream he understood its meaning and was perplexed or stunned. For a while, he sat silently in the presence of Nebuchadnezzar. He loved his king and had to confront him with the answer, an answer he found awesome and terrifying. Nebuchadnezzar recognized Daniel's reluctance to reveal the interpretation. But he wanted to know, so he implored Daniel not to let it bother him. Daniel began by wishing these bad things applied to Nebuchadnezzar's enemies instead of his beloved king, but they did not. God's best servants can wish that bad things would not happen to people they love, but such things are in the hands of God.

Restating the Dream

tree
Judges 9:6–15

> **DANIEL 4:20** *The tree that you saw, which grew and became strong, whose height reached to the heavens and which could be seen by all the earth,* (NKJV)

Daniel is simply restating the dream for Nebuchadnezzar. He is reminding the king that he dreamed about a magnificent tree; the tallest tree known to man, touching the sky, and visible to the whole earth.

Continuing the Restatement

> **DANIEL 4:21** *whose leaves were lovely and its fruit abundant, in which was food for all, under which the beasts of the field dwelt, and in whose branches the birds of the heaven had their home—* (NKJV)

This is more of Daniel's restatement of the dream. The magnificent tree had not only grown strong and visible to the whole world, but it had gained great glory (become beautiful) and had prospered (was providing food and shelter for the people and creatures of the earth).

You Are That Tree

> **DANIEL 4:22** *it is you, O king, who have grown and become strong; for your greatness has grown and reaches to the heavens, and your dominion to the end of the earth.* (NKJV)

We could do no better than the wise men without this information, but now we know. Daniel told Nebuchadnezzar he was that tree. He had become great and strong. His greatness reached to the heavens, and his dominion covered the earth. Some question it, but as far as God was concerned, Nebuchadnezzar's kingdom was a world kingdom. Nebuchadnezzar had won all his wars, put down all his enemies, rebuilt all his cities, invigorated his nation's agriculture, built great buildings such as temples and places of worship, and

Bible tells us
Daniel 2:41–45

gained so much wealth his kingdom had become known as the "kingdom of gold." For a pagan king ruling a pagan people it was an amazing record. But remember, God's people, the Jews, had abandoned him, so he put this man in power and gave great glory to this pagan king.

It is obvious that Nebuchadnezzar never ruled the whole earth. His kingdom was geographically smaller than that of the Medes and Persians, Greeks, or Romans who followed him, but he was the world's only superpower during his time. His kingdom was vertical from earth to the heavens, or as high as anyone could go. It was horizontal, extending in every direction on earth. It was without question the richest, most powerful, and largest kingdom on earth at this time.

what others say

M. R. De Haan

Just as Nebuchadnezzar succeeded in conquering the entire world and uniting all the people under one great Babylonian system of government, so too the Bible tells us that toward the end of this age there will emerge a world government, a world federation of nations under one federal headship which shall guarantee unto man a man-made prosperity, a time when war shall cease, when there will be no poverty, no strife, no disagreement, but the Utopia of man's dreams, the millennium of man's making shall find its fulfillment [the Tribulation Period].[10]

Forty years earlier Daniel interpreted a dream for the king and said, "You, O king, are a king of kings. For the God of heaven has given you a kingdom, power, strength, and glory; and wherever the children of men dwell, or the beasts of the field and the birds of the heaven, He has given them into your hand, and has made you ruler over them all—you are this head of gold" (Daniel 2:37–38 NKJV).

Judgment and Grace

DANIEL 4:23 *"And inasmuch as the king saw a watcher, a holy one, coming down from heaven and saying, 'Chop down the tree and destroy it, but leave its stump and roots in the earth, bound with a band of iron and bronze in the tender grass of the field; let it be wet with the dew of heaven, and let him graze with the beasts of the field, till seven times pass over him'; (NKJV)*

This is a continuation of Daniel's recounting of the dream. The heavenly messenger said:

1. "Chop down the tree and destroy it" (Daniel 4:23 NKJV) symbolized God's plan to judge Nebuchadnezzar.

2. "Leave its stump and roots" (4:23 NKJV) symbolized the grace of God in his desire to judge, but not reject, the king. It shows God's desire to preserve what was left of Nebuchadnezzar's life after he was judged (punished).

3. "Let it be wet with the dew of heaven, and let him graze with the beasts of the field" (4:23 NKJV) reveals what the king's judgment would be. He would be driven out of his palace where his body would get wet from the dew of heaven, and his mind and life would be like that of an animal.

4. "Till seven times pass over him" (4:23 NKJV) is a statement showing how long this <u>judgment</u> would last—seven years.

go to

judgment
Romans 14:10;
2 Corinthians 5:10;
Revelation 20:11–15

what others say

Tim LaHaye and Ed Hindson

Watchers is the term Daniel uses to show that angels watch over humans and observe their behavior. The Bible often depicts them as calling out to God to intervene in human affairs.[11]

The Wycliffe Bible Commentary

The intent of these words was that the king personally would experience a great disaster, losing his position for a period of seven times. The Aramaic is no more specific than the English translation in regard to the length of time involved. Inasmuch as days, weeks, or months would hardly have allowed time for the developments of verse 33b, it seems best to follow most commentators in adopting "years" as the meaning.[12]

Some experts see a double fulfillment in this prophecy about Nebuchadnezzar. They believe it was literally fulfilled the first time when Nebuchadnezzar went out of his mind and acted like a beast in the field. But they also think there is reason to believe it will be fulfilled a second time when the Antichrist comes on the scene. The Antichrist will be a world leader just like Nebuchadnezzar was. His deceit, treachery, wars, and persecution of Christians and Jews will

beast
Revelation 13:1

false prophets
2 Corinthians
11:1–15

be the deeds of a mad man. He will be so evil the Bible calls him a beast. Nebuchadnezzar went insane for seven years, and the folly of the Antichrist will last for seven years in the Tribulation Period.

So Let It Be Done

> DANIEL 4:24 *this is the interpretation, O king, and this is the decree of the Most High, which has come upon my lord the king:* (NKJV)

This is the prophecy about what would happen to Nebuchadnezzar. Notice that it is by decree of the Most High, a decree that he personally issued against the king of Babylon. If this was the decision of a council of angels, it was also the decision of God. They were in perfect agreement.

The message to Nebuchadnezzar and the world says there is a God who removes kings and raises up kings (Daniel 2:21). He is in control. He rules over the affairs of kings and kingdoms. This ruler had decided to demonstrate his authority by temporarily replacing Nebuchadnezzar.

It would be good if we could trust everyone who claims to speak for Christ or in the name of God, but we simply cannot. Concerning the End of the Age Jesus said, "Many false prophets will rise up and deceive many" (Matthew 24:11 NKJV). The apostle Paul warned that "Satan himself transforms himself into an angel of light" (2 Corinthians 11:14 NKJV). Beware of people who preach a Jesus other than the Jesus of the Bible, a gospel other than the gospel of the Bible, or a Christianity other than historical Christianity. Beware of people who boast of special revelations, private knowledge, or previously uncovered secrets. Beware of people who want to involve you in a fantastic new movement that ties you to their organization. These are the kinds of things false prophets will do. Messengers of God (angels) never draw attention to themselves but ascribe the glory to God.

Driven from His Home

> DANIEL 4:25 *They shall drive you from men, your dwelling shall be with the beasts of the field, and they shall make you eat grass like oxen. They shall wet you with the dew of heaven, and seven times shall pass over you, till you know that the Most High*

rules in the kingdom of men, and gives it to whomever He chooses. (NKJV)

beast coming out of the sea
Revelation 13:1

The king would be driven out of his palace. He would be driven away from the people and attention he loved so much, away from the power and glory he exalted in, away from all the delicacies, comforts, and servants. Where would he go? He would live in the fields with the wild animals, cattle, sheep, camels, and donkeys. His body would be wet from being outside in the dew. Seven years would pass before he would finally acknowledge that God rules over the nations and puts in power anyone he wishes.

The Bible declares that men will reap what they sow (Galatians 6:7). There are several contrasts in this chapter. Notice the following:

1. In verse 6, Nebuchadnezzar issued a decree that could not be fulfilled when he said "bring in all the wise men" to interpret his dream, but in verse 17 the watchers issued a decree that would be fulfilled.

2. In verse 9, Nebuchadnezzar told Daniel, "No secret troubles you," but in verse 19 he told Daniel, "Do not let the dream or its interpretation trouble you."

3. In verse 12, Nebuchadnezzar was like a tree in the field providing food and shelter for the beasts, but in verse 25 Nebuchadnezzar would be like one of the beasts in the field searching for food.

4. In verse 27, Daniel urged Nebuchadnezzar to stop sinning and be merciful to the poor, which he did not do, but in verse 23 God was merciful to Nebuchadnezzar by limiting his affliction to seven years and then healing him.

5. In chapter 3, Nebuchadnezzar commanded people to worship him, but in chapter 4 verse 34 worshiped God.

6. In chapter 3 verse 9, the wise men said "O King live forever," but in verse 34 Nebuchadnezzar honored Daniel's God who lives forever.

7. In chapter 3, Nebuchadnezzar erected a statue to declare that his dominion would be forever, but in chapter 4 verse 34 he acknowledged that God's dominion is an everlasting dominion.

The Bible refers to the Antichrist as a beast. He is the (the first beast of Revelation) <u>beast coming out of the sea</u> and his number

number of the beast
Revelation 13:18

coming out of the earth
Revelation 13:11

mark of the Beast
Revelation 13:14–17

receive
1 Corinthians 4:7

pride
Proverbs 16:18

(666) is the <u>number of the beast</u>. The Bible also refers to the False Prophet as a beast. He is (the second beast of Revelation) another beast, <u>coming out of the earth</u>; he is the one who will set up an image to honor the first beast (Antichrist) and the one who will order people to worship the Antichrist. He will also force people to take the <u>mark of the Beast</u>.

He Will Return

DANIEL 4:26 *"And inasmuch as they gave the command to leave the stump and roots of the tree, your kingdom shall be assured to you, after you come to know that Heaven rules. (NKJV)*

After reading the harsh judgments of Daniel 4:25, who could imagine that Nebuchadnezzar would ever get his throne back? Who could imagine the people of Babylon accepting him back and trusting his decisions as king, after seeing him going out of his mind and living like an animal? But that was Daniel's interpretation of the dream. Nebuchadnezzar would be out of his mind for seven years, and would eventually acknowledge that heaven rules. Only then would he <u>receive</u> his kingdom back.

God's words do not fail or return void. His judgments, as severe as some may be, are a gift from heaven. The decree of the watchers would accomplish their purpose and Nebuchadnezzar's illness would be a blessing in disguise.

Grace Before Judgment

DANIEL 4:27 *Therefore, O king, let my advice be acceptable to you; break off your sins by being righteous, and your iniquities by showing mercy to the poor. Perhaps there may be a lengthening of your prosperity." (NKJV)*

If we tried we could compile a fairly long list of sins in Nebuchadnezzar's life—abuse of power, anger, arrogance, cruelty to Israel, idolatry, oppression of the poor, <u>pride</u>, etc.—but that is not needed. The most important thing is that Nebuchadnezzar was in the presence of a man of God, the chief of all his wise men, and he knew it. This man of God, leader of the wise men, and friend offered him some kindly advice.

God always gives ample warning. Preachers call it "grace before judgment." God does not enjoy using the paddle, and only true repentance can turn away his wrath.

In spite of everything he had seen and heard, the king did not take the advice of his good friend and adviser Daniel. There is no indication that he changed anything. It seems that many people are making the same mistake today. What do you think?

God's judgments will fall upon the earth during the Tribulation Period. In just seven years millions will perish, but the grace of God will come into play before these judgments. This grace is called the Rapture. It is possible to leave in the Rapture and miss God's terrible judgments. Anyone can do that by repenting of their sins and sincerely accepting Jesus as their Savior.

go to

millions will perish
Revelation 6:7–8;
8:10–11; 9:15, 18;
11:13; 13:15

foolish
Proverbs 1:7; 19:29;
Ephesians 5:15–17

speedily
Ecclesiastes 8:11

So Be It

DANIEL 4:28 *All this came upon King Nebuchadnezzar.* (*NKJV*)

Again, we should keep in mind that this is Nebuchadnezzar's personal testimony written for all the world to read. He does not say that he foolishly ignored Daniel's advice, but apparently he must have since God's judgment fell. The following is his own account of what happened to him.

God Never Forgets

DANIEL 4:29 *At the end of the twelve months he was walking about the royal palace of Babylon.* (*NKJV*)

God's judgment did not come speedily. One week passed after Daniel advised the king to repent and nothing happened. Soon one month was gone, then six months, and then one year later Nebuchadnezzar was walking around his royal palace. It was the custom in those days to build a flat roof on at least part of the building and use it for a patio, which is where we find Nebuchadnezzar.

He was walking on the roof of his palace, but he had not heard that famous sermon that says there's a payday someday. In this case, payday had arrived. Every individual needs to pay attention to this, because ready or not Judgment Day will arrive. God even has an

thanking
1 Thessalonians 5:18

forgotten God
Deuteronomy
8:6–18;
Psalm 9:17

glory
Psalm 96:1–13

proud
Proverbs 16:5; 29:23

self-exaltation
elevate one's own
self, brag, boast

appointed time for the judgment of the nations. He is patient and may wait a long time, but the time will pass and the day will arrive.

Wow, Look What I've Done

DANIEL 4:30 *The king spoke, saying, "Is not this great Babylon, that I have built for a royal dwelling by my mighty power and for the honor of my majesty?" (NKJV)*

Nebuchadnezzar was out on his patio admiring the beautiful kingdom God had already said was given to him. He should have been thanking God for what he saw and received, but he had forgotten God. He should have done these things for God's glory, but he did them for his own glory. This proud king was patting himself on the back.

Everything comes from God. He can take it away or restore it anytime he chooses.

Self-exaltation runs contrary to the teachings of Jesus. He said, "Whoever exalts himself will be humbled, and he who humbles himself will be exalted" (Matthew 23:12 NKJV). True greatness is service to God and others.

Pride caused the downfall of Satan (Ezekiel 28:13–17). It is a sign of the end of the age (2 Timothy 3:1–2). It was Nebuchadnezzar's poor master. Some of what the Bible says about pride is shown in the following chart.

Pride

Characteristics	Scripture
It is one of the seven deadly sins.	Proverbs 6:16–19
It makes a person an abomination to God.	Proverbs 16:5
It is one step away from destruction.	Proverbs 16:18
It keeps a person from confessing his sin.	Luke 18:11
It causes a person to run up against the resistance of God.	James 4:6

Gone in a Word

DANIEL 4:31 *While the word was still in the king's mouth, a voice fell from heaven: "King Nebuchadnezzar, to you it is spoken: the kingdom has departed from you! (NKJV)*

The Bible teaches that God knows our very <u>thoughts</u>, even every <u>word</u> we speak. These words were not even off the lips of Nebuchadnezzar when there came a <u>voice from heaven</u>. The heavenly council had decided that the time to dethrone the king had come. He was seeking to be superhuman, to be glorified and worshipped, but he was about to become subhuman, reviled and scorned. Many people say God doesn't make people sick. They fail to understand that God has a loving purpose for everything he does. Here God sent an affliction upon Nebuchadnezzar to humble him, to teach him, and to save him.

Notice that this would be a seven-year affliction and that the Tribulation Period will be a seven-year affliction. Notice that God sent delusion upon Nebuchadnezzar and that after the Rapture God will send strong delusion on those who refused to believe the Word and be saved (2 Thessalonians 2:11–12). Notice that Nebuchadnezzar barely got the words out of his mouth when his affliction struck, and understand that Paul said when they say peace and safety, sudden destruction will come upon them (1 Thessalonians 5:3). Consider the following names of the Tribulation Period in light of Nebuchadnezzar's illness:

go to

thoughts
Psalm 94:11;
1 Corinthians 3:20

word
Matthew 12:36

voice from heaven
Matthew 3:17;
John 12:28;
Acts 11:9

1. The Indignation (Isaiah 26:20).

2. The Time of Jacob's Trouble (Jeremiah 30:7).

3. A Day of Trouble and Distress (Zephaniah 1:15).

4. The Day of the Lord's Wrath (Zephaniah 1:18).

5. The Great Tribulation (Matthew 24:21).

6. The Hour of Trial (Revelation 3:10).

7. The Hour of Judgment (Revelation 14:7).

what others say

Frank Ramirez

When the exile is delayed, Nebuchadnezzar has a chance to change his ways. Bible scholar Graydon Snyder points out that in scripture virtually all predictions of the Day of the Lord, or a day of doom, have a delay clause. There is time for people to change their ways. That most powerful of words—if— was offered as an out. If we do not change our ways, then doom will fall. This is an offer of hope.[13]

kingdom
1 Corinthians 15:24

repented
turned away from
sin and turned
toward God

Then Daniel blessed the God of heaven and said: "Blessed be the name of God forever and ever, for wisdom and might are His. And He changes the times and the seasons; He removes kings and raises up kings" (Daniel 2:20–21 NKJV).

No Repentance

> DANIEL **4:32** *And they shall drive you from men, and your dwelling shall be with the beasts of the field. They shall make you eat grass like oxen; and seven times shall pass over you, until you know that the Most High rules in the kingdom of men, and gives it to whomever He chooses." (NKJV)*

Look at the list! He could have **repented**. Perhaps, the angelic council would have changed its mind if he had, but he did not.

1. Your <u>kingdom</u> has been taken from you (Daniel 4:31).

2. You will be driven away from people (Daniel 4:32).

3. You will live with the wild animals.

4. Seven times (years) will pass by for you.

5. You will acknowledge that the Most High rules in the kingdom of men.

6. You will acknowledge that he gives kingdoms to anyone he wishes.

Birdman of Babylon

> DANIEL **4:33** *That very hour the word was fulfilled concerning Nebuchadnezzar; he was driven from men and ate grass like oxen; his body was wet with the dew of heaven till his hair had grown like eagles' feathers and his nails like birds' claws. (NKJV)*

The instant the heavenly voice ceased speaking the defiant king received exactly what God said. This rebellious man was driven out of his wonderful palace where he became a monstrosity of a man. He crawled around on his hands and knees, ate grass like ordinary cattle, and his body stayed wet all the time. He was covered with hair—hair so thick it looked like the feathers of an eagle. His fingernails and toenails grew out and looked like the claws of a bird. He would not repent and for seven long years he paid a terrible price.

We are not told where he lived or anything about his interim government during the seven years of his insanity. We suspect that everyone knew from Daniel's interpretation of the dream that his illness would be only temporary. From Daniel 4:15, "Leave the stump and roots in the earth, bound with a band of iron and bronze, in the tender grass of the field" (NKJV), we would assume that he was confined to a well-cared-for field, surrounded by an iron fence decorated with brass. Daniel and the king's other advisers probably ran things until he recovered.

As is the case with almost everything in the Bible, there are skeptics who say this is just a good story. It really didn't happen. There is no such illness. Nebuchadnezzar didn't experience anything like this. However, at least one historical source has been found that mentions Nebuchadnezzar's strange illness. There have been documented cases of similar illnesses. The Babylonian Talmud says Daniel cared for Nebuchadnezzar. Also, Nebuchadnezzar's name is strangely absent from all historical and governmental documents for a period of about four years, which coincides with the time of this reported illness. His name reappears shortly before his death. The case of the skeptics is nonexistent.

Most High
Psalm 47:1–9

healed
Deuteronomy
32:39–43

I Was Wrong

> DANIEL 4:34 *And at the end of the time I, Nebuchadnezzar, lifted my eyes to heaven, and my understanding returned to me; and I blessed the **Most High** and praised and honored Him who lives forever:*
>   *For His dominion is an everlasting dominion,*
>   *And His kingdom is from generation to generation. (NKJV)*

"At the end of the time" (Daniel 4:34 NKJV) means there was no parole. Nebuchadnezzar served his full sentence before he finally raised his eyes toward heaven. Then he was <u>healed</u>, and while in his right mind, he understood that God is in charge. So he began to praise God—the eternal God who lives forever, the God who will always reign, the God whose kingdom will never end.

go to

powers
Romans 8:38;
Colossians 1:15–16

heavenly places
Ephesians 6:12

Creator
Genesis 1:1

Donald E. Gowan

Since the intention of the chastisement was to teach Nebuchadnezzar that "the Most High has sovereignty over the kingdom of mortals, and gives it to whom he will" (verse 25), the fulfillment of the dream includes his acceptance of that truth.[14]

John Phillips

The words of the restored Babylonian should be graven with an iron pen and lead in the rock forever and placed over the portals of every throne room and every congress on earth—especially in times like these, when terror stalks the earth, and when men have within their grasp weapons of mass destruction, and when men have shrugged off all fear of God.[15]

When Daniel interpreted Nebuchadnezzar's dream he said, "Inasmuch as they gave the command to leave the stump and roots of the tree, your kingdom shall be assured to you, after you come to know that Heaven rules" (Daniel 4:26 NKJV).

No One but Me

DANIEL 4:35
All the inhabitants of the earth are reputed as nothing;
He does according to His will in the army of heaven
And among the inhabitants of the earth.
No one can restrain His hand
Or say to Him, "What have You done?" (NKJV)

God is great. All the peoples of the earth are nothing compared to him. He does as he pleases whether it be with spiritual powers in the heavenly places or with peoples of the earth. He is so powerful no one can resist him, not even a strong world leader. He has done such marvelous things no one can ask, What have you done? Nebuchadnezzar learned his lesson. God is the Creator; he is in charge, and he does what he wants to do.

People sometimes ask why God told Pharaoh to let the Hebrews go and then hardened his heart so he wouldn't do it. Pharaoh was the head of a Gentile world government, and God did it to show the world that no one is rich enough, powerful enough, or has an army strong enough to resist him. After God finished sending the ten plagues, Pharaoh gladly told Moses to take the Hebrews and go. World leaders should avoid a confrontation with God. They will lose. But one is coming over the land of Israel.

Greater Than Before

DANIEL 4:36 *At the same time my reason returned to me, and for the glory of my kingdom, my honor and splendor returned to me. My counselors and nobles resorted to me, I was restored to my kingdom, and excellent majesty was added to me.* (NKJV)

God always does what he says he will do. Nebuchadnezzar got his <u>good name</u> back and his kingdom. His officials did not shun him, and for the remainder of his life (about one year), he was greater than ever.

God will do it again. Following the seven-year Tribulation Period, Jesus will return and restore sensible government to the world. It will be even better than anything the world has ever experienced. The world will know "He who is the blessed and only Potentate, the King of kings and Lord of lords" (1 Timothy 6:15 NKJV). The world will know what Nebuchadnezzar learned. We are not gods, we are the subjects of God.

Humble Thyself Before the Lord

DANIEL 4:37 *Now I, Nebuchadnezzar, praise and extol and honor the King of heaven, all of whose works are truth, and His ways justice. And those who walk in pride He is able to put down.* (NKJV)

This testimony shows the great change that came about in Nebuchadnezzar. He turned away from the false gods of Babylon, and to the world he wrote, "I, Nebuchadnezzar, praise and extol and honor the King of heaven" (Daniel 4:37 NKJV). Why? Because:

1. Everything God does is <u>right</u>.

2. All his ways are <u>just</u>.

3. All those who walk in pride he is able to <u>humble</u>.

go to

good name
Proverbs 22:1–4

right
Psalm 33:4

just
Deuteronomy 32:4

humble
Deuteronomy 8:1–5;
Matthew 18:1–4;
Luke 14:7–11

For most of his life, Nebuchadnezzar was a wicked man. He conquered Israel, destroyed Jerusalem and the Temple, killed and enslaved multitudes, and emasculated others. He tried to establish a one-world pagan religion, would have killed Daniel and all the wise men, threw Shadrach, Meshach and Abed-Nego into the fiery furnace, was full of pride, and much more. But God in his amazing grace chose to save him. It doesn't matter how bad a person has been. God loves that person and stands ready to save all who will turn to him.

A King's Understanding of God

1. He called him Daniel's God. The king said to Daniel, "Truly your God is the God of gods, the Lord of kings, and a revealer of secrets, since you could reveal this secret" (Daniel 2:47 NKJV).

2. He called him the God of Shadrach, Meshach, and Abed-Nego. Then Nebuchadnezzar said, "Blessed be the God of Shadrach, Meshach, and Abed-Nego, who sent His Angel and delivered His servants who trusted in Him, and they have frustrated the king's word, and yielded their bodies, that they should not serve nor worship any god except their own God!" (Daniel 3:28 NKJV).

3. He recognized that God is great. "I thought it good to declare the signs and wonders that the Most High God has worked for me. How great are His signs, and how mighty His wonders! His kingdom is an everlasting kingdom, and His dominion is from generation to generation" (Daniel 4:2–3 NKJV).

4. He recognized that God is everybody's God. "I blessed the Most High and praised and honored Him who lives forever: For His dominion is an everlasting dominion, and His kingdom is from generation to generation. All the inhabitants of the earth are reputed as nothing; He does according to His will in the army of heaven and among the inhabitants of the earth. No one can restrain His hand or say to Him, 'What have You done?'" (Daniel 4:34–35 NKJV).

5. He recognized that God is his God. "Now I, Nebuchadnezzar, praise and extol and honor the King of heaven, all of whose works are truth, and His ways justice. And those who walk in pride He is able to put down" (Daniel 4:37 NKJV).

Chapter Wrap-Up

- This chapter is an account of N€
  ten testimony of one who initia
  and proud of his accomplishme

- Nebuchadnezzar had a second (
  men, but they could not explai
  first, Daniel was stunned, but
  4:5–8; 19–26)

- Daniel recommended that th
  ignored the advice. God's j
  the king went insane and
  This affliction of madness

- The king's affliction even
  to look toward heaven, ackน.
  4:34)

- When Nebuchadnezzar looked to God he was healed บ1 ..
  insanity. Then his throne was restored and he became greater
  than ever. (Daniel 4:34–36)

Study Questions

1. How could Daniel interpret the dream when the other wise men
   could not?

2. Who said, "Cut down the tree"? Who or what are they? How
   was mercy shown?

3. What important thing does God want the living to know? Why?

4. Are we in charge of our own destiny?

5. What control does God have over the proud? Does he do
   wrong? How did this help Nebuchadnezzar?

Daniel 5 The King Who Defied God

Chapter Highlights:
- A Big Party
- A Big Boast
- A Big Hand
- A Big Invasion
- A Big Change

Let's Get Started

A little more than twenty years has now passed (see Time Line #1, Appendix A) since Nebuchadnezzar's testimony; much has changed. Nebuchadnezzar is dead and Daniel is about eighty years old. Infighting has struck the royal family and the crown has changed heads several times. The palace has been declared off-limits to Daniel and many of the advisers who served former kings. The winds of change have blown hard on Babylon.

Chapter 5 details the last night of Babylon's existence, the last night of the empire of gold on God's Statue (see Illustration #5) of Nebuchadnezzar's famous dream about gentile world kingdoms. A combined army of Medes and Persians has surrounded the city (see Illustration #14). They represent the empire of silver in Nebuchadnezzar's famous dream. Before dawn the empire of gold will be gone and the empire of silver will rule the world.

The main character is now one of Nebuchadnezzar's **despotic** grandsons, a man named Belshazzar. He is serving as **co-regent** with his father, Nabonidus, who had taken an army outside the walls to engage the Medes and Persians in battle. But Nabonidus was defeated, then fled, and is now in hiding. Major changes have taken place since the death of Nebuchadnezzar. Keep in mind that Nebuchadnezzar was Belshazzar's grandfather. This is important in order to understand Daniel 5:2, 11, 13, and 18.

As is the case with several other facts we have already studied, there is a long list of Bible critics who once said the book of Daniel is filled with error. As far as chapter 5 is concerned, they based their claim on two facts. First, they could find no record of anyone named Belshazzar, so they said he was a figment of Daniel's imagination, and, second, they could find no record of a king other than Nabonidus. Then, during the 1920s, a batch of Babylonian documents was discovered that solved both problems. Belshazzar was the oldest son of Nabonidus. His father wanted to go off to Arabia. He crowned Belshazzar king of Babylon, took a trip, and left him in

despotic
a tyrant; a cruel, unjust ruler

co-regent
a co-ruler; an acting ruler in the absence of the main ruler

charge. Nabonidus didn't give up his crown. He was still king and served as co-ruler. It's just that he chose to place a crown on his son's head while he toured and ruled other areas of the kingdom. The critics quieted down, but not completely. Then, in 1956 two cylinders were discovered that verified previous information, and, for the most part, the skeptics have been silenced.

The book of Daniel is an amazing book. It is quoted by other Bible writers many times. Jesus even quoted it. Few, if any other, books of the Bible contain as many prophecies. Several dozen incredible facts have been literally fulfilled. Critics know this, so they have jumped on it with a vengeance. But over and over again, they have been proven wrong by archaeology, and it has been proven right.

Rulers of Babylon

Beginning of Reign	King	Years Reigned	Death	Replaced by
626 BC	Nabopolassar	21	Not known	His son, Nebuchadnezzar
605 BC	Nebuchadnezzar	44	Natural	His son, Evil-merodach
561 BC	Evil-merodach	2	Murdered by Neriglissar	His brother-in-law, (married to Nebuchadnezzar's daughter)
559 BC	Neriglissar	4	Killed in battle	His son, Labosoar-chad (Nebuchadnezzar's grandson)
556 BC	Labosoar-chad	9 mos.	Murdered by Nabonidus	His step-grandfather, Nabonidus (married to Neriglissaris widow)
555 BC	Nabonidus	16	Not dead, in hiding	Not replaced. Belshazzar, his son is co-regent
544 BC	Belshazzar	5	Killed when Babylon fell	Darius, King of the Medes and Persians

what others say

Henry M. Morris

The famous image of Nebuchadnezzar's dream had been interpreted by Daniel to mean that four great empires would dominate future world history, the first being Babylon itself. The other three, as practically all Bible expositors agree, turned out to be Persia, Greece, and Rome, in that order. Each of these endured for centuries as the most important nation in the world, but each eventually fell. Each played a key role in the plan of God, contributing significantly (though unknowingly) in carrying forward the dominion mandate and also in God's spiritual program.[1]

When Daniel interpreted Nebuchadnezzar's first dream about the great statue he told the king, "After you shall arise another kingdom [the chest and arms of silver] inferior to yours" (Daniel 2:32, 39 NKJV).

A BIG Party

> DANIEL 5:1 *Belshazzar the king made a great feast for a thousand of his lords, and drank wine in the presence of the thousand.* (NKJV)

The Medes and the Persians had joined forces in an effort to defeat Babylon. Nabonidus had come out of the city to attack them, but he was defeated. Cyrus now had the city of Babylon under siege. His combined army of Medes and Persians was just outside the city walls, and he was preparing to attack. Belshazzar, however, did not seem to care because he undoubtedly had been told that he was secure behind the walls of Babylon. He seemed to believe it, because he was proud and defiant. He feared no one; not his enemies, not Cyrus, not the empire of silver, not even God. He even decided to show everyone how unafraid he was. He threw a big party while enemy troops were outside his beautiful city. He invited a thousand nobles from his kingdom, brought out the best wine, and they drank together.

Cyrus was the son of King Cambyses I of Persia and Queen Mandan, daughter of King Astyages of the Medes. Their marriage was a major factor in the alliance between the Medes and the Persians. Cyrus was the "commander" of the combined army of the Medes and Persians that conquered Babylon. He was a shrewd, compassionate leader who would come to be known as "Cyrus the Great." After Cyrus captured Babylon, Darius, who was then king of the Medes, became king of the new world empire. When Darius died two years later, Cyrus replaced him on the throne.

Bring in Those Hebrew Goblets

> DANIEL 5:2 *While he tasted the wine, Belshazzar gave the command to bring the gold and silver vessels which his father Nebuchadnezzar had taken from the temple which had been in Jerusalem, that the king and his lords, his wives, and his concubines might drink from them.* (NKJV)

Illustration #14
Ancient City of Babylon—One of the greatest cities of all times. The palace alone took up six square miles, and the Hanging Gardens were one of the Seven Wonders of the Ancient World.

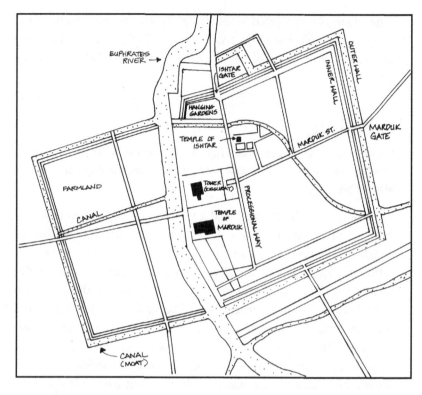

go to

vessels
Daniel 1:2;
2 Chronicles
36:11–21

Most High
Daniel 4:17

sacred
belonging to, or set apart for, God

concubines
his least-favored wives

sacrilege
disrespect for God

reveler
pleasure seeker

polygamist
has more than one wife

blasphemer
shows contempt for God

As the evening wore on, the wine became both a comfort and a curse to Belshazzar. With each drink he seemed to become more bold and more foolish. In a moment of daring he sent for the **sacred** <u>vessels</u> his grandfather, Nebuchadnezzar, had plundered from the Jewish Temple. He decided to defy the <u>Most High</u> who rules in the kingdom of men by drinking wine out of these vessels. He wanted his nobles, his wives, and his **concubines** to do the same. It was a grave **sacrilege**. We will learn in Daniel 5:22 that he knew better.

But it's hard to imagine that he could have found a way to insult God more than this or that he could have elected to do anything more unnecessary or stupid. God is longsuffering, but this man was asking for trouble.

what others say

Union Gospel Press

Some rulers, in spite of their vices, have redeeming qualities that give their lives some worth. This brief glimpse of Belshazzar, however, reveals nothing to be admired. He was a carefree **reveler**, an immoral **polygamist**, an arrogant **blasphemer**.[2]

Remember, Nebuchadnezzar was Belshazzar's grandfather and not his father, as this verse says. This is not an error in the Bible. It should be understood that we are using a translation of an original text, and in the original language (Aramaic) there is no word for *grandfather* or *grandson*. The word *father* in the original language means "ancestor." Nebuchadnezzar was Belshazzar's ancestor—his grandfather.

A Big Boast

DANIEL 5:3 *Then they brought the gold vessels that had been taken from the temple of the house of God which had been in Jerusalem; and the king and his lords, his wives, and his concubines drank from them. (NKJV)*

There is much in the Bible about the love of God. He is love, but he is also to be feared (respected) above all else. And while he is loving and longsuffering there is usually a line that no man should cross. It is that line that the foolish Belshazzar crossed. He made a big mistake when he requested the sacred vessels for use at his drunken party and drank from them. In doing so, he openly mocked God.

How many vessels were used is not indicated. It probably took several to accommodate such a large crowd. But the use of just one vessel in this degrading manner by Babylon's reprobate king was enough to justify the swift judgment of God.

Praise Be to Our Gods

DANIEL 5:4 *They drank wine, and praised the gods of gold and silver, bronze and iron, wood and stone. (NKJV)*

This was the crowning event in Belshazzar's contempt for God. It shows just how far he was willing to go with his anti-God attitude. The golden vessels had not come from some pagan temple but from God's own house. It was a <u>foolish</u> thing to do, but Belshazzar used the sacred vessels to praise the false gods of Babylon.

It is good to keep in mind the prophetic nature of Daniel's book. This deliberate defiance of God, blasphemy and idolatry, foreshadows the actions of the Antichrist and his False Prophet during the

Tribulation Period (Revelation 13:1–18). This drunken anti-God attitude is typical of the coming Mystery, Babylon the Great, the Mother of Harlots and of the Abominations of the Earth who will be drunk with the blood of the saints and with the blood of the martyrs of Jesus (Revelation 17:5–6).

Alcohol is a depressant. Specifically, alcohol affects the control centers of the brain. As a result, intoxicated people may lose their self-control and behave in ways that are unacceptable to others. They may experience mental confusion and an inability to walk steadily or talk clearly.

A Big Hand

DANIEL **5:5** *In the same hour the fingers of a man's hand appeared and wrote opposite the lampstand on the plaster of the wall of the king's palace; and the king saw the part of the hand that wrote.* (NKJV)

"In the same hour" is a reminder that God often acts in the blink of an eye. When the Antichrist signs the seven-year covenant for peace in the Middle East, sudden destruction will come upon the earth. When the Second Coming takes place at the end of the Tribulation Period, it will be suddenly like lightning streaking across the sky. Here "in the same hour" means as soon as Belshazzar desecrated the Temple vessels God crashed the party. He was gulping down liquor when the Holy God of Israel entered the room.

Suddenly, the fingers of a man's hand appeared and, as the king watched, they wrote on the wall. Were these drunken idolaters hallucinating? Was this the product of their intoxicated imagination? No. This was painfully real.

The hand wrote on the **plaster** near the lampstand in the royal palace. This may have been the **golden lampstand** (see Illustration #15) taken from the Jewish Temple. Archaeologists have discovered that it was used by the Babylonians as a trophy or a symbol of their victory over Israel. It is also possible that God wants us to know that the hand appeared in a well-lit area of the banquet hall.

What a change! Turn the clock back a few minutes, and the king was defying God and demonstrating that he was not afraid of anything. Suddenly, the fingers of a hand appeared, and suddenly the

go to

suddenly
1 Thessalonians
5:1–3

fingers
Exodus 8:19

golden lampstand
1 Chronicles 28:15

plaster
a soft chalky covering on the wall

golden lampstand
a seven-branched candlestick that stood in the Temple at Jerusalem

king was shaking in his shoes. This is the way it was before the Flood. People were eating and drinking, marrying and giving in marriage, and suddenly it started to rain (Matthew 24:38). This is the way it will be when Jesus returns. People will be drinking and partying, and suddenly they will be caught unprepared for eternity.

foolish
Luke 12:16–21

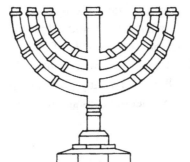

Illustration #15
Golden Lampstand—Before the Temple was destroyed, Jewish priests kept this lit day and night.

His Knees Were a-Knockin'

> DANIEL 5:6 *Then the king's countenance changed, and his thoughts troubled him, so that the joints of his hips were loosened and his knees knocked against each other.* (NKJV)

I imagine there was no more tinkling of glasses and no more loud laughter. It appears Belshazzar now realized that he had made a terrible mistake. The color drained from his face, he began to tremble, and his knees started knocking. He was so weak with fear that his legs gave way.

This was the hand of the supernatural. Aramaic scholars say it was a palm with fingers. it's probably the same hand that wrote the **Ten Commandments** on tablets of stone (Exodus 31:18). Some think it may be the same hand that wrote on the ground when the scribes and Pharisees brought the woman taken in adultery to Jesus (John 8:1–11).

Bring in My Wise Men

> DANIEL 5:7 *The king cried aloud to bring in the astrologers, the Chaldeans, and the soothsayers. The king spoke, saying to the wise men of Babylon, "Whoever reads this writing, and tells me*

Ten Commandments
ten laws for Israel that God revealed to Moses

go to

called
Daniel 2:2

wise men
Daniel 4:6

sin
1 John 1:9

its interpretation, shall be clothed with purple and have a chain of gold around his neck; and he shall be the third ruler in the kingdom." (NKJV)

It was time for Belshazzar to confess his sin, repent, and pray, but he did not. He was too defiant and proud. So he made the same mistake his once pagan grandfather Nebuchadnezzar often made. He called his ever-failing wise men. He needed to know what the writing was all about—what it said and what it meant. His wise men were called, and he offered rewards of expensive clothing, jewelry, power, and position to anyone who could tell him. He was desperate, scared, and willing to pay any price except the one that might possibly work—acknowledging his sin and recognizing God.

What Does It Mean?

DANIEL 5:8 *Now all the king's wise men came, but they could not read the writing, or make known to the king its interpretation. (NKJV)*

In came the unfortunate crew of so-called wise men. They looked at the message, but it was from God, so they obviously didn't understand it. The Bible says, "The natural man does not receive the things of the Spirit of God, for they are foolishness to him; nor can he know them, because they are spiritually discerned" (1 Corinthians 2:14 NKJV). So, once again, the enchanters, astrologers, and diviners failed.

This Can't Be Happening Again

DANIEL 5:9 *Then King Belshazzar was greatly troubled, his countenance was changed, and his lords were astonished. (NKJV)*

The failure of Belshazzar's wise men drove the intensity of the crisis even higher. The pale, knee-knocking king was now terrified. The ashen color of his face grew even whiter than before. No one there could claim his great rewards because no one could tell him what he wanted to know.

O King, Take It Easy

DANIEL 5:10 *The queen, because of the words of the king and his lords, came to the banquet hall. The queen spoke, saying, "O king, live forever! Do not let your thoughts trouble you, nor let your countenance change.* (NKJV)

There may have been some shouting and yelling going on and perhaps some shrieks of terror, because the queen heard the voices of Belshazzar and his rulers as she went to the banquet hall to learn what was going on.

Notice something here. This queen was probably not the wife of Belshazzar. Daniel 5:3 tells us that his wives and concubines were already present. So, although it cannot be said for certain, this queen was most likely the Queen Mother—the daughter of Nebuchadnezzar, the one who first married Neriglissar and later Nabonidus.

This queen, whoever she was, entered the banquet hall, quickly sized up the situation, and began to try to calm Belshazzar down. She had seen other crises, other times when the wise men were baffled, and knew this mystery was not impossible to solve.

Don't You Remember Daniel?

DANIEL 5:11 *There is a man in your kingdom in whom is the Spirit of the Holy God. And in the days of your father, light and understanding and wisdom, like the wisdom of the gods, were found in him; and King Nebuchadnezzar your father—your*

go to

in charge
Daniel 2:48

spirit of the holy gods
Daniel 4:8–9, 18

light
illumination and
awareness

understanding
comprehension and
enlightened
intelligence

wisdom
the right use of
knowledge

father the king—made him chief of the magicians, astrologers, Chaldeans, and soothsayers. (NKJV)

The Queen Mother's calmness grew out of her knowledge of Daniel and his God-given ability to solve mysteries for her father, Nebuchadnezzar. She informed the king that he had a man in his kingdom who could help. She reminded him that Daniel had proven his **light**, his **understanding**, and his **wisdom** during the days of Nebuchadnezzar, and that Daniel was placed in charge of all the wise men. This is another great testimony about Daniel and the things he had done—the Queen Mother knew all about him. Daniel had proven his ability to understand the mysteries of God.

Nebuchadnezzar placed Daniel <u>in charge</u> of all the wise men. He knew that Daniel had the <u>spirit of the holy gods</u> in him.

He'll Know the Answer

> DANIEL 5:12 *Inasmuch as an excellent spirit, knowledge, understanding, interpreting dreams, solving riddles, and explaining enigmas were found in this Daniel, whom the king named Belteshazzar, now let Daniel be called, and he will give the interpretation." (NKJV)*

In essence the Queen Mother told Belshazzar that Daniel had proven himself, and he should be called to explain this. Daniel was up to the task, but it might be worth noting that the situation was a little different this time. This was not a dream, riddle, or difficult problem. It was a plain statement of fact written by the hand of Almighty God.

According to *Strong's Exhaustive Concordance of the Bible*, the word *enigma* means "untie" or "loose." It was normally used for untying or loosing knots. In essence, the Queen Mother was saying that Daniel can break this riddle down and solve it. He can unravel it and tell you what it means.

Are You the One?

> DANIEL 5:13 *Then Daniel was brought in before the king. The king spoke, and said to Daniel, "Are you that Daniel who is one of the captives from Judah, whom my father the king brought from Judah? (NKJV)*

Belshazzar took the Queen Mother's advice. He called for Daniel to be brought before him. It is obvious that Daniel was living within the city walls, and he was probably not far away. It wasn't long until someone brought him to the palace where he entered the banquet hall.

As he entered, we learn something strange: the drunken king did not even know him. He had to ask Daniel if he was one of the exiles Nebuchadnezzar had brought from Judah. We wonder why but can only speculate. Maybe Daniel had been shoved aside at some point during the power struggle following Nebuchadnezzar's death. His age may have been a factor. He was now about eighty years old. His religion may have been a factor. He and the king were certainly at opposite ends of the spectrum on that. Whatever the case, it is obvious that he did not currently hold the high position he once held and that Belshazzar definitely had not been consulting with him about anything.

Insight, Intelligence, and Wisdom

DANIEL 5:14 *I have heard of you, that the Spirit of God is in you, and that light and understanding and excellent wisdom are found in you.* (NKJV)

Belshazzar told Daniel that his reputation had preceded him. He explained that he had heard of Daniel and began to praise him for his abilities. He had been neglecting Daniel, but now he wanted something and was trying to butter him up. There can be little doubt that Daniel, with all his abilities, was well aware of what this hypocrite was doing.

what others say

H. A. Ironside

I would address a word of warning to the unsaved. Belshazzar's great offense was this: though he knew of God's dealings with Nebuchadnezzar, he sinned right on, going against light and knowledge. None are so guilty as those who so act. And to all such the word comes with awful force, "He, that being often reproved hardened his neck, shall suddenly be destroyed, and that without remedy" (Proverbs 29:1).[5]

go to

wise men of babylon
Daniel 2:10–11; 4:7

earthly minded
only concerned
about the things of
this life

Those Buffoons Don't Know

DANIEL 5:15 *Now the wise men, the astrologers, have been brought in before me, that they should read this writing and make known to me its interpretation, but they could not give the interpretation of the thing. (NKJV)*

The king summarized the events for Daniel:

1. He summoned the wise men and astrologers.

2. He showed them the message on the wall.

3. He asked them to interpret it.

4. They failed.

The wise men were frauds having no knowledge of the things of God.

There were two other times when the wise men of Babylon could not do what the king asked.

Money, Position, and Power

DANIEL 5:16 *And I have heard of you, that you can give interpretations and explain enigmas. Now if you can read the writing and make known to me its interpretation, you shall be clothed with purple and have a chain of gold around your neck, and shall be the third ruler in the kingdom." (NKJV)*

This is the same offer that Belshazzar made to his unenlightened wise men: expensive gifts, a prominent position in the kingdom, and power. These are the things that most **earthly minded** people want—money, position and power. All Daniel had to do to receive them was interpret the handwriting.

Keep Your Gifts

DANIEL 5:17 *Then Daniel answered, and said before the king, "Let your gifts be for yourself, and give your rewards to another; yet I will read the writing to the king, and make known to him the interpretation." (NKJV)*

Daniel was unusually disrespectful to the king. He did not answer with, "O King, live forever" but immediately rejected the king's gifts and rewards. He probably knew they wouldn't be worth much, because he wouldn't be keeping them very long. What good is a raise and promotion the day before your company folds?

However, there is another point here: when God gives someone a gift, such as Daniel's gift of interpreting dreams, that gift is meant to be used for God's glory and not for the profit or glory of the one who receives it. Daniel did not want to make <u>money</u> with the gift God had given him, so he told the king to keep the gifts. A true man of God will not use the things of God for his own glory. It seems obvious that Daniel did not like the king, but he assured Belshazzar that he would still read the message and interpret it.

go to

money
Acts 8:17–20

foolish
1 Samuel 13:13–14

> **what others say**
>
> **Kenneth O. Gangel**
>
> The casual Bible reader might consider this chapter valuable information about ancient empires, and the beginning and the end of the chapter certainly provide that. But the great bulk of the verses center on the foolishness and wickedness of a pagan king and how God's heavenly judgment ended his kingdom.[6]

This was not the first time Daniel refused something. "Daniel purposed in his heart that he would not defile himself with the portion of the king's delicacies, nor with the wine which he drank; therefore he requested of the chief of the eunuchs that he might not defile himself" (Daniel 1:8 NKJV).

Remember Old Nebuchadnezzar

DANIEL 5:18 *O king, the Most High God gave Nebuchadnezzar your father a kingdom and majesty, glory and honor. (NKJV)*

Daniel let Belshazzar tremble a little longer. Before reading the message to him, he reminded the <u>foolish</u> king of a few things.

First, he reminded him of the source of Nebuchadnezzar's kingdom, majesty, glory, and honor. Nebuchadnezzar did not earn or deserve the things he had. They were gifts from the Most High God. The next five verses are a six-point sermon that would do any preacher proud. Daniel's text was chapter 4. His message was the sovereignty of God. It was a toe-stomper, short and right to the point.

The Greatest of Them All

DANIEL 5:19 *And because of the majesty that He gave him, all peoples, nations, and languages trembled and feared before him. Whomever he wished, he executed; whomever he wished, he kept alive; whomever he wished, he set up; and whomever he wished, he put down.* *(NKJV)*

Second, Daniel reminded Belshazzar that <u>Nebuchadnezzar</u> had absolute power. He was known and feared all over the earth. He killed those he wanted to kill and spared those he wanted to spare. He was so powerful no human being could prevent him from doing whatever he wished.

God Sat Him Down

DANIEL 5:20 *But when his heart was lifted up, and his spirit was hardened in pride, he was deposed from his kingly throne, and they took his glory from him.* *(NKJV)*

Third, Daniel pointed out Nebuchadnezzar's sin. His heart was filled with arrogance and <u>pride</u>. He took sole credit for all his accomplishments and believed everything he did was for his own <u>glory</u>. It was only after God put him down that he developed a right perspective and began to glorify God. The purpose of Daniel's words was to show the trembling king that he had made the same mistake his grandfather made, and Belshazzar had no right to expect to get away with it.

God cannot lead people who will not submit. If we would humble ourselves and submit to him, he would reward instead of having to humble us. The Bible says, "God resists the proud, but gives grace to the humble" (1 Peter 5:5 NKJV).

Out to Pasture

DANIEL 5:21 *Then he was driven from the sons of men, his heart was made like the beasts, and his dwelling was with the wild*

Nebuchadnezzar
Jeremiah 27:6–7

pride
Proverbs 16:18

glory
Daniel 4:30

donkeys. They fed him with grass like oxen, and his body was wet with the dew of heaven, till he knew that the Most High God rules in the kingdom of men, and appoints over it whomever He chooses. (NKJV)

Fourth, Daniel reminded Belshazzar of what happened to Nebuchadnezzar. God deposed him and caused him to go insane. He had the mind of a beast, lived with the wild donkeys, and ate <u>grass</u> like an ordinary cow. His body was always wet with dew, and his mental illness continued until he admitted that the Most High God controls all kingdoms and chooses all rulers.

go to

grass
Daniel 4:30–33

deliberately
2 Peter 3:3–7

what others say

Charles R. Swindoll

All crowns of authority belong to the Lord, who gives them and takes them away with the same sovereign hand. Not even kings have a right to boast before God.[7]

Oh, Foolish You

DANIEL 5:22 *But you his son, Belshazzar, have not humbled your heart, although you knew all this. (NKJV)*

Fifth, Daniel reminded Belshazzar that he was a descendant of Nebuchadnezzar, which is a way of saying he had personal knowledge of the things that happened to him. Also, that Belshazzar had committed the same sin Nebuchadnezzar committed by not humbling himself before God. And to make matters worse, Belshazzar was fully aware of all these things. Daniel was making the point that Belshazzar could not plead ignorance; he had <u>deliberately</u> ignored these things.

what others say

Arno Froese

Chapter 5 paints a prophetic picture of the Gentile world. In spite of the offer of grace, forgiveness and restoration, the Gentiles defy the living God and will continue to do so until their ultimate demise.[8]

How Could You Be So Stupid?

DANIEL 5:23 *And you have lifted yourself up against the Lord of heaven. They have brought the vessels of His house before you,*

desecrating
abusing or showing
contempt for the
things of God

*and you and your lords, your wives and your concubines, have
drunk wine from them. And you have praised the gods of silver
and gold, bronze and iron, wood and stone, which do not see or
hear or know; and the God who holds your breath in His hand
and owns all your ways, you have not glorified. (NKJV)*

Sixth, Daniel charged Belshazzar with being an enemy of God by
opposing and setting himself against him. He charged the king with
committing a grave sacrilege by sending for the Temple vessels and
desecrating them at his drunken feast. He also charged the king
with idolatry by praising man-made gods that are deaf and dumb
while ignoring the God who held the king's life and ways in his
hands.

These harsh and embarrassing charges were leveled against
Belshazzar in front of all his guests and family. He could have had
Daniel killed for saying these things, but Daniel did not soften his
words. He laid it on the line.

Belshazzar's grandfather Nebuchadnezzar had said, "I make a
decree that any people, nation, or language which speaks anything
amiss against the God of Shadrach, Meshach, and Abed-Nego shall
be cut in pieces, and their houses shall be made an ash heap; because
there is no other God who can deliver like this" (Daniel 3:29 NKJV).
He decreed the death penalty and the destruction of their house.
Who would have thought Nebuchadnezzar's own grandson would
have violated it?

Daniel Reminded Belshazzar

- that God was the source of Nebuchadnezzar's sovereignty,
  greatness, glory, and splendor,

- that God gave Nebuchadnezzar absolute power,

- of Nebuchadnezzar's sin—a heart filled with arrogance and pride,

- of what happened to Nebuchadnezzar—God deposed him and caused him to go insane,

- that he was a descendant of Nebuchadnezzar so he should remember what happened to him, and

- that he was acting as an enemy of God by opposing and setting himself against him.

key point

The Hand

DANIEL 5:24 *Then the fingers of the hand were sent from Him, and this writing was written.* (NKJV)

Because of what Daniel has already said, God sent the hand that wrote on the wall. In short, God made Belshazzar's grandfather great and gave him absolute power. But his grandfather became arrogant and proud, ignoring God and glorifying himself, So God humbled him. Belshazzar knew this but did not care. He did not use the information God had placed before him or take advantage of the opportunities he had. And, to make matters worse, he even made himself an enemy of God by defiling the sacred vessels taken from the Temple. This is what provoked the handwriting on the wall.

The opposite of pride is humility. God wants his people to be humble, but he does not ask his people to be a doormat or a jellyfish in the face of sin. He asks his people to take a stand and speak against evil, to be strong in the world, and to boldly confess Christ. There is nothing wrong with being proud of hard work, doing a good job, accepting Christ, or trying to honor him. Humility refers to our relationship with God and others. It means confessing our sins, seeking forgiveness, overlooking the faults of others, being willing to let others go first, and more. People should be humble before God and resist the devil. Unfortunately, many people humble themselves before the devil to do his will and resist God to avoid doing what he wants. This is what Belshazzar was doing.

number
Psalm 90:12

What Was That?

DANIEL 5:25 *"And this is the inscription that was written: MENE, MENE, TEKEL, UPHARSIN. (NKJV)*

The hand had disappeared, but the message remained on the wall. Daniel looked at it and read it. No one can definitely say what language it was written in, but it was certainly not that of the Babylonians. If it had been, Belshazzar would have read it himself. It was probably not Hebrew either, since some of his wise men could have read it. All that can be said for sure is that it was written by God, and the Holy Spirit revealed it to Daniel.

Your Number Is Up

DANIEL 5:26 *This is the interpretation of each word. MENE: God has numbered your kingdom, and finished it; (NKJV)*

This is Daniel's interpretation of the message. Each word has a short definition. The word *Mene* is similar to the English word "number" or "numbered." It meant that God had numbered the days of Belshazzar's reign, and they were all used up. His reign was over. The word *Mene* was repeated (Mene, Mene or numbered, numbered) to add emphasis to the decision or to show that it was final. Belshazzar may not have been afraid of that army outside his walls when he drank the wine out of the temple vessels, but he should have been. God was emphatic about bringing him down.

An interesting thing about this is the fact that God knew about all the sin that would exist in Babylon and the palace before it ever happened. The Jews were supposed to let their land rest one year out of every seven, but they didn't. They stole one crop every seven years until they had stolen seventy crops over a period of 490 years. This will be studied in chapter 9, but here it is important to understand that God had decided to make the evil Babylonians his servants until he had removed the Jews from their land for a period of seventy years to punish them for stealing the seventy crops (Jeremiah 25:9–11). He even promised to punish the Babylonians after seventy years and to have the Jews released after the Babylonian's time was up (Jeremiah 25:12; 29:10).

God also knows when the Tribulation Period will begin and the date of the Second Coming, but no one else knows (Matthew

key point

24:36). He is omniscient. He knows everything, including total knowledge of all future events. He has known all of this from the beginning of the world (Acts 15:14–18).

go to

weigh
Job 31:6

weighed
1 Samuel 2:3;
Psalm 62:9

what others say

F. B. Huey Jr.

Only through revelation would Jeremiah have been able to know that the empire days of Babylon would be so brief—seventy years. When Babylon fell, Judah's time of punishment would end, and restoration would begin.[10]

You Don't Measure Up

DANIEL 5:27 *TEKEL: You have been weighed in the balances, and found wanting;* (NKJV)

The word *Tekel* is similar to the English words "<u>weigh</u>," "weight" or "<u>weighed</u>." It meant that God had put Belshazzar on his divine scales and found that he did not measure up. He was undeserving of the blessings he was enjoying and not qualified to lead a world government.

what others say

Paul Benware

Men are accountable to the Lord God for what they do with His truth and His people. Some people might think that God is not watching, but the Scriptures reveal that God knows everything man does and says.[11]

A Double Meaning

DANIEL 5:28 *PERES: Your kingdom has been divided, and given to the Medes and Persians."* (NKJV)

Here the word is *Peres*. In Daniel 5:25 it was *Upharsin*. Most scholars say *Peres* and *Upharsin* are the same word with *Peres* being the singular form and *Upharsin* being the plural form. Like most words, it had more than one meaning. The first meaning is similar to the English words "divide," "divided," or "division," and the second meaning is a reference to the kingdom of Persia. The thought is that Babylon would be divided and given to the Persians. At that time, the Persians formed a dual empire with the Medes, so Daniel rightly interpreted the word to mean "Your kingdom has been divided, and given to the Medes and Persians."

Now, we ask, "Could God really do that?" It seems impossible. Belshazzar was the head of a world power and the city of Babylon was an armed fortress. It was one of the most fantastic and greatest cities of all time. Its hanging gardens were among the seven wonders of the world. The city was essentially a square (see Illustration #14). Each side was fourteen miles long. If you set out to walk around it, you would walk fourteeen miles across the front, fourteeen miles down one side, fourteeen miles across the back, and fourteeen miles up the other side for a total of fifty-six miles.

You have heard of the Great Wall of China. The city of Babylon was circled by two great walls. The outer wall was 311 feet high, 87 feet thick, and 56 miles long. There was a road on top of the wall. It was wide enough for six chariots to ride side by side. There were 250 towers on top of that wall. Each tower was manned with troops.

Down below, on the outside of the wall, was a canal or moat. It surrounded the city and was filled with water. People crossed it on drawbridges. Huge gates closed off the city. There was a second wall inside the outer wall with more soldiers and another road that was used for the rapid deployment of troops and supplies. The river Euphrates flowed under these walls. It went through the city and out the other side. It provided a constant supply of drinking water.

Several hundred acres of land had been set aside for farming inside the walls. Vegetables and cattle were grown to support the inhabitants of the city. There was enough food and provisions in storage to last for years, and more food could be grown if needed. At the time of Belshazzar's big feast, the ever-flowing Euphrates River was full of water, the drawbridges were raised, the gates were closed, sentinels were posted on the walls, and a great army was entrenched behind them. This is why Belshazzar felt so secure. He believed he was safe and had all he needed, but God had other plans.

Could it happen? Belshazzar must have given it some thought. He knew the Medes and Persians had an army outside the city, but how could they get across the moat? It was filled with water. How could they get over the first wall? It was 311 feet high. How could they get through the wall? It was 87 feet thick. And even if they did get past it, they still had to penetrate the second wall and defeat the

Babylonian army. But God said Belshazzar's time was up, so even the most impressive defenses in the world couldn't save him.

Take Your Gifts; You Have Them Coming

DANIEL 5:29 *Then Belshazzar gave the command, and they clothed Daniel with purple and put a chain of gold around his neck, and made a proclamation concerning him that he should be the third ruler in the kingdom.* (NKJV)

If Belshazzar was angry with Daniel for his bold denunciation, nothing is said about it. His word was law, and he kept it. He ignored Daniel's suggestion to keep the gifts and give the rewards to someone else. A **purple** robe was placed on Daniel's shoulders, a gold chain was placed around his neck, and he was proclaimed the third highest ruler in Babylon.

The first ruler and true king was Nabonidus. The second ruler and co-regent was Belshazzar. That is why Daniel was made the third highest ruler. Belshazzar could not replace his father, and would not replace himself, so he put Daniel in the next highest position.

A Big Invasion

DANIEL 5:30 *That very night Belshazzar, king of the Chaldeans, was slain.* (NKJV)

Here we have the end result, but we have to rely on secular history for the details. About two weeks before the drunken party Cyrus, commander of the Medes and Persians, started preparing for an invasion. He divided his army and sent several thousand troops to the south side of the city. It was their job to stay near the place where the Euphrates River exited the city, to watch for the river to stop flowing, and stay out of sight. He sent several thousand more troops to the north side of the city. It was their job to stay near the place where the Euphrates River entered the city. They were also supposed to watch for the river to stop flowing and stay out of sight (see Illustration #14).

About ten miles north of the city there was a very large swamp not far from the river. Cyrus had his troops dig a channel from the river to within just a few feet of the swamp. He also had the dirt piled on the banks of the river, so he could dam it up at the time of his choosing.

go to

purple
Judges 8:26;
Luke 16:19

purple
the most expensive
color available

go to

inferior kingdom
Daniel 2:39

foreordained
decreed by God
before it happened

On the night of the invasion, he had some of his troops complete the unfinished part of the channel to the swamp. He had thousands of other troops pushing dirt into the river to block the flow of water. All of that sent the water flowing in a different direction. The river bed emptied and the moat drained. That left only the river bed under the wall with no water. When the troops on each side of the city saw the water drop, they went under both walls of the city, killed the guards, lowered the drawbridges, and let in the rest of the army.

This caught Belshazzar and his lords by complete surprise. The handwriting on the wall had them rattled, the wine had them drunk, and as a result, they were unable to direct their army. Belshazzar was a proud, unrepentant pleasure seeker who was living under a false sense of security. He assumed he had everything under control. He provoked God, and in one night his world empire fell. He failed to consider the power of God and was killed.

A Big Change

DANIEL 5:31 *And Darius the Mede received the kingdom, being about sixty-two years old. (NKJV)*

After Cyrus and his troops captured the city, several weeks passed. Eventually, his uncle, Darius the Mede, went to Babylon and took over the world kingdom (see Time Line #1, Appendix A). He was sixty-two years old at the time. Later we will learn that this seems to be **foreordained** by God because this new empire will release the Jewish captives Nebuchadnezzar had taken years before and allow them to return home to rebuild Jerusalem and the Temple.

It is an interesting fact of history that the mother of Cyrus was a Mede and his father a Persian. It was their marriage that brought this coalition

what others say

J. G. Hall

Two prophecies were fulfilled as Darius entered the reveling city and conquered it that night. The head of gold on Nebuchadnezzar's dream-image gave way to the breast and arms of silver as an inferior kingdom came to power, and the handwriting on the wall was fulfilled to the letter.[12]

Chapter Wrap-Up

- The Medes and Persians had Babylon surrounded, so Belshazzar threw a big party to show everyone that he was not afraid. He invited a thousand of his top leaders, his wives, and his concubines. (Daniel 5:1)

- Belshazzar decided to demonstrate that he was not even afraid of Israel's God, so he stupidly committed a sacrilege by drinking wine out of the vessels taken from the Temple in Jerusalem. All his guests foolishly joined in. (Daniel 5:2–4)

- Suddenly a supernatural event took place at the party. A ghostly hand appeared, and its finger wrote a strange message on the wall. Everyone was dumbfounded. (Daniel 5:5–12)

- When no one at the party could interpret the message, Daniel was summoned. He told the king that the message meant the king's reign was over, he had been judged and found lacking, and the Medes and Persians would take control of the kingdom. (Daniel 5:13–28)

- Although Daniel was rewarded for his service to the king, it meant little to him. For that same night Babylon fell, Beshazzar was killed, and the Medes and Persians took over the empire. (Daniel 5:29–30)

Study Questions

1. What rewards were offered to Daniel to interpret the handwriting? What was his response, and what happened?

2. Did Daniel respect his king or gloss over Belshazzar's terrible sin?

3. Are people secure in an armed fortress? Were the Babylonians?

4. Are people and nations accountable to God for what they do? What happened to Babylon?

5. How did Belshazzar change when the hand wrote the message on the wall? Did he repent?

Daniel 6 The Conspiracy Against Daniel

Chapter Highlights:
- **A Plan to Promote**
- **A Plot to Eliminate**
- **Prayer and Protection**
- **Punishment of Accusers**
- **King's Decree**

Let's Get Started

Now we come to the best-known chapter in Daniel. In fact, the story of Daniel in the lions' den, and the story in chapter 3 about Shadrach, Meshach, and Abed-Nego are two of the most popular children's stories in the entire Bible. Many Christians have probably never heard of God's Statue (Nebuchadnezzar's dream statue) in chapter 2 or the Seventy Weeks of Daniel in chapter 9, but they are well aware of the courage and faith of Daniel as he stood before the den of lions, and that of Shadrach, Meshach, and Abed-Nego as they stood before the fiery furnace. We can learn a great deal from these stories about God's **sustaining grace**. Not much time has passed since the handwriting on the wall, but there are many dramatic changes taking place in Babylon. The head of gold, Babylon (the first Gentile world kingdom), on God's Statue (see Illustration #5) is gone. Medo-Persia (the second Gentile world kingdom), the chest and arms of silver, is now in power. Belshazzar, the last and most foolhardy king of Babylon, is dead, and Darius, the sixty-two-year-old king of Medo-Persia, is on the throne. However, he is sick, and this is how we know that not much time has passed. Historians tell us Darius died about two years after he became king of the empire. Daniel was still about eighty years old (see Time Line #1, Appendix A).

go to

sustaining
Nehemiah 9:21;
Psalm 55:22

grace
1 Corinthians 1:4;
15:10

satraps
Daniel 3:2–3

sustaining
the helping power of God

grace
the undeserved favor of God

satraps
princes or people of authority

Divvy It Up

> **DANIEL 6:1** *It pleased Darius to set over the kingdom one hundred and twenty satraps, to be over the whole kingdom;* (NKJV)

This is another reason why we know not much time had passed since the handwriting on the wall. Darius was in the process of setting up his government. He divided his newly conquered kingdom into 120 divisions or provinces. Then came the political appointments, which usually, but not always, went to members of the royal family. It pleased Darius to make 120 appointments, one ruler for each division or province of his kingdom. These rulers were called **satraps**.

Daniel Finds Favor

second in command
Genesis 41:39–44

DANIEL 6:2 *and over these, three governors, of whom Daniel was one, that the satraps might give account to them, so that the king would suffer no loss.* (NKJV)

The 120 divisions or provinces of the kingdom were divided up into three groups, probably forty in each group. Then three administrators were appointed, one over each group, and Daniel was one of the three. It was the job of these administrators to protect the interests of the king. They were probably told to watch the satraps for things like corruption, disloyalty, theft, and poor administration.

Daniel was qualified for this position. More than sixty years earlier, while he was in his late teens, Daniel interpreted a dream for Nebuchadnezzar, and the king made him ruler over the whole province of Babylon and chief administrator over all the wise men of Babylon (Daniel 2:48). When he interpreted the handwriting on the wall for Belshazzar, he was placed in position as the third highest ruler in the kingdom, which was his title when Darius took over (Daniel 5:29). He had the approval of God, the benefit of experience, a record of distinguished service, a reputation for being ten times better than the other wise men of Babylon, knowledge of the kingdom, and all the qualifications he needed to do this job. It is obvious that Darius wanted the best man for the job rather than a relative or political crony.

Promote Daniel

DANIEL 6:3 *Then this Daniel distinguished himself above the governors and satraps, because an excellent spirit was in him; and the king gave thought to setting him over the whole realm.* (NKJV)

Daniel was superior to everyone else Darius had appointed. He quickly distinguished himself among the other leaders, and it did not go unnoticed. The king made plans to set Daniel over the whole kingdom. He would have Daniel second in command only to himself.

When Nebuchadnezzar dreamed his frightening dream about the great tree, he said, "In him [Daniel] is the Spirit of the Holy God" (Daniel 4:8 NKJV). When the handwriting appeared on the wall the

Queen Mother heard a commotion and entered the banquet hall to determine what the noise was all about. Upon learning about the handwriting and that Belshazzar's wise men could not interpret it, she declared, "There is a man [Daniel] in your kingdom in whom is the Spirit of the Holy God" (Daniel 5:11 NKJV). This verse reveals that Darius found an excellent spirit in Daniel. it's obvious that God had a purpose for Daniel's life and that the Holy Spirit was working through him.

go to

charges
Acts 24:13–21

blameless
Philippians 2:15

no fault
Luke 23:4

regard for good things in the sight of all men
Romans 12:17

what others say

John C. Whitcomb

Even though the last kings of Babylon and most of the Babylonians (and probably many complacent Israelites in the exile as well) had ignored Daniel for many years, God, in His marvelous providence, saw to it that His faithful prophet received the honor that was due him.[1]

We've Got to Get Rid of Him

> DANIEL 6:4 *So the governors and satraps sought to find some charge against Daniel concerning the kingdom; but they could find no charge or fault, because he was faithful; nor was there any error or fault found in him.* (NKJV)

The idea of making Daniel second in command found opposition among the other two administrators and all 120 satraps. They organized and tried to formulate <u>charges</u> to bring against Daniel.

They wanted to discredit his service to the king, but could not find a way to do it. His conduct was <u>blameless</u>, and Pilate found <u>no fault</u> in this man. He was trustworthy, honest, and had <u>regard for good things in the sight of all men</u>.

what others say

Union Gospel Press

While Daniel's competence and honesty pleased the king, they infuriated the other officials. There may have been several reasons for this. First, jealousy is a normal reaction in people who are passed over when promotions are made. Second, some may have considered Daniel's high status unfair since he was advanced in years, a hold-over from the enemy administration, and a Jew. Furthermore, since his office involved a

go to

strict accounting of money
Daniel 6:2

Daniel himself was faultless
Daniel 6:4

subversive
intending to overthrow the one-world government

strict accounting of money and since Daniel himself was faultless, he may have been thwarting other officials' corrupt schemes for enriching themselves.[2]

Sinclair B. Ferguson

The second theme is that of the perpetual conflict of the kingdom of darkness against the kingdom of light, the kingdom of God. On this occasion it has its focus on the laws of these two kingdoms. The unchangeable law of the Medes and the Persians was used by devious men to attempt to overcome the laws of God's kingdom.[3]

Concerning the End of the Age, the apostle Paul said, "In the last days perilous times will come: For men will be lovers of themselves, lovers of money, boasters, proud, blasphemers, disobedient to parents, unthankful, unholy, unloving, unforgiving, slanderers, without self-control, brutal, despisers of good, traitors, headstrong, haughty, lovers of pleasure rather than lovers of God, having a form of godliness but denying its power. And from such people turn away!" (2 Timothy 3:1–5 NKJV).

Anti-Semitism will be a major problem, and there will be a worldwide effort to wipe Israel off the face of the earth (Zechariah 12:1–3; 14:1–2). The Antichrist will seek to change times and laws (Daniel 7:25). This is coming on the scene today with the crackdown on faith groups and their prayers in schools, in the military, and elsewhere; with the extreme Muslim hatred and violence toward Jews; and with the efforts to remove all references to Jesus from American history and laws.

During the Tribulation Period the False Prophet will use the Mark of the Beast to make Christians appear **subversive**. He will use it to create a conflict between world government and Christianity, thereby trying to justify the execution of Christians.

Something Must Be Done

DANIEL 6:5 *Then these men said, "We shall not find any charge against this Daniel unless we find it against him concerning the law of his God." (NKJV)*

Daniel led a godly life that was above reproach. Look at the steps of this determined group. First, they tried to find something wrong with Daniel's service to the king, but they found no errors. Second, they tried to find something wrong with Daniel's character, but they found no flaws. Finally, they came to the conclusion that the only way to get him was to attack his commitment to God.

This was not a new idea. It comes from Satan and it was used before. At this time some astrologers came forward and denounced the Jews. They said to King Nebuchadnezzar, "O king, live forever! You, O king, have made a decree that everyone who hears the sound of the horn, flute, harp, lyre, and psaltery, in symphony with all kinds of music, shall fall down and worship the gold image; and whoever does not fall down and worship shall be cast into the midst of a burning fiery furnace. There are certain Jews whom you have set over the affairs of the province of Babylon: Shadrach, Meshach, and Abed-Nego; these men, O king, have not paid due regard to you. They do not serve your gods or worship the gold image which you have set up" (Daniel 3:9–12 NKJV).

O Gracious Darius, Listen to Us

DANIEL 6:6 *So these governors and satraps thronged before the king, and said thus to him: "King Darius, live forever! (NKJV)*

The administrators and satraps assembled themselves together in or near the palace. They probably selected a spokesperson, and then they went in as a group to have an audience with the king. They were very <u>cunning</u> and **subtle**. They approached the king like <u>angels of light</u> with sweet-sounding words: "King Darius, live forever!" (Daniel 6:6 NKJV).

The Bible teaches that people will live forever, but not in the body we now have. Jesus said, "Because I live, you will live also" (John 14:19 NKJV). He was referring to the resurrection of the righteous with a new immortal body. Unbelievers will be raised too, but the awful difference is where each will spend eternity.

cunning
Genesis 3:1

angel of light
2 Corinthians 11:14

subtle
cunning, clever, tricky, sly

what others say

Jack W. Hayford

It is conceded that in living out biblical principles there will inevitably be confrontational assaults made upon believers by

go to

lied
Psalm 62:4

conspiracy of the administrators and satraps
Daniel 6:4

God
Isaiah 45:5, 21–22; 46:9

conspiracy against Jesus
Psalms 59:3; 64:2–4

Even Daniel Wants This

DANIEL 6:7 *All the governors of the kingdom, the administrators and satraps, the counselors and advisors, have consulted together to establish a royal statute and to make a firm decree, that whoever petitions any god or man for thirty days, except you, O king, shall be cast into the den of lions.* (NKJV)

They exaggerated the situation and even <u>lied</u>. This was a <u>conspiracy of the administrators and satraps</u>. They exaggerated the situation by telling the king that the prefects, advisers, and governors were in on it too, so they lied by acting like Daniel was included in the decision.

They wanted two things: a decree and a penalty. The decree would forbid all prayers for thirty days except those directed to Darius. This would force everyone to do one of three things: not pray, recognize Darius as a <u>god</u>, or break the law. They were asking the king to establish a world religion for thirty days. The penalty they wanted called for violators to be thrown into the lions' den. This was similar to the <u>conspiracy against Jesus</u>: "The chief priests, the elders, and all the council sought false testimony against Jesus to put Him to death" (Matthew 26:59 NKJV). This will be a problem at the end of the age. Jesus said, "Then they will deliver you up to tribulation and kill you, and you will be hated by all nations for My name's sake" (Matthew 24:9 NKJV).

The thirty-day time limit is a great compliment to Daniel. He definitely was committed and obviously was an effective witness for his God in Babylon. These conspirators believed thirty days would be more than enough time to catch him praying to the same God he always prayed to.

So Let It Be Written

DANIEL 6:8 *Now, O king, establish the decree and sign the writing, so that it cannot be changed, according to the law of the Medes and Persians, which does not alter."* (NKJV)

They not only asked the king to issue this decree, they also asked him to put it in writing. According to the law of the Medes and Persians, if he put it in writing, it could not be changed, not even by him. It was a very sinister plan.

According to the belief of the Medes and Persians, the king was a god. If he changed a law, he would be admitting that he had made a mistake, but no god could do that. So he had to obey the law. In fact, the only law he had to obey was his own.

Most religions believe their gods are infallible and <u>changeless</u>. And since their gods are infallible and changeless, the decrees of their gods are infallible and changeless. Apply this to our time because some modern New Age cults teach that we are gods. If it is true then why do we make so many mistakes? Why do we age? Why aren't we surrounded by millions of infallible and changeless people? How many god-men or god-women do you know? The fact is that none of us are infallible or changeless. Satan is the first one to say humans can be <u>like God</u>. God says there are <u>no other</u> gods. We can never be like God.

go to

changeless
Malachi 3:6

like God
Genesis 3:5

no other
Isaiah 45:5, 14, 21–22

something to ponder

So Let It Be Done

DANIEL 6:9 *Therefore King Darius signed the written decree.* *(NKJV)*

The king was deceived. He did not see the diabolical plan behind the decree. He thought his advisers and satraps were asking for a good thing, so he gave in, put the decree in writing, signed it, and was stuck with it.

These so-called wise men probably left the palace gloating and patting themselves on the back. They surely believed their plot was well conceived. They probably envisioned promotions, profits and pleasure on the horizon. But they had forgotten about the God who delivered Shadrach, Meshach, and Abed-Nego out of the fiery furnace. The Bible says "Do not boast about tomorrow, for you do not know what a day may bring forth" (Proverbs 27:1 NKJV). And it would be quite a day.

The day will come when anti-Christ forces will face the God of Daniel and all the others. It is the same in many Muslim countries, where worship of any deity other than Allah is prohibited under

go to

city
1 Kings 8:44–45

knelt
Ephesians 3:14

three times
Psalm 55:17

prayed and gave thanks
1 Thessalonians 5:17–18

penalty of trial, torture, and death, the latter usually being after the third offense. In China, beatings and imprisonment have forced many Christians into underground churches.

The practice [in Saudi Arabia] of any religion besides Islam is banned, and conversion to another faith is punishable by execution. Non-Muslims caught worshiping (even in private), and wearing religious symbols such as crosses, or uttering prayers have faced arrest, imprisonment without trial, torture, and in some cases death.

Back on His Knees

DANIEL 6:10 *Now when Daniel knew that the writing was signed, he went home. And in his upper room, with his windows open toward Jerusalem, he knelt down on his knees three times that day, and prayed and gave thanks before his God, as was his custom since early days.* (NKJV)

Daniel did not know about the decree until after it had been published. But learning about it did not change anything. It seemed, from a human standpoint, that his life was on the line, but he did not back down. He did not stop praying. He did not pray in secret, nor did he pray to Darius. He simply did what he had always done—went home, opened a window facing the <u>city</u> of Jerusalem, and humbly <u>knelt</u> and prayed. <u>Three times</u> a day he <u>prayed and gave thanks</u> to God.

Some argue that the Jews lost their national identity while in exile, that God's promises to Israel have been canceled, and even that the Church is a later replacement for Israel. Daniel's opening his window toward Jerusalem is one argument against this. The Jews have never given up on returning to their land or abandoned the idea that God has a role for them and Jerusalem at the end of the age. They will worship again at the Temple. His prophetic plan will be fulfilled.

Notice the prayer. There is no indication that Daniel was afraid, crying, or pleading with God to deliver him. Instead of folding under pressure, he bowed and gave thanks to God. Giving thanks in the face of danger demonstrates his strong faith and is something he did over and over again.

Frank Ramirez

The early Christians faced the same choice—obey God or earthly rulers. In some cases those who obeyed God and suffered were delivered, as when Peter was released from prison in Acts 12. But others who obeyed were executed, as were Stephen and James the brother of the Lord. It's not that God failed them. Their deaths were their victories, for their martyrdom proved the ultimate validation of their faith.[5]

obey their government
Romans 13:1–7

interferes
Daniel 3:17–18;
Acts 5:29

pray
Matthew 6:9–15

As a general rule Christians are supposed to <u>obey their government</u>. But when government <u>interferes</u> with the worship of God civil disobedience is both acceptable and necessary. Daniel prayed on his knees three times each day, and gave thanks to God. Daniel would not compromise any of his beliefs.

shining shores of eternity
heaven

Just Like We Thought

DANIEL 6:11 *Then these men assembled and found Daniel praying and making supplication before his God. (NKJV)*

It is only speculation, but it seems almost certain that at least some of these men knew how many times a day Daniel <u>prayed</u> and when. The two administrators and the 120 satraps went as a group to catch Daniel disobeying the law. They were out to make things hard for God's man, so he wouldn't get the promotion he so well deserved.

David Breese

There are many people who ask the foolish question, "If there is a God, why is there so much evil in the world?" "Why is life so hard?" The answer to this is that life is supposed to be hard . . . because it is not final reality but the prelude to reality. Ultimate joy, peace, and fulfillment will only come when we arrive on the **shining shores of eternity**.[6]

Theodore H. Epp

A Christian in such company [among unbelievers] is a marked man when his life is consistent before God. The reason is that Satan hates men of prayer and will stir up foes against them. Daniel's prayer life brought not only recognition from his king, but it also led to persecution from his enemies.[7]

Daniel was one of the chief administrators in a world kingdom. He had many important and pressing responsibilities. And he also had a group of corrupt individuals to supervise, but he was never too busy to pray. Daniel:

1. Prayed regularly (daily).

2. Had a set time of prayer (three times a day).

3. Had a set place of prayer (upstairs by the window facing Jerusalem).

4. Was humble (he kneeled).

5. Showed gratitude (he gave thanks to God).

6. Was persistent (he prayed just as he had done before).

The Law Stands

> **DANIEL 6:12** *And they went before the king, and spoke concerning the king's decree: "Have you not signed a decree that every man who petitions any god or man within thirty days, except you, O king, shall be cast into the den of lions?" The king answered and said, "The thing is true, according to the law of the Medes and Persians, which does not alter."* (NKJV)

They did not waste any time. They had what they wanted, and they rushed back to the king. Notice the hypocrisy of their question. They are the ones who got the king to publish the fiendish decree, but they asked, "Have you not signed a decree that every man who petitions any god or man within thirty days, except you, O king, shall be cast into the den of lions?" (Daniel 6:12 NKJV). Of course the king did, and he made it clear that the decree still stood. He even confirmed that the law of the Medes and Persians would not allow the decree to be repealed.

"Millions of American Christians pray in their churches each week, oblivious to the fact that Christians in many parts of the world suffer brutal torture, arrest, imprisonment, and even death—their homes and communities laid waste—for no other reason than that they are Christians," writes Nina Shea, director of Puebla Program of Freedom House, in her book *In the Lion's Den*. "The shocking untold story of our time is that more Christians have died this century simply for being Christians than in the first 19 centuries after the birth of Christ. They have been persecuted and martyred before an unknowing, indifferent world and a largely silent Christian community."[8]

Three Times a Day

DANIEL 6:13 *So they answered and said before the king, "That Daniel, who is one of the captives from Judah, does not show due regard for you, O king, or for the decree that you have signed, but makes his petition three times a day." (NKJV)*

Notice several things here about the conspirators:

1. They are guilty of anti-Semitism for unnecessarily pointing out that Daniel was one of the exiles from Judah.

2. They tried to cause a rift between Daniel and the king by pointing out that Daniel was ignoring the king.

3. They tried to put pressure on the king by pointing out that Daniel was ignoring the decree.

4. They tried to pressure the king even more by pointing out that the decree was in writing.

What was Daniel's crime? He was still praying three times a day.

what others say

Kenneth O. Gangel

This sounds like déjà vu all over again. A similar crowd approached Nebuchadnezzar a couple of generations earlier and said exactly the same thing about Daniel's three friends (3:12). One thing seems absolutely clear throughout this book: the people of God will serve no god but God himself.[9]

Time Has Run Out

DANIEL 6:14 *And the king, when he heard these words, was greatly displeased with himself, and set his heart on Daniel to deliver him; and he labored till the going down of the sun to deliver him. (NKJV)*

The administrators and satraps were unsuccessful with their attempt to cause a rift between Daniel and the king. He fully understood what had happened and instead of being angry with Daniel, he was distressed with himself for being duped into creating this dilemma. He was determined to keep Daniel out of the lions' den and made every effort to find a way to do so. But the trap was firmly set, and both Daniel and the king were caught in it.

Remember Your Word

DANIEL 6:15 *Then these men approached the king, and said to the king, "Know, O king, that it is the law of the Medes and Persians that no decree or statute which the king establishes may be changed." (NKJV)*

Daniel's enemies were still assembled together at sundown and went as a group to see the king. They reminded him that the law of the Medes and Persians would not permit him to change the decree.

what others say

Leon J. Wood

Pieces of the overall picture may then have fallen into place. These men had been the ones to persuade him to sign the decree; they had been conveniently on hand to observe Daniel in his praying; and now they were insisting that the decree be carried out. These men, then, had plotted Daniel's death, and had used him, the king, as an instrument to bring it about.[10]

Merrill F. Unger

Once again the conspirators assembled to cause confusion and thus prevent any delay in the execution, lest the king should find some way to prevent Daniel's death.[11]

Into the Lions' Den

DANIEL 6:16 *So the king gave the command, and they brought Daniel and cast him into the den of lions. But the king spoke, saying to Daniel, "Your God, whom you serve continually, He will deliver you." (NKJV)*

Darius had no choice but to give the order. He reluctantly ordered Daniel to be taken and thrown into the lions' den (see Illustration #16). The king loved Daniel and went along, so he could be with Daniel. When his friend was thrown in he said, "Your God, whom you serve continually, He will <u>deliver</u> you" (Daniel 6:16 NKJV). Daniel never stopped serving God regardless of what came his way.

Are we accomplishing what God wants us to accomplish? Christians are not only the objects of God's love, we are also the means through which he works to show others his love. Our behavior impacts others and we are witnesses whether we intend to be or not. If Daniel's faith, loyalty, and service could greatly impact two powerful heathen kings like Nebuchadnezzar and Darius, shouldn't we also be a factor in changing our society for the better?

Roll in the Stone

> **DANIEL 6:17** *Then a stone was brought and laid on the mouth of the den, and the king sealed it with his own signet ring and with the signets of his lords, that the purpose concerning Daniel might not be changed. (NKJV)*

After shoving Daniel into the lions' den, a large stone was rolled over the opening. Next, a layer of warm wax was poured between the stone and the den wall to make sure it was sealed. Then, the king used his **signet ring** to make an impression in the wax. Finally, some of the administrators and satraps also used their signet rings to make impressions in the wax. All of this was done to make sure the rock was not moved during the night. When the administrators and satraps returned the next morning, they wanted to be sure that Daniel had not been set free.

When Daniel was thrown into the lions' den, they rolled a large stone over the opening and sealed it. When Jesus was crucified, Joseph took the body, wrapped it in a clean linen cloth, and placed it in his own new tomb that he had cut out of the rock. He rolled a big stone in front of the entrance to the tomb and went away. Mary Magdalene and the other Mary were sitting there opposite the tomb. The next day, the one after **Preparation Day**, the chief priests and the Pharisees went to Pilate: "'Sir, we remember, while He was still alive, how that deceiver said, "After three days I will rise." Therefore command that the tomb be made secure until the third day, lest His

deliver
Psalms 34:7, 19;
37:39–40; 50:15;
1 Thessalonians
1:10;
2 Peter 2:9

signet ring
Esther 3:12; 8:8–10

signet ring
a ring used to make an official stamp or mark on something

Preparation Day
the day before the Sabbath (people prepared for the Sabbath because they could not work on the Sabbath)

fasting
Isaiah 58:4–7

Illustration #16
Lions' Den—Where
Daniel trusted God
for his deliverance.

fasting
the act of denying
oneself something
such as food or
drink to show humil-
ity, mourning, or sor-
row before God,
and to gain his favor

disciples come by night and steal Him away, and say to the people, "He has risen from the dead." So the last deception will be worse than the first.' Pilate said to them, 'You have a guard; go your way, make it as secure as you know how.' So they went and made the tomb secure, sealing the stone and setting the guard" (Matthew 27:63–66 NKJV).

No Sleep

DANIEL 6:18 *Now the king went to his palace and spent the night fasting; and no musicians were brought before him. Also his sleep went from him.* (NKJV)

Darius left the site of the lions' den grieving and worried. He returned to his palace and spent the restless night **fasting**. He even refused all entertainment and pleasure.

Fasting

Many Christians fast by going without food, but not because they want to lose weight. They do it for spiritual reasons. They want to demonstrate:

1. Sincerity before God (sincere grief, humility, repentance, or faith).

2. That they are willing to exchange things they need or enjoy for a closer relationship with God.

3. That spiritual things are more important to them than physical things.

4. That the answer to their prayers is more important to them than their own comfort.

go to

dawn
Matthew 28:1

They seek things like forgiveness of their sins, a revelation from God, help with problems they cannot solve, deliverance from a national crisis, and healing for someone. They fast for different periods of time: one day (Judges 20:26), three days (Esther 4:16), forty days (Luke 4:1–2), or a period of time of their own choosing. They usually spend a great deal of time in prayer when they are fasting and they often read their Bibles. It is even possible for groups of Christians to fast. However, it is best to see a doctor before fasting. People with diseases like diabetes should not fast without a doctor's approval.

During the lifetime of Isaiah, the Jews were noted for fasting, but they were not fasting to draw closer to God. They were fasting for their own glory, to gain a reputation and to gain the applause of men. Fasting that is done for selfish reasons is worthless. Instead of giving up a few meals, a candy bar and a coke, God would prefer that we give up our sins. Instead of putting on ashes and sackcloth, God would prefer that we put on a genuine attitude of holiness and caring. It is far better to stop living a self-centered life, to stop using the Lord's Day for our business and pleasure, and to stop trying to bring religious glory to ourselves than it is to stop eating a particular treat for a while. This is not to say that fasting is wrong, but it does mean that we can fast for the wrong reasons.

something to ponder

Fasting is good, but we can fast for the wrong reasons.

Back to the Lions' Den

DANIEL 6:19 *Then the king arose very early in the morning and went in haste to the den of lions.* (NKJV)

The king could have sent legions of soldiers to check on Daniel, but he did not. He wanted to do that personally. So early the next morning, at the first light of <u>dawn</u>, he rushed out of his palace and headed to the lions' den.

go to

able
Romans 14:4

living God
the giver of life, the
one who is alive, the
eternal God

adulation
praise or flattery

A Hedge of Protection

DANIEL 6:20 *And when he came to the den, he cried out with a lamenting voice to Daniel. The king spoke, saying to Daniel, "Daniel, servant of the living God, has your God, whom you serve continually, been able to deliver you from the lions?" (NKJV)*

Darius was so anxious to find out about Daniel's condition he could not wait until he arrived at the lions' den. He started calling out as soon as he got close enough for Daniel to hear. There was anguish in his voice. He called Daniel's God the **living God**. He repeated the fact that Daniel constantly—not part of the time or when he felt like it—served the living God, and he asked if Daniel's God was <u>able</u> to save him.

Jesus said, "If you abide in Me, and My words abide in you, you will ask what you desire, and it shall be done for you" (John 15:7 NKJV). Daniel continually served God.

Yes, I Am Here

DANIEL 6:21 *Then Daniel said to the king, "O king, live forever! (NKJV)*

This is the fourth time we have seen this expression in Daniel. It seems to be the usual way of addressing kings in Babylon. It was supposed to convey **adulation** or respect. But it seems a little ridiculous because, regardless of the way the kings were addressed, they all died.

We see the words "O king, live forever" also in Daniel 2:4; 3:9; 5:10 (NKJV).

what others say

Kay Arthur

May we not join the ranks of those who have compromised the Word of God in adverse circumstances. Let us join in heart with the martyrs of the faith who swore to be faithful unto death because our God is able to deliver us from the furnace of blazing fire—and from the lion's den. But even if He does not deliver us, may it be known that we will not serve nor worship any other god but our Most High God![12]

He Shut the Mouths of the Lions

DANIEL 6:22 *My God sent His angel and shut the lions' mouths, so that they have not hurt me, because I was found innocent before Him; and also, O king, I have done no wrong before you.* (NKJV)

power
Romans 4:20–21

nothing too hard
Jeremiah 32:17

furnace
Daniel 3:19–25

What Darius desperately wanted to do, but could not, God had the <u>power</u> to do. <u>Nothing is too hard</u> for him. God sent an angel (some say this angel was Jesus) to shut the mouths of the lions. Daniel told the king he was not hurt because he was innocent in God's eyes; not according to the man-made laws of the Medes and Persians, but according to the laws of God. Daniel also added that he was innocent before the king. He could honestly claim this because he was not supposed to worship any human being.

Notice that Daniel was innocent before God. This is true success: learning God's will and carrying it out. He has a plan for every person. When we stand before the Judgment Bar, our success in life will not be measured by the fortune we amassed, or the people we supervised, or the problems we overcame, or anything like that. Our success will be measured by our response to God's plan. Were we committed? Did we give, forgive, witness, and set an example for others? Are we innocent before God?

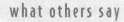

what others say

Billy Graham

Spiritual forces and resources are available to all Christians. Because our resources are unlimited, Christians will be winners. Millions of angels are at God's command and at our service. The hosts of heaven stand at attention as we make our way from earth to glory, and Satan's BB guns are no match for God's heavy artillery. So don't be afraid. God is for you. He has committed his angels to wage war in the conflict of the ages—and they will win the victory.[13]

When Shadrach, Meshach, and Abed-Nego were thrown into the fiery <u>furnace</u> Nebuchadnezzar looked into the fire and said, "I see four men loose, walking in the midst of the fire; and they are not hurt, and the form of the fourth is like the Son of God" (Daniel 3:25 NKJV). When Daniel was thrown into the lions' den God sent his angel, and he shut the mouths of the lions.

go to

flee to the mountains
Matthew 24:16;
Revelation 12:13–16

foreshadows
illustrates or pictures

Petra
an ancient city south
of the Dead Sea in
Jordan

Not Even a Scratch

DANIEL 6:23 *Now the king was exceedingly glad for him, and commanded that they should take Daniel up out of the den. So Daniel was taken up out of the den, and no injury whatever was found on him, because he believed in his God.* (NKJV)

The administrators and satraps had tricked Darius into signing a devilish decree. They even forced him into condemning Daniel and carrying out the penalty it prescribed. The sentence was executed, but Daniel survived. The king was truly delighted and immediately commanded his troops to lift Daniel out of the lions' den. Daniel was pulled up and examined. They didn't find even one scratch on him because he had believed in his God.

what others say

Henry H. Halley

Let us remember that for a thousand years God had been nurturing the Hebrew Nation for the purpose of through that nation establishing in a world of Idol-worshipping nations the idea that God is God. Now God's nation had been destroyed by a nation that worshiped Idols. That was plain evidence to all the world that the gods of Babylon were more powerful than the God of the Jews. It was a crisis in God's struggle with Idolatry. If ever there was a time when God needed to do something to show who is God it was during the Babylonian Captivity. Strange indeed would it have been had nothing unusual happened.[14]

Many students of prophecy believe the deliverance of Daniel from the lions' den **foreshadows** the deliverance of the Jews from the Antichrist during the Tribulation Period. Those Jews who trust in their God and <u>flee to the mountains</u> will be saved. The mountains referred to here are probably those at the ancient site of **Petra** (see Illustration #2).

Throw Them In

DANIEL 6:24 *And the king gave the command, and they brought those men who had accused Daniel, and they cast them into the den of lions—them, their children, and their wives; and the lions overpowered them, and broke all their bones in pieces before they ever came to the bottom of the den.* (NKJV)

Darius did not see through the plot when his administrators and satraps first approached him seeking the decree, but before this event was over he figured it out and did not like being used. Not once did he get angry with Daniel, but now he was furious with the conspirators. He sent his troops to round up the conspirators and their families. They were taken to the lions' den and given the same treatment they so eagerly sought for Daniel. And the lions were so vicious and hungry they attacked and killed their victims while they were still falling through the air.

Daniel's accusers reaped what they sowed, and, according to the law of the Medes and the Persians, their families also suffered for their crimes. The conspirators, their children, and their wives would be a large number of people. This would imply a large number of lions. Critics say Daniel survived because the lions were not hungry, but the fate of so many other people says otherwise. Other critics condemn the fate of the children and wives, but it must be remembered that the kingdom of Medes and Persians was a pagan kingdom, not a Jewish or Christian kingdom. It didn't operate by God's rules.

Those in power should understand that it is a mistake to unjustly mistreat people who trust in the living God.

go to

peace
Daniel 4:1

Prosper Greatly

DANIEL 6:25 *Then King Darius wrote:*
To all peoples, nations, and languages that dwell in all the earth:
Peace be multiplied to you. (NKJV)

This incident prompted another decree from Darius. It went to everyone in his worldwide kingdom. It began in the normal way: <u>Peace</u> be multiplied to you.

what others say

Donald E. Gowan

Darius's encyclical letter begins with the same words as Nebuchadnezzar's (3:29; 4:1) and praises Daniel's God with similar language, but he goes beyond Nebuchadnezzar, who threatened severe punishment for anyone who spoke against God (3:29). Darius's decree seems to call for a positive acknowledgement of Daniel's God, for all peoples, nations, and languages are to "tremble and fear" before him.[15]

fear
respect

The Living God

DANIEL 6:26
I make a decree that in every dominion of my kingdom men must tremble and fear before the God of Daniel.
   For He is the living God,
   And steadfast forever;
   His kingdom is the one which shall not be destroyed,
   And His dominion shall endure to the end. (NKJV)

The decree then gave a warning to everyone in the kingdom; everyone was required to tremble and **fear** the God of Daniel. King Darius gave several reasons:

1. He is the living God (not a dead god, false god, or idol).

2. He is steadfast forever (is alive and well in every generation).

3. His kingdom will not be destroyed (earthly kingdoms will end, but his spiritual kingdom will never end).

4. His dominion will endure to the end (nothing can replace him or prevail against him).

key point

what others say

Uriah Smith

In this case, and in the case of the three Hebrews in the fiery furnace, the seal of God is set in favor of two great lines of duty: 1) As in the case of the three in the fiery furnace, not to yield to any known sin; and 2) As in the present case, not to omit any known duty. And from these instances, the people of God in all ages are to derive encouragement.[16]

He Does It All

DANIEL 6:27
   He delivers and rescues,
   And He works signs and wonders
   In heaven and on earth,
   Who has delivered Daniel from the power of the lions. (NKJV)

Here are more reasons why everyone should fear and reverence Daniel's God:

1. He delivers (He delivered Daniel from his enemies; also, Shadrach, Meshach, and Abed-Nego).

2. He rescues (He rescued Daniel from the lions and Shadrach, Meshach, and Abed-Nego from the fiery furnace).

3. He performs signs and wonders in heaven and on earth (He has the power to perform miracles not just in heaven, but also on earth).

So Daniel Lives On

DANIEL 6:28 *So this Daniel prospered in the reign of Darius and in the reign of Cyrus the Persian. (NKJV)*

Daniel was safe, secure, and successful during the reign of Darius and also that of Cyrus. There were no more conspiracies or attempts to overthrow and kill him.

"The devil walks about like a roaring lion, seeking whom he may devour" (1 Peter 5:8 NKJV), but God is able to deal with roaring lions. He defeated Satan when Jesus died on the cross. He defeated the roaring lions in Babylon by giving them lockjaw. The safest road is to trust him.

what others say

John F. Walvoord

When the power of God is finally demonstrated at the second coming of Christ, the persecutors of Israel and the enemies of God will be judged and destroyed much like the enemies of Daniel. Like Daniel, however, the people of God in persecution must remain true regardless of the cost.[17]

Chapter Wrap-Up

- After capturing Babylon, Darius made several political appointments. One of them was Daniel, who excelled to where the king planned to promote him over everyone else. (Daniel 6:1–3)

- Daniel's honesty and integrity worried the administrators and satraps. They could not find any flaws in his character or the way he did his job, so they devised a plan to use his religion against him. They proposed an unjust law that they knew Daniel would not obey. Then they got the king to make it official. (Daniel 6:4–9)

- The administrators and satraps caught Daniel breaking the new law by praying to God instead of Darius. They turned Daniel over to the king and had him thrown into the lions' den. But God protected Daniel; he survived and was released. (Daniel 6:10–23)

- The administrators and satraps, along with their wives and children, were given the same treatment they sought for Daniel—they were killed by the lions. (Daniel 6:24)

- The king issued a decree honoring Daniel's God. Daniel prospered during the remainder of Darius's reign and through the reign of King Cyrus. (Daniel 6:25–28)

Study Questions

1. Why did the administrators and satraps object to Daniel being in charge?

2. What is wrong with having a one-world religion?

3. Which is more important, the laws of man or the laws of God?

4. Why was Daniel delivered from the lions?

5. Was Daniel's deliverance a miracle?

Part Two
DANIEL'S PROPHECIES

Daniel 7 Daniel's Vision of Things to Come

Chapter Highlights:
- Four Beasts
- The Heavenly Court
- A Heavenly Being
- Daniel's Interpretation
- The End of Things

Let's Get Started

The book of Daniel has twelve easily divided chapters: Chapters 1–6 are **historical** and chapters 7–12 are **prophetic** (see Time Line #1, Appendix A). Because Daniel divided them into these two simple sections, he did not put them in chronological order. Instead, he used the first verse of each chapter to let us know how they fit chronologically. Notice the chronology for the last six chapters on the time line. The visions found in these chapters were all given after the death of Nebuchadnezzar. Chronologically, chapters 7 and 8 took place before chapter 5 (the handwriting on the wall and death of Belshazzar), but chapters 9 through 12 took place after chapter 5 (during the reign of the Medo-Persian Empire).

All of this means we have come to a turning point in the book of Daniel. Chapters 7–12 deal with prophecy. It was future prophecy to Daniel, but it is partly future and partly past prophecy to us. For example, the rise of the Old Roman Empire was future to Daniel but past to us. And the rise of the Revived Roman Empire was future not only to Daniel but to us as well. Concerning that which is future to us, a very important thing to remember is the fact that at least some of it may be sealed and not yet explained. Keep in mind the instructions to Daniel near the end of this book, "Shut up the words, and seal the book until the time of the end" (Daniel 12:4 NKJV). The word *until* is a key. It implies that some mysteries will be unexplainable for a while, but they will start to unravel as we approach the End of the Age of the Gentiles.

Two Viewpoints

Viewpoint #1—Chapter 7 may be one of those unexplainable chapters. It tells about four strange beasts Daniel saw in a series of visions from God. Many great Bible experts believe these four strange beasts represent the same four world kingdoms Nebuchadnezzar saw in his scary dream found in chapter 2, and therefore also relate to God's Statue (Nebuchadnezzar's dream statue; see Illustration #5) as follows:

historical
about past events

prophetic
about future events

1. The head of gold is the kingdom of Babylon.

2. The breast of silver is the kingdom of Medo-Persia.

3. The belly and thighs of bronze is the kingdom of Greece.

4. The legs of iron and feet of partly iron and partly clay are the kingdoms of the Old Roman Empire and Revived Roman Empire.

Viewpoint #2—But this author and a few other prophecy experts disagree. Because there are so many experts on both sides of the issue it is recommended that careful consideration be given to the following:

1. The *symbols* are different. Chapter 2 is about materials in a statue, but chapter 7 is about beasts.

2. The *number of symbols* is different. Chapter 2 has five materials (gold, silver, bronze, iron, a mixture of iron and clay), but chapter 7 has four beasts (lion, bear, leopard, terrifying animal).

3. The *timing* is different. Chapter 7 was given in the first year of Belshazzar (Daniel 7:1); and the four beasts are four kingdoms that will rise from the earth (Daniel 7:17). The first beast (lion) cannot be the first material (gold) because Babylon had "already" risen and, in fact, was near its demise.

4. The *end of the kingdoms* is different. In chapter 2, the first material (head of gold) did not outlive the last material (feet of iron and clay); the second material (breast and arms of silver) did not outlive the last material (feet of iron and clay); nor did the third material (belly of bronze). But in chapter 7, the first three beasts will outlive the fourth beast (see Daniel 7:11–12).

5. The *relationship between the kingdoms* is different. In chapter 2, the five materials of the statue lived at different times. The gold kingdom existed, then the silver kingdom existed, then the bronze kingdom existed, etc. But in chapter 7, the four beasts all live at the same time. The first three even witness the destruction of the fourth.

6. In chapter 2, the gold, silver, and bronze kingdoms will not exist when Jesus returns. They are past history. But in chapter 7 all the beasts will be alive when Jesus returns.

7. In chapter 2, Daniel knew who the head of gold was (Babylon). But in chapter 7, he *did not know* who the winged lion was.

8. The first three beasts in chapter 7 appear to be the same kingdoms associated with the kingdom of Antichrist in Revelation 13:2 and *all of them are future*, not past.

9. In chapter 8, a *two-horned ram* represents Medo-Persia not a bear (Daniel 8:20). And a male goat represents Greece not a four-winged, four-headed leopard (Daniel 8:21).

So what does all of this mean? First, there is no question that those who think chapter 2 and chapter 7 deal with the same thing have excellent reasons for believing so. They can accurately point to many historical fulfillments that seem to bare their viewpoint out. Second, while that is true we still have the differences in the list above. And, although we might be able to find an explanation for some of them, there is no explanation for all of them. Third, we should keep in mind the fact that the Bible often gives us an initial partial fulfillment of a prophecy, but there is a greater, more complete fulfillment in the future. That will work. The four beasts do correspond to the materials in God's Statue (Nebuchadnezzar's dream statue) up to a point. But the final fulfillment is at the Time of the End.

key point

This is too important to skim over. Many of the great Bible experts who say chapter 2 and chapter 7 deal with the same thing are inconsistent when they say the first three beasts of chapter 7 are now past and not to be treated as having a future fulfillment. For example, most of these same experts say Shadrach, Meshach, and Abed-Nego in the fiery furnace is past, but they prefigure the Jews in the future Tribulation Period. Most say the absence of Daniel at the fiery furnace is past, but it prefigures the absence of the Church in the Tribulation Period (it prefigures the Pre-Tribulation Rapture). Most say the appearance of Antiochus Epiphanes is now past, but he prefigures the coming Antichrist. Most say the Abomination of Desolation is now past, but it prefigures a future defilement of the Temple (Jesus agreed). Most say Nebuchadnezzar's seven-year illness is now past, but it is typical of the seven-year madness of the Antichrist and others during the Tribulation Period. There is more, but the point is well taken: if these past historical events are predictive truth, it is both consistent and reasonable to believe the first three beasts of chapter 7 are both historical and prophetic. This is shown in the following chart.

The Times of the Gentiles

Chapter 2	Past Fulfillment	Chapter 7	Prophetic Application
Head of gold	Babylon	Winged Lion	English Coalition
Chest of Silver	Medes & Persians	Bear	Russian Coalition
Belly of Brass	Greece	Leopard	African Coalition
Legs of Iron	Rome	Not Mentioned	Not Mentioned
Feet of Iron & Clay	Still Future	Terrible Beast	Rome Plus Others
Rock	Still Future (Jesus)	Ancient of Days	Second Coming

what others say

David Hocking

You may ask me, "Are you sure, David [that chapter 2 and chapter 7 are about different things]?" I must answer, "Absolutely not!" However, I'll tell you one thing, because of certain details, I cannot believe the standard view [that chapter 2 and chapter 7 are about the same thing] because it doesn't match with what the Bible says! I don't know if what I'm saying is right or not, but I believe that these visions [in chapter 7] apply to the Time of the End before the Messiah comes to set up his kingdom. So this is more likely to refer to something in the endtime than to three kingdoms that fell long before Rome was ever in existence. There's something wrong here with **traditional** interpretation.[1]

key point

The Bible often gives us an initial partial fulfillment of a prophecy, but there is a greater, more complete fulfillment in the future.

what others say

Wallace Emerson

The first vision (chapter 7), seen by Daniel in the first year of Belshazzar, carries us directly to the Time of the End, as we interpret it. It exhibits to our eyes four empires that will occupy the world stage at the End of the Age [not four empires that existed hundreds of years ago].[2]

Noah Hutchings

It is difficult to understand how anyone could be so dogmatic as to say that the lion has to be ancient Babylon, the bear has to be Medo-Persia, and the leopard has to be Greece. The forces of Satan deceiving the nations, and preparing them to be drawn into the Middle East at the battle of Armageddon; the waves and the seas roaring; wars and rumors of wars; the major world powers' interest in the Mediterranean—all these things would place the setting entirely in the last generation [not a previous generation].[3]

visions
Revelation 9:17

wrote
Revelation 1:19

substance
the main points

Isle of Patmos
small island in the Mediterranean Sea

Daniel's Dream

DANIEL 7:1 *In the first year of Belshazzar king of Babylon, Daniel had a dream and visions of his head while on his bed. Then he wrote down the dream, telling the main facts.* (NKJV)

In chapter 5, it was stated that Nabonidus became king of Babylon around 555 BC and Belshazzar, his son, was a co-regent when Babylon fell around 539 BC. Depending upon what source we use, Belshazzar reigned for about three to five years. From that we can deduce that the first year of his reign as co-regent and the date of these visions was approximately 544–542 BC (see Time Line #1, Appendix A).

So far as we can tell, Daniel was asleep and dreaming when these visions started passing through his mind. The word *visions* suggests more than one. The following chart explains what this means.

When the dream and <u>visions</u> ended, Daniel awoke. Realizing that something significant had occurred, he <u>wrote</u> down the **substance** of what he saw. This is the practice John followed when he recorded Revelation on the **Isle of Patmos.**

Visions of the Four Beasts

Part	Verses	Phrase	Vision
1	2–3	I saw	the four beasts (kingdoms) will rise up
2	9	I watched	God will sit on the throne
3	11	I watched	the four beasts (kingdoms) will be judged
4	13	I was watching	Jesus will receive dominion

what others say

David Breese

Nothing is clearer in the Word of God than the fact that God wants us to understand himself and his working in the lives of men.[4]

go to

darkness
Zephaniah 1:14–16;
Joel 2:2

night
1 Thessalonians 5:2

winds
Revelation 7:1

storm
Jeremiah 25:32–33

sea
Joshua 15:12;
Isaiah 57:20;
Revelation 13:1–10;
15:2

waters
Revelation 17:1, 15;
19:6

Wind, Wind, Everywhere Wind (Visions of the Four Beasts, Part 1)

DANIEL 7:2 *Daniel spoke, saying, "I saw in my vision by night, and behold, the four winds of heaven were stirring up the Great Sea.* (NKJV)

1. One of the names of the Tribulation Period is a day of <u>darkness</u> and gloom, and it will come as a thief in the <u>night</u>, so some interpreters think this vision is something that will be fulfilled during the Tribulation Period. There are other reasons to think that they may be right, but here, at night probably refers to the time of day when Daniel had the vision.

2. The Bible talks about the four <u>winds</u> of the earth coming from the four corners of the earth (north, south, east, and west), so a small minority of prophecy experts think this is a reference to the natural winds causing a <u>storm</u>. Since these are called "the four winds of heaven," a few argue that the winds are caused by heavenly forces. But the four winds of heaven probably refers to demonic forces because Satan is the "prince of the power of the air, the spirit who now works in the sons of disobedience" (Ephesians 2:2 NKJV).

3. "The Great Sea" is a Bible expression with more than one meaning. It sometimes refers to the Mediterranean <u>Sea</u>, and it sometimes refers to the sea or <u>waters</u> of humanity (people).

We should not be dogmatic about the exact meaning of this verse, but it probably means that demonic forces will cause war in the Middle East at the End of the Age. Those demonic forces will upset nations all over the earth, but the main focus of their disturbance will be concentrated around the Mediterranean Sea as the Times of the Gentiles runs out. The Mediterranean is approximately 2,200 miles long. Europe lies to the north, Africa to the south, Asia to the east, and the Atlantic Ocean to the west.

what others say

Wallace Emerson

Some have interpreted the great sea literally as meaning the Mediterranean and as indicating that the action in the vision will take place around this sea. Others regard it as symbolic of humanity at large; i.e., the nations. There may even be a double reference here since there is no incompatibility between these two meanings. The action may, indeed, take place around the great sea and involve all nations.[5]

J. Vernon McGee

Customarily the wind blows from only one direction at a time, but here it is a tornado of great violence with the wind coming from all directions. It refers not only to the disturbed conditions out of which these four nations arose, but particularly to the last stage of the fourth kingdom (Daniel 7:11, 12, 17) in which certain ideologies shall strive to capture the thinking of the disturbed masses of all nations and tribes.[6]

Hal Lindsey

There has hardly been an era where there has not been war. And some of the greatest achievements of mankind have been achieved in connection with building machines of war. . . . Like ravenous beasts the gentile powers of the earth have continued in carnage.[7]

In Daniel 7:2 we see the "four winds of heaven" churning up the great sea. This could mean demonic forces from every direction on the compass would cause a struggle around the Mediterranean Sea at the End of the Age. Daniel 7:3 points out that four beasts came up out of the sea. Daniel 7:4 shows the first beast located west of the Sea, Daniel 7:5 shows the second beast located north and east of the Sea, and Daniel 7:6 shows the third beast located south of the Sea. The fourth beast is the rise of the final Gentile world kingdom.

Jesus was talking about the signs of the End of the Age when he said, "Nation will rise against nation, and kingdom against kingdom. And there will be great earthquakes in various places, and famines and pestilences; and there will be fearful sights and great signs from heaven . . . There will be signs in the sun, in the moon, and in the stars; and on the earth distress of nations, with perplexity, the sea and the waves roaring" (Luke 21:10–11, 25 NKJV).

something to ponder

Four Big Beasts

DANIEL 7:3 *And four great beasts came up from the sea, each different from the other.* (NKJV)

four great beasts
Daniel 7:17

lion
Jeremiah 4:7–13;
Ezekiel 38:13

heart
Jeremiah 17:9

ideology
beliefs, opinions,
doctrines, etc.

One result of this worldwide disturbance will be the rise of <u>four great beasts</u>. These beasts will be four kingdoms and this verse tells us they are different from each other.

The important thing to remember is that some kind of strife will cause four kingdoms (probably four groups or four coalitions of nations) to appear on the scene near the end of the Gentile age. We are not told what will cause their appearance or the disturbing strife, but we are told some of the characteristics of the four kingdoms and there is reason to believe that the greatest turmoil will be in the Middle East.

what others say

Edward Tracy

The next thing [Daniel 7:3] we note is that there is a difference between these powers on the earth in the end-time. This difference may be expressed in their **ideology**, their form of government, or pride of race, but whatever it is, the basic "difference" between them is what leads to the strife of the previous verse. . . . The manner of their striving would not be limited to war alone, but to all forms of political intrigue and power politics which are so characteristic of nations today. There is struggling for supremacy and predominance among these four world powers [at the end-time].[8]

The First Beast

DANIEL 7:4 *The first was like a lion, and had eagle's wings. I watched till its wings were plucked off; and it was lifted up from the earth and made to stand on two feet like a man, and a man's heart was given to it. (NKJV)*

The symbol used to represent this empire is not that of a lion. It is something that looks like a lion. And it does not look like an ordinary <u>lion</u>. It looks like a lion with the wings of an eagle.

This beast will have its wings torn off and will stand on its hind legs like a man. It will be given the wicked <u>heart</u> of a man. But it will still be a beast (a nation or coalition of nations).

In general, experts agree that the wings represent the rapid movement, victory, and expansion of this kingdom while the plucking of the wings represents an inability to continue to do these things. At first this kingdom will be very powerful and unrestrained. Then it will weaken and become somewhat restrained. Many also agree that standing on its feet represents a decline militarily. A lion on the attack crouches low, runs on all fours, and leaps or pounces. It does not stand up and walk on its hind legs because it would lose power and speed in that position.

The United States lies west of the Mediterranean Sea and, along with England, was very instrumental in the reestablishment of Israel as a nation.

what others say

Noah Hutchings

The United States, since World War I, has been England's protective wings. This nation had to come to England's aid in World War I and again in World War II, but England and the United States have drifted apart and England has declined as a world colonial power. . . . With the withdrawal of England from the Mediterranean after World War II, the eagle's wings that were plucked off, the United States, controlled the great sea. Thus, for twenty years the Mediterranean was an American sea and the United States dictated policy in the Middle East.[9]

David Hocking

All it [the lion] will become is a political voice in the world, saying what it wants to say but without its past glory. That would explain Daniel 7:12 where the lives were prolonged for a season and a time (KJV). It may have existed for a time as a great nation, but its wings were plucked and all of a sudden it was lifted up from the earth—no longer having the effectiveness it once had. It becomes nothing more than a man speaking and acting like he has power when, in fact, he does not have it anymore.[10]

Some experts believe Babylon's symbol was the lion while others claim it wasn't. In either case, Babylon's symbol was not a standing lion. England is the only nation to ever use the standing lion for its symbol, and since the United States largely came out of England, it is possible that our nation is like a lion in its language and culture.

The Second Beast

DANIEL 7:5 *And suddenly another beast, a second, like a bear. It was raised up on one side, and had three ribs in its mouth*

rapacious
predatory, hungry,
grasping, greedy

warlike
belligerent, willing
to fight

Gog and Magog
Russia and her allies

between its teeth. And they said thus to it: 'Arise, devour much flesh!' (NKJV)

The symbol used to represent this empire is not that of a bear. It is something that looks like a bear. But it will not be like a cuddly teddy bear. It will be like an angry or hostile grizzly bear threatening anything in its path. It will have three ribs (parts of other beasts or empires) in its mouth between its huge teeth (representing a **rapacious** and **warlike** nature). It will be told to eat its fill of flesh (attack and devour other beasts or empires).

what others say

Wallace Emerson

The first thought that comes to one when Russia is mentioned is the Russian bear. For generations, this animal has been used to designate this vast, ungainly country. Can any one country on the face of the earth be so aptly described as having devoured much flesh? Even Hitler, with his demonic lust for power and willingness to shed much blood, cannot equal the human loss of Russia in the First World War, the Russian Revolution, the prison camps of Siberia (20,000,000), the Volga famines (6,000,000), the murders and liquidations that took place under Stalin (wholesale murder of Polish officers), and the human loss during the Second World War. How could anyone describe Russia in better terms?[11]

Edward Tracy

Other expositors have painstakingly investigated the identification of **Gog and Magog**, etc. of Ezekiel 38–39. It is their considered consensus, with scarcely a dissent, that the nations referred to are Russia and her satellites in league with Islamic nations who pose the final threat to Israel's sovereignty.[12]

Hal Lindsey

If you are in a time of constant conflict, if you want to stay a free and peaceful nation, what do you have to do? You have to prepare for war. And you have to be willing to use it if you have to. That's been the order of the day during the "Times of the Gentiles." Only the strong have stayed free.[13]

Ezekiel 38 and 39 record an unfulfilled prophecy about a future attack on Israel in the last days. The list of experts who say the aggressors will be Russia and some of her allies is very impressive. These nations will prepare for war and decide to devour and plunder the land of Israel. Several nations, including those from the <u>lion empire</u>, will question the attack but not stop it. Since Russia will be the leader, and main supplier of troops, weapons, and fighter planes in this group of nations, could we not say the group will be "like a bear"?

Russia and some of the nations that will join her (Iran, Iraq, etc.) in an end-time <u>invasion</u> of Israel lies to the north and east of the Mediterranean Sea (see Illustration #2).

Some prophecy experts say Medo-Persia's symbol was the bear while others claim it wasn't. While there may be some basis for agreeing with those who say Medo-Persia's symbol was the bear, we must still keep in mind the fact that many prophecies have an initial, partial fulfillment, and then later they have a final, total fulfillment. And we must not forget that this empire will be on the scene when the Antichrist arrives. Could it be that the bear represents Russia and the three ribs represent parts of three nations known to have bears: southern Turkey, Northern Syria and Iran?

go to

lion empire
Ezekiel 38:13

invasion
Ezekiel 38:10–13

The Third Beast

> **DANIEL 7:6** *After this I looked, and there was another, like a leopard, which had on its back four wings of a bird. The beast also had four heads, and dominion was given to it.* (NKJV)

The symbol used to represent this empire is something that looks "like a leopard." It will be a strange leopard indeed with four wings and four heads. Instead of seizing authority as a conqueror, it will be given authority by someone or something more powerful than it is (perhaps an alliance of nations such as NATO or the United Nations).

If the four winds of heaven churning the great sea in Daniel 7:2 represent turmoil coming from all directions around the sea, we must, at some point, expect trouble from a coalition of nations in the South (see Illustration #2). That could only mean Africa and Arab nations.

key point

The traditional interpretation says this strange leopard was Greece, the belly and thighs of bronze on God's Statue from Nebuchadnezzar's dream. As with the lion beast in Daniel 7:4, the wings are supposed to represent rapid movement and conquest, but with one dif-

heads
Revelation 12:3;
13:1; 17:3, 7–10

ference: this beast with four wings would have to be faster than the lion with just two wings. So the traditional interpretation is that Alexander the Great fulfilled this by conquering the world in a short time. And the final aspect of that view says the four heads represent the generals who divided up Alexander's empire after he died.

There are several problems with that. And it seems more likely that this beast represents a four-nation Arab/African coalition of the future. The coalition has not yet appeared nor can it until after the second beast of Daniel 7:5 (Russia and her allies) invades the Middle East. Notice that it receives its power between the decline of the second beast and the rise of the fourth beast.

Wallace Emerson

Could the leopard be an alliance of Arab nations? Most especially those that are closer to the old Babylonian world and which are found in the areas now designated as Iraq, Syria, Jordan, Egypt, Libya, and Arabia? Some of these Arabian states in North Africa belonged to the Old Roman Empire in its greatest extent and might conceivably belong to the new one but not necessarily so. . . . That some fourfold federation could rather suddenly appear in the Arab world should not seem too far-fetched or impossible.[14]

Noah Hutchings

After the bear is chased from the Mediterranean, the four-headed leopard with four wings on its back appears. We cannot tell a great deal about this particular beast because it has not made its appearance yet, and it cannot appear until after the battle of Ezekiel Chapters 38 and 39. Leopards are not native to Palestine; however, from the Song of Solomon 4:8, it is evident that there were some of these animals in the mountains to the south of Israel. . . . The nature and characteristics of this third beast are indicative of the African bloc of nations, or an Afro-Asian alliance.[15]

David Hocking

The heads of the beast certainly represent empires as they do in Revelation where we find the beast with seven heads and on the seventh head, there are ten horns. If they represent empires or kingdoms, why don't they represent that here? So who in the world might this third beast be? Is it not possible that this leopard that comes to power in the midst of the con-

The Smart Guide to the Bible

tinuance of the lion and the bear nations (although they have lessened powers) is something different than we have ever thought before? Could this refer to some sort of Arab alliance of the end-time? Could the leopard who strikes very quickly be someone like Saddam Hussein? Could the result of handling the difficult Middle East problems be the emergence of an Arab empire with four powerful nations all looking at the question of domination? We simply don't know.[16]

Every jot and tittle in the Word of God is important. Notice the words after this in Daniel 7:6–7. And notice that they do not appear in Daniel 7:5. Could this suggest a sequence of events; namely, that the third empire cannot come on the scene until after the power and influence of the first two wane; and that the fourth cannot control things until after the third has been organized and given power?

It is not difficult to find prophecy experts who say Greece's symbol was the leopard. And it is also not difficult to find experts who say it wasn't. But the four heads in this vision are not what is left of the beast after Alexander died. They are part and parcel of the beast when it comes to power. Also, Alexander the Great was not given authority. He seized it. The amazing rise and breakup of Greece may foreshadow the life and death of this empire, but we must remember that this will be an End of the Age empire.

The Fourth Beast

> **DANIEL 7:7** *After this I saw in the night visions, and behold, a fourth beast, dreadful and terrible, exceedingly strong. It had huge iron teeth; it was devouring, breaking in pieces, and trampling the residue with its feet. It was different from all the beasts that were before it, and it had ten horns. (NKJV)*

We now come to something that most prophecy experts agree on; namely, this fourth beast represents the development of the final Gentile world kingdom. It will be a wicked world kingdom. And here God has given us more information about it than all of the other three kingdoms combined.

After seeing the first two beasts rise to power in the Middle East, and after seeing a third beast being given power there, Daniel saw this fourth beast. He did not find any of the first three beasts terrifying and frightening, but this fourth beast put terror in his coura-

go to

kingdom
Daniel 7:23

horns
Daniel 7:24; 8:22

king
Daniel 7:24

man
2 Thessalonians 2:3;
Revelation 13:18

mouth
Revelation 13:5

Lamb
a name of Jesus

geous heart. It will be a very powerful world <u>kingdom</u> or world government with large iron teeth (larger and stronger than the bear's teeth) that will be used to crush its victims. Then, whatever is left of the victim will be trampled underfoot.

When this beast (world government) comes to power it will be different from any government that has ever existed before. It will begin with ten <u>horns</u> (or ten leaders) that will rule over the ten divisions of the earth.

> **what others say**
>
> **Grant R. Jeffrey**
>
> This tenfold division of the Roman Empire describes the embryonic power base of the Antichrist's world government at the close of "the Times of the Gentiles" and immediately prior to the Second Coming of Christ.[17]

We have more information about these ten kings in Revelation. John said, "The ten horns which you saw are ten kings who have received no kingdom as yet, but they receive authority for one hour as kings with the beast. These are of one mind, and they will give their power and authority to the beast. These will make war with the **Lamb**, and the Lamb will overcome them, for He is Lord of lords and King of kings; and those who are with Him are called, chosen, and faithful" (Revelation 17:12–14 NKJV).

The Little Horn

> **DANIEL 7:8** *I was considering the horns, and there was another horn, a little one, coming up among them, before whom three of the first horns were plucked out by the roots. And there, in this horn, were eyes like the eyes of a man, and a mouth speaking pompous words. (NKJV)*

While Daniel was thinking about the ten horns (future leaders), he saw another horn (<u>king</u> or future leader). At first, he will be an insignificant leader on the rise to power in a world that already has ten powerful leaders over its ten divisions. But he will quickly become strong enough to oppose and defeat one of the ten leaders, then he will oppose and defeat a second, and then a third. He will have eyes like the eyes of a <u>man</u> and a <u>mouth</u> that speaks pompous word. Most experts agree that this "little horn" is the Antichrist.

what others say

John Hagee

In Daniel's vision, the "little horn" sprouted among the other ten, which we know are somehow ten divisions of the Old Roman Empire. In his rise to power, the Antichrist will weave his hypnotic spell, first over one nation in the ten-kingdom federation, then over all ten. He will conquer three of the ten nations and then assume primacy over all of them; next he will turn his ravenous eyes toward the Apple of God's eye—Israel.[18]

At first, the Antichrist will seem relatively ordinary and unimportant compared to the ten world leaders, but the look in his eyes will indicate insight, shrewdness, and cunning. And the words of his mouth will indicate pride and arrogance.

World Government During the Times of the Gentiles

Gentile Kingdoms	Ten Divisions
1. Babylonian (gold)	
2. Medo-Persian (silver)	
3. Greek (bronze)	
4. Old Roman Empire (iron)	
5. United Nations (iron + clay)	l_____1

l_____2

l_____3

Nations from the Old Roman Empire (iron) plus others (clay)
l_____4
l_____5
l_____6
l_____7

Antichrist appears and overthrows three divisions

l_____8 _____Antichrist rules world

l_____9 *3 1/2 years Satan rules Antichrist* — **Tribulation Period**

l_____10 *3 1/2 years Second Coming of Jesus*

what others say

Jack Van Impe

Europe is increasingly moving toward unification, and the rest of the world is forming regional military and economic alliances that will make eventual global convergence inevitable (Daniel 7:8, 20, 23, 24).[19]

go to

carrying a bow but no arrows
Revelation 6:2

heaven/thrones
Revelation 4:1–11

throne
Psalms 45:6; 93:2

Ancient of Days
Micah 5:2

clothing
Mark 9:2–3

wheels
Ezekiel 10:1–19

fire
Deuteronomy 4:24

judgment
2 Corinthians 5:10

Ancient of Days
a name for God

what others say

David Breese

"Why isn't the world better," many people say? It's because this world is not our final dwelling place. God works upon the troubled sea of wicked men in order to cause them to be anxious about their human destiny, and look upward to the Lord, and see his plan, and as a result, receive Christ as personal Saviour.[20]

When the Antichrist makes his first appearance in Revelation he is <u>carrying a bow but no arrows</u>. He does not appear with powerful weapons nor does he seem to be Satan's man. He seems to be more like a docile lamb than an indescribable beast.

Some people think the Antichrist will be one of the original ten leaders, But Daniel was thinking about those ten leaders when he saw another leader come up.

The Vision of God's Throne (Visions of the Four Beasts, Part 2)

DANIEL 7:9
"I watched till thrones were put in place,
And the Ancient of Days was seated;
His garment was white as snow,
And the hair of His head was like pure wool.
His throne was a fiery flame,
Its wheels a burning fire; (NKJV)

Here Daniel's dream shifts from a vision of the Antichrist on earth to a vision of future things in <u>heaven</u>. While the Antichrist is ravaging the earth, several <u>thrones</u> will be set in place including the throne of God. Then the **Ancient of Days** will take his seat. God's <u>clothing</u> and hair will be dazzling white (like the brightness and purity of heaven). God's throne and its <u>wheels</u> (a symbol of mobility) will be burning with <u>fire</u> (a symbol of wrath and <u>judgment</u>).

Picture this scene. God is the Judge on the throne, and he is in human form. In the Bible, Jesus is usually the Judge on the throne, and God is a spirit. But this is God, and there are several visions. First, Daniel sees the judgment of unbelievers (verse 10). Second, Daniel sees and hears the Antichrist and the judgment against him (verse 11). Third, Daniel sees One like the Son of Man (Jesus) appear before the Judge seeking a judgment that will give him authority over the earth (verses 13–14). Guess who is really in charge?

The Ancient of Days is mentioned three times in this one chapter (7:9, 13, 22), but the title or name is not used anywhere else in the Bible. He is the God whose throne is forever and ever (Psalm 45:6), the God who is everlasting (Psalm 93:2), the Holy One (Habakkuk 1:12). Jesus is like him. He was born in Bethlehem Ephrathah, but his goings forth are from of old, from everlasting (Micah 5:2).

what others say

Stephen R. Miller

An awesome scene is now unfolded before Daniel's eyes as the "Ancient of Days" (the eternal God) takes his seat upon the throne and exercises his prerogative as the great Judge (or Chief Justice) of the universe.[21]

John's vision of Jesus reads: "Then I turned to see the voice that spoke with me. And having turned I saw seven golden lampstands, and in the midst of the seven lampstands One like the Son of Man, clothed with a garment down to the feet and girded about the chest with a golden band. His head and hair were white like wool, as white as snow, and His eyes like a flame of fire; His feet were like fine brass, as if refined in a furnace, and His voice as the sound of many waters; He had in His right hand seven stars, out of His mouth went a sharp two-edged sword, and His countenance was like the sun shining in its strength" (Revelation 1:12–16 NKJV).

A Day in Court

DANIEL 7:10
A fiery stream issued
And came forth from before Him.
A thousand thousands ministered to Him;
Ten thousand times ten thousand stood before Him.
The court was seated,
And the books were opened. (NKJV)

Fire symbolizes judgment and a fiery stream symbolizes overwhelming and unending judgment. The Antichrist and his wicked

thousands
Revelation 5:11

stand
Romans 14:10–11

books
Exodus 32:33;
Revelation 3:4–5;
20:12; 21:27; 22:19

every
Philippians 2:11

ten thousand times
ten thousand
a Hebrew expres-
sion meaning "a
great multitude"

followers will provoke a continuous flood of God's wrath. God's throne will be surrounded by a thousand <u>thousands</u> of angels who minister to him, and **ten thousand times ten thousand** of the saved from the world. In the presence of the angels and the saved, God's court will go into session. As it begins, everyone will <u>stand</u> and be seated before the <u>books</u> will be opened.

These books (plural) are Books of Works or Books of Deeds and books containing the names of the saved. Opening them indicates an evaluation or judgment. This is not the judgment of the saved; it is the judgment of the nations and the lost. We must understand that all people are accountable for their sins. God keeps records, and what people do while they are here on this planet will come up in the future. The deeds of believers will bring the gain or loss of rewards. The deeds of unbelievers will determine degrees of punishment.

Today, God is unimportant in the lives of multitudes, but the Bible teaches that the day is coming when every individual will spend some time in God's court. Some may never bow their knee on earth, but <u>every</u> knee will bow in heaven. Think about these judgments mentioned in the Bible:

1. The judgment of the believer's sin when Jesus died (John 5:24; Romans 5:9; 8:1; Galatians 3:13).

2. The individual's judgment of self (1 Corinthians 11:31–32; Hebrews 12:5–12).

3. The judgment of the believer's works (1 Corinthians 3:11–15; 2 Corinthians 5:12).

4. The judgment of the nations (Matthew 25:31–46).

5. The judgment of Israel (Ezekiel 20:30–38).

6. The believer's judgment of the angels (Jude 1:6).

7. The judgment of all unbelievers (Revelation 20:11–15).

Shut Your Big Mouth (Visions of the Four Beasts, Part 3)

go to

fire
Matthew 25:46

DANIEL 7:11 *I watched then because of the sound of the pompous words which the horn was speaking; I watched till the beast was slain, and its body destroyed and given to the burning flame. (NKJV)*

Daniel switched to another vision and kept watching because of the pompous words the little horn (Antichrist) was speaking. He kept watching until the fourth beast (the fourth kingdom) was killed and destroyed in the Lake of (eternal) <u>Fire</u>.

This scene prefigures Revelation 19:11–21. Here God's throne is a fiery flame. There Jesus returns with eyes like a flame of fire. Here the Antichrist is judged. There Jesus returns to judge and make war. Here the Antichrist is speaking pompous words. There the name of Jesus is called the Word of God and out of his mouth comes a sharp sword that is the Word of God. Here the kingdom of Antichrist was given to the burning flame. There the Antichrist is cast into the Lake of Fire.

Also, notice that this is not a scene of the gradual triumph of good over evil or the gradual conversion of the world by the Church. This is a scene of the sudden end of the kingdom of Antichrist and the immediate beginning of the reign of Christ on earth. The Antichrist will appear just before the end of the age or just before the Second Coming of Jesus; he will last a short time, be forcefully seized, and all that he stands for will be destroyed.

what others say

Henry M. Morris

Their fright (the armies at Armageddon) was nothing compared to that of the beast and the prophet, as they were suddenly seized and translated at unimaginable speed to a vast fiery lake boiling with brimstone. There, while still alive in their human bodies of flesh and blood, they were hurled into the flaming cauldron, where they would remain throughout eternity.[22]

A Big Power Loss

DANIEL 7:12 *As for the rest of the beasts, they had their dominion taken away, yet their lives were prolonged for a season and a time. (NKJV)*

Son of Man
Luke 5:24; 6:5; 7:34;
Revelation 1:13

Jesus
Matthew 24:1–3;
Revelation 22:20

clouds
Matthew 24:30;
Acts 1:9;
Revelation 1:7

fragments
perhaps individual
nations, counties,
possessions, etc.

Millennium
the 1,000-year reign
of Christ on earth

At the judgment it will be decided that the first three beasts (groups of nations) will lose their right to ever rule again, but they will not suffer the same swift and total destruction as the fourth beast (kingdom of Antichrist). The court will decide to let **fragments** of their kingdoms (some of their territories) and some of their people continue to exist for a period of time beyond the judgment of the fourth kingdom.

what others say

Noah Hutchings

This part of Daniel's vision extends beyond the destruction of the fourth beast kingdom. This relates to the future and not to the past. In other words, England, Russia, and the Afro-Asian alliance will be stripped of all their power and territories, but they will continue to exist as nations during the **Millennium.**[26]

The Son of Man (Visions of the Four Beasts, Part 4)

DANIEL 7:13
"I was watching in the night visions,
And behold, One like the Son of Man,
Coming with the clouds of heaven!
He came to the Ancient of Days,
And they brought Him near before Him. (NKJV)

Here Daniel's dream shifts to a vision of One like the Son of Man. We know from other Scriptures that this is a reference to Jesus. Daniel saw Jesus coming with the clouds of heaven, and other Scriptures tell us this is his Second Coming. Jesus will approach the Ancient of Days and be led into his awesome presence.

Some scholars say the Hebrew expression translated "Son of Man" is similar to the English expression "human being." So Daniel saw Someone like a human being come with the clouds, the chariot of God and the Lord, to appear before God (Psalm 104:3; Isaiah 19:1). He saw two members of the Trinity appearing in a vision at the same time in the Old Testament and both are deity.

The Real CEO

go to

government
Isaiah 9:6–7

those who are left
Revelation 20:4

reign
Luke 1:31–33

kingdom
Revelation 5:9–10;
11:15

troubled
Genesis 41:8

DANIEL 7:14
Then to Him was given dominion and glory and a kingdom,
That all peoples, nations, and languages should serve Him.
*His **dominion** is an everlasting dominion,*
Which shall not pass away,
And His kingdom the one
Which shall not be destroyed. (NKJV)

God's court will give the authority that was stripped from the beasts and all other authority, to the Son of Man. Every <u>government</u> and all power on earth will be turned over to him. The peoples, nations, and men that will worship him are the saved—<u>those who are left</u> after the wicked are destroyed. Jesus will <u>reign</u> over his <u>kingdom</u> forever.

This will be the end of Gentile world government and the end of the Times of the Gentiles. It is the kingdom that will be established when the stone strikes the statue upon its feet of iron and potter's clay (Daniel 2). It is still future because it will come upon the scene after one final Gentile world government, and it shall not be destroyed. This hasn't happened yet.

dominion
power and permission to rule

what others say

Renald E. Showers

Now that God in His sovereignty had ended Gentile world dominion, the earth needed a new kingdom with a new king. Just as God had foretold in Psalm 2, He sovereignty gave all the peoples and nations of the earth to His Son to rule over as king.[24]

An Anxiety Attack

DANIEL 7:15 *"I, Daniel, was grieved in my spirit within my body, and the visions of my head troubled me. (NKJV)*

Daniel had seen a vision of God and one of Jesus, but he did not find his visions something to brag about. He was too upset for that. The other visions <u>troubled</u> him; something in them disturbed and frightened him.

When Nebuchadnezzar dreamed about the awesome statue his mind was troubled and he could not sleep (Daniel 2:1). He was so

go to

winged lion
Daniel 7:4

upset he threatened to have all his wise men killed if they did not reveal the dream and its interpretation. When he dreamed about the great tree he said, "The thoughts on my bed and the visions of my head troubled me" (Daniel 4:5 NKJV).

I Wanted to Know

> DANIEL 7:16 *I came near to one of those who stood by, and asked him the truth of all this. So he told me and made known to me the interpretation of these things:* (NKJV)

There were thousands upon thousands of angels around God's throne and a great multitude of the saved. Daniel did not understand these things but wanted to know what they meant, so he approached one of the heavenly beings, probably an angel, and asked for an explanation. It happened to be a being that could explain things to Daniel.

what others say

Charles H. Dyer

We shrink back when we read of multi-metaled statues or beasts that seem to leap from the pages of horror novels. Somehow we imagine Daniel eating a pepperoni pizza before going to bed and recording his nightmares to frustrate the saints throughout history. Daniel's visions may be bizarre, but they are not incomprehensible. After each vision God interpreted the various parts, and his interpretation makes perfect sense when we examine it carefully.[25]

We Are Talking About the Future

> DANIEL 7:17 *Those great beasts, which are four, are four kings which arise out of the earth.* (NKJV)

In his vision Daniel saw the four beasts come up out of the sea (Daniel 7:3). Now the heavenly being tells him the four great beasts are four kingdoms that will rise from the earth.

This is important because many experts believe the <u>winged lion</u> is Babylon, a kingdom that had already risen and was at this time near its fall. However, that explanation does not fit because all four of these kingdoms were in Daniel's future.

And the Winner Is . . .

DANIEL 7:18 *But the saints of the Most High shall receive the kingdom, and possess the kingdom forever, even forever and ever.' (NKJV)*

The identity of the saints of the Most High is a problem because several different groups of people are called saints in the Bible, and it is impossible to say if this is a reference to just one of the groups or all of the groups. One group of saints is called the **Church**, another is called the **Tribulation Saints**, and yet another is called **believing Israel**. However, most experts believe this verse is a reference to believing Israel.

A debate about the identity of the saints, however, is not the point. The heavenly being was making it clear that none of the four beasts would receive God's kingdom. It will go to God's people who will possess it forever; it is repeated to add emphasis—forever, even forever and ever.

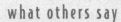

what others say

Uriah Smith

The saints; those of all others in low esteem in this world, despised, reproached, persecuted, cast out; those who were considered the least likely of all men ever to realize their hopes; these shall take the kingdom, and possess it forever. The **usurpation** and **misrule** of the wicked shall come to an end.[26]

Leon J. Wood

These saints receive the kingdom, not in the sense of kings (true only for the Son of Man), but in being permitted to enter into and enjoy this time of perfect rule. Those who are not saints, according to Matthew 25:31–46, will not be given this privilege.[27]

I Also Wanted to Know

DANIEL 7:19 *Then I wished to know the truth about the fourth beast, which was different from all the others, exceedingly dreadful, with its teeth of iron and its nails of bronze, which devoured, broke in pieces, and trampled the residue with its feet; (NKJV)*

go to

Church
Romans 1:7

Tribulation Saints
Revelation 13:7

believing Israel
Matthew 27:52–53

Church
people who accept Christ as Savior before the Rapture

Tribulation Saints
people who accept Christ as Savior after the Rapture

believing Israel
Old and New Testament Jews who believe in the Messiah

usurpation
seizing of power

misrule
bad, poor, or unwise rule

go to

fourth beast
Daniel 7:7

kingdom
Daniel 7:17

greater
impressive

The next thing Daniel wanted the heavenly being to tell him was the meaning of the <u>fourth beast</u>. The thing that seemed to bother him most was the fact that it will be so different from the first three beasts or kingdoms and so much more terrifying with its iron teeth and bronze nails. It will be a ferocious <u>kingdom</u>, crushing and devouring anyone it chooses and trampling underfoot anything left. All four beasts (kingdoms) would rise in Daniel's future.

Many nations have selected animals to be their symbol. As already noted, I believe the United States is the eagle, England is the lion, Russia is the bear, and the Arab/African coalition is the leopard. In order to depict groups of nations that are very fast, the Holy Spirit puts wings on the animal (Daniel 7:4). In order to depict groups of nations that are very fierce, he puts ribs between the animal's teeth (Daniel 7:5). But there is no animal ferocious enough to depict the Antichrist's kingdom, so it is aptly called a terrifying and frightening and powerful beast (verse 7). In order to depict its fierceness it is pictured with large iron teeth and bronze claws. How terrible it must be when there are no animals strange enough, bad enough, or horrible enough to depict this coming kingdom.

And Then I Wanted to Know

DANIEL 7:20 *and the ten horns that were on its head, and the other horn which came up, before which three fell, namely, that horn which had eyes and a mouth which spoke pompous words, whose appearance was greater than his fellows. (NKJV)*

Daniel also wanted the heavenly being to explain the ten horns on the head of this fourth kingdom and the other "little horn."

By seeking this information Daniel repeats four things about the other horn (the Antichrist):

1. Three of the first ten will fall before him.

2. His appearance will be **greater** than the other ten.

3. He will have eyes.

4. He will speak pompous words.

In a vision of Jesus, John said Jesus had seven eyes. He told us the seven eyes represented the seven spirits of God (Revelation 5:6). In other words, the seven eyes represented the all-seeing **omniscient** vision of the Holy Spirit. Since the eyes of a good man can represent the eyes of a good spirit, what do you think is so important about the eyes of this wicked man (the Antichrist)?

We should pay attention to everything mentioned in the Bible, but especially when something is repeated. Here in Daniel 7, the boasting of the Antichrist is mentioned in three different verses (8, 11, and 12). This will surely be one of his dominant characteristics.

go to

horn
Daniel 7:24

flee
Revelation 12:6

saints
Revelation 13:5–7

omniscient
knows everything

> ### what others say
>
> #### Henry M. Morris
>
> Although full understanding of these and other related prophecies must await their fulfillment, it does seem clear enough that these ten prominent nations of the last days will be joined also by many other "peoples, and multitudes, and nations, and tongues" (Revelation 17:15).[28]

The Coming Battle Between Good and Evil

DANIEL 7:21 *I was watching; and the same horn was making war against the saints, and prevailing against them,* *(NKJV)*

Daniel is continuing to tell the heavenly being what he saw and what he would like to have explained. He saw a <u>horn</u> (the Antichrist) waging war against the saints and killing them. From studying Revelation, we know that the Antichrist will attack Israel (the woman) and the Jews will <u>flee</u> into the desert. We also know that he will speak against God and kill all the <u>saints</u> he can during the Tribulation Period. This coming war against the saints is one of the terrible things that attracted Daniel's attention, and the fact that the Antichrist is going to win tells us that it will be a horrible war. The Antichrist will persecute and kill Christians and Jews during the Tribulation Period.

Daniel saw the Antichrist prevailing against the saints, but Jesus said the gates of Hades shall not prevail against the Church (Matthew 16:18). Unless the Church is raptured before the Tribulation Period arrives, there is a contradiction in the Bible. But there is no contradiction in the Bible. This verse supports the Pre-Tribulation Rapture. The Antichrist will prevail against the Tribulation Saints.

go to

vision of God's court
Daniel 7:10

judgment
Revelation 20:1–4

saints
1 Corinthians 6:1–2

kingdom
Matthew 25:31–34

truth
Daniel 7:19

whole earth
be a world kingdom

what others say

Ed Hindson

From the very beginning of the Christian era, believers were convinced that a world ruler would eventually come on the scene who was the embodiment of Satan. The book of Revelation (chapters 12–13) presents an "unholy trinity" that aligns Satan (vs. Father), Antichrist (vs. Son), and False Prophet (vs. Holy Spirit). Thus, the real power behind the Antichrist is Satan.[29]

Tell Me More

DANIEL 7:22 *until the Ancient of Days came, and a judgment was made in favor of the saints of the Most High, and the time came for the saints to possess the kingdom. (NKJV)*

This is more of what Daniel saw and wanted the heavenly being to explain. He is referring back to his vision of God's court, and he wanted information about three things:

1. The Ancient of Days who will come and take a seat in the court.

2. The judgment that will be pronounced in favor of God's saints.

3. The fact that God's saints will possess the kingdom.

This Is His Answer

DANIEL 7:23 *"Thus he said:*
'The fourth beast shall be
A fourth kingdom on earth,
Which shall be different from all other kingdoms,
And shall devour the whole earth,
Trample it and break it in pieces. (NKJV)

Daniel had asked the heavenly being for the truth about the fourth beast. His answer demands our close attention. Notice four things:

1. The fourth beast is an earthly kingdom.

2. The fourth beast will be different from all the other kingdoms.

3. The fourth beast will devour the **whole earth**.

4. The fourth beast will **trample and break** the earth in pieces.

You Asked About Those Horns

DANIEL 7:24
The ten horns are ten kings
Who shall arise from this kingdom.
And another shall rise after them;
He shall be different from the first ones,
And shall subdue three kings. (NKJV)

In the previous verse we learned that a world kingdom is on the way. The thing to notice in this verse is that ten <u>horns</u> (ten kings or ten divisions) will arise out of that future world kingdom. Then another (an eleventh) king will arise. This reveals a step-by-step development of the "last" Times of the Gentiles empire. Exactly what the heavenly being meant when he said the Antichrist will be different from the first ten kings is a matter of speculation. But when we add what Daniel gives us to information given in other books of the Bible we develop a picture of an evil man who will make Adolf Hitler look like a friendly little angel. This eleventh leader (the Antichrist) will have satanic powers. He will be a polished, brilliant, <u>self-exalting</u>, <u>miracle-working</u> blasphemer who comes straight out of the **bottomless pit** and **subdues** three of the first ten kings.

The verses about toes, horns, and kings quickly confuse those who do not spend much time with Bible prophecy, but they are clear to those who love to study this portion of God's Word. The following chart demonstrates how the Bible interprets itself.

horn
Daniel 7:20

self-exalting
2 Thessalonians 2:4

miracle-working
2 Thessalonians 2:9

bottomless pit
Revelation 17:8

trample and break
be brutal and destructive

bottomless pit
the place where God holds the most vicious demonic spirits

subdues
takes their power; overthrows, or conquers

Toes and Horns Are Kings

Toes	Scripture
The toes of the feet were partly of iron and partly of clay.	Daniel 2:42
In the days of these kings the God of heaven will set up a kingdom.	Daniel 2:44

Horns	Scripture
The beast had ten horns.	Daniel 7:7, 20
The ten horns are ten kings.	Daniel 7:24

Kings	Scripture
The beast has seven heads and ten horns.	Revelation 13:1
The ten horns which you saw are ten kings.	Revelation 17:12
They have received no kingdom as yet, but they receive authority as kings with the beast.	Revelation 17:12
They are of one mind [with the beast] and will give their power and authority to the beast.	Revelation 17:13

what others say

Grant R. Jeffrey

The ten regions of the new world government:

Region 1—Canada and the United States of America

Region 2—European Union—Western Europe

Region 3—Japan

Region 4—Australia, New Zealand, South Africa, Israel, and Pacific Islands

Region 5—Eastern Europe

Region 6—Latin America—Mexico, Central and South America

Region 7—North Africa and the Middle East (Moslems)

Region 8—Central Africa

Region 9—South and Southeast Asia

Region 10—Central Asia[31]

Irvin Baxter Jr.

The Bible prophesies one-world government and one-world religion for the end-times. We have watched the United Nations become more and more prominent in world governance during the decade of the nineties. . . . We have witnessed the changing of governments in Rhodesia, South Africa and Haiti through the concerted actions of the U.N. In spite of these "successes," peace on earth still seems as elusive as ever.

Because many armed confrontations are rooted in religious conflicts, insiders at the U.N. are stating that world peace can never be realized unless unity and cooperation can be achieved among the religions of the world. A major step has now been taken toward global cooperation and unity among the world's religions. On June 23–27, 1997, the process for creation of the charter of the United Religions Organization was begun.[32]

go to

four specific things
Revelation 13:6

created
Genesis 1:1

forty-two
Revelation 13:5

distress
Matthew 24:21–22

You Asked About the Saints

DANIEL 7:25

He shall speak pompous words against the Most High,
Shall persecute the saints of the Most High,
And shall intend to change times and law.
Then the saints shall be given into his hand
For a time and times and half a time. (NKJV)

"He shall speak pompous words against the Most High" (Daniel 7:25 NKJV) means he will be anti-God. He will do <u>four specific things</u> against God: (1) blaspheme God; (2) slander the name of God; (3) slander the dwelling place of God (the Church); and (4) slander those who live in heaven. It is safe to predict that the Antichrist will oppose everything connected with God.

"Persecute the saints" (7:25 NKJV) foretells a coming persecution of Christians and Jews. There will be a satanic philosophy behind his government. He will be anti-Christ and anti-Semitic.

"Intend to change times and law" (7:25 NKJV) probably means he will try to change our calendar and our Judeo-Christian values. The Christian calendar is based upon the year Jesus Christ was born.

BC is before his birth while AD is after his birth. The Jewish calendar is based upon the time God <u>created</u> the heavens and the earth. God is the One who changes the times and seasons (Daniel 2:21). The Antichrist will not like these things or anything based upon the teachings of God or Jesus Christ. He will probably claim he needs to change them so as not to offend people of other faiths. Time, times, and half a time is explained in Daniel 4:16. It is three and one-half years or <u>forty-two</u> months. This will be the last three and one-half years (second half) of the Tribulation Period, and the <u>distress</u> upon earth will be terrible.

go to

Mark of the Beast
Revelation 13:16–18

Mark of the Beast
the mark, number,
or name of the
Antichrist

J. R. Church

It is my feeling that this designates the time in which the "**Mark of the Beast**" will be introduced. He will tighten his control on all nations by requiring a personal identification for every citizen. No one will be able to participate in the marketplace without complete government control. . . . During these crucial three-and-a-half years, God will pour out his wrath upon the nations. Earthquakes will be commonplace. Drought and famine will be widespread. Disease will be rampant. All nations will face seeming certain destruction—and the world dictator will be powerless to stop it.[33]

John Hagee

Every single new world order, including the coming Antichrist's, has had one common trait: an attempt to cast God out of the affairs of men. Why? As long as we believe the Word of God and are loyal to the kingdom of God, we represent a government within a government. We are pilgrims and strangers who worship another King and have another citizenship, and as such, we are a hindrance to the New World Order. When our government condones what God condemns, those who have trusted in him become the enemy. And so the Bible-believing Christians of America are labeled dangerous, "intolerant," and enemies of the state.[34]

It is important to understand the lengths of time mentioned in the Bible. The New Testament confirms the Old Testament, and the following chart will help.

God's Calendar

Biblical Term	Scripture	Today's Time
Seven times	Daniel 4:16, 23, 25, 32	Seven times = 7 x 1 time = 7 years
Time, and times and half a time	Daniel 7:25; 12:7; Revelation 12:14	Time = 360 days = one year Times = 720 days = two years Half a time = 180 days = half a year Time, and times and half a time = 360 + 720 + 180 = 1260 days or 3 1/2 years (Note: times means two years unless preceded by a numeral indicating otherwise)
One week	Daniel 9:27; Genesis 29:20–30	One week of years = 360 days/year x 7 years = 2520 days
Middle of the week	Daniel 9:27	7 years/2 = 1260 days = 3 1/2 years
Forty-two months	Revelation 11:2; 13:5	The same as time and times and half a time = 1260 days = 3 1/2 years

God's Calendar (cont'd)

Biblical Term	Scripture	Today's Time
One thousand two hundred and sixty days	Revelation 11:3; 12:6	The same as forty-two months

go to

court
Daniel 7:9–10

lake of fire
Revelation 19:19–20

kingdom
Daniel 7:22

It Is the Decision of This Court . . .

DANIEL 7:26
> 'But the court shall be seated,
> And they shall take away his dominion,
> To consume and destroy it forever. *(NKJV)*

In just one short sentence we have the judgment of the Antichrist. And this brief statement seems almost prophetic itself because it reveals that the Antichrist will come to a quick end. At some point during the Tribulation Period God's <u>court</u> will go into session. Before it is over the decision will be made that the Antichrist should be stripped of his authority and destroyed. Revelation tells us that the Antichrist will be cast into the <u>lake of fire</u> burning with brimstone.

Some experts teach that the Church will start a great revival, convert the world, and usher in the kingdom of God on earth. This is known as *Kingdom Theology*. But these visions indicate just the opposite. The last Gentile world power will come close to wiping out God's people.

A Fifth and Last Kingdom

DANIEL 7:27
> *Then the kingdom and dominion,*
> *And the greatness of the kingdoms under the whole heaven,*
> *Shall be given to the people, the saints of the Most High.*
> *His kingdom is an everlasting kingdom,*
> *And all dominions shall serve and obey Him.' (NKJV)*

When the Antichrist is dethroned the <u>kingdom</u> will be handed over to God's people. This includes the lion kingdom, the bear kingdom, the leopard kingdom, the world kingdom of the Antichrist, and all other kingdoms on earth. God's kingdom is an everlasting kingdom. Every ruler will eventually worship and obey God whether they want to or not.

Could the last five verses be a time line or an outline of how events will progress at the End of the (Gentile) Age? Notice the following:

1. A world government will be established (Daniel 7:23).

2. Ten kings or ten divisions will come up from this world government (Daniel 7:24).

3. After the ten kings rise to power over the ten divisions, another king, the Antichrist, will rise to power (Daniel 7:24).

4. After the Antichrist rises to power he will have complete control over God's people for three and one-half years (Daniel 7:25).

5. God will judge the Antichrist and take his power away (Daniel 7:26).

6. The kingdom will be turned over to God's people (Daniel 7:27).

Notice what these verses say about the saints:

1. The saints of the Most High will receive the kingdom and will possess it forever (Daniel 7:18).

2. This horn was waging war against the saints and defeating them (Daniel 7:21).

3. The Ancient of Days came and pronounced judgment in favor of the saints of the Most High, and the time came when they possessed the kingdom (Daniel 7:22).

4. He [the Antichrist] will speak against the Most High and persecute his saints (Daniel 7:25).

5. The saints will be handed over to him for a time, times, and half a time [three and one-half years] (Daniel 7:25).

6. Then the dominion and greatness of the kingdoms under the whole heaven will be handed over to the saints (Daniel 7:27).

I Don't Feel So Good

> DANIEL 7:28 *"This is the end of the account. As for me, Daniel, my thoughts greatly troubled me, and my countenance changed; but I kept the matter in my heart."* (NKJV)

The vision ended when the heavenly being finished saying, *all dominions shall serve and obey* him, but that was not the end of the matter for Daniel. When he had this vision he said, "I, Daniel, was grieved in my spirit within my body, and the visions of my head troubled me" (verse 15). When he got the interpretation he said, "My thoughts greatly troubled me, and my countenance changed." "My thoughts" means he pondered the awful nature of the coming one-world government, the Antichrist, the war against Christ, the persecution of the saints, the Tribulation Period, and all that will happen, and it stressed him out so much the very expression on his face changed. The original language indicates that the color drained out of his face and he became pale. He wrote down the vision and its interpretation, but he didn't tell Shadrach, Meshach, and Abed-Nego or anyone else. He may have thought it would impact them the same way.

Chapter Wrap-Up

- Daniel had a vision of four beasts (or kingdoms) rising to power out of the Sea of Humanity: the first like a lion with eagle's wings (perhaps England and the U.S.); the second like a lopsided bear with three ribs in its mouth (perhaps Russia and her allies); the third like a four-winged, four-headed leopard (perhaps an Arab/African coalition); and the fourth terrifying, frightening and powerful (the kingdom of the Antichrist). The fourth had ten horns (kings) and a little horn (the Antichrist); three of the ten horns were overthrown by the little horn. (Daniel 7:1–8)

- Daniel had a vision of God sitting in judgment upon the fourth kingdom and its ruler, the Antichrist. Multitudes of angels and saints surrounded his throne, the books were opened, the Antichrist was judged and punished, and the other beasts were stripped of their authority and allowed to live for a time. (Daniel 7:9–12)

- Daniel saw a heavenly being standing nearby, so he repeated his visions and asked for an interpretation. The heavenly being gave him an explanation. (Daniel 7:15–23)

- The four beasts represent four kingdoms in Daniel's future. The fourth kingdom will establish ten divisions, and the Antichrist will rise and subdue three of these divisions. Then all power on earth will be turned over to him for 3 1/2 years. He will be anti-God and persecute and kill God's saints. (Daniel 7:24–25)

- The end of things will come when Jesus returns. He will destroy the Antichrist, seize his authority, and turn it over to his people. His will be the final kingdom, and it will last forever. (Daniel 7:26–27)

Study Questions

1. Who is the "little horn" and what are some of the things he will do?

2. What titles does Daniel use for God in this chapter? For Jesus?

3. What will cause the defeat of the Antichrist, and when will it happen?

4. Do you think Daniel's vision from God made him proud? Can you name three ways he was affected by it?

5. What do the four beasts symbolize, and why do you think God uses beasts to symbolize them?

Chapter Highlights:
- Two-Horned Ram
- Male Goat
- Next World Leader
- God Reigns
- Daniel's Reaction

Daniel 8
Three End-of-the-Age Powers

Let's Get Started

So far, our main focus has been on matters concerning the Gentiles. This is about to change, because we are now going to start focusing on how Gentile matters have, and will, affect the Jews and Jerusalem. We can say it like this: we are about to start studying how the Times of the Gentiles will affect Israel in Daniel's future, and especially how it will affect Israel during the Tribulation Period.

first
Daniel 7:1

Most of this vision, usually called "the Vision of the Ram and the Goat," has already been fulfilled, which makes it past history to us. (Even this fulfilled part is very important since it attests to the fact that Daniel was a true prophet, and his writings were inspired by God.) But Daniel makes it clear that it also has an End of the Age application. Part of it is sealed up so we may not be able to understand all of the details. However, we will learn what we can.

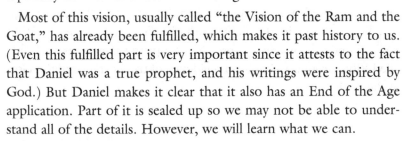

what others say

Tim LaHaye

The accuracy of this prophecy as fulfilled in history has caused many critics to suggest that a "latter Daniel" wrote the book of Daniel because the original Daniel was dead long before the Greeks rose to prominence. However, no such evidence can be found to support this notion, and the discovery of the book of Daniel among the Dead Sea Scrolls has provided ample evidence that the book is of ancient origin and consequently, is prophetic Scripture.[1]

The Time: Two Years Later (The Vision of the Ram and the Goat)

DANIEL 8:1 *In the third year of the reign of King Belshazzar a vision appeared to me—to me, Daniel—after the one that appeared to me the first time. (NKJV)*

The visions in chapter 7 were in the <u>first</u> year of Belshazzar's reign (see Time Line #1, Appendix A); but this vision was in the third year

night
Daniel 5:30

wrote
Daniel 5:5

of his reign. Two years have passed and the date is about 540–542 BC. It is about one to three years *before* the <u>night</u> the hand <u>wrote</u> on the wall, signaling Babylon's fall and Belshazzar's death.

It is helpful to understand the situation surrounding this vision. Belshazzar was the last king of Babylon; his Gentile world kingdom would soon fall. The next Gentile world kingdom on God's Statue (the chest and arms of silver—the Medes and Persians) would soon take over (see Illustration #5). Then they would be followed by another Gentile world kingdom (the belly and thighs of bronze—Greece). This vision provides details about those next two Gentile world kingdoms.

Some people say, "I will never believe in a miracle unless I see one." But the reality of miracles is evident throughout the Bible. Jesus performed miracles and multitudes accepted them as a sign that he was God in the flesh. Isn't the fact that Daniel foretold events hundreds of years before they happened a miracle? Isn't fulfilled Bible prophecy significant evidence of the existence of the God of the Bible?

what others say

C. I. Scofield

The remarkably precise predictions in chs. 8 and 11 about the reign, character, and antecedents of Antiochus Epiphanes, the Hellenistic king who cruelly persecuted the Jews 400 years after the time of Nebuchadnezzar, were advanced by Porphyry, an anti-Christian philosopher of the third century A.D., as proof that the Book of Daniel could not have been written before that time. This view has been followed by many modern critics but should not keep any believer in predictive prophecy from accepting the traditional date.[2]

Two Languages of Daniel—Hebrew and Aramaic

Language	Reason for Use	Scripture
Hebrew	Written for Israel	Daniel 1–2:3
Aramaic	Written for all nations	Daniel 2:4–7:28
Hebrew	Written about events important to Israel	Daniel 8–12

The Place: Shusan in Elam Near the River Ulai

DANIEL 8:2 *I saw in the vision, and it so happened while I was looking, that I was in Shushan, the citadel, which is in the province of Elam; and I saw in the vision that I was by the River Ulai.* (NKJV)

In this vision Daniel was transported to the Babylonian fortress at Shushan (see Illustration #2). That was a small city and military base in the province of Elam. Its commander, Abradates, would soon revolt and join the Medes and Persians in their <u>attack</u> on Babylon, so Daniel was taken to this soon-to-be Medo-Persian fortress and found himself beside the Ulai River. Daniel knew Shushan would be the capital of the Persian Empire while it was still a small nondescript city about 200–250 miles east of Babylon.

go to

attack
Isaiah 21:1–2

represent the kings
Daniel 8:20

took over the kingdom
Daniel 5:31

> what others say
>
> ### Kenneth O. Gangel
>
> The deliverance of Daniel's people is more than ten years away with Babylonia still very much in control, although battles with the Persians are already underway. Yet God wanted Daniel to see not only what would happen in order to get his people back home but also how the flow of history will change.[3]

The Ram with Two Horns

DANIEL 8:3 *Then I lifted my eyes and saw, and there, standing beside the river, was a ram which had two horns, and the two horns were high; but one was higher than the other, and the higher one came up last.* (NKJV)

In his vision of the future, Daniel saw a ram with two horns. The two horns <u>represent the kings</u> (kingdom) of Media and Persia. We now know them as Darius and Cyrus (see chart at Daniel 7:24).

The two horns, Darius and Cyrus, were very long. But one horn, Cyrus, was longer than the other and came up last. Darius the Mede, the first and shorter horn, <u>took over the kingdom </u>when Babylon fell. He ruled for about two years and died. Then Cyrus the Persian, the second and longer horn, took over the kingdom and ruled for about twenty more years.

horns
Revelation 17:12

kingdom
Daniel 2:32, 39

key point

go to

what others say

Uriah Smith

The two horns represented the two nationalities of which the empire consisted. The higher came up last. This represented the Persian element, which, from being at first simply an ally of the Medes, came to be the leading division of the empire.[4]

In Bible prophecy <u>horns</u> are symbolic of kings, rulers, and leaders. This is very important and can be confusing since Revelation talks of two beasts with horns. In Daniel 8:20 we are told that the two horns represent the king of Media and Persia. So when you see horns mentioned in a symbolic way in the Bible, remember they represent kings, rulers, and teachers (see chart at Daniel 7:24).

Charge

> **DANIEL 8:4** *I saw the ram pushing westward, northward, and southward, so that no animal could withstand him; nor was there any that could deliver from his hand, but he did according to his will and became great.* (NKJV)

As Daniel was watching the ram it charged first to the west, then to the north, and finally to the south. No nation or empire was strong enough to resist it. And no nation or empire was strong enough to rescue those it defeated. The ram did as it pleased and became a great <u>kingdom</u>.

An amazing point is the fact that Daniel prophesied the plan of attack used by the Medes and the Persians. Their first, and greatest push, was to the west, just as Daniel said. After that, they pushed north, the direction Daniel noted second, and, at a later time, they pushed south in the last mentioned direction. But they never pushed east in the direction not mentioned. Daniel not only announced the exact sequence of attack, but he also announced that the attack would end after the campaign to the south. No one but God could know how it would go and how it would end before it happened.

The Male Goat with One Horn

> **DANIEL 8:5** *And as I was considering, suddenly a male goat came from the west, across the surface of the whole earth, without touching the ground; and the goat had a notable horn between his eyes.* (NKJV)

As Daniel's vision of the future continued, he saw a male goat with one large horn between its eyes. This male goat represents the king (kingdom) of Greece and adds that the large horn represents the first king of Greece. Crossing the whole earth without touching the ground is like saying it had wings; it flew or moved very fast.

Greece was to the west of Persia. Its first king, after the fall of the Medes and Persians, was Alexander the Great (the large horn on the goat). Alexander came across the earth and crushed everything in front of him. His kingdom of bronze of Greece defeated the million-man Persian army in a little less than three years.

male goat
Daniel 8:21

kingdom of bronze
Daniel 2:32, 39

what others say

The Nelson Study Bible

The goat represents Greece (v. 21). The notable horn symbolizes Alexander the Great (v. 21) who launched his attack against Persia in 334 BC. By 332 BC he had essentially subdued the Persian Empire. Alexander's conquest was so rapid that it seemed as if he flew across the earth.[5]

Noah Hutchings

Inasmuch as these two nations are so clearly identified by their national emblems, we should also expect the beasts of Chapter 7 to relate to nations with similar emblems—namely, England, the United States, Russia, the Afro-Asian bloc, and the Revived Roman Empire.[6]

A Furious Attack

DANIEL 8:6 *Then he came to the ram that had two horns, which I had seen standing beside the river, and ran at him with furious power. (NKJV)*

The male goat with one horn (Greece under Alexander the Great) charged the ram with two horns (the kingdom of the Medes and Persians) with a furious rage.

what others say

Leon J. Wood

The word for "fury" comes from a root meaning "to be hot." Hatred for the Persians had built up within the Greeks since the days of Cyrus, because of constant tension and quarreling. Normal strength becomes heightened when backed by emotional heat.[10]

The Ram Goes Down

DANIEL 8:7 *And I saw him confronting the ram; he was moved with rage against him, attacked the ram, and broke his two horns. There was no power in the ram to withstand him, but he cast him down to the ground and trampled him; and there was no one that could deliver the ram from his hand.* (NKJV)

In his vision of the future, Daniel saw the following:

1. The goat butted the ram furiously (the Greeks attacked the Medes and Persians without mercy).

2. The ram's horns were broken (the Greeks inflicted terrible losses on the Medes and Persians).

3. The ram was powerless (the Greeks defeated the Medo-Persian military).

4. The ram was knocked to the ground (the Medo-Persian people were subdued and humbled).

5. The ram was trampled upon (the Medo-Persian people were crushed).

6. The ram could not be rescued (no one could stop the Greeks).

what others say

Kay Arthur

God told Daniel what was going to transpire in regard to the Medo-Persian Empire and the Grecian Empire when neither was a major world power. In the days when the Babylonians still ruled, God gave Daniel a vision—a sure word of prophecy that would explain the future to the nation of Israel. . . Whom will you believe child of God? Man, who is limited by his understanding, his education—or the Word of God given to us by an infinite God who cannot lie and knows the beginning from the end? Will you believe the God who rules over history?[8]

Rodney Stortz

It is important to understand that Alexander's rise to power was two centuries after Daniel made this prophecy—two hundred years! These four kingdoms could not have been imagined by any normal human mind.[9]

The Broken Horn

go to

four other horns
Daniel 8:22

four winds of heaven
Daniel 7:2

DANIEL 8:8 *Therefore the male goat grew very great; but when he became strong, the large horn was broken, and in place of it four notable ones came up toward the four winds of heaven. (NKJV)*

In his vision of the future, Daniel learned that the goat (the Greek Empire) would become very great after it defeated the ram (the Medes and Persians). But what about the large horn (Alexander the Great)? At the height of his power he would be broken off (die). <u>Four other horns</u> (leaders) would take his place and grow toward the <u>four winds of heaven</u> (north, south, east, and west).

This is exactly what happened. History and tradition tell us that Alexander the Great expanded the Greek Empire until he sat down and wept because he had no more worlds to conquer. Then, at the height of his power and prime of his life (just under thirty-three years old), he suddenly died.

What happened to the Greek Empire upon Alexander's death? The Greek Empire was divided into four parts and Alexander the Great was replaced by four prominent horns, which history identifies as his four top generals.

> **what others say**
>
> ### John F. Walvoord
>
> Alexander, who had conquered more of the world than any previous ruler, was not able to conquer himself. Partly due to a strenuous exertion, his dissipated life, and a raging fever, Alexander died in a drunken debauch at Babylon, not yet thirty-three years of age. His death left a great conquest without an effective single leader, and it took about twenty years for the empire to be successfully divided.[10]

Out of Seleucus came a king called Antiochus IV or Antiochus Epiphanes (215–163 BC). He was anti-Semitic (hostile to all Jews), anti-God, and in many ways he prefigured the coming Antichrist. There is wide agreement that he literally committed the terrible sins recorded in the book of Daniel and in the Apocrypha book called I Maccabees, but many things he did are typical of what the coming Antichrist will do. The following chart shows the division of the one-world Gentile government of Greece into four groups. The area ruled by Seleucus brought forth Antiochus Epiphanes, a type of the Antichrist. At the end of the age, the final one-world government of the United Nations will divide into ten groups. The Antichrist will overthrow three of them and then be given control of all ten.

Antiochus Ephiphanes and the Antichrist

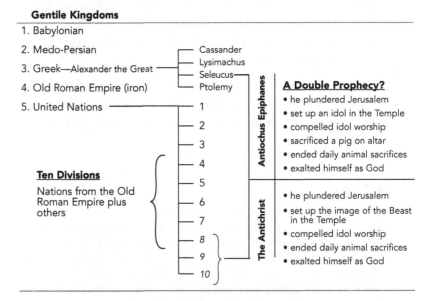

Will the Real Horn Please Stand Up?

DANIEL 8:9 *And out of one of them came a little horn which grew exceedingly great toward the south, toward the east, and toward the Glorious Land. (NKJV)*

"Out of one of them" means out of one of the four parts of the divided Greek Empire. "Came a little horn" means there would arise another leader. He would start small and then grow in power in three directions: (1) toward the south, (2) toward the east, and (3) toward the **Glorious Land**.

The Wycliffe Bible Commentary

These verses [9–14] predict the sad conflict of the Jews, in the second half of the second century BC with the Seleucid king, Antiochus IV, called Epiphanes ("Magnificent") by friends, Epimanes ("Madman") by enemies. Many evangelical interpreters see here a type of Antichrist and his conflict with Christ and his people in the end time. This may very well be.[11]

John Phillips

Here we have one of those remarkable evidences of Scripture that each word in the sacred original text was "God-breathed" because the words for "little horn" in chapters 7 and 8 are not equivalents. This careful choice of words is designed to underline the fact that the two little horns are not the same. The coming world dictator depicted in chapter 7 is described by an Aramaic word that can be translated "a horn, a little one" (7:8). The vile dictator in chapter 8 is described by a Hebrew word that can mean "a horn less than little" or "a horn from littleness" (arising from a small beginning), pointing to his development from insignificant beginnings.[12]

distant future
Daniel 7:26

sealed up
hidden until a certain time

A Double Prophecy?

Here we run into a big problem. Many prophecy experts believe this leader (another horn) turned out to be Antiochus Epiphanes, a descendant of Seleucus who took over Syria and Babylonia when Alexander the Great died. But many other, equally good, experts believe this leader was not Antiochus Epiphanes. The Bible itself says this prophecy is **sealed up** and concerns the distant future. The friendly disagreement and lack of certainty are fueled by the fact that Antiochus Epiphanes fulfilled many of the requirements of this prophecy but definitely not all. What is the most likely answer? As bad as he was, Antiochus Epiphanes was only an incomplete imitation of the real little horn. God may have let him exist to reveal many things about the real horn, but the world will not know the real horn until the Tribulation Period arrives.

Because Antiochus Epiphanes was a Syrian some experts suggest that the Antichrist will be a Syrian, but that is just speculation. He may be a Syrian, but it is impossible to know for sure. Do not forget that the Antichrist will not be revealed until after the Rapture, and his nationality will not be nearly as important as his evil deeds. The

go to

small
Daniel 8:9

power
Revelation 13:2

little horn
Daniel 7:8

trampling
Daniel 7:7, 23

stars/angels
Revelation 1:20

stars/Jews
Genesis 15:5; 26:4;
37:9–11;
Revelation 12:1

emphasis in this chapter is on his inconspicuous beginning, the great power he attains, and his great wickedness.

He Will Grow and Grow and Grow . . .

DANIEL 8:10 *And it grew up to the host of heaven; and it cast down some of the host and some of the stars to the ground, and trampled them. (NKJV)*

One thing to notice here is the phenomenal growth of the Antichrist. We learned that he will start out <u>small</u> and grow in <u>power</u>, and we learned that he will start out as a "<u>little horn</u>" and grow until he takes over the whole world. Here we are told that he will grow until he reaches the host of heaven. This is a biblical phrase referring to the residents of heaven. The point here is that the Antichrist will become exceedingly powerful.

Another thing to notice is this matter of throwing some of the starry host down to the earth and <u>trampling</u> on them. In the Bible stars symbolize two things: (1) <u>angels</u>, and (2) the <u>Jews</u>. Since this chapter is dealing with Daniel's prophecies about the Jews, this probably means the Antichrist will cause the fall and destruction of many Jews. Those who think this is a reference to Antiochus Epiphanes can point to history and show that he forced many Jews to blaspheme God and worship idols. He even killed approximately 100,000 Jews and sold another 40,000 into slavery.

Here is a small sample of the crimes of Antiochus:

1. He plundered Jerusalem.

2. He outlawed the Jewish religion and replaced it with Greek worship.

3. He outlawed the observance of the Sabbath.

4. He outlawed circumcision.

5. He outlawed the reading of the Scriptures.

6. He burned whatever Scriptures he could find.

7. He sacrificed a pig on the altar at the Temple.

8. He set up an idol in the Temple.

9. He compelled idol worship.

10. He claimed he was God manifest in the flesh.

He Will Make Himself Like the Most High

DANIEL **8:11** *He even exalted himself as high as the **Prince of the host**; and by him the daily sacrifices were taken away, and the place of His sanctuary was cast down. (NKJV)*

In chapter 7 we learned about the <u>pompous</u> words of the Antichrist. He will be like Satan, the <u>morning star</u>—arrogant, proud, and pretending to be <u>God</u>. He will put an end to the daily <u>animal sacrifices</u> at the rebuilt Jewish Temple. He may even temporarily establish his headquarters in the Temple, thereby bringing God's sanctuary low. But God will remove the Antichrist's <u>power</u> at the Second Coming of Christ.

This verse is clearly a reference to Antiochus Epiphanes, who portrayed himself as God, stopped the Jewish animal sacrifices, defiled the Temple, dedicated it to his pagan god Zeus, and more. No one doubts that he is in view here. But there has to be more because Gabriel interpreted the vision for Daniel and said *I am making known to you what shall happen in the latter time of the indignation* (the Tribulation Period). So Antiochus Epiphanes was a type or forerunner of the coming Antichrist. His actions reveal the future.

The fact that Daniel saw the sanctuary being cast down does not mean that he saw it being demolished into rubble. It means the desecration or pollution he saw was total or as bad as it could possibly be. The Apocryphal book of 1 Maccabees reveals that it was so bad the Jews completely remodeled the interior and totally replaced the altar that was used for burnt offerings (1 Maccabees 4:43–48)

One of the great sins of Antiochus Epiphanes was the act of setting up an idol of Zeus in the Temple and forcing the Jews to worship it. In a similar fashion the False Prophet will <u>set up an image</u> of the Antichrist during the Tribulation Period and compel people to worship it. The Lord Jesus referred to that and told the Jews to

go to

pompous
Daniel 7:8, 11, 20

morning star
Isaiah 14:13–17

God
2 Thessalonians 2:4

animal sacrifices
Daniel 9:27

power
Daniel 7:26

set up an image
Revelation 13:13–15

Prince of the host
Jesus or God

go to

flee to the mountains
Matthew 24:15–16

Saints
Revelation 13:7;
Daniel 7:21, 25

Christ
Matthew 27:22–26

truth
Proverbs 12:17

deceit
Matthew 24:5, 11,
24;
2 Thessalonians
2:9–12

**sacrifices animals for
their sins**
Numbers 28:1–8

Petra
an ancient city in the
mountains of Jordan

transgression
ignoring or
disobeying God

watch for it. They should <u>flee to the mountains</u> (probably to **Petra**) when they see it happen. From that time to the end of the Tribulation Period there will be great persecution with multitudes being killed.

The High Cost of Low Living

DANIEL 8:12 *Because of transgression, an army was given over to the horn to oppose the daily sacrifices; and he cast truth down to the ground. He did all this and prospered. (NKJV)*

Because of **transgression** by those on earth, and most especially the Jews, all those who accept Christ during the Tribulation Period, all the Tribulation <u>Saints</u>, and all the Jews (believing Israel) will be given over to the power of the Antichrist. This will be the high cost of low living. Because the sacrifice of <u>Christ</u> upon the cross was rejected by the Jews, the daily sacrifice of animals at the rebuilt Jewish Temple will be rejected by God. Those sacrifices will be sinful, so authority over them will be handed to the Antichrist. He will be permitted to stop the sacrifices, and he will prosper in all his endeavors. <u>Truth</u> will be ignored in favor of <u>deceit</u> and lies.

In the Old Testament God told the Jews to <u>sacrifice animals for their sins</u>. Their animal sacrifices pictured or illustrated the sacrifice of Jesus on the cross for the sins of those who believe in Jesus. When Jesus was crucified God stopped accepting the animal sacrifices. But the Jews continued to offer them until their nation and Temple were destroyed. Now that their nation has been reestablished they want to rebuild the Temple and start offering animal sacrifices again. The problem is that God will not accept their offerings. The Jews have rejected the sacrifice of God's Son, so he will reject the sacrifice of their animals.

What an Angel Wanted to Know

DANIEL 8:13 *Then I heard a holy one speaking; and another holy one said to that certain one who was speaking, "How long will the vision be, concerning the daily sacrifices and the transgression of desolation, the giving of both the sanctuary and the host to be trampled underfoot?" (NKJV)*

Have you ever gone through a terrible time and asked, "How long? How long will God let this go on?" In his vision Daniel heard two holy ones discussing the situation. These <u>holy ones</u> were angels, and one was asking the other several questions:

holy ones
Daniel 4:13, 17, 23

desolate
Daniel 9:27

42 months
Revelation 11:2;
13:5

sanctuary
the Temple

cleansed
reconsecrated and
made fit for worship
of Almighty God

1. How long will it take for this vision of the Antichrist to be fulfilled?

2. How long will God let the Antichrist have authority over the animal sacrifices at the Temple?

3. How long will God let the Temple be <u>desolate</u> because of the rebellion?

4. How long will God let the **sanctuary** be under the Antichrist's control?

5. How long will God let his people be under the Antichrist's power?

---

what others say

Billy Graham

Our certainty that angels right now witness how we are walking through life should mightily influence the decisions we make. God is watching, and his angels are interested spectators too. The Amplified Bible expresses 1 Corinthians 4:9 this way: God has made an exhibit of us . . . a show in the world's amphitheatre—with both men and angels (as spectators).[13]

2,300 Days (Daniel's Seventy Weeks)

DANIEL 8:14 *And he said to me, "For two thousand three hundred days; then the sanctuary shall be **cleansed**." (NKJV)*

This is a very difficult passage; it may be that the interpretation is still hidden, but we do have some ideas. 2,300 days is almost 6 years and 5 months. But we know from other Scriptures that Jerusalem will be trodden down for 3 ½ years, or <u>42 months</u>, or 1,260 days. So what is the answer?

Perhaps there is a clue in the actions of Antiochus Epiphanes. It can be shown that exactly 2,300 days passed between the time he first began his persecution of the Jews and the time it ended. It can also be shown that he captured Jerusalem and started the persecutions almost three years (probably 1,040 days) before he stopped the Jewish sacrifices. If this is correct, it means the Antichrist will start

---

defilement
used for unholy or
sinful things

persecuting the Jews about 7 months after the Tribulation Period begins (6 years and 5 months plus 7 months =7 years), but the most severe persecution and **defilement** of the Temple will not begin until the Tribulation Period midpoint.

The Apocryphal book of 1 Maccabees is not recognized as Scripture but is highly regarded as historically accurate records of many of these events. For example, the rise of Antiochus Epiphanes and his desecration of the Temple can be found in chapter 1, and the purification and rededication of the Temple can be found in chapter 4. The rededication was *on the twenty-fifth of the ninth month, Chislev, in the year one hundred and forty-eight* (December 25, 164 BC). Since this would be an actual event that also refers to what will happen at the time of the end (verse 17), one can expect the Antichrist to start persecuting the Jews 2,300 days before the Tribulation Period ends (220 days after the Antichrist signs the seven-year covenant).

what others say

William E. Biederwolf

Antiochus Epiphanes took Jerusalem in 170 BC. Three years later, 167 BC, in June he sent Appolonius against the city who at that time caused all sacrifices to cease. On December of this same year Appolonius set up the heathen altar in the Temple and on December 25 the heathen sacrifices began. Three years later on this date, December 25, 164 BC, Judas Maccabeus restored the true sacrifice. The three-and-a-half years dating from June, 167 BC was a period of severe oppression and sacrilege against the Temple.[14]

There have been several unusual interpretations of this 2,300-day period. One well-known group (Seventh-Day Adventists) said it meant 2,300 years. Based on that, many Seventh-Day Adventists unwisely predicted the date of the Second Coming to be in 1843. Others have said it means 1,150 evenings and 1,150 mornings, but there are many problems with that, including the fact that it does not fit anything else in the Bible. It is best to take the 2,300 days literally.

Many people have tried to predict the date of the Second Coming, but everyone who has tried has failed. Date-setting is inconsistent with Bible teaching and a good sign of a lack of spiritual maturity.

I Was Confused

> **DANIEL 8:15** *Then it happened, when I, Daniel, had seen the vision and was seeking the meaning, that suddenly there stood before me one having the appearance of a man. (NKJV)*

While Daniel was watching the vision someone suddenly appeared in front of him. He looked like a man, but he was actually the angel Gabriel.

Gabriel, Explain the Vision

> **DANIEL 8:16** *And I heard a man's voice between the banks of the Ulai, who called, and said, "Gabriel, make this man understand the vision." (NKJV)*

Daniel was standing beside the <u>Ulai</u> River when he had this vision (the Vision of the Ram and the Goat). After seeing many things, someone who looked like a man suddenly appeared in front of him. Then there came a voice that said, "Gabriel, make this man understand the vision" (Daniel 8:16 NKJV).

This is the first time an angel is identified by name in the Bible. Only two angels are identified by name, both are identified in the book of Daniel, and both are also identified in the New Testament. The two angels are <u>Gabriel</u> and <u>Michael</u>. Gabriel will appear to Daniel again (9:21), and to Zacharias (Luke 1:19) and to Mary more than five hundred years later in the New Testament (Luke 1:26–27). Michael will appear to Daniel (10:21), and be the one who leads the war against Satan at the middle of the Tribulation Period (Revelation 12:7). This is clear evidence that angels are eternal beings.

An Important Point

> **DANIEL 8:17** *So he came near where I stood, and when he came I was afraid and fell on my face; but he said to me, "Understand, son of man, that the vision refers to the time of the end." (NKJV)*

As Gabriel came near where Daniel was standing, Daniel was overwhelmed with fear and fell on his face. Gabriel called Daniel "**<u>son of man</u>**" and told him the vision concerns the **Time of the End**.

<u>Ulai</u>
Daniel 8:2

Gabriel
Daniel 9:21;
Luke 1:19, 26

Michael
Daniel 10:21;
Jude 1:9;
Revelation 12:7

son of man
Ezekiel 2:1, 3, 6, 8;
Matthew 8:20; 9:6

son of man
son of Adam

Time of the End
End of the Times of
the Gentiles

go to

face
Matthew 17:1–9

chasten
persecute

time of the
indignation
another name for
the Tribulation
Period

Notice, he said, Time of the End and not the "end of time." The Time of the End refers to the End of the Times of the Gentiles not the end of the world.

The point of Gabriel's message is this: the fulfillment of the vision is set for some future date. The time when God will let the Antichrist take authority over the sacrifices, make the Temple desolate, and **chasten** his people is set for the End of the Times of the Gentiles.

I Couldn't Take It

DANIEL 8:18 *Now, as he was speaking with me, I was in a deep sleep with my face to the ground; but he touched me, and stood me upright. (NKJV)*

The stress was too much for Daniel. While Gabriel was speaking Daniel fainted—fell into a trance. It was a deep sleep, and he fell with his <u>face</u> to the ground. Gabriel had to revive him before continuing.

I Have News for You

DANIEL 8:19 *And he said, "Look, I am making known to you what shall happen in the latter time of the indignation; for at the appointed time the end shall be. (NKJV)*

Gabriel informed Daniel that he was going to tell him what will happen in the **time of the indignation**. Again he emphasized that the vision concerns the Time of the End, which means at the End of the Times of the Gentiles. No one can deny that there were many similarities during the reign of Antiochus Epiphanes, but that definitely was not the Tribulation Period. The terrible things in this vision are still future. All of it was future to Daniel, but to students of Bible prophecy today, these are now historical events that contain prophetic revelations about the coming Antichrist, the soon-to-be rebuilt Jewish Temple, and the approaching Tribulation Period (Other names of the Tribulation Period can be found in this book at Daniel 12:1).

Messengers from on High

One of the main tasks of an angel is that of being a messenger. God used the following angels:

1. Angels urged Lot to leave Sodom and Gomorrah. (Genesis 19:1–26)

2. An angel revealed prophecies to Zechariah. (Zechariah 1:9; 2:3; 4:1, 5; 5:5; 6:4–5)

3. An Angel told the women at the tomb that Jesus had been raised from the dead. (Matthew 28:1–7)

4. An angel announced the coming birth of John the Baptist to Zechariah. (Luke 1:11–20)

5. An angel revealed the birth of Jesus to Joseph. (Luke 1:26–38; Matthew 1:20–21)

6. Angels announced the birth of Jesus to shepherds. (Luke 2:8–20)

7. An angel told Peter to wake up, put on his clothes, and follow him. (Acts 12:1–11)

8. An angel told Paul he would stand trial before Caesar. (Acts 27:21–26)

ram
Daniel 8:3–7

goat
Daniel 8:5–8

The Two-Horned Ram Explained

DANIEL 8:20 *The ram which you saw, having the two horns— they are the kings of Media and Persia.* (NKJV)

Without this interpretation from God there is no telling what kind of strange explanations people would come up with. However, Gabriel clearly identified the <u>ram</u> with the two horns as representing the combined kingdom of the Medes and Persians.

The Male Goat Explained

DANIEL 8:21 *And the male goat is the kingdom of Greece. The large horn that is between its eyes is the first king.* (NKJV)

Gabriel's next revelation was the identity of the male <u>goat</u>. After learning what the two-horned ram symbolized we could probably figure this one out, but we do not have to. The male goat represents the kingdom of Greece. The large horn represents its first king. History has revealed him to be Alexander the Great.

four
Daniel 8:8

horn
Daniel 8:9

fierce features
a striking, stern-faced appearance

sinister schemes
satanic deceit and treachery

It helps to know that most or all of the Old Testament empires were influenced by astrology. All of them had professionals who studied the stars and the signs of the Zodiac. Persia chose as its symbol the sign of Aries or the ram, and Greece chose as its symbol the sign of Capricorn or the goat. Thus, our all-knowing God used the appropriate symbols in Daniel's vision to depict these empires.

The Four Horns Explained

DANIEL 8:22 *As for the broken horn and the <u>four</u> that stood up in its place, four kingdoms shall arise out of that nation, but not with its power. (NKJV)*

Here Gabriel explained the meaning of the four horns. They represent the four kingdoms that would emerge from the kingdom of the horn that was broken off (emerge from the kingdom of Greece). These were the four generals who divided up the Greek Empire following the death of Alexander the Great: Cassander, Lysemachus, Seleucus, and Ptolemy. The strongest of the four eventually turned out to be Seleucus. It was his empire that produced Antiochus Epiphanes, but none of these four, even at their greatest strength, ever approached the power of Alexander the Great.

The Next World Leader

DANIEL 8:23
"And in the latter time of their kingdom,
When the transgressors have reached their fullness,
A king shall arise,
Having fierce features,
Who understands sinister schemes. (NKJV)

This is the small <u>horn</u>. He will appear at the Time of the End. What he does will take place in the Time of Indignation. It will be near the end of the reign of the empires that emerged from the Greek empire. The wickedness on earth, and most especially the wickedness in Israel, will be great. This sinful era will provoke the terrible wrath of God. He will permit a king with **fierce features** to arise; a man who is bold, determined, and reckless. This man will understand **sinister schemes** and will be a man (the Antichrist) with supernatural occultic powers.

This verse predicts the rise of Antiochus Epiphanes, but it also foreshadows the rise of Antichrist. One (Antiochus) would appear in the latter time of the four kingdoms coming out of the Greek Empire, and the other will appear at the time of the end. One (Antiochus) would be a madman with demonic characteristics, and the other will be far more evil and satanic (Revelation 13:4–8). One (Antiochus) would spread evil and destruction in the Middle East, and the other will spread it all over the world. This is critical to our understanding of where this modern drive toward Globalism will wind up.

go to

power and authority
Revelation 13:5–8

whole earth
Daniel 7:23–24

satanic
2 Thessalonians 2:9;
Revelation 13:2, 4

The word *Antichrist* appears only four times in the Bible (1 John 2:18, 22; 4:3; 2 John 1:7), but he will be so prominent at the end of the age the Scriptures mention him more than 100 times. The book of Revelation calls him a beast more than 30 times. The following chart gives a glimpse of what he will be like:

Titles of the Antichrist

Term Used	Scripture
Vile person	Daniel 11:21
Worthless shepherd	Zechariah 11:17
Man of sin	2 Thessalonians 2:3
Son of perdition	2 Thessalonians 2:3
Lawless one	2 Thessalonians 2:8
Beast out of the bottomless pit	Revelation 11:7
Beast that will go to perdition	Revelation 17:8

key point

More About the Next World Leader

DANIEL 8:24
His power shall be mighty, but not by his own power;
He shall destroy fearfully,
And shall prosper and thrive;
He shall destroy the mighty, and also the holy people. (NKJV)

"His power shall be mighty" is shown in other Scriptures to mean that he will have <u>power and authority</u> over the <u>whole earth</u>. But not by his power is usually thought to be a reference to his <u>satanic</u> power. "He sshall destroy fearfully" could be a reference to his amazing high-tech weapons (nuclear bombs, smart bombs, laser-guided missiles, biological and chemical weapons) or it could refer to the great devastation these weapons will cause during the Tribulation Period.

"He shall destroy the mighty, and also the holy people" refers to all those who oppose him but especially to those who accept Christ after the Rapture and, of course, the Jews (believing Israel), God's chosen people.

Prophetic scholars understand that the word *Antichrist* can be translated "against the Christ" (anti) and "instead of the Christ" (a phony replacement for the Christ). Other identifying characteristics are shown in the following chart:

Characteristics of the Antichrist

Attribute	Scripture
He will rise to power at the time of the end or latter time.	Daniel 8:19–23
He will be cunning, cause deceit, and exalt himself.	Daniel 8:25
He will oppose Jesus and claim to be God.	Daniel 8:25; 2 Thessalonians 2:4
He will sign a seven-year peace treaty and break it.	Daniel 9:27
He will locate his government and religion in Babylon.	Zechariah 5:5–11
He will be given power over the final world government.	Revelation 13:7
He and the False Prophet will control global trade.	Revelation 13:16–18

The Rise and Fall of a World Leader

DANIEL 8:25
Through his cunning
He shall cause deceit to prosper under his rule;
And he shall exalt himself in his heart.
He shall destroy many in their prosperity.
He shall even rise against the Prince of princes;
But he shall be broken without human means. (NKJV)

This is more of Gabriel's revelation about the Antichrist. Satan's man will come out of the <u>bottomless pit</u> and quickly rise to power over the whole world. Notice the following:

1. *"He shall cause <u>deceit</u> to prosper"* (Daniel 8:25 NKJV) speaks of his corruption and treachery. More often than not he will use deceit to achieve his goals.

2. *"He shall exalt himself in his heart"* (8:25 NKJV) refers to his <u>self-exaltation</u> and his views of others. He will magnify himself and think what he does is right because he is better than others.

go to

bottomless pit
Revelation 17:8

deceit
Matthew 24:4;
2 John 1:7

self-exaltation
2 Thessalonians 2:4

3. *"In their prosperity"* (8:25 NKJV) refers to another one of his favorite tools. He will make covenants and treaties to lull people into a false sense of security. Then he will break them.

4. *"He shall destroy many"* (8:25 NKJV) describes the result of his treachery and false <u>covenants</u>. Multitudes of betrayed people will be struck down and <u>perish</u>.

5. *"He shall even rise against the Prince of princes [Jesus]"* (8:25 NKJV) means he will be against the Christ. He will even take an army and try to make <u>war</u> against Jesus.

6. *"He shall be broken"* (8:25 NKJV) refers to the fact that he will be cast alive into the <u>lake of fire</u> burning with brimstone.

7. *"He shall be broken without human means"* (8:25 NKJV) but by Jesus, the <u>King</u> of kings and Lord of lords.

go to

covenants
Daniel 9:27

perish
Zechariah 13:8

war
Revelation 19:19

lake of fire
Revelation 19:20

King
Revelation 19:16–21

evenings
Daniel 9:21

The Antichrist will be a failure in God's eyes, but for a time the world will view him as one of the greatest leaders it has ever known. His ability to lead is highlighted in the following

Leadership of the Antichrist

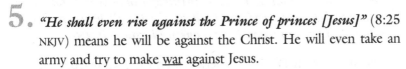

Attribute	Scripture
He will be very intelligent.	Daniel 8:23
He will be a great orator.	Daniel 11:36
He will be a master politician.	Revelation 17:11–12
He will control global trade.	Daniel 11:43; Revelation 13:16–17
He will be a military expert.	Revelation 6:2; 13:2
He will be religious but lost.	2 Thessalonians 2:4; Revelation 13:8

key point

It Is Hard to Believe

DANIEL 8:26
> *And the vision of the evenings and mornings*
> *Which was told is true;*
> *Therefore seal up the vision,*
> *For it refers to many days in the future."* (NKJV)

Daniel must have been appalled at the fact that the Temple will be desecrated for 2,300 <u>evenings</u> and mornings. Most would think that people would have more respect or that God would put a stop to it sooner, but Gabriel assured Daniel that it will end. Then he told

go to

coming
Luke 21:26

understand
Daniel 9:22

Daniel to seal up the vision, which is generally understood as "do not reveal the interpretation (keep it a secret)." This vision will be fulfilled during the Tribulation Period.

It Was Sickening

DANIEL 8:27 *And I, Daniel, fainted and was sick for days; afterward I arose and went about the king's business. I was astonished by the vision, but no one understood it.* (NKJV)

The stress from Daniel's experience and the knowledge of those things <u>coming</u> on the world were almost too much for him. He was tired and became sick with an illness that lasted for several days. Afterward, he got up and went back to work. But he was devastated by the vision and there was still much that he did not <u>understand</u>. It may be that Gabriel did not tell him more because Daniel could not handle it all at once. We will see in chapter 9 that Daniel was told more at a later time.

what others say

H. A. Ironside

The centuries since have borne witness to the truth of much of it; the days to come will manifest the balance.[15]

Chapter Wrap-Up

- Daniel had a vision in the third year of King Belshazzar. First, he saw a two-horned ram with one horn longer than the other. The ram (Medo-Persia) was powerful and became great. Its two horns represented the kings of Media and Persia. The short horn represented Darius and the long horn represented Cyrus. Their kingdom defeated Babylon and became the next great Gentile kingdom (Daniel 8:1–4, 21).

- Next Daniel saw a male goat (Greece) with one large horn moving swiftly across the whole earth. The goat attacked the ram with great rage and defeated it. At the peak of the goat's power the large horn broke off and four weaker horns grew up in its place. The male goat represents Greece, and its large horn represents Alexander the Great. The goat defeated the two-horned ram of Medo-Persia, but died shortly thereafter. The four weaker horns represent Alexander's four generals who took his place (Daniel 8:5–8, 21–23).

- Then Daniel saw another horn. It was very small at first, but it grew to the heavens, opposed Jesus, stopped the Jewish sacrifices, desecrated the Temple, and made war on God's people. It was successful in everything it did. This horn represents the Antichrist. He will begin as a little horn but will grow until he rules the world. He will be deceitful and corrupt, cause great destruction on earth, kill most of God's people, and be anti-God and anti-Christ (Daniel 8:9–13, 23–25).

- The Antichrist will be very powerful, but God is greater. This future world leader will be destroyed (Daniel 8:25).

- These things were almost too much for Daniel to handle. In his vision, the angel Gabriel appeared to him and terrified him to the point he fell on his face and went into a deep sleep. Afterward he was exhausted and sick for several days, and found the whole event appalling and beyond his understanding (Daniel 8:17–18, 27).

Study Questions

1. Why would a loving God permit an evil man like the Antichrist to rise to power and do these terrible things?

2. Who or what should people rely on to interpret Bible prophecy?

3. What is the relationship between Bible prophecy and history?

4. When the world gets a one-world government will it have freedom of religion, peace, and safety?

5. Where will the Antichrist get his power? How much will he have and what will be his final end?

Daniel 9 A Fantastic Prayer— A Fantastic Answer

Chapter Highlights:
• Daniel's Discovery
• Daniel's Confession
• Daniel's Plea for Forgiveness
• Gabriel Appears
• Seventy Weeks

Let's Get Started

In order to fully understand Daniel's prayer found in chapter 9 we need to begin with some background on the covenant God made with Israel. God had promised <u>Abraham</u>, <u>Isaac</u>, and <u>Jacob</u> many descendants, prosperity, and land. When Jacob had an encounter with God his <u>name</u> was changed to Israel, his children became known as the children of Israel, and his country became known as the land of Israel. During a great famine the children of Israel migrated to the land of Egypt where they eventually became slaves. They remained slaves until <u>Moses</u> led them out of Egypt 430 years later. He took them to Mount Sinai where God swore to keep the promises he made to their <u>forefathers</u>. He made a special covenant with them and gave them specific instructions about keeping it. A major provision concerned the <u>land</u>: they agreed to let the land rest every seventh year. If they kept their part of the covenant, God promised to bless them. If they did not, God said he would chastise them. If the chastisement didn't work, he said he would destroy their nation and <u>scatter</u> the people among the nations. For hundreds of years, Israel went through cycles of rebellion and chastisement that kept them in line. But eventually the nation of Israel split into a Northern Kingdom called Israel and a Southern Kingdom called Judah (see Illustration #4). At first, the Northern Kingdom of Israel was the most rebellious. It would not listen and was taken captive by the Assyrians. Then things worsened in the Southern Kingdom and God began to deal with it through the prophet Jeremiah. He had <u>Jeremiah</u> warn the people of Judah that they should repent or he would destroy their nation and turn them over to the Babylonians for seventy years. Of course they didn't listen, and that's why we find them in Babylonian hands in the book of Daniel.

But that is just part of the story. The time off the land would be for the sin of stealing crops by planting one in the Sabbath year when the land should be resting. But keeping the Sabbath of the land is just one of the commandments. There are nine more. And the rest

go to

Abraham
Genesis 11:31–12:7

Isaac
Genesis 26:1–5

Jacob
Genesis 28:1–22

name
Genesis 32:22–32

Moses
Exodus 12:31–42

forefathers
Deuteronomy 7:6–8

land
Leviticus 25; 26

scatter
Leviticus 26:30–34

Jeremiah
Jeremiah 25:1–13

Darius
Daniel 5:31

of the story is the fact that God made it clear that he would punish them seven times more for the sin of breaking the other commandments: adultery, idolatry, lying, killing the prophets, and all the rest. He warned them about this over and over again (Leviticus 26:18, 21, 24, 28).

Now, with this background information covered we can turn our attention to chapter 9. This chapter can be divided into two parts: (1) Daniel's famous prayer, and (2) God's answer to his prayer. The prayer is unquestionably one of the greatest prayers in the Bible, and God's answer is unquestionably one of the greatest prophetic revelations in the Bible. We have in these two things an excellent example of how to pray, and a compact and comprehensive outline of the End of the (Gentile) Age.

It is very important to keep the Sabbath and all the commandments. If the Jews would do it, God would bless them. If they didn't, God would give them time to repent. Repentance would bring restoration. No repentance would bring punishment. Ignoring the punishment would eventually get their nation destroyed and they would be punished seven times more. We will soon learn that they would eventually steal 70 crops, be off the land 70 years, and be punished another 490 years (7 x 70) for their other sins.

God's Standard of Punishment

If the Jews Stole	They Would Be Off the Land	They Would Be Punished 7 Times More for Their Sins
1 crop in 7 years	1 year	7 years
2 crops in 14 years	2 years	14 years
3 crops in 21 years	3 years	21 years
70 crops in 490 years	70 years	490 years

The Time

DANIEL 9:1 *In the first year of Darius the son of Ahasuerus, of the lineage of the Medes, who was made king over the realm of the Chaldeans—* (NKJV)

We have shown that Babylon fell around 539 BC (see Time Line #1, Appendix A) and Darius the Mede took over the kingdom. Historians tell us he died about two years later. Since our present verse took place during the first year of his reign, the time of this event is established at around 538–537 BC, which is probably the same year as chapter 6 when Daniel was thrown into the lions' den. Also, since chapter 1 opens around the year 605 BC when Daniel was about thirteen or fourteen years old, we can calculate that Daniel and all Israel had been in captivity about sixty-nine years, and Daniel was now a little more than eighty years old.

Daniel's Discovery

> **DANIEL 9:2** *in the first year of his reign I, Daniel, understood by the books the number of the years specified by the word of the LORD through Jeremiah the prophet, that He would accomplish seventy years in the desolations of Jerusalem. (NKJV)*

We know that it was a time of upheaval in Daniel's life. Babylon had just fallen, a new empire had taken over, and a sick king was on the throne. We also know that Daniel regularly <u>prayed</u> three times a day. It is not unreasonable to assume that he also read the Scriptures when he prayed.

While reading the book of Jeremiah, which Daniel considered to be the Word of God, Daniel made an interesting discovery. He read that Jerusalem would be desolate for <u>seventy years</u>. He was probably concerned about his people, and even though he was a prophet, he wanted to know what the other prophets had to say about the future of the Jews. So he read prophecy. Isn't it fascinating that we still have that same prophecy 2,500 years later?

We can read what God said would happen before it took place. We can read what God said about the punishment of Babylon before Belshazzar was born, before he drank out of the Temple vessels, and before the hand wrote on the wall. We can read that Daniel, whom Jesus called a prophet, interpreted Jeremiah's prophecies literally. It is amazing!

But we do not want to go too far. Daniel only read about the first phase of Judah's punishment, the part that said the Jews would be off the land seventy years for stealing seventy crops. At this point, he did not know about the second phase, whereby the Jews would be punished seven times more (another 490 years) for their other sins.

One would be wise to note that God said the land would be desolate seventy years. He even said the Jews would spend the seventy

prayed
Daniel 6:10

seventy years
Jeremiah 25:1–13;
29:10;
2 Chronicles
36:15–21

go to

prayer
Jonah 2:1–10

fasting
Matthew 4:2

sackcloth
Genesis 37:34

ashes
Jonah 3:6;
Job 2:8

supplications
humble prayers

sackcloth
a very coarse
material similar
to burlap

years in Babylon (Jeremiah 25:11). He also said he would punish Babylon after the seventy years (Jeremiah 25:12). He added that the Jews would return home after being off the land seventy years (Jeremiah 29:10). And afterward he said he did it to fulfill his words by the mouth of Jeremiah so he could get the seventy stolen crops (Sabbaths) back (2 Chronicles 36:21).

Daniel's Response

DANIEL 9:3 *Then I set my face toward the Lord God to make request by prayer and supplications, with fasting, sackcloth, and ashes.* (NKJV)

After discovering in the Word of God the fact that Jerusalem would be desolate for seventy years Daniel began to fast and pray. Aside from the fact that he was obviously praying for God's will, notice these things:

1. The God he turned to was the Lord God.

2. He pleaded with God in <u>prayer</u>.

3. He pleaded with God in **supplications**.

4. He pleaded with God by denying himself through <u>fasting</u>.

5. He pleaded with God by wearing drab and uncomfortable **<u>sackcloth</u>**.

6. He pleaded with God by dirtying himself with <u>ashes</u> (sitting in them and/or putting them on his face or head).

This is a good example of what prophetic study will do. The knowledge that God is in control caused this great government leader, Daniel, to set aside what he was doing to find a place where he could think about the things of God. It caused him to humble himself (make pleading requests of God), deny himself (fasting), and humiliate himself (wear sackcloth and ashes). Other verses show he prayed for himself (confession) and others (intercession). Knowledge of Bible prophecy causes spiritual purity and growth.

go to

pray
1 Thessalonians
5:17–18

what others say

Theodore H. Epp

We cannot be second Daniels, but we have Daniel's God as our God. The same prayer privileges are ours as were his. We have an excellent spirit within, the Holy Spirit of God Himself who indwells us.[2]

God has asked his people to approach him in prayer. This is an important way Christians show their faith and dependence upon him. But prayer is more than talking to God. It is more than an outward show of humility. True prayer is deliberate, humble, and sincere. On occasion, God's people endeavor to show this by making sacrifices, chastening themselves, and demonstrating their grief. When done for the right reason the goal is to get God's attention and not the attention of human beings.

apply it

It does no good to fast, wear sackcloth, or sit in ashes if it is done for show or not done sincerely. Also understand that for health reasons some people should not fast without consulting a doctor first.

He Is My God

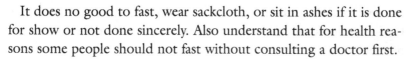

DANIEL 9:4 *And I prayed to the* LORD *my God, and made confession, and said, "O Lord, great and awesome God, who keeps His covenant and mercy with those who love Him, and with those who keep His commandments,* (NKJV)

Daniel addressed his <u>prayer</u> to "the LORD my God." "My God" shows humility, submission, and a personal relationship. True prayer is deliberate, humble, and sincere. He followed that up with praise and respect by calling God the great and awesome God. This recognizes God's amazing ability to do mighty things. Daniel continued his praise by acknowledging that God is a God who keeps his covenant of love with all who love him and obey his commands. This is an acknowledgment that Judah's problems were not because of a

go to

confess
Romans 14:11–12

emasculated
made eunuchs

lack of faithfulness on God's part, but rather, Judah's problems were because the nation did not keep its part of the covenant.

God makes covenants because he loves people, and he absolutely will not go back on them. His covenants are the driving force of prophecy. When God makes promises he has to fulfill them. If he doesn't fulfill them, he lied or the Bible is wrong. Neither option is acceptable. Therefore, students of the Bible should expect every detail of every covenant to be literally fulfilled.

What Is Confession?

We need to know because it is written: "At the name of Jesus every knee should bow, of those in heaven, and of those on earth, and of those under the earth, and that every tongue should <u>confess</u> that Jesus Christ is Lord, to the glory of God the Father" (Philippians 2:10–11 NKJV). So then, each of us will give an account of himself to God. Webster's dictionary says *confession* means "to admit one's guilt" or "to acknowledge one's sins." That is good, but not good enough. A better definition says *confession* means "to say the same thing." We have to say the same thing that is in our heart and the same thing that God says about our sin. We have to be sincere because there is nothing that we do and nothing in our heart that God does not know. We have to say the same thing because we cannot fool God.

<u>We Are Guilty</u>

> **DANIEL 9:5** *we have sinned and committed iniquity, we have done wickedly and rebelled, even by departing from Your precepts and Your judgments. (NKJV)*

This is true confession and the word "we" is prominent in this prayer. Notice three things:

1. We have sinned and committed iniquity.

2. We have done wickedly and rebelled.

3. We have departed from your precepts and judgments.

Why were Judah, Jerusalem, and the Temple destroyed? Why were hundreds of thousands of people killed, **emasculated**, and raped?

Why were so many people made slaves? The answers to these questions—sin, rebellion, and breaking God's commands and laws. Who did Daniel blame? Did he blame the leaders of Judah? Did he blame the wicked people in his nation? No. He identified himself with his people by saying we are at fault.

We Have Not Listened

> **DANIEL 9:6** *Neither have we heeded Your servants the prophets, who spoke in Your name to our kings and our princes, to our fathers and all the people of the land. (NKJV)*

Daniel confessed that he and the people of Judah were not only guilty of **sins of commission** but were guilty of **sins of omission** as well. More specifically, he confessed that everyone <u>refused to listen</u> to the prophets of God who tried to warn them about the impending danger.

This is a major problem today in all of society, including the Church. More than 25 percent of the Bible is prophecy, but most people do not want to know what it says. Jesus told his people to watch the signs, but the vast majority of Church members are not interested and are not looking. The same God who dealt with Israel's refusal to listen is still on the throne. To him, Gentile rebellion is no different from Jewish rebellion. Ignoring his Word is a sure way to invite his judgment.

The seriousness of this cannot be overstated. God said he will gather all nations for judgment at the Battle of Armageddon because they have scattered the Jews and divided his land (Joel 3:2). This has been pointed out to world leaders, but they insist on driving the Jews off the West Bank so they can divide the land and create a Palestinian state there. Hearing and obeying the Word of God would avoid the Battle of Armageddon, but this deliberate decision to ignore it will eventually bring the Gentile nations to their destruction.

go to

refused to listen
Jeremiah 25:2–11

sins of commission
wrongdoing, all thoughts and acts contrary to God's will and laws

sins of omission
not doing God's will or keeping his laws

what others say

Sinclair B. Ferguson

Throughout his prayer Daniel refers to God's word in a variety of ways. It expresses His "covenant" and His "commandments" (v. 4); it contains His "precepts" and His "judgments" (v. 5). It was written by "Your servants the prophets who spoke

> in Your name" (v. 6). It is "the voice of the Lord our God" (vv. 10, 11, 14) and contains His "law" (v. 10, 11). In it are found "the curse and the oath written in the Law of Moses the servant of God" (v. 11). They are God's own "words" (v. 12).[3]

Daniel 9:4 mentions the <u>love</u> of God, and we know that the Bible teaches that God is love. We can be thankful for that. But should preachers then preach nothing but that? Should preachers just stick to sugar-coated messages about the love of God, Fatherhood of God, and brotherhood of man? Should society brand as fanatics those preachers who say our nation and the Church are sick, and unless there is repentance we will all come under the judgment of God? Would we be wise to do like Judah and not listen to the call for repentance?

Unfaithfulness Has a Price

DANIEL 9:7 *O Lord, righteousness belongs to You, but to us shame of face, as it is this day—to the men of Judah, to the inhabitants of Jerusalem and all Israel, those near and those far off in all the countries to which You have driven them, because of the unfaithfulness which they have committed against You.* (NKJV)

Here Daniel made a comparison between God and all the people of Israel and Judah. He noted that God is **righteous**, but all the people were covered with <u>shame</u>. Because of their unfaithfulness to God, wherever they went they would carry their shame. God was right, they were wrong, and it was a disgrace.

Notice how specific Daniel got in this prayer. In verse 6, he said God's servants the prophets spoke in his name to our kings and to our princes, to our fathers and to all the people of the land. In this verse, he said shame belongs to the men of Judah, to the inhabitants of Jerusalem and all Israel, those near and those far off in all the countries to which you have driven them. No matter their lot in life they heard God's Word, and no matter where they lived they should be ashamed. Every Israelite on earth was guilty.

Some experts teach that the ten tribes that made up the Northern <u>Kingdom</u> called Israel were lost or extinct by this time. But Daniel did not believe this. It is true that the nation had been destroyed and

love
Daniel 9:4;
Ephesians 2:4;
1 John 4:8

righteous
Isaiah 5:16

shame
Proverbs 3:33–35;
13:18

kingdom
Ezekiel 37:15–22

righteous
sinless, God always
does the right thing

taken captive by Assyria, but pay close attention to the fact that Daniel mentions all Israel, both near and far. In his opinion the ten tribes of Israel were scattered with those that were close to him and those that were far away in other countries.

go to

sinned
Romans 3:23;
1 John 1:8, 10

Shame! Shame!

> **DANIEL 9:8** *O Lord, to us belongs shame of face, to our kings, our princes, and our fathers, because we have sinned against You. (NKJV)*

mercy
showing pity, love; and forgiveness

forgiveness
acting as though it never happened

Daniel was earnestly humbling himself. He was also acting as a priest confessing sin on behalf of the entire nation. He was admitting guilt on behalf of everyone; that everyone was literally covered with shame. Why? Because everyone had <u>sinned</u> against God.

Consider Seven Biblical Reasons Why Your Prayer May Not Be Answered

1. Unbelief or doubting God (James 1:6; Hebrews 11:6)

2. Asking for the wrong reason (James 4:3)

3. Sin in your life (Isaiah 59:2; John 9:31; 1 Peter 3:7)

4. Neglecting the needs of others (Proverbs 21:13)

5. Failure to forgive others (Mark 11:25)

6. It is not God's will (Luke 22:42)

7. Self-exaltation (Luke 18:9–14)

key point

The Character of God

> **DANIEL 9:9** *To the Lord our God belong mercy and forgiveness, though we have rebelled against Him. (NKJV)*

Daniel was simply reminding God of his **mercy** and **forgiveness**. He knew that God could not abandon his people even though the people had rebelled.

In verse 7, he talked of God's righteousness. God was right to do what he did. It was Israel's fault. The Jews deserved to have Jerusalem and the Temple destroyed. There was no reason to restore Israel except for the mercy and forgiveness of God.

If you were God, would you <u>forgive</u> the Jews? They were guilty. They rebelled. They broke the covenant. They ignored and killed the prophets. They lied. They committed adultery. They worshiped idols. If you were God, would you show <u>mercy</u> and take them back? Obviously you are just a human being, but the Lord is slow to <u>anger</u>, abounding in <u>love</u>, and forgiving of sin and <u>rebellion</u>.

We Have Been Unfaithful

> DANIEL 9:10 *We have not obeyed the voice of the LORD our God, to walk in His laws, which He set before us by His servants the prophets. (NKJV)*

Israel and Judah had the Scriptures and prided themselves on following God, but Daniel confesses that they did not obey God.

They also prided themselves on following <u>Moses</u>, but again we hear Daniel confess that they did not keep the **Law of Moses**. Actually, they did not keep any of the other laws given through God's servants the <u>prophets</u> either.

Consider This Bible Prayer List

1. For those in authority over us (1 Timothy 2:2)

2. For people to do God's work (Matthew 9:38)

3. For those who persecute us (Matthew 5:44)

4. For God's kingdom to come, his will to be done, food, forgiveness, and deliverance from temptation (Matthew 6:9–13)

5. For the peace of Jerusalem (Psalm 122:6)

6. For others (Ephesians 6:18; 3:14–19)

7. For wisdom (James 1:5)

We Chose to Be Cursed

> DANIEL 9:11 *Yes, all Israel has transgressed Your law, and has departed so as not to obey Your voice; therefore the curse and the*

go to

forgive
Nehemiah 9:17;
Matthew 6:14–15;
Mark 11:25;
1 John 1:9

mercy
Deuteronomy 4:31;
Matthew 5:7

anger
Exodus 34:6–7

love
Romans 5:8

rebellion
Numbers 14:18

Moses
Exodus 2:1–10

Law of Moses
Exodus 24:12–18;
Deuteronomy
5:1–21

prophets
Matthew 23:29–32;
Luke 11:47–48;
1 Thessalonians
2:14–15

Law of Moses
all the rules God
gave to Moses

oath written in the Law of Moses the servant of God have been poured out on us, because we have sinned against Him. (NKJV)

Daniel confessed that everyone had broken the **law** and everyone had <u>turned away</u> from God. It wasn't a matter of ignorance or misunderstanding. It was a deliberate refusal to obey God. Notice the terrible result. They were under the **curses** and judgments of God written in the Law of Moses. These were clearly spelled out, but many people simply could not accept the fact that God would put anyone under a curse. The problem was they were blaming God instead of themselves. The reason Israel came under the curses was because they sinned against God.

The Law of Moses includes the Ten Commandments. God gave them. They contain his will for our lives. In the United States, some people want them taken out of the courthouses and off of all public property. They want to act like the commandments do not exist. Everyone would be wise to pay attention to what happened to Israel when they did this.

Daniel had already confessed that God is <u>righteous</u>. God never does wrong. Take the time to study Deuteronomy 28 and notice that God's covenant with Israel was conditional. If Israel kept the covenant he would bless the nation in many ways. If Israel broke the covenant, kept breaking it, and refused to repent, many curses would come upon the nation. This was Israel's choice: (1) obedience with blessings, or (2) disobedience with curses. Israel eventually chose the wrong thing.

<u>You Have Fulfilled Your Words</u>

DANIEL 9:12 *And He has confirmed His words, which He spoke against us and against our judges who judged us, by bringing upon us a great disaster; for under the whole heaven such has never been done as what has been done to Jerusalem. (NKJV)*

Daniel acknowledged that God simply did what he promised if Israel refused to keep the <u>covenant</u>. And it was terrible. No city had ever been attacked, plundered, and destroyed like Jerusalem. No temple had ever been desecrated and destroyed like the Temple at Jerusalem. Nebuchadnezzar struck Jerusalem with a vengeance unlike anything known before.

go to

law
Leviticus 26:14–17

turned away
Isaiah 53:6

curses
Deuteronomy 28:15–68

righteous
Daniel 9:7

covenant
Exodus 24:8

law
the Law of Moses

curses
the predictions of harm that would befall them

key point

According to several polls most Americans and most church members believe in a place called <u>hell</u>. But for many seminary professors, theologians, and liberal pastors the idea of a place called hell is repulsive and unbelievable. They say God is too loving and compassionate to cast people into hell. The idea of hell is a relic of pagan thinking, and those who believe in hell believe in a God who is cruel, vindictive, and capable of doing evil. It is up to each person to choose what they want to believe, but there is no escaping the fact that the Bible plainly teaches the existence of hell and the fact that God fulfills his words. Please read all of Deuteronomy 28 again and then re-read this verse. What do you think?

We Refused to Change

> DANIEL 9:13 *As it is written in the Law of Moses, all this disaster has come upon us; yet we have not made our prayer before the LORD our God, that we might turn from our iniquities and understand Your truth. (NKJV)*

Daniel is confessing that the disasters had come upon him and his people in exactly the same way it was written in the Law of Moses. God did not deviate from what was written. Even though the disasters had struck the people, they still refused to <u>seek</u> the Lord. They still refused to repent of their sins, and they still refused to <u>listen</u> to the truths in the <u>Word</u> of God.

God Is Righteous

> DANIEL 9:14 *Therefore the LORD has kept the disaster in mind, and brought it upon us; for the LORD our God is righteous in all the works which He does, though we have not obeyed His voice. (NKJV)*

Some complain about the slow pace and lack of justice in the United States. It is no secret that some cases drag through the courts for years and some criminals get light sentences because judges hesitate to enforce the penalties of the law. It is different with God. He is patient, but he does not hesitate to enforce his Word. He did not hesitate to bring disaster upon the Jews, and he will not hesitate to send a Tribulation Period to punish others.

hell
Matthew 10:28–33;
Mark 9:42–49;
Luke 16:19–31

seek
2 Chronicles 7:14

listen
Leviticus 26:14–46

Word
Matthew 24:35

Here Daniel repeats the fact that God is <u>righteous</u>. God never mistreats people. His character will not allow him to do that. Nevertheless, he will not allow sin to go unpunished. The Jews knew that, and still disobeyed him.

When Noah was alive the earth was corrupt and filled with violence. The wickedness of man was great, and his thoughts were constantly on evil. So God told Noah he intended to destroy the earth with a <u>flood</u>, and he had Noah warn the wicked. No one listened, yet God did not hesitate to send the flood.

Today we have a large amount of historical and scientific evidence to show that the flood did happen. In our modern society multitudes are disobeying God. But according to the Bible he is still righteous and disobedience will bring his wrath. This is something the Church should be concerned about too. Many church members are asking for prayer in schools when they never have prayer in their homes. Many others cry out for character in our government leaders, but they never cry out for character in their church. What does a righteous God think of all this?

go to

righteous
Psalm 96:11–13

flood
Genesis 6–8

mighty hand
Jeremiah 32:17–25

plagues
Exodus 7:14–12:30

God's Name Is Great

DANIEL 9:15 *And now, O LORD our God, who brought Your people out of the land of Egypt with a mighty hand, and made Yourself a name, as it is this day—we have sinned, we have done wickedly! (NKJV)*

Here Daniel was remembering that God delivered the children of Israel out of the land of Egypt. "With a <u>mighty hand</u>" refers to the ten <u>plagues</u> or ten great miracles God performed to convince Pharoah to let them go. Daniel called attention to the fact that God's great acts gained God great fame. Then Daniel repeated something he had already said in several ways: the people of Israel and Judah had sinned. It was not God who had done wrong. It was the Jews. We know Israel's God is the true God because he works through them and refuses to let their nation be destroyed.

what others say

John White

I need to believe two things when I pray: first, that God exists; and, second, that he rewards those who earnestly seek him. I

holy mountain
Psalm 2:6

anger
Psalm 7:11

seventy years
Jeremiah 25:1–13;
29:10

holy
God declares it is
different or separate
from any other city.

iniquities
general term refer-
ring to all kinds of
wickedness

found it easy enough to believe that God exists, but I have had great difficulty in believing that he would answer me. I sought him earnestly enough, but I felt neither good enough nor spiritual enough to deserve answers. I know that this is nonsense, but my feelings interfered with my faith and, in my case, it became a serious problem. Then one day it was as though God said, "Don't you trust me?" Light began to break around me, and my heart melted. Even now that question brings tears to my eyes. Not trust him? How could I do anything but trust him after all his goodness to me? I need to have confidence in the person whom I know and love.[4]

Is God's name Jehovah, Allah, Diana, Gaia, Ishtar, Mother Earth, or what? His name is very important. The world cannot know who to worship unless it knows God's name. What is God's name, and who do we worship? That is one reason why Jehovah works through Israel and refuses to let the tiny nation be wiped out. He is showing the world that Israel's God, the Lord God Jehovah, is God.

Jerusalem Is God's City

DANIEL 9:16 *O Lord, according to all Your righteousness, I pray, let Your anger and Your fury be turned away from Your city Jerusalem, Your **holy mountain**; because for our sins, and for the **iniquities** of our fathers, Jerusalem and Your people are a reproach to all those around us. (NKJV)*

Does God get angry? Would God pour out his anger on anyone or anything? The person who says no either does not know or does not believe what's in the Bible. God does get angry, and he did use wicked nations to vent his wrath on Israel and Judah.

But let's notice something. Daniel said, "I, Daniel, understood by the books the number of the years specified by the word of the LORD through Jeremiah the prophet, that He would accomplish seventy years in the desolations of Jerusalem" (Daniel 9:2 NKJV). He also said, "The LORD our God is righteous in all the works which He does" (Daniel 9:14 NKJV). And we know righteous means God always does the right thing. In this verse, Daniel 9:16, Daniel is appealing to God's righteousness to turn away his anger and fury from Jerusalem because the seventy years is almost up. A righteous God would not allow that time to be exceeded.

Who owns Jerusalem? God. Does Jerusalem have a special status? Yes. God has kept it and plans to use it for his own purposes. Anyone who tries to do anything with it other than what God wants is going against his will. What has caused Jerusalem to be such a problem for the world? Sin on behalf of the Jews.

For Your Glory

DANIEL 9:17 *Now therefore, our God, hear the prayer of Your servant, and his supplications, and for the Lord's sake cause Your face to shine on Your sanctuary, which is desolate. (NKJV)*

God does not have to listen to our prayers and petitions. Daniel was well aware of that, so he asked God to hear him. The thoughts of his mind were focusing upon the Temple, which was God's house, God's own dwelling place on earth when the nation was faithful. Daniel pleaded with God to look upon his requests favorably and restore the Temple.

But his request went beyond the restoration of the Temple. He called for God's face to shine on the sanctuary. This was a request for the presence of God to return to a rebuilt Temple. God is light. He was present with his people in the wilderness in the form of a cloud that hovered above the Tabernacle by day, and a fire that hovered above it by night. When Moses came down from Mount Sinai with the Ten Commandments his face shone from being in the presence of God. When Jesus was transfigured his face shone as the sun and his robe was as light. When the Church began, tongues as of fire rested on those gathered in the Upper Room. These were manifestations of the presence of God. Daniel wanted the brightness of God's face on the Temple.

Also, he wanted this for the Lord's sake. All of the prophecies have to be fulfilled. If just one prophecy is not fulfilled, the Bible is wrong or God did not tell the truth. This would cause people to blaspheme God. This is bad news for the militant Muslims and all those who want to give Jerusalem and the Temple Mount away. God will not allow them to stop the fulfillment of his Word.

what others say

Uriah Smith

[It is] not that God is moved with motives of ambition and vain glory; but when his people are jealous for the honor of his

city
Daniel 9:16

evince
to show clearly

name, when they **evince** their love for him by pleading with him to work, not for their own personal benefit, but for his own glory, that his name may not be reproached and blasphemed among the heathen, this is acceptable with him.[5]

We Ask for Mercy

DANIEL 9:18 *O my God, incline Your ear and hear; open Your eyes and see our desolations, and the city which is called by Your name; for we do not present our supplications before You because of our righteous deeds, but because of Your great mercies. (NKJV)*

In Daniel 9:17, Daniel asked God to look with favor on the desolate sanctuary. In this verse he asked God to notice the desolation of his city Jerusalem. Daniel based his request not on the righteousness of the Jews but on the great mercy of God. Our righteousness is not good enough for us to ask anything of God. Our righteousness is like filthy rags (Isaiah 64:6). We need to go to God in the righteousness of Jesus and depend on his mercy.

Consider the situation. Daniel had been fasting. He was wearing sackcloth and sitting in ashes. He was earnestly pleading with God to hear his request, see the desolation of Jerusalem, and respond with mercy on the Jews.

what others say

Randall Price

If Jerusalem did not retain its sanctity or purpose with the expulsion of the Jewish people, as some people argue, then why should Daniel have opened his windows toward Jerusalem and prayed so fervently for its restoration (Daniel 9:16–19)? Though in ruins and under the rule of Gentile powers, Jerusalem, for Daniel, was still "The city Jerusalem" (Daniel 9:16) and "the holy mountain of my God" (Daniel 9:20). That being the case, we cannot say that the Jewish people's expulsion from Jerusalem in AD 70 severed it from God's past promises for the future. In order for the specific prophecies relating to Jerusalem's future to be fulfilled, the city must once again come under Jewish control yet remain in a vulnerable position under the greater dominion of the Gentile nations.[6]

A Final Request

> DANIEL 9:19 *O Lord, hear! O Lord, forgive! O Lord, listen and act! Do not delay for Your own sake, my God, for Your city and Your people are called by Your name." (NKJV)*

city of God
Psalm 87:2–3

people of God
Exodus 3:7; 5:1

sinned
Romans 3:23

governors
Daniel 6:4–5

These are the last words of Daniel's prayer. Israel and Judah had not listened to God, but Daniel asked God to listen to him. He pled for forgiveness for his people. He wanted God to hear him, act on his prayer, and not delay because the seventy years was almost up and because God's name was at stake. He was concerned about God's name and glory. And he did something noteworthy: he linked the city of Jerusalem to the Jews. Both bear the name of God: Jerusalem is the City of God and the Jews are the people of God. And this God is not Allah or any other god. In verses 15–19, Daniel's prayer is directed to Adonai and Elohim, familiar names of the Hebrew God.

what others say

Jim Combs

Forty-one times he uses a personal pronoun, like "I" or "we" or "our" in this intensely personal prayer. No note of self-justification, no excuse, no pride, no arrogance, no appeal to any supposed good works appears anywhere in this "effectual fervent prayer of a righteous man."[7]

Before My Prayer Ended

> DANIEL 9:20 *Now while I was speaking, praying, and confessing my sin and the sin of my people Israel, and presenting my supplication before the LORD my God for the holy mountain of my God, (NKJV)*

While Daniel was talking to God and confessing his sin and the sin of his people Israel, and while he was talking to God about the Temple, something happened. We will find out what in Daniel 9:21, but for the moment let us focus on the fact that Daniel was confessing his sin. He may have been the best man on earth, but he still sinned. Two of his fellow governors and 120 satraps diligently tried to find something to accuse him of, but they could not find anything. Still, Daniel was a sinner. And so is everyone else.

delay
Daniel 9:19

Gabriel
Daniel 8:16

vision
Daniel 8:27

A Heavenly Visitor

DANIEL 9:21 *yes, while I was speaking in prayer, the man Gabriel, whom I had seen in the vision at the beginning, being caused to fly swiftly, reached me about the time of the evening offering.* (NKJV)

Daniel had asked God not to delay; he didn't. Daniel didn't even get to say, "Amen" before the angel Gabriel appeared. This is the same Gabriel Daniel had seen in the Vision of the Ram and the Goat. He came in swift flight at about three in the afternoon (the time the evening sacrifice was offered before the Temple was destroyed).

Notice that Daniel said the man Gabriel appeared unto him. Gabriel is a powerful angel, but he appeared in human form. Abraham and others had a similar experience (Genesis 18:1–16). Paul said some have entertained angels unawares (Hebrews 13:2).

what others say

M. R. De Haan

The sacrifices in Jerusalem had been discontinued, but Daniel, even though there was no actual sacrificing going on, still observed the time that God has instituted, the time of day when the sacrifice was to be offered. During that time he was upon his face before Almighty God, still continuing his regular habit of prayer and still spiritually sacrificing unto the Lord God, and it was at this time that the angel Gabriel came.[8]

I Have More Information for You

DANIEL 9:22 *And he informed me, and talked with me, and said, "O Daniel, I have now come forth to give you skill to understand.* (NKJV)

At the close of chapter 8, we learned that Daniel's vision of the Antichrist (the Vision of the Ram and the Goat) had left him appalled, exhausted, and ill for several days. We also learned that Gabriel had explained many things to Daniel, but there was much more that he did not understand. In this verse we learn that Gabriel returned while Daniel was praying to provide more insight and understanding. Thus we see that what we are about to learn is more about the Antichrist of chapter 8. To be more specific, Daniel has been praying about Jerusalem, the Temple, and his people, so we are going to be told what will happen to the city, the Temple, and the people starting with Daniel's lifetime and working toward the End of the (Gentile) Age (the Time of the End).

fierce features
Daniel 8:23

holy people
Daniel 8:24

Prince of princes
Daniel 8:25

I Am Here to Help You

> DANIEL 9:23 *At the beginning of your supplications the command went out, and I have come to tell you, for you are greatly beloved; therefore consider the matter, and understand the vision: (NKJV)*

As soon as Daniel started praying, Gabriel was given an answer to this prayer and authorized to take it to Daniel. He appeared to Daniel and told Daniel what he was authorized to do and why: he was authorized to help Daniel understand the Vision of the Ram and the Goat because Daniel was greatly beloved. When we refer back to the vision it is important to notice that it concerned the king with <u>fierce features</u> (the Antichrist), the <u>holy people</u> (all of God's people, but particularly the Jews), and the <u>Prince of princes</u> (Jesus). It is a great honor that God would give this revelation to Daniel.

The swiftness of this answer is interesting. A close reading of this verse indicates that Daniel had already started praying when the answer was given to Gabriel. Thus we see that Gabriel left heaven, located Daniel, and appeared to Daniel almost instantaneously. This lets us know that when there is no hindrance from Satan or his evil forces it is possible for our prayers to be answered in the blink of an eye.

what others say

Uriah Smith

Think of celestial beings, the highest in the universe—the Father, the Son, the holy angels—having such regard and esteem for a mortal man here upon earth as to authorize an angel to bear the message to him that he is greatly beloved! This is one of the highest pinnacles of glory to which mortals can attain.[9]

King James Bible Commentary

We should strive before God to be able to have the same words spoken of us. Certainly Daniel's great concern for God's honor, and for his people, must have been part of the reason he was so dearly loved of God.[10]

go to

Jeremiah's prophecy
Daniel 9:2

years
Jeremiah 25:1–13

years
Jewish year is 360
days

490 Years Are Decreed to Do Six Things

DANIEL 9:24
"Seventy weeks are determined
For your people and for your holy city,
To finish the transgression,
To make an end of sins,
To make reconciliation for iniquity,
To bring in everlasting righteousness,
To seal up vision and prophecy,
And to anoint the Most Holy. (NKJV)

Gabriel told Daniel a decree had been issued. Since Gabriel came from heaven we can believe the decree was issued by God in heaven. Gabriel's appearance is similar to that of the watcher that delivered a decree from God to Nebuchadnezzar (Daniel 4:23–25). That decree was the result of the holy ones' going into session and issuing a verdict (Daniel 4:13–17). God endorsed their verdict. It will happen again when the Ancient of Days sits on his throne and issues a verdict against the Antichrist (Daniel 7:9–28)

Gabriel told Daniel that seventy weeks are determined for "your people" and for "your holy city" (see Time Line #3, Appendix A). This brings up three questions: (1) How long is "seventy weeks," (2) Who does "your people" refer to, and (3) What does "your holy city" refer to?

First, the Hebrew word translated "weeks" is *shavuah*. It means "sevens." In Hebrew the phrase "seventy weeks" is "seventy sevens." It is possible to have seventy sevens of minutes, seventy sevens of days, seventy sevens of weeks, seventy sevens of years, or seventy sevens of anything. However, because Daniel was reading <u>Jeremiah's prophecy</u> about Judah spending seventy years of captivity in Babylon when he started praying—a prophecy about **years**, the first phase of Israel's punishment for stealing crops every seventh year—most prophecy experts agree that Gabriel is talking about years, the second phase of Israel's punishment (seven times more or seven times seventy years) for breaking the other commandments of God. The first phase of Israel's punishment was almost complete, but the second phase was still future. This has been verified by history, as you will see later in this chapter. Seventy weeks means seventy weeks of years, or 490 years. This is shown in the following charts.

How Long Is One Week?

Week of Years	Scripture
Jacob worked seven years and was tricked into marrying Leah. Then, he fulfilled Rachel's week by serving Laban seven more years. He worked another week or seven more years.	Genesis 29:21–30
God told Ezekiel to lie on his side to picture the judgment of Israel and Jerusalem. God said, "I have laid on you a day for each year." Seven days represented seven years. One week of days represented seven years.	Ezekiel 4:4–6
Concerning the Year of Jubilee, God told Moses to count seven Sabbaths of years, seven times seven years. He said the seven Sabbaths of years shall be forty-nine years. One Sabbath would be seven years. One week is seven years long.	Leviticus 25:8

How Many Days in One Week?

Number of Years per Week	Number of Days per Week
1 week equals 7 years or 2,520 days.	7 years X 360 days/year
7 weeks equals 49 years or 17,640 days.	7 weeks X 2,520 days/week
62 weeks equals 434 years or 156,240 days.	62 weeks X 2,520 days/week
69 weeks equals 483 years or 173,880 days.	69 weeks X 2,520 days/week

How Many Days in One Year?

1. Jesus told the Jews to flee into the mountains when they see the Abomination of Desolation stand in the holy place (Matthew 24:15–16). This will happen at the middle of the Tribulation Period when the Antichrist breaks the covenant (Daniel 9:27). They will flee into the mountains for 1,260 days (Revelation 12:6). There will be three and one-half years or 42 months left in the Tribulation Period. This means there are 30 days per month (1,260 days divided by 42 months).

2. One year equals 360 days (12 months X 30 days/month). This is called one prophetic year.

Second, "your people" refers to Daniel's people, the Jews. Daniel was praying about the captivity of his people, the Jews. He said shame belongs to the men of Judah, to the inhabitants of Jerusalem and all Israel (verse 7). He said all Israel has transgressed your law (verse 11).

go to

hardened
Romans 11:25–27

transgression
rebellion against
God

sin
missing the mark,
wrongdoing

kingdom of
Everlasting
Righteousness
when God's perfect
rule completely
prevails forever

Millennium
the thousand-year
reign of Christ on
earth

anoint
set apart or conse-
crate

Third, "your holy city" refers to Jerusalem. Daniel was reading what Jeremiah said about the desolation of Jerusalem (verse 2). He was praying for the inhabitants of Jerusalem (verse 7). He asked God to let his anger and fury be turned away from "Your city Jerusalem" (verse 16).

All of this means that Gabriel's first words to Daniel were that the seventy years of captivity for stealing seventy crops were just part of the punishment. The other part was an additional punishment of 490 years for the Jews and Jerusalem because they had broken the other commandments of God. The additional punishment would accomplish six things:

1. *To finish the transgression*—God has decreed that he will finish (shut up or arrest) all **transgression**.

2. *To make an end of sins*—God has decreed that he will put an end to all **sin**.

3. *To make reconciliation for iniquity*—God has decreed that he will make reconciliation for iniquity. (Note: Christians believe this occurred when Jesus died on the cross, but the Jews, as a nation, have had their hearts <u>hardened</u> and will not accept it until after these 490 years have passed.)

4. *To bring in everlasting righteousness*—God has decreed that he will bring in a **kingdom of Everlasting Righteousness.** (Note: It will begin with the **Millennium.**)

5. *To seal up vision and prophecy*—God has decreed that he will ful-fill everything he has promised in visions and prophecies, includ-ing punishing the Jews seven times more.

6. *To anoint the Most Holy*—God has decreed that he will **anoint** the most holy. (Some experts say this means anoint a new Temple; oth-ers say it means anoint Jesus as the Messiah. It probably means both.)

what others say

Randall Price and Thomas Ice

In answer to Daniel's prayer, a Jewish remnant returned to Judah to resettle the Land and to rebuild Jerusalem and the Temple. Also, a Jewish Messiah came to the Land of Israel to "make atonement for iniquity" (9:24). In the same way that these events were fulfilled literally, the six prophetic goals of the 70 weeks should also be expected to be fulfilled literally. These six goals have not been fulfilled in the church in this age; rather, they apply to the Jewish nation in the age to come.[11]

Grant R. Jeffrey

One of Daniel's most significant prophecies was that the coming Messiah would be anointed with this special oil of anointing. It is significant that the title "Messiah" and "Christ" mean "anointed." . . . While Jesus was never anointed with this sacred oil during His First Coming, He will finally be anointed when He returns as Israel's acknowledged King at His Second Coming.[12]

Look this list over again. There are some wonderful things here. But two things are required for these things to come true: (1) Jesus had to die on the cross, and (2) Jesus will have to come back to establish his kingdom here on earth. The First Coming was fulfilled literally, and there is every reason to believe the second event will be fulfilled literally.

Let's pause and recognize an important point here. There are many people who do not believe in a Tribulation Period. They teach that the Church will succeed in converting the world and bringing in the kingdom of everlasting righteousness (Kingdom Theology) without the world going through a terrible ordeal like the Tribulation. But here we see it plainly stated that Israel must go through all 490 years (the last seven are the Tribulation Period) before the kingdom of everlasting righteousness can begin.

Some experts call Daniel 9:24–27 the four most important prophetic verses in the Bible. These verses span more than 2,500 years, predict the rebuilding of Jerusalem, reveal the date of the First Coming of Jesus, his death, the destruction of Israel and Jerusalem, facts about the Antichrist and Tribulation Period, and more, but they are not easy to understand. The following chart will help.

The Seventy Weeks of Daniel

Verse	Scope	Event
9:24	70 weeks or 490 years required	fulfill prophecy, deal with Israel's sin, etc.
9:25	the first 69 weeks or 483 years	has two consecutive parts (7 weeks + 62 weeks)

go to

Cyrus
2 Chronicles
36:22–23;
Ezra 1:1–4

Darius
Ezra 6:1–12

Artaxerxes
Ezra 7:11–26

Jerusalem
Nehemiah 2:1–8;
17–18

The Seventy Weeks of Daniel (cont'd)

Verse	Scope	Event
9:26	an interval before last week	kill Messiah, destroy city and Temple, land desolate
9:27	the last week (final 7 years)	7-year covenant, rebuild Temple, war

When God's Clock Will Start

DANIEL 9:25
Know therefore and understand,
That from the going forth of the command
To restore and build Jerusalem
Until Messiah the Prince,
There shall be seven weeks and sixty-two weeks;
The street shall be built again, and the wall,
Even in troublesome times. (NKJV)

Here Gabriel revealed the fact that God would start keeping time on the seventy weeks (490 years) when a certain decree was issued. Pay attention to this starting point because it means that God's 490-year clock was not running when Gabriel met with Daniel. His clock was not ticking at that time but when it did start, it would not tick continuously through to the 490 years. God was going to use this clock like a stop watch; he would turn it on and off as he wished (see Time Line #3, Appendix A).

So we learn that God planned to start his 490-year clock when a certain decree was issued. Again we need to pay close attention to every word here because over the next few years there would be several decrees concerning the Jews going back to Israel and rebuilding the Temple and Jerusalem, but there would be only one decree that would fulfill all the words in this passage.

Cyrus issued a decree in 538 BC to release the Jews, but it did not fit this prophecy because it made no mention of rebuilding Jerusalem. Darius issued a decree in 519 BC, but all it did was repeat the decree of Cyrus with the exception that it allowed the Jews to rebuild the Temple. Artaxerxes issued a decree in 458 BC, but it did not fit because it made no mention of rebuilding Jerusalem. But he issued a second decree in 445 BC that fulfills the words of this prophecy, and that is when the rebuilding of Jerusalem began. So the commencement date or the starting of God's clock on the seventy sevens (490 years) would turn out to be a decree in the month of Nisan in the twentieth year of King Artaxerxes.

But there is more. This verse mentions two very important events: the <u>rebuilding of Jerusalem</u> and the <u>Messiah, the Prince</u>. And it gives two time periods: seven weeks (7 x 7 = 49 years) and sixty-two weeks (62 x 7 = 434 years). The first time period (49 years) relates to the rebuilding of Jerusalem; the second time period (434 years) relates to the coming of the Messiah, the Prince.

Concerning the rebuilding of Jerusalem, it took 49 years to accomplish that. The Bible and secular historians record many things about it. The Ammonites, Moabites, and Samaritans all <u>opposed the rebuilding</u> of Jerusalem. They laughed at the Jews, ridiculed them, plotted to kill Nehemiah, and threatened war. They caused so much trouble the Jews stationed guards with weapons and trumpets at 500-foot intervals around the wall; the Jews wore swords while they worked and kept shields within a few feet of every man.

Concerning the Messiah the Prince (Jesus), Gabriel said the decree would be issued, seven weeks (49 years) would pass, sixty-two weeks (434 years) would pass, and then he would come. This is a reference to the First Coming of Jesus, and we learn that he would appear 483 years (49 years + 434 years = 483 years) after the proper decree. But let's be careful here. This is a reference to his <u>Triumphal Entry</u>, not his birth. Notice these words spoken during his Triumphal Entry about his coming, As he approached Jerusalem and saw the city, he wept over it and said, "If you had known, even you, especially in this your day, the things that make for your peace! But now they are hidden from your eyes. For days will come upon you when your enemies will build an embankment around you, surround you and close you in on every side, and level you, and your children within you, to the ground; and they will not leave in you one stone upon another, because you did not know the time of your visitation" (Luke 19:41–44 NKJV).

It is obvious that Jesus expected the Jews of his day to know and understand this prophecy. He even held them accountable because they didn't. When he made his Triumphal Entry, he made it plain that he expected them to know that this was their day and the time of their visitation. Their failure to know and understand this is why they are blinded today (hidden from your eyes), and why God allowed the Romans to destroy Jerusalem and the Temple. It is why

go to

rebuilding of Jerusalem
Nehemiah 2:17–3:32

Messiah, the Prince
Acts 10:38–43

opposed the rebuilding
Nehemiah 4

Triumphal Entry
Matthew 21:1–11

Jesus allowed the people to call him their king on this occasion, but he refused to allow them to do it at any other time. This was the exact day the angel Gabriel said he would appear. Notice the words "from" and "until" in Daniel 9:25. They reveal exactly when the first coming of Messiah would take place.

This is what we have: (1) the starting date, which is the date Artaxerxes issued his second decree, and (2) the ending date, which is the date Jesus made his Triumphal Entry into Jerusalem. We only need to determine if that spans the required 483 years. And the answer is, yes, right to the very day.

Sir Robert Anderson, a highly respected English lawyer and former head of Scotland Yard, figured it out. He multiplied 483 years times the Jewish prophetic year of 360 days per year and found that 483 Jewish years equals 173,880 days. Then he took the date of the decree (March 14, 445 BC) and calculated the number of days to the Triumphal Entry (April 6, AD 32), taking into account leap year and the fact that there was only one year between 1 BC and AD 1 (no year numbered 0), and the total was 173,880 days. So we see that exactly 483 years passed between the decree and the First Coming (Triumphal Entry) of Jesus.

It should be pointed out that Sir Robert Anderson's valuable work has been checked out and praised by several of the top prophetic scholars, including Dr. Harold Hoehner, Dr. John Walvoord, Dr. Tim LaHaye, and Dr. Thomas Ice, to name a few. They believe he is right about everything, except that they say the starting date is March 5, 444 BC, and the ending date is March 30, 33 AD. It is not unusual to find people who think the date of an Old Testament event is off by one year. But these great scholars still believe Gabriel revealed the exact date of the First Coming of Jesus and he made his Triumphal Entry on the very day it was predicted he would arrive.

God's clock is like a stop watch that can be started and stopped at will. He would start it when the decree was issued. He would allow two time periods to tick off: 49 years and 434 years. Then he would stop it. And he would not restart it for a long time.

Three time periods are given. The following chart shows that the length, the beginning, and the end of each one can be identified.

How Gabriel Divided the 490 Years

Period	Length	Begins	Ends
1st	7 weeks (49 years)	Decree to rebuild city	49 years later
2nd	62 weeks (434 years)	After 1st period	When Messiah appears (Triumphal Entry)
3rd	1 week (7 years)	After city and Temple are destroyed and land is desolate—when the Antichrist confirms a 7-year covenant	7 years later or 3 1/2 after sacrifices end at rebuilt Temple

what others say

Grant R. Jeffrey

According to the Talmud (a collection of ancient Jewish religious writings and law), "The first day of the month of Nisan is the New Year for the computation of the reign of kings and for festivals." In other words, when no other date is given, we assume the event occurred on the first day of Nisan. The Royal Observatory in Greenwich, U.K., has calculated that the first of Nisan in the twentieth year of the reign of King Artaxerxes occurred on March 14, 445 BC.[13]

After the Sixty-Two Weeks (434 Years)

DANIEL 9:26

And after the sixty-two weeks
Messiah shall be cut off, but not for Himself;
And the people of the prince who is to come
Shall destroy the city and the sanctuary.
The end of it shall be with a flood,
And till the end of the war desolations are determined. (NKJV)

Gabriel was telling Daniel that after the second time period of sixty-two weeks (434 years) Jesus would be cut off (crucified). He would have nothing; no earthly possessions, home, throne, or kingdom. In fact, he would not have put an end to sin, finished transgression, or fulfilled all the visions and prophecies either. Jesus would die before doing everything that God decreed for him to do. This was done at the cross in AD 32.

And there was more bad news. Following the death of Jesus, Jerusalem and the rebuilt Temple would be destroyed again. This was done by a Roman General named Titus in AD 70. He sacked and burned Jerusalem, killed five million Jews, and tore the Temple apart stone by stone.

wars
Matthew 24:6–7

Armageddon
Revelation 16:16

But there was another important point. Gabriel mentioned a prince who is to come. This is a reference to the coming Antichrist, and it is important because it identifies the group of nations he will come out of. We just pointed out that the Romans destroyed Jerusalem and the Temple in AD 70, so the Romans are the people of the prince who is to come. This tells us that when the Antichrist comes he will come out of the nations that made up the Old Roman Empire during the earthly life of Jesus.

This brings us to a final point. We have looked at the first two time periods: seven weeks (49 years) and sixty-two weeks (434 years). This is a total of sixty-nine weeks or 483 years. But God decreed seventy weeks or 490 years would pass before everything was fulfilled. This means he must start his clock again so the last 7 years can tick off. We have also noticed four things that would happen after the period of sixty-two weeks (434 years): (1) Jesus would be killed (AD 32), (2) Jerusalem would be destroyed (AD 70), (3) the Temple would be destroyed (AD 70), and (4) Jerusalem and the Temple would be desolate until the Time of the End. These four things had to happen before God would restart his clock. His clock is stopped right now. It has been stopped for over 1,900 years, and we do not know when he will restart it. However, most prophetic experts think it will be soon because Jerusalem is no longer desolate and many of the Jews are seeking to rebuild the Temple.

How will the seventy weeks (490 years) end? They will end with a flood of destruction. Nations will rise against nations and there will be <u>wars</u> and rumors of wars all through history until the last and greatest war called the Battle of <u>Armageddon</u>. The Jews themselves would suffer many things and Jerusalem would be desolate until the Time of the End.

The failure to accomplish everything God wanted was not on the part of Jesus but on the part of the Jews. Jesus prepared to make his Triumphal Entry by sending two disciples after a donkey and her colt. He said, "'If anyone says anything to you, you shall say, "The Lord has need of them," and immediately he will send them.' All this was done that it might be fulfilled which was spoken by the prophet, saying: 'Tell the daughter of Zion, "Behold, your King is coming to you, lowly, and sitting on a donkey, a colt, the foal of a donkey"'" (Matthew 21:3–5; Zechariah 9:9 NKJV). Referring to himself as "Lord" in fulfillment of Bible prophecy amounted to a public declaration of his Messiahship. He approached Jerusalem as the Messiah weeping over the city. He said, "If you had known, even you, especially in this your day, the things that make for your peace! But now they are hidden from your eyes" (Luke 19:42 NKJV). If the Jews had realized this was the prophesied day that their Messiah would arrive, that accepting him would bring them peace, and if they would have done that, he would have fulfilled everything and established his kingdom right away. But they failed to recognize the day and to accept him as the Messiah. Jesus knew that would happen. He knew that his crucifixion was near and he would soon be cut off. Because of the Jewish failure their nation was spiritually separated from God, the Church was brought in to take their place, and the last seven years of Gabriel's message (the Tribulation Period) remain to be fulfilled. This will happen before the Second Coming of Jesus.

what others say

The Wycliffe Bible Commentary

It is agreed by almost all evangelical interpreters that these two events, the cutting off of the Messiah (*Anointed One*) and the destruction of the sanctuary refer to the crucifixion of Christ and the destruction of Jerusalem by the Romans. These two events were separated by a period of nearly forty years. Yet, in the literary order of the passage, they are both after the sixty-ninth week and before the final "one week" mentioned in the next verse. Thus the very syntax, grammar, and word-meaning indicate a gap in the succession of the seventy weeks.[14]

John R. Rice

This prophecy was fulfilled in A.D. 70, some forty years after Christ was crucified. Titus, the Roman general, led his army against Jerusalem. The city was utterly destroyed and hundreds and thousands of Jews put to death. From that time on, the Jews have had no national history, no separate nation, no temple, no worship. The temple was destroyed, and there has never been one since at Jerusalem.[15]

The Antichrist will come out of a group of nations called the Revived Roman Empire. Most experts believe this group of nations has now come on the scene and is called by the modern, nonbiblical name of the European Union. Following the Rapture, a popular leader will arise unlike anyone the world has ever seen. He will gain strength in Europe and then take over the world government.

go to

same people
Daniel 9:26

confirm
he will cause the
signing of an agree-
ment

covenant
a comprehensive
Middle East peace
agreement

many
representatives of
many nations and
groups of nations

The Final Seven Years (The Seventieth Week of Daniel)

DANIEL 9:27
Then he shall confirm a covenant with many for one week;
But in the middle of the week
He shall bring an end to sacrifice and offering.
And on the wing of abominations shall be one
who makes desolate,
Even until the consummation, which is determined,
Is poured out on the desolate." (NKJV)

The final 7 years of the 490 did not occur before the Triumphal Entry in AD 32 because that ended the 434 year period. They also did not take place between AD 32 and AD 70, because Jerusalem and the Temple had to be destroyed before they could begin. They also have not taken place since AD 70, because they cannot take place without the Temple. This means everything in this verse is still future.

Commentators call these final seven years the Tribulation Period. "He" refers to the Antichrist. He has more than thirty titles in the Bible, but Christians try to simplify what is said by calling him the Antichrist. This man of sin will come from the <u>same people</u> who destroyed Jerusalem and the Temple in AD 70 (the Romans). Today, the modern equivalent is the European Union (EU). In ancient times there was an Eastern Roman Empire and a Western Roman Empire. The nations that form the European Union today are primarily from the Western Roman Empire. Most prophetic scholars expect this group to produce the Antichrist. However, one of the titles of the Antichrist is the Assyrian, so several good scholars believe the European Union needs to expand more. It is their opinion that the Eastern leg must come back into being to produce the Antichrist.

This verse tells us he will **confirm** a **covenant** with **many** for one week (seven years). The word *confirm* indicates the treaty may exist a short while before he signs it. Thus, the beginning of the Tribulation Period is not when the various parties reach an agreement. It is when the Antichrist signs it. It is interesting to know that the European Union met some time ago and voted to confirm any covenant that can be worked out for peace in the Middle East. They used the exact word that is found here in this verse. The world does not know who the Antichrist is today, but this will be a sure sign of his identity. However, it will be after the Rapture, so the Church will learn about it in heaven.

peace
1 Thessalonians 5:3

Another interesting point is the fact that modern Jews say they do not trust the Palestinians to keep an agreement, so they do not want to sign a permanent treaty. They want a long-term agreement at first. If the Palestinians keep that, then they will sign a permanent treaty. And on the Palestinian side, some have expressed a desire to sign a *hudna* (temporary agreement) for up to ten years, but not more. The question is, will the two sides settle on an agreement of seven years.

Gabriel does not spell out the conditions of this covenant, but other verses indicate that Israel will think it has <u>peace</u> and safety. However, the Jews will be deceived because it will be a false peace. In fact, Jesus will break the second seal and remove peace from the earth (Revelation 6:3–4).

Most modern Jews believe they must get permission from their Messiah to rebuild the Temple. Many conservative Christians believe they will wrongly accept the Antichrist as their Messiah (John 5:43). If this is true, it places the rebuilding of the Temple at some point during the first half of the Tribulation Period after the Antichrist appears, but before the Tribulation period midpoint. The Jewish Sanhedrin wants to build a prefabricated Temple off-site today, take it apart in sections, store it, and have it ready to erect in as little as six weeks from the time they get permission. They have already located the place where the red heifers were offered in Old Testament times and say from this they can determine exactly where the next Temple should be erected. All of the utensils for the animal sacrifices, all of the garments for the priests, and all of the music instruments for the worship services are now complete. Priests have been selected and trained. Some are actually sacrificing animals at rabbinic schools near the Temple Mount because they believe they cannot make mistakes when they do it at the Temple, and they believe the only way to do it right at that time is to practice on real animals now. Red heifers are needed to make the water of purification to cleanse the Temple Mount and the priests who erect the Temple. The herd was thought to be extinct for almost two thousand years, but it has been reestablished, and heifers without blemish and spot are available.

go to

Temple
2 Thessalonians 2:4

image
Revelation 13:14–18

flee
Matthew 24:15–16

Temple Mount
area in Jerusalem
where all the Jewish
Temples have been
located

Gabriel did not spell out who the "many" refers to, and there have been several partial agreements to date, but the latest negotiations involve more people than ever before. President George W. Bush initiated the Road Map for peace in the Middle East and established the Quartet (UN, EU, Russia, and US) to help bring it about. How can we have more "many" than the United Nations? And notice that the EU, the home of the Antichrist, is involved. This is the first time for these two groups. So the current negotiations involve the Israelis, the Palestinians, the United States, the Russians, the Europeans, and the United Nations, and for 2,500 years the Bible has said it will be a covenant with many.

"In the middle of the week" divides the seven-year Tribulation Period into two equal segments of 3 1/2 years each. The first 3 1/2 years will be bad, but the last 3 1/2 years will be terrible. So the Tribulation Period midpoint is significant. Gabriel said, "He [the Antichrist)] shall bring an end to sacrifice and offering" (Daniel 9:27 NKJV). He will declare the highly touted covenant with many signatures invalid. It is even likely that he will send a so-called peacekeeping force into Jerusalem to prevent sacrifices and offerings from being made. Today, the EU has established its own military. They call it a "peacekeeping force," or their "army of peace."

"He shall bring an end to sacrifice and offering" implies the rebuilding of the Temple. Offerings and sacrifices have to start before they can be stopped and they have always been made at the Temple. This lets us know that, at least for a very short time, Israel will have, at the very least, some sort of limited sovereignty over East Jerusalem and the **Temple Mount**. Also, at the middle of the Tribulation Period, the Antichrist will set up "an abomination that causes desolation" (Abomination of Desolation). That will be something that desecrates or contaminates the Temple. Gabriel does not say what it is, but there is good reason to believe that it is an image of the Antichrist. Whatever it is, the Jews should flee into the mountains when it happens because tribulation and death will be their lot in Jerusalem. Here we see too that the Temple will be defiled "Even until the consummation, which is determined, is poured out on the desolate" (Daniel 9:27 NKJV). This means until the 490 years are complete and the Antichrist is captured and cast into the lake of burning sulfur (the Lake of Fire).

One final comment on this chapter. Much has been said about the critics who suggest that the traditional Daniel didn't write this book. Many believe a substitute Daniel wrote it around 100–200 BC. There is an overwhelming pile of evidence to prove they are wrong. But suppose they are right and the book was written when they say. Their substitute Daniel still predicted the exact day the Messiah would arrive and what would happen to him more than one hundred years before it happened. If someone could foretell it one hundred years before it happened, someone could foretell it five hundred to six hundred years before it happened.

what others say

Grant R. Jeffrey

It is intriguing to note that the ancient Jewish sages also interpreted the prophecy of Daniel 9:24–27 to teach that the Messiah, "the son of David," will literally appear at the end of a seven-year period of great troubles, suffering, and distress. For example, the Babylonian Talmud contains the following statement regarding the return of the Messiah: "Our rabbis taught: In the seven-year cycle at the end of which the son of David will come . . . At the conclusion of the septennate [7 year period] the son of David will come." In another passage, the Babylonian Talmud reported, "The advent of the Messiah was pictured as being preceded by years of great distress."[16]

Chapter Wrap-Up

- Daniel was reading the book of Jeremiah when he discovered that Jerusalem would be desolate for seventy years. He knew that period was almost over and wanted God to cause the city and the Temple to be rebuilt. (Daniel 9:1–3)

- He confessed that he and his people had sinned, done wrong, been wicked, rebelled, broke God's laws, ignored the prophets, been unfaithful, disobeyed God, and transgressed God's law. (Daniel 9:3–15)

- Daniel asked God to turn away his anger and wrath, to hear his prayer and petitions, to look with favor on the desolate Temple, to have mercy, to consider his (God's) name, to forgive, and to act without delay. (Daniel 9:16–19)

- Gabriel appeared with a message for Daniel. He said he had come to give Daniel insight and to help him understand the vision. (Daniel 9:20–23)

- Gabriel said God had decreed 490 more years of dealing with his people. A decree would be issued, and it would take 49 years to rebuild Jerusalem. Then 434 more years and Jesus would come. Jesus would be killed and Jerusalem and the Temple would be destroyed. The last 7 years would begin with a covenant, but it would be broken after 3 1/2 years. The animal sacrifices would cease and the Temple would be defiled and made desolate. (Daniel 9: 24–27)

Study Questions

1. What evidence do we have that Daniel knew the Scriptures?

2. What does this chapter teach about forgiveness?

3. What characteristics of God are identified by Daniel?

4. What is the object of Daniel's prayer?

5. What are some of the things associated with the Tribulation Period?

Daniel 10 Demonic Warfare

Chapter Highlights:
- Fasting and Praying
- Vision of the Anointed One
- Effect on Daniel
- A Heavenly Being
- Strength and Assurance

Let's Get Started

Chapters 10–12 of Daniel are all one vision, the "Vision of the Anointed One." This is the last and longest of Daniel's visions. Chapter 10 can be considered an introduction to the vision, chapter 11 the vision itself, and chapter 12 an epilogue or postscript to the vision.

Many of the verses in these three chapters concern the unseen **spirit world**. This may be an eerie thought for some, but the Bible plainly <u>teaches</u> that **fallen angels** and **demonic spirits** are real and must be faced. How else can we account for all of the evil in the world? How else can we explain World War I, the Holocaust, Satan worship, witchcraft, and other horrors? Biblically speaking, <u>Satan</u> and his followers are ultimately responsible for all of these things.

go to

teaches
Luke 7:21; 8:2;
Acts 19:12–13;
Jude 1:6

Satan
Revelation 12:7–9

spirit world
personalities in the invisible, non-physical realm

fallen angels
angels that sinned by rebelling against God

demonic spirits
spirits that bring or cause evil to human beings

what others say

William L. Owens

For approximately two centuries the Church has not openly discussed the subject of demonic powers. This hesitancy is probably due to the emerging Age of Reason. It almost seems that the church has been afraid to admit that demons are real. Social pressure in an enlightened era has probably accounted for the reluctance on the part of the Church to acknowledge this subject. In this writer's opinion, Satan has been the personality behind the Church's silence. The devil does not want to be exposed, and he will exert his entire force in active resistance against exposure.[1]

The Time and the Subject

DANIEL 10:1 *In the third year of Cyrus king of Persia a message was revealed to Daniel, whose name was called Belteshazzar. The message was true, but the appointed time was long; and he understood the message, and had understanding of the vision.* (NKJV)

go to

king of Babylon
Daniel 5:30

"The third year of Cyrus king of Persia" (Daniel 10:1 NKJV) establishes the time (see Time Line #1, Appendix A). Belshazzar, the <u>king of Babylon</u>, was killed around 539 BC. Darius the Mede took over the kingdom, and ruled for about two years before he died. Cyrus the Persian became king, and in the third year of his reign Daniel received this vision. So the time is around 534 BC, roughly five years after the fall of Babylon, and Daniel would be in his mid-eighties..

We shall soon be studying this vision that God revealed to Daniel. Since it is from God we know it is true. It concerned a great war, but not the typical kind of war. It concerned a war in the spirit world, a war among the supernatural. Along with this vision Daniel received understanding of it.

Jesus said, "Ye must be born again," but he also taught that the new birth is not the end of the matter. We need to grow in our relationship with God. Paul said we should increase in knowledge. Peter said we should grow in grace and in knowledge, and he said we should add to our faith. Daniel may have been the most godly teenager who ever lived, but he still grew as the following chart shows.

Daniel's Growth as a Man of God

Event	Scripture
Daniel interpreted Nebuchadnezzar's dream about the future, but only after he received the answer in a vision.	Daniel 2:19
Daniel interpreted a later dream about the future for Nebuchadnezzar, but he didn't need a vision of any kind.	Daniel 4:19
Daniel started having his own dreams and visions about the future.	Daniel 7:1
Daniel was transported from Babylon to Shushan in a vision.	Daniel 8
Daniel was visited by the angel Gabriel.	Daniel 9:21
Daniel was visited by the post-incarnate Christ.	Daniel 10:4–5

Twenty-one Days

DANIEL 10:2 *In those days I, Daniel, was mourning three full weeks. (NKJV)*

Daniel does not say why he was mourning. Some experts think it was because only a small number of his people returned home after being released from captivity in Babylon. Others think it was because those who did return home were having a difficult time. Actually, it appears that he was mourning because he was trying to understand this war in the spirit world (verse 12). The reality of evil and a universal conflict in the spirit world with devastating effects on all human beings is somewhat difficult to comprehend, but the Bible teaches this and it should not be ignored.

fast
Nehemiah 9:1–3;
Esther 4:1–4

A Partial Fast

> DANIEL 10:3 *I ate no pleasant food, no meat or wine came into my mouth, nor did I anoint myself at all, till three whole weeks were fulfilled. (NKJV)*

This was not a total <u>fast</u>, but it was certainly a partial fast. Daniel ate no choice foods; he ate no meat and refused wine. He used no lotions, did not anoint his body with oil, and did not use any perfumes. He chose to do these things as a sign to God showing that he was sincere about his grief; he continued this for twenty-one days.

what others say

Charles Stanley

[In the Sermon on the Mount] Jesus talked about three things that we should refrain from doing in public. First, we should not give for public notoriety (Matthew 6:2). Second, we are admonished to pray in private (Matthew 6:5). Third, we should fast in private (Matthew 6:16). Nothing is intrinsically wrong with doing these things publicly, but I believe Jesus understood the tendency of people to do things for the admiration and respect of their peers rather than for the glory of God.[2]

The Date and Place (The Vision of the Anointed One)

> DANIEL 10:4 *Now on the twenty-fourth day of the first month, as I was by the side of the great river, that is, the Tigris, (NKJV)*

It was the twenty-fourth day of the first month, and Daniel was standing on the bank of the great Tigris River (see Illustration #2). On the Jewish calendar it is the month of Nisan. On our calendar it would be April 24, 534 BC.

Could It Be Jesus?

> DANIEL 10:5 *I lifted my eyes and looked, and behold, a certain man clothed in linen, whose waist was girded with gold of Uphaz! (NKJV)*

sash
Leviticus 8:6–9

High Priest
Hebrews 4:14–16

golden
Revelation 1:13

face
Matthew 17:2

bronze
Micah 4:13

created
Genesis 1:1–13

raise the dead
1 Thessalonians
4:13–18

ordained
officially appointed
to be a priest

high priest
spiritual head of Old
Testament Israel

Daniel looked up and saw a man in front of him. He did not say who the man was so we will try to identify him by his dress and features. The man was dressed in linen and had a belt of fine gold around his waist.

This brings to mind two events in the Bible. When Aaron was **ordained** to be the **high priest** of Israel Moses tied a <u>sash</u> around his waist. And when Jesus, our <u>High Priest</u>, appeared to John on the Isle of Patmos he was wearing a <u>golden</u> sash around his chest. Not all experts agree, but Daniel probably saw Jesus.

> ## what others say
>
> ### Arno Froese
>
> In Daniel's vision, the Lord was ready to do the task that the Father had entrusted to Him. But in the book of Revelation, this golden girdle was around His chest, signifying that the work had already been done. John reveals that the chest—that is, the location of the heart—is covered. He no longer is the servant, but has become the Judge, the King of kings and Lord of lords. The time of grace will have expired.[3]

His Features

> DANIEL 10:6 *His body was like beryl, his face like the appearance of lightning, his eyes like torches of fire, his arms and feet like burnished bronze in color, and the sound of his words like the voice of a multitude.* (NKJV)

Although Daniel did not call this man by name his features were similar to those of the resurrected Christ in Revelation 1:13–16: His <u>face</u> like lightning reminds us of the shekinah glory of God.

"His eyes like torches of fire" (Daniel 10:6 NKJV) speaks of his great insight and ability to see everything. "His arms and feet like burnished <u>bronze</u> in color" (10:6 NKJV) are symbols of judgment. "The sound of his words like the voice of a multitude" (10:6 NKJV) reminds us of the voice that <u>created</u> everything, the voice of the one who will <u>raise the dead</u> in the Rapture.

Not everyone agrees that this man was Jesus, but it is the view of most scholars. The following chart compares Daniel's description of this man with Jesus as he appeared to John in Revelation chapter 1.

God's Servant Is the Coming Judge

Daniel 10	Revelation 1
dressed in linen	a robe reaching down to his feet
a belt of fine gold around his waist	a golden band around his chest
face like lightning	countenance like sun shining in its strength
eyes like torches of fire	eyes like flame of fire
arms and feet like burnished bronze	feet like fine brass
sound of words like voice of a multitude	voice as sound of many waters

go to

Jesus
Acts 9:1–9

what others say

Tim LaHaye

If this "certain man" is indeed Jesus Christ, then a glimpse of the Son of God is befitting for this last vision given to Daniel, for it is a most significant prophecy of the End Times (Daniel 10–12).[4]

My Companions Were Terrified

DANIEL 10:7 *And I, Daniel, alone saw the vision, for the men who were with me did not see the vision; but a great terror fell upon them, so that they fled to hide themselves.* (NKJV)

Daniel does not say who was with him, but he does mention that none of them saw the vision. The apostle Paul had a similar experience while traveling on the road to Damascus. There Paul had a vision of Jesus, but none of his companions saw anything.

Although Daniel's companions did not see anything, something happened to scare them terribly. They were so affected by this event that they ran and hid. They may not have realized it, but they were dealing with the supernatural.

I Was Overwhelmed

DANIEL 10:8 *Therefore I was left alone when I saw this great vision, and no strength remained in me; for my vigor was turned to frailty in me, and I retained no strength.* (NKJV)

Daniel's companions abandoned him, forcing Daniel to stare at this great vision alone. If he was as scared as they were, he couldn't

fell
Matthew 17:6;
Revelation 1:17

sleep
Daniel 8:18

do anything about it because his strength abandoned him, leaving him too weak to run. He found himself standing there alone and helpless.

The Lights Went Out

DANIEL 10:9 *Yet I heard the sound of his words; and while I heard the sound of his words I was in a deep sleep on my face, with my face to the ground.* (NKJV)

We are not told that Daniel <u>fell</u> to the ground, but it seems that way. He was pale and weak, heard a voice, and listened, but something happened to him. He may have fainted or passed out because he says he fell into a deep <u>sleep</u> with his face to the ground. We can't be sure what happened, but it would appear that some change came over him to prepare him to receive this vision.

Someone Touched Me

DANIEL 10:10 *Suddenly, a hand touched me, which made me tremble on my knees and on the palms of my hands.* (NKJV)

Daniel was on the ground, in a deep sleep, and too weak to move when a hand touched him. We don't know who it was, but we do know it was someone from the supernatural realm, probably an angel. The purpose of the touch was to strengthen Daniel, but when the hand touched him, he started trembling. He was terrified, and the hand pulled him up to his hands and knees.

We know that angels can appear out of nowhere. Gabriel did that when he delivered that great message to Daniel in chapter 9. Angels appeared when Jesus was born, tempted, transfigured, raised from the dead, and more. Some people have entertained angels unawares. Angels seem to be different from demons in that they can materialize in a body, but demons can't. Demons want a body. They prefer to possess a person, but they would rather dwell in a pig than not have a body.

what others say

M. R. De Haan

Then after a period of great amazement on the part of Daniel, with his face toward the ground, the heavenly messenger

> touched him and strengthened him and gave him the message which he was to put down for these **latter days** for our instruction.[5]

greatly beloved
Daniel 9:23

man
Daniel 10:5

feet
Daniel 8:18

latter days
the last days of the Times of the Gentiles

I Want Your Undivided Attention

DANIEL 10:11 *And he said to me, "O Daniel, man greatly beloved, understand the words that I speak to you, and stand upright, for I have now been sent to you." While he was speaking this word to me, I stood trembling. (NKJV)*

The angel's first words mention that Daniel was <u>greatly beloved</u>. This was a repeat of what the angel Gabriel said in chapter 9. It was a great compliment to Daniel. Abraham was called a friend of God. Jesus was called the beloved Son of God. John was called the disciple whom Jesus loved. It seems more than interesting that the human authors of the two greatest prophetic books in the Bible, Daniel and John, are called beloved and the disciple whom Jesus loved. This explains much about why God chose them to reveal these prophecies.

The angel urged Daniel to make a special effort to understand what he was about to reveal. He told Daniel to stand up. He explained that the reason he appeared was because he had been sent. It is not said who sent him, but it was probably the <u>man</u> (Jesus) whom Daniel had just seen. Daniel obeyed and stood on his <u>feet</u>, even though he was still shaking.

what others say

Henry H. Halley

In this chapter, they [angels] are represented as being interested in the destiny of Israel; in Revelation, the destiny of the Church. In Revelation 12:7–9 Michael and his angels are in war with Satan and his angels. In Ephesians 6:12 powers of the unseen world are the chief enemies against which Christians have to fight.[6]

God Heard You

DANIEL 10:12 *Then he said to me, "Do not fear, Daniel, for from the first day that you set your heart to understand, and to humble yourself before your God, your words were heard; and I have come because of your words. (NKJV)*

Daniel 10 Demonic Warfare ———————— 271

three weeks
Daniel 10:2–3

visions
Daniel 7:15; 8:15;
9:23

fall of Satan
Isaiah 14:12–17

heavenly realm
Ephesians 6:11–12

spirit
1 John 4:1–3

personification
the creature or
source of evil

The angel could tell that Daniel was afraid, so he tried to calm Daniel down before beginning.

Daniel had been fasting and praying for <u>three weeks</u>, and the angel knew it. He informed Daniel that his prayers were heard the first day Daniel started praying. Daniel was asking for understanding concerning the <u>visions</u> of chapters 7, 8, and 9, and the angel said that providing understanding was the purpose behind his visit.

what others say

William L. Owens

One cannot understand the purpose of evil spirits or the reason for evil unless the person of Satan is considered. The Bible presents Satan as the **personification** of evil and the archenemy of the eternal God. The Scriptures are not clear about the origin of demons; however, it is probable that demons fell from heaven with the <u>fall of Satan</u>. Evil spirits are so closely related in nature and character to Satan that it is difficult to imagine them apart from him. Therefore, one may conclude through deduction, that demons are created beings, like unto Satan, who followed him in his rebellion.[7]

Billy Graham

Lucifer [another name for Satan], our archenemy, controls one of the most powerful and well-oiled war machines in the universe. He controls principalities, powers, and dominions. Every nation, city, village, and individual has felt the hot breath of his evil power. He is already gathering the nations of the world for the last great battle in the war against Christ—Armageddon.[8]

A War in the Heavenlies

DANIEL 10:13 *But the prince of the kingdom of Persia withstood me twenty-one days; and behold, Michael, one of the chief princes, came to help me, for I had been left alone there with the kings of Persia.* (NKJV)

Here the angel pulled back a curtain, so to speak, to show Daniel a cosmic struggle in the <u>heavenly realm</u>. He revealed that more is going on in the world than most people realize. Behind the scenes is an unseen war between God and Satan, the angels of God and the demons of Satan, the Spirit of Christ and the <u>spirit</u> of Antichrist. The angel told Daniel that the prince of the Persian kingdom (a fallen angel or evil spirit) had prevented him from getting through with an answer to his prayer. The evil spirit was so powerful he managed to hold off this good angel for twenty-one days—the same length of time Daniel had been fasting and praying. Furthermore, the only way the good angel finally got through to Daniel was for Michael, one of the chief angels, to render assistance.

It appears from the Scriptures that different angels have different functions. The angel Gabriel appears several times, but each time he shows up it is with a message. On the other hand, Michael appears to be a war angel. He turned up here to help this angel in his struggle with the prince of Persia. He fights for Israel (Daniel 12:1). He disputed with Satan over the body of Moses (Jude 1:9). And he will lead a group of angels that will cast Satan and his angels out of heaven (Revelation 12:7).

go to

ruler
Ephesians 2:2

god of this age
2 Corinthians 4:4

what others say

The Nelson Study Bible

The Prince of the kingdom of Persia cannot be a human ruler because the conflict referred to here is in the spiritual, heavenly realm, as the allusion to Michael makes clear. This prince, therefore, must be understood as a satanic figure who was to supervise the affairs of Persia, inspiring its religious, social, and political structures to works of evil.[9]

The Bible teaches that this present world is evil and there is a <u>ruler</u> called the prince of the power of the air influencing people to sin. He is also called the <u>god of this age</u> (Satan) who is blinding those who refuse to accept Christ. So we see that there is a wicked personality operating behind the scenes to cause sin and unbelief.

key point

The Target

DANIEL 10:14 *Now I have come to make you understand what will happen to your people in the latter days, for the vision refers to many days yet to come." (NKJV)*

This may well be the key verse in this chapter. From it we learn that what follows in chapters 10–12 concerns two things:

1. "Your people" means Daniel's people, the nation of Israel, and

2. the future.

speaking
Luke 1:20, 64

lips
Isaiah 6:6–7

seraphim, cherubim
creatures that guard
the throne of God

Do not overlook this. The next chapter clearly reveals events concerning Israel during the Medo-Persian Empire and the Greek Empire, but these events are pictures or types of events that will take place in the latter days or the End of the Age.

I Couldn't Talk

DANIEL 10:15 *When he had spoken such words to me, I turned my face toward the ground and became speechless.* (NKJV)

While the angel was revealing these things to Daniel, he simply looked down and said nothing. The next verse indicates it was not that Daniel did not know what to say but that something stopped him from speaking.

Someone Else Touched Me

DANIEL 10:16 *And suddenly, one having the likeness of the sons of men touched my lips; then I opened my mouth and spoke, saying to him who stood before me, "My lord, because of the vision my sorrows have overwhelmed me, and I have retained no strength.* (NKJV)

We are dealing with the spirit world here and do not know how many beings are involved. At times we do not even know if we are dealing with Jesus, angels, **seraphim, cherubim**, who or what. Here, someone who looked like a man touched Daniel on his lips. This was done to enable Daniel to speak. After it happened, Daniel addressed the being by saying that he was overcome with sorrow and had no strength.

Something like this should cause people to stop and reflect. There are those who try to contact the spirit world without knowing what might happen. It is a supernatural world filled with powerful spirit beings, both good and evil. At least some have the power to possess people. They have the ability to talk, afflict people, and cause people to do things they wouldn't otherwise do. They cannot be dealt with in ordinary ways. Spiritual weapons are required. Prayer in the name of Jesus is a starting point. Also, knowledge of the Word of God. But it is best to be cautious and not get involved in things one has very little knowledge of.

go to

strength
Daniel 10:8

touched
Daniel 10:10, 16, 18

I Am Weak and Out of Breath

DANIEL 10:17 *For how can this servant of my lord talk with you, my lord? As for me, no strength remains in me now, nor is any breath left in me."* (NKJV)

Daniel respectfully addressed the being about his own physical condition. His vision and this experience were having such a tremendous effect upon him that his <u>strength</u> was gone and breathing was difficult.

Touched a Third Time

DANIEL 10:18 *Then again, the one having the likeness of a man touched me and strengthened me.* (NKJV)

As Daniel stood there physically shaken and weak, this being <u>touched</u> him again. The first touch strengthened Daniel a little and left him trembling on his hands and knees. The second touch enabled him to speak. This third touch energized him with even more strength.

God Loves You

DANIEL 10:19 *And he said, "O man greatly beloved, fear not! Peace be to you; be strong, yes, be strong!" So when he spoke to me*

sorrow
Daniel 10:16

peace
John 14:27

strong
Ephesians 6:10

understand
Daniel 10:14

prince
Daniel 10:13

evil spirits
Acts 19:13–16

kings
Revelation 16:13–14

Medes
Daniel 5:30–31

I was strengthened, and said, "Let my lord speak, for you have strengthened me." (NKJV)

The being comforted Daniel and again tried to settle him down. He reminded Daniel that Daniel was highly esteemed in heaven, which is similar to saying, "God loves you."

Daniel had experienced <u>sorrow</u> over this vision so the being wished him <u>peace</u> and told Daniel to be <u>strong</u> After this encouragement Daniel was immediately strengthened and felt better, so he asked the being to continue with the message.

A Time Yet to Come

DANIEL 10:20 *Then he said, "Do you know why I have come to you? And now I must return to fight with the prince of Persia; and when I have gone forth, indeed the prince of Greece will come. (NKJV)*

The heavenly being asked Daniel a question but did not wait for an answer. He had already given the answer: he came to make Daniel <u>understand</u> what would happen to the Jews in the future.

The heavenly being then told Daniel, "Now I must return to fight with the prince of Persia" (Daniel 10:20 NKJV). In other words, he had appeared to Daniel for the express purpose of delivering a message, but he needed to return to the heavenlies because there was a spiritual war going on that required his involvement. The <u>prince</u> of Persia (evil spirit in charge of Persia) needed to be opposed, but when he went back to oppose the prince of Persia, the prince of Greece (evil spirit in charge of Greece) would move in and take over. This demonstrates that the spiritual war was ongoing. Overcoming the prince of Persia to allow the heavenly being to get through wasn't the end of the matter.

The Bible not only teaches that there are <u>evil spirits</u> in charge of the nations on earth, it also teaches that evil spirits can possess people. It is easy to believe this is what happened to Adolf Hitler, Joseph Stalin, and others. This is what will happen to the Antichrist, what will give him power to take over the world government, and what will summon the <u>kings</u> of the earth to the Battle of Armageddon.

The <u>Medes</u> and Persians defeated Babylon. Darius the Mede, the short horn on the ram with two horns, took over and was followed by Cyrus, king of <u>Persia</u>, the <u>long horn</u>, two years later. But Alexander the Great of Greece, the <u>male goat</u>, replaced him. These events have already happened.

And the thing to notice is that these events followed the sequence given in Scripture. They are evidence that God knows the end from the beginning. They also show that angels such as Michael may have been involved in the fall of Babylon, the Medes and Persians, the Greeks, and the Romans. Furthermore, behind every prophecy there may be a host of angels assigned to see that it gets fulfilled the way the Word of God predicts.

It Is Written

> DANIEL 10:21 *But I will tell you what is noted in the Scripture of Truth. (No one upholds me against these, except Michael your prince.)"* (NKJV)

The angel came to Daniel to explain what will happen to the Jews in the future. The heavenly being informed Daniel that he would tell Daniel what has already been recorded about the future in God's heavenly Scriptures. That revelation will come in chapters 11 and 12, but first this messenger wanted Daniel to know that no one was helping him fight the princes of Persia or Greece except Michael. "Your prince" is Daniel's prince and it identifies <u>Michael</u> as the angel or prince that God has placed in charge of Israel. This is the same Michael who helped the heavenly being get through with the answer to Daniel's prayer.

The Bible is the Scripture of Truth and the greatest book ever written. It has been published in more than 600 different languages and dialects, has probably more than 100 billion copies in print, and has weathered attacks in every generation and on every continent. It is time now for people to understand that the Bible has a heavenly origin and a heavenly or supernatural protection.

People also need to understand that human beings are pawns in an unseen supernatural war. But they are more than the least important pieces on a chessboard. They are the trophy or the prize. The future of every person depends upon which side they are on and who wins this war.

Persia
Daniel 10:1

long horn
Daniel 8:3, 20

male goat
Daniel 8:5–7, 21

Michael
Daniel 10:13

Chapter Wrap-Up

- During the third year of the reign of Cyrus king of Persia, Daniel was fasting and praying when he received a message. (He had gone without choice food, meat, wine, and lotions for twent-one days.) (Daniel 10:1–4)

- While standing by the Tigris River, Daniel looked up and saw a vision of someone believed to be Jesus (the Anointed One). Daniel's companions did not see the vision, but something scared them into running and hiding. (Daniel 10:5–7)

- Daniel became weak, turned pale, was helpless, and fell to the ground in a deep sleep. (Daniel 10:8–9)

- The hand of a heavenly being touched Daniel, putting him on his hands and knees, and causing him to tremble. A voice told Daniel to stand up and listen. The voice assured Daniel that God heard his prayers and sent an answer, but the prince (evil spirit) in charge of the kingdom of Persia detained him. The Archangel Michael helped the heavenly being get past the evil spirit. (Daniel 10:10–14)

- Daniel couldn't talk until someone touched his lips. Then he told the heavenly being he was in anguish, helpless, and having trouble breathing. The heavenly being assured him that he was highly esteemed, wished him peace, and strengthened him. (Daniel 10:15–21)

Study Questions

1. Should we believe the things in this vision? Why?

2. What does this chapter tell us about prayer?

3. Was Daniel's meeting with angels a glorious experience? What happened to him?

4. What does this chapter teach us about angels?

5. What does this chapter tell us about evil spirits?

The Smart Guide to the Bible

Chapter Highlights:
- Persia and Greece
- North Versus South
- Antiochus Epiphanes
- The Antichrist
- Time of the End

Daniel 11 Past Pictures of Future Events

Let's Get Started

As previously noted, chapters 10–12 deal with one vision (the Vision of the Anointed One). Chapter 10 is the prologue, chapter 12 is the epilogue, and Daniel 11 is the vision itself.

This remarkable chapter is forty-five verses long, with each verse being in Daniel's future. However, from our point in time, much of it has been fulfilled, and it would be easy for us to divide it into two convenient sections:

- thirty-five verses of historical background

- ten verses of future prophecy

This chapter could be divided that way but not without making it a little misleading. The first 35 verses are historical events that also foreshadow future events. They predict historical struggles that, to us, have already happened, but those historical struggles are also examples of future things that will happen at the End of the Age. Someone has said, "history repeats itself." These historical events illustrate things that will be repeated in the future.

It might help us to grasp this concept if we recall that Babylon was defeated by the <u>Medes and Persians</u>. The Medes and Persians were defeated by Alexander the Great of <u>Greece</u>. When he died his kingdom was divided and given to four <u>horns</u>, his four generals: Cassander took Greece and Macedon, Lysimachus took Asia Minor (now Turkey and Thrace), Seleucus took Syria and Babylonia, and Ptolemy took Egypt and Palestine. For the next two hundred to three hundred years these empires fought each other in a continuous struggle for supremacy. Israel was often caught in the middle and greatly harmed by their constant fighting. In this chapter the angel accurately predicted some of their battles and their effect upon Israel. But God also revealed their battles because they are excellent examples of the turmoil that will exist in the Middle East at the End of the Age.

Medes and Persians
Daniel 5:28–31

Greece
Daniel 8:5–8, 20–21

horns
Daniel 8:8

go to

Darius
Daniel 5:31

prince
Daniel 10:13

decree
Ezra 6:1–12;
Daniel 9:25

Cyrus
Daniel 10:1

The Wycliffe Bible Commentary

Egypt (v. 8) is mentioned by name in such a manner as to identify it as the "king of the south" (v. 9); but Syria (actually much larger than Syria, and unrelated historically to the OT kingdom of that name) is left unnamed. This appears to be because Egypt had long been known as a kingdom in Daniel's time, but the kingdom of the Seleucids was not yet in existence. If Daniel had been written in the second century, as some critics say, the kingdom of Syria would almost certainly have been named.[1]

Who Took a Stand?

DANIEL 11:1 *"(Also in the first year of Darius the Mede, I, even I, stood up to confirm and strengthen him.)* (NKJV)

The facts in this chapter are so accurate the critics claim it couldn't possibly have been written by Daniel. They emphatically declare that it would be humanly impossible for him to predict these things before they happened. This is a big reason behind their argument that Daniel was written two hundred to three hundred years later than it claims, and a good reason why we need to identify the speaker in this verse. Forget the chapter and verse divisions because they were not in the original writings. This verse follows the last verse of chapter 10 where the speaker is a heavenly being. He is the same one speaking here. We have not been told his name, but it seems likely that he is the angel Gabriel. And Daniel is the secretary recording this vision.

Keep in mind two facts from previous chapters: (1) Darius the Mede ruled over the combined kingdom of the Medes and Persians, and (2) Satan had placed an evil spirit called the prince of the Persian Kingdom in charge of Persia. When Darius came to power Satan had an evil spirit in charge of Persia, so this good angel took a stand to support and protect Darius. We are not sure why but it might be because Darius was kind to the Jews. He even issued a decree to let them rebuild their Temple in Jerusalem.

Notice that Daniel received this vision in the third year of Cyrus (see Time Line #1, Appendix A). Now notice in this verse that the angel is talking about something that happened in the first year of Darius. In other words, the angel is looking back and telling Daniel that he supported and protected Darius a few years earlier.

kingdom
Daniel 2:39

Cyrus king of Persia
Daniel 10:1

what others say

Billy Graham

The Bible teaches that the demons are dedicated to controlling this planet for their master, Satan. Even Jesus called him the prince of this world (John 12:31). He is the master-organizer and strategist. Many times throughout Biblical history, and possibly even today, angels and demons engage in warfare. Many of the events of our times may very well be involved in this unseen struggle.[2]

America has experienced an explosion of interest in satanic activity in recent years. There have been several cases of young people killing parents, teachers, and classmates. Many have gone from believing in aliens, ghosts, and UFOs to believing in the occult and trying to make contact with Satan or his fallen angels. Is it possible that a struggle is going on in the spirit world for control over people in this world? The Bible says, "Yes."

Persia's Future

DANIEL 11:2 *And now I will tell you the truth: Behold, three more kings will arise in Persia, and the fourth shall be far richer than them all; by his strength, through his riches, he shall stir up all against the realm of Greece. (NKJV)*

Keep in mind the time of this vision. Persia was the ruling world kingdom, and it was the third year of Cyrus king of Persia. The angel was telling Daniel the fact that this vision was a truth about Persia's future. Following Cyrus, four more kings would reign in Persia. The fourth king, a man by the name of Xerxes, would be richer than all the others. He would use his great wealth to gain power, build a great army, and stir up his people against the Greeks. Xerxes attacked the Greeks, had some initial successes, took some slaves, and did a lot of damage, but he eventually suffered a terrible defeat.

according to his will
Daniel 11:36

Greece
Daniel 8:3–8, 19–21

kingdom
Daniel 2:39

four
Daniel 8:5–8, 21–22

Greece's Future

DANIEL 11:3 *Then a mighty king shall arise, who shall rule with great dominion, and do according to his will. (NKJV)*

This is what the angel told Daniel about the rise of Greece: "A mighty king shall arise, who shall rule with great dominion, and do according to his will" (Daniel 11:3 NKJV).

What happened? The Persian king Xerxes did have some success against the Greek Empire, but he never gained the upper hand. What he did do was stir up a lot of Greek hatred against Persia, and cause the Greeks to look forward to an opportune time for revenge. That happened when a mighty king named Alexander the Great came on the scene. No one could resist Alexander. He quickly conquered Persia and assumed authority over the entire kingdom.

The mighty king was Alexander the Great. History tells us he was unquestionably the most successful military man on earth in his day. He extended the Greek kingdom until there were no other kingdoms to conquer. He had an insatiable desire for war and no one could stop him. The Bible says there will be another king who will do as he pleases. We call that power-hungry man the Antichrist. It is hard to believe the world will turn complete control over to one man, and especially when that one man belongs to Satan. The world will obviously not be like the world we live in today.

Greece Will Be Divided

DANIEL 11:4 *And when he has arisen, his kingdom shall be broken up and divided toward the four winds of heaven, but not among his posterity nor according to his dominion with which he ruled; for his kingdom shall be uprooted, even for others besides these. (NKJV)*

Here the angel predicted the future of Greece. The empire would break up and be divided in four directions. It would not go to a descendant of the mighty king. It would be weakened and divided among others.

History records that Alexander the Great died as a young man. He was about thirty-three years old, an alcoholic, suffering from malaria, and fighting depression because there were no more kingdoms to conquer. Historians say that he was asked whom he wanted to take over the kingdom and he replied, "Give it to the strong." The result of that was a power struggle, the murder of his entire family, and the eventual division of the empire into four parts.

This occurred over a period of about twenty years. Alexander left a half brother named Philip, who was mentally ill; an illegitimate son named Hercules, who was very young; and a yet-to-be-born son, who was also named Alexander. The decision was made to let Philip and Alexander rule as co-regents under the decision-making influence of others, but the appointment of the "others" became the source of a power struggle. Six years after Alexander died, the uprooting of his kingdom started. The next eight years saw the murder of Philip, Hercules, and Alexander, and the division of the Greek Empire into four parts ruled by the four most powerful generals: Cassander, Lysimachus, Seleucus, and Ptolemy.

Egypt: The King of the South

DANIEL 11:5 *"Also the king of the South shall become strong, as well as one of his princes; and he shall gain power over him and have dominion. His dominion shall be a great dominion.* (NKJV)

The angel narrowed his prophecy down to two of the four kingdoms that would come into existence following the division of the Greek Empire. The kingdom to the south of Israel would become strong. A commander from that kingdom would become even stronger, and he would rule his own kingdom.

History records that one of the four generals under Alexander the Great was a man named Ptolemy. He acquired Egypt and Palestine when the kingdom was divided. Egypt soon rose to prominence, and Ptolemy became rich and powerful.

One of the other three generals, Seleucus, acquired Syria, but he had problems ruling and once had to flee for his life. He went to Egypt where his old friend Ptolemy ruled. Ptolemy took him in, gave him a high position in Egypt, and provided money and assistance so that Seleucus was soon able to go back and retake the Syrian kingdom. This time he was so successful that he soon became stronger than Ptolemy.

When the Bible mentions a direction such as north or south, that direction is always in relation to the land of Israel. The king of the

dynasties
a long line of kings

given up
made powerless

North will always refer to a power north of Israel and the king of the South will always refer to a power south of Israel.

Ptolemy and Seleucus were generals who took over two parts of Alexander's empire. As the first rulers in their new empires they established **dynasties** that would rule for years to come. There were several kings named Ptolemy who ruled in Egypt over the next 300 years and several kings named Seleucus who ruled in Syria over the next 250 years.

The discussion in this verse refers to Ptolemy I and Seleucus I. They were the founders of two ruling families or empires often referred to as the Ptolemies and Seleucids. Some may not find these historic events interesting, but it will soon become apparent that the angel was taking Daniel down through the ancestry of a coming Seleucid king named Antiochus Epiphanes and on to the time of the end and a man Christians call the Antichrist. Some say he will be a Syrian. We have come from four kings to two kings and will go to one king. Notice the following chart.

The King of the South— Ptolemies (Egypt)	The King of the North— Seleucids (Syria)
Ptolemy I (Soter) 323–285	Seleucus I (Nicator) 312–280
Ptolemy II (Philadelphus) 285–246	Antiochus I (Soter) 280–261 Antiochus II (Theos) 261–246
Ptolemy III (Euergetes) 246–221	Seleucus II (Callinicus) 246–226 Seleucus III (Ceraunus) 226–223
Ptolemy IV (Philopator) 221–204	Antiochus III (the Great) 223–187
Ptolemy V (Epiphanes) 204–181	Seleucus IV (Philopator) 187–175
Ptolemy VI (Philometor) 181–145	Antiochus IV (Epiphanes) 175–164

Sometimes Everything Goes Wrong

DANIEL 11:6 *And at the end of some years they shall join forces, for the daughter of the king of the South shall go to the king of the North to make an agreement; but she shall not retain the power of her authority, and neither he nor his authority shall stand; but she shall be **given up**, with those who brought her, and with him who begot her, and with him who strengthened her in those times. (NKJV)*

The angel now skips over several years to a new generation of kings. He tells Daniel that the king of the South and the king of the

North (Egypt and Syria) would become allies. He predicted that the daughter of the king of the South would go to the king of the North to seal the alliance. He also predicted that the idea would not work, that the daughter would lose her power, and then the king would lose his power. Furthermore, the angel predicted that she would be handed over together with everyone who had anything to do with her.

By this time fifty or more years had passed. The king of the South was an Egyptian king named Ptolemy Philadelphus. The king of the North was a Seleucid who called himself Antiochus Theos (Antiochus the God). The two kingdoms were having trouble getting along and these two kings wanted to change things. They thought it would be wise to forge an alliance, so Ptolemy Philadelphus offered to let his daughter, Bernice, marry Antiochus Theos. There was just one problem—Antiochus Theos was already married, so Antiochus Theos divorced his wife, Laodice, and disowned their children. He quickly married Bernice, and the alliance was sealed. But it wasn't long until Ptolemy Philadelphus died. Antiochus then changed the status of Bernice to **concubine** and remarried Laodice. Although Laodice married him, she wanted revenge, so she poisoned Antiochus, had Bernice murdered, and named one of her sons king. Thus, the attempt to forge an alliance was a total failure.

War Between the South and the North

DANIEL 11:7 *But from a branch of her roots one shall arise in his place, who shall come with an army, enter the fortress of the king of the North, and deal with them and prevail.* (NKJV)

As the angel continued the prophecy he told Daniel that one from the daughter's (Bernice) family would arise to take her place. He said this relative would attack the king of the North, enter into his stronghold, and win the battle.

When Ptolemy Philadelphus died, his son Ptolemy Euergetes assumed the throne in Egypt. He was the brother of Bernice and was angry over what happened to his sister. Revenge was one of his first acts. He gathered a large army and attacked the fortress of Seleucia where Laodice was. He won the battle, captured Laodice, and put her to death.

love
Matthew 5:44

revenge
Ezekiel 25:15–17

judgment of God
2 Corinthians
5:10–11

Jerome
a famous Bible
expert who trans-
lated ancient writ-
ings into Latin

God tells us to <u>love</u> our enemies, but <u>revenge</u> is just the opposite. It is something God hates and has even been known to make him angry. Some say revenge is sweet, but it is unlikely that Laodice would say that. Before taking revenge one should ponder the fact that it is a terrible thing to come under the <u>judgment of God</u>.

Helpless Gods

DANIEL 11:8 *And he shall also carry their gods captive to Egypt, with their princes and their precious articles of silver and gold; and he shall continue more years than the king of the North.* (NKJV)

The angel focused his prophecy on the gods and riches of Syria. Ptolemy Euergetes (Bernice's brother) would seize the Syrian gods, images, and valuables and take them back to Egypt. And it would be a long time before the two kingdoms fought each other again. Historians say Ptolemy Euergetes was on the verge of capturing all of Syria when he received word of an insurrection back home in Egypt. He quickly grabbed up all the valuables he could find and returned to Egypt. According to **Jerome** he took 4,000 talents of gold, 40,000 talents of silver, and 2,500 Syrian idols.

Listen to what the Bible says about idols: "Their idols are silver and gold, the work of men's hands. They have mouths, but they do not speak; eyes they have, but they do not see; they have ears, but they do not hear; noses they have, but they do not smell; they have hands, but they do not handle; feet they have, but they do not walk; nor do they mutter through their throat. Those who make them are like them; so is everyone who trusts in them" (Psalm 115:4–8 NKJV). Worshiping idols is a waste of time, but multitudes will worship the image of the Antichrist during the Tribulation Period.

The North Strikes Back

DANIEL 11:9 *Also the king of the North shall come to the kingdom of the king of the South, but shall return to his own land.* (NKJV)

The next angelic prediction was that Syria would invade Egypt. However, Syria would not be successful and would have to retreat to their own country.

The Syrian king Callinicus directed an attack on Egypt but lost the battle and had to return home empty-handed.

Back and Forth

DANIEL 11:10 *However his sons shall stir up strife, and assemble a multitude of great forces; and one shall certainly come and overwhelm and pass through; then he shall return to his fortress and stir up strife.* (NKJV)

The next angelic prediction was that the sons of Callinicus would prepare for war, organize an army, and quickly move against one of the main Egyptian fortresses.

Callinicus had two sons. History reveals that the oldest became king first. He prepared to attack Egypt but was a poor and unpopular leader, so two of his generals poisoned him. Then the youngest son, Antiochus the Great, assumed the throne. He continued the war preparations, was a better leader, and launched an attack. He won a big victory against the Egyptians at **Gaza** (see Illustration #2) and considered trying to conquer the entire nation.

Egypt
Daniel 11:42

Gaza
narrow strip of land between Egypt and Israel

> **what others say**
>
> **King James Bible Commentary**
>
> The sons of Seleucus II were Seleucus III, called variously Ceraunus or Soter, and Antiochus III, the Great. Seleucus III was assassinated in 223 BC, so Antiochus III took over, eventually running roughshod over Ptolemy IV in the land of Egypt. Later, he was defeated in the north; but he eventually captured the fortress of Gaza in Palestine.[3]

The Antichrist will move into the Middle East. He will then take an army and move south through Gaza and take Egypt. Several other nations will also fall at that time.

Seesaw

DANIEL 11:11 *"And the king of the South shall be moved with rage, and go out and fight with him, with the king of the North, who shall muster a great multitude; but the multitude shall be given into the hand of his enemy.* (NKJV)

go to

army
Psalm 33:16

pride
Proverbs 16:18

The angel told Daniel that Egypt would be angered and go out to fight Syria. Syria would have a great army, but it would be defeated.

Ptolemy Philopator replaced his father, Euergetes, as king of Egypt. He had a terrible temper and was greatly angered by Syria's victory at Gaza. He finally struck back and defeated Syria's great <u>army</u>.

what others say

Stephen R. Miller

In response Ptolemy IV Philopator (221–203) launched a counterattack. Both armies were quite large. According to Polybius, Ptolemy's forces consisted of 70,000 infantry, 5,000 cavalry, and 73 elephants; whereas Antiochus's army had 62,000 infantry, 6,000 cavalry, and 102 elephants. . . . [In 217 BC] Ptolemy had won a great victory over the Syrians at Raphia (located in Palestine).[4]

Tremper Longman III

The story of Antiochus III the Great's reign continues through verse 19. The significance given to his reign likely has much to do with the fact that it was through his agency that Palestine finally shifted from Ptolemaic control to Seleucid control, thus setting the scene for the horrors of his son's reign (cf. below on vv. 21ff.).[5]

Pride Goes Before Destruction

DANIEL 11:12 *When he has taken away the multitude, his heart will be lifted up; and he will cast down tens of thousands, but he will not prevail.* (NKJV)

Here the angel told Daniel that the victory of Ptolemy Philopator over Antiochus the Great would cause Philopator to be lifted up with <u>pride</u>. He would slaughter many thousands, but his victory would not turn out to be a great triumph.

When Ptolemy Philopator defeated Antiochus the Great at Raphia he killed ten thousand Syrians and took several thousand prisoners, but because of his pride, he did not follow up on his great victory. Instead of continuing on into Syria to capture the whole kingdom he signed a foolish peace treaty with Antiochus the Great and returned home to receive glory and have a good time.

The Antichrist will be filled with pride and will defeat many nations. His move through the Middle East will be a **blitzkrieg**, but his triumphs will come to an <u>end</u>, and he will have no one to help him.

end
Daniel 11:45

covenants
Daniel 9:27

blitzkrieg
sudden and violent war

A Broken Peace Treaty

> DANIEL 11:13 *For the king of the North will return and muster a multitude greater than the former, and shall certainly come at the end of some years with a great army and much equipment.* (NKJV)

This time the angel prophesied that Syria would muster a larger and better-equipped army. And after several years he would advance on Egypt once again.

The peace treaty that Ptolemy Philopator signed with Antiochus the Great let the Syrian king take his army and return home. Upon his return, Antiochus started a program to rebuild his military. Some <u>covenants</u> are just tools to buy time or gain an advantage. Over the next fourteen years he built a powerful force, suppressed all his enemies, enriched his nation, and began to reach out and take whatever he wanted. Soon he received word that the Egyptian king Ptolemy Philopator had died and his five-year-old son Ptolemy Epiphanes had succeeded him. Antiochus the Great looked at the situation and decided it would be a good time to attack Egypt, so he broke his covenant and struck Egypt thinking he would have an easy victory.

Who Wants a Five-Year-Old King?

> DANIEL 11:14 *Now in those times many shall rise up against the king of the South. Also, violent men of your people shall exalt themselves in fulfillment of the vision, but they shall fall.* (NKJV)

The angel predicted rebellion against Egypt. "Your own people" refers to Daniel's people, the Jews. The angel predicted that wicked Jews would join the rebellion against Egypt but without success.

Many of Egypt's most influential citizens were greatly disappointed when Ptolemy Epiphanes was crowned king. Some of them banded together and rebelled against his leadership, killing several of

people
Daniel 9:26

Anointed One
Jesus

the king's most faithful subjects. There were also Jews within Egypt and back in Israel who joined in the rebellion. All these rebels believed that Antiochus the Great would defeat Egypt, so they wanted to be on the right side. What they did not count on was Egypt signing a mutual-aid treaty with Rome. That powerful nation entered the picture and changed everything. There will be wicked Jews during the Tribulation Period who will join forces with the Antichrist. Many Jews will oppose the covenant with Antichrist, but some wicked Jews will betray their people and sign it.

"In fulfillment of the vision" is an interesting phrase. It reminds us of the Vision of the Ram and the Goat in chapter 9. That vision reveals that the <u>people</u> of the ruler who will come (the Romans) would destroy Jerusalem and the Temple after the **Anointed One** was killed. We know the Romans did this in AD 70, but this present verse has them moving into the Middle East in fulfillment of the vision. In other words, it was the providence of God that Rome went to Egypt's aid. That put them in position to fulfill the Vision of the Ram and the Goat.

A Northern Victory

DANIEL 11:15 *So the king of the North shall come and build a siege mound, and take a fortified city; and the forces of the South shall not withstand him. Even his choice troops shall have no strength to resist. (NKJV)*

This is more detail from the angel concerning the previous verse. He predicted that Syria would capture an Egyptian-fortified city. He added that Egypt's forces would be powerless to stop him and that even the best Egyptian troops would not be strong enough to stop Syria.

The rebellion resulting from crowning a five-year-old boy as king of Egypt and the insurrection of the Jews greatly weakened Egypt. This was just what Antiochus wanted, so he set out to attack Egypt. Unfortunately for Antiochus, the Romans had entered the picture, and they had one of their experienced ministers serving as guardian and assistant to the young king. He called on a famous Egyptian general named Scopas to help. Scopas quickly organized an army and went out to meet Antiochus the Great. But he wasn't strong enough, and Antiochus the Great defeated his army. After defeat, Scopas and a few of his troops fled to the fortress city of Sidon, but Antiochus the Great pursued them and laid seige to the city. Egypt got word and sent troops to help, but they were not strong enough to defeat Antiochus either. He defeated them, starved out the besieged Egyptians, captured the fortress city of Sidon, and sent the surviving troops away stark naked. Everything the angel said was accomplished.

Glorious Land
Daniel 11:41

Poor Israel

> DANIEL 11:16 *But he who comes against him shall do according to his own will, and no one shall stand against him. He shall stand in the Glorious Land with destruction in his power.* (NKJV)

The angel is providing all this information about Syria and Egypt because their struggles greatly affected Israel. Every time one country attacked the other the invading army had to pass through Israel. It didn't happen every time, but the Jews often took a beating.

The angel revealed these things for Daniel's understanding, and although we are receiving a lot of information about Syria and Egypt, this is really a message about Daniel's people Israel.

Here the angel predicted that Antiochus the Great would do as he pleased. No one would be strong enough to stop him. He would settle down in the <u>Glorious Land</u> and be strong enough to destroy it.

The Egyptians were weak and knew it. They had signed a mutual-aid treaty with Rome, so they asked Rome for help. The Romans were rapidly becoming a great power, so they warned Antiochus the Great not to invade Egypt. So Antiochus held back and settled down in Israel while he pondered his options. He had the power to destroy Israel, but did not because of the Jews who had rebelled and supported him in Egypt.

what others say

Rodney Stortz

This fulfilled prophecy shows us that God is sovereign in the affairs of men and nations. No one comes to power except those God places in that position of authority. Paul says in Romans 13:1, "Everyone must submit himself to the govern-

go to

mountain
Daniel 11:45

join forces
Daniel 11:6

peace
Jeremiah 6:14

ing authorities, for there is no authority except that which God has established. The authorities that exist have been established by God." Daniel 11:2–20 shows this to be true.[6]

During the Tribulation Period the Antichrist will invade the Glorious Land and use it as a base to attack other nations. He will receive power from Satan and do as he pleases for three and one-half years. John said people will worship him, saying, "Who is like the beast? Who is able to make war with him?" (Revelation 13:4 NKJV). He will be like Lucifer, who said, "I will ascend into heaven, I will exalt my throne above the stars of God; I will also sit on the mount of the congregation on the farthest sides of the north; I will ascend above the heights of the clouds, I will be like the Most High" (Isaiah 14:13–14 NKJV). God said he will be cast down into Sheol (hell or the pit). That is what will happen to the Antichrist. He will locate his headquarters at the glorious holy <u>mountain</u>, and that is where he will be when he is captured and cast into the Lake of Fire (Revelation 19:20).

Try Diplomacy: A False Peace Treaty

DANIEL 11:17 *He shall also set his face to enter with the strength of his whole kingdom, and upright ones with him; thus shall he do. And he shall give him the daughter of women to destroy it; but she shall not stand with him, or be for him. (NKJV)*

The angel told Daniel that Antiochus would be determined in his desire to capture Egypt. In order to do that he would <u>join forces</u> with Egypt. He would give one of his daughters in marriage to the king of Egypt in order to overthrow the Egyptian kingdom, but it would not work.

Fear of drawing the Romans into the conflict on the side of Egypt and having to fight both nations at the same time caused Antiochus the Great to occupy the land of Israel while he waited and strengthened his forces. But his fear did not deter him from wanting to conquer Egypt. It just caused him to change his tactics.

By this time Ptolemy Epiphanes, the child-king of Egypt, was about seven years old and Antiochus the Great had a daughter who was a little older, perhaps as much as five or six years older. Her name was Cleopatra. Antiochus the Great suggested that Syria and Egypt stop fighting and sign a <u>peace</u> treaty. He suggested that Ptolemy and

Cleopatra marry to seal the treaty. Antiochus the Great thought his daughter would be loyal to him, dominate the young Egyptian king, and help bring about Syria's acquisition of Egypt, but Cleopatra did not cooperate. She was loyal to her husband and sided with the Egyptians against her own father. The false treaty did not work.

go to

man of peace
Revelation 6:2

break the treaty
Daniel 9:27

destroy the Jews
Revelation 12:13–17

what others say

Merrill F. Unger

In his strategy, Antiochus was seeking to destroy Egypt without openly attacking her, for he feared intervention from Rome if he did so. So he arranged to give him (the young king, Ptolemy V Epiphanes) his daughter, Cleopatra, as a wife. Antiochus's ultimate plan was to use that marriage to ruin Egypt in order to further his own ambitions of conquest.[7]

Saladin
a Muslim leader who
broke a peace treaty

Today the Arabs and PA are suggesting that Israel should swap "land for peace." But there are two definitions of *peace* in the Arab language. The first definition is the true peace we Americans think of. It is the kind of peace that has existed between the United States and Canada for many years. The second definition is the "peace of **Saladin**." That is a truce that can be broken at a convenient time. When Arab leaders speak to their Arab brothers they make it plain that "land for peace" means the "peace of Saladin." They are talking about a peace that can be broken to bring about the destruction of Israel. When Muslim militants say Islam is a peaceful religion, it should be understood that they are really warmongers trying to bring about peace by forcing the whole world to convert to Islam. They are at war with non-Muslims, and there can be no peace until there are no non-Muslims.

The Antichrist will be a wolf in sheep's clothing. This means he will actually be a warmonger, but he will come on the scene as a man of peace. He will sign a peace treaty to protect Israel, but he will break the treaty three and half years later. Then he will try to destroy the Jews. His sweet-sounding words will be a charade and his written agreements will be worthless pieces of paper.

This is not the same Cleopatra who was famous for her relationship with the great Roman leaders Julius Caesar and Mark Antony. That Cleopatra reigned between 69 and 30 BC, but this Syrian Cleopatra reigned more than one hundred years earlier. There were seven Egyptian queens named Cleopatra.

In Come the Romans

go to

reap
Galatians 6:7

people
Daniel 9:26

ships
Daniel 11:40

DANIEL 11:18 *After this he shall turn his face to the coastlands, and shall take many. But a ruler shall bring the reproach against them to an end; and with the reproach removed, he shall turn back on him. (NKJV)*

The next thing the angel prophesied was that Antiochus would abandon his plans to take Egypt and go after the coastlands. He would be successful at first, but a commander would end his rampage, and Antiochus would <u>reap</u> what he sowed.

Antiochus the Great was furious over Rome's protection of Egypt and his daughter's betrayal. He assembled a three-hundred-ship navy and started seizing the cities and islands along the coasts of the Mediterranean Sea. However, most of these coastal cities were under Roman control and Rome was not about to let Antiochus the Great take their territory. To prevent this, the Romans commissioned a young naval commander named Scipio to take a fleet of Roman warships and go after the Syrian vessels. Scipio found and sank most of the Syrian navy, thereby turning Antiochus the Great's insolence back upon himself.

The Romans would be in control of Israel when the Anointed One (Jesus) came. They are the <u>people</u> who would destroy Jerusalem and the Temple. This verse points to their arrival on the scene in the Middle East. They (the Old Roman Empire) would be there for the First Coming, and they (the Revived Roman Empire) will be back for the Second Coming of Jesus. In fact, the king of the North will attack them with many <u>ships</u> during the Tribulation Period, but he will be defeated.

The Tax Man Cometh

DANIEL 11:19 *Then he shall turn his face toward the fortress of his own land; but he shall stumble and fall, and not be found. (NKJV)*

The angel continued revealing the vision to Daniel. He predicted that Antiochus would return to his own country following his defeat along the coastlands. But things would not go well in his homeland. He would stumble and be seen no more.

Antiochus the Great returned home with one eye looking over his shoulder. He expected the Roman army to be right on his heels. As soon as he got home he sent messengers to Rome seeking peace. The Romans had the upper hand and were in no mood to be generous. They offered peace, but at a very high price. Antiochus the Great had to give them all the territory he controlled in Europe, a big chunk of what he controlled in Asia, all but ten of his warships, an enormous tribute, and heavy taxes every year for the next twelve years. He agreed to their terms but had trouble coming up with the money and was killed while trying to seize it a few months later.

go to

wages of sin
Romans 6:23

for us
Romans 8:31

lake of fire
Revelation 19:20

No Tax Cuts Under This Administration

> DANIEL 11:20 *"There shall arise in his place one who imposes taxes on the glorious kingdom; but within a few days he shall be destroyed, but not in anger or in battle. (NKJV)*

Here the angel prophesied the future of the successor to Antiochus the Great. He would send out the tax collector to keep payments going, but shortly thereafter would be destroyed. He would not die, however, in anger or in battle.

Antiochus the Great was succeeded by his oldest son Seleucus Philopator. Seleucus inherited the large debt his father agreed to pay in order to obtain peace with Rome. He raised taxes to meet the agreement, but his nation was so impoverished he had trouble collecting them. By the time he neared the last year of the twelve-year taxation clause he was in a financial crisis. He desperately instructed his treasurer to go to Jerusalem and confiscate the gold and silver vessels that were being used at the Temple. A short time later someone poisoned him.

what others say

Oliver B. Greene

In each instance concerning the battles, the victories, and the defeats of these kings of the North and of the South, we see over and over again that the <u>wages of sin</u> is death, and God is not mocked. . . . Whether we are king or peasant, if God is <u>for us</u>, who can be against us? But by the same token, whether we are king or peasant, if God is against us we are defeated.[8]

The Antichrist will not die in battle. He will be captured by Jesus at the Second Coming and thrown alive into the <u>lake of fire</u> burning with brimstone.

The Contemptible Person

sinister schemes
Daniel 8:23

horn
Daniel 8:9

precursor
a living example

DANIEL 11:21 *And in his place shall arise a vile person, to whom they will not give the honor of royalty; but he shall come in peaceably, and seize the kingdom by intrigue.* (NKJV)

The angel told Daniel the next king to rule would be a vile person. Although he would be the king, he would not be the true heir to the throne. He would invade the kingdom (Israel) during a time of peace and seize it by intrigue (sinister schemes).

Antiochus Epiphanes was not the true heir to the throne. (See "Antiochus Epiphanes and the Antichrist" chart in chapter 8.)

After Seleucus Philopator tried to confiscate the Temple vessels he was poisoned. He had two sons—Demetrius, the oldest, was in position to be crowned king, but Seleucus Philopator had a younger brother, Antiochus, who was an extraordinarily good manipulator. Like his father Antiochus the Great, Antiochus was wicked and cunning, and like his sister Cleopatra, who was married off to Ptolemy Epiphanes of Egypt, he was deceitful and treacherous. He used his manipulative skills, treachery, and deceit to acquire the crown over his nephew Demetrius, the rightful heir. Antiochus later became known as Antiochus Epiphanes. He is widely recognized by prophecy experts as a **precursor** or forerunner of the horn in chapter 8. What the angel has to say about this man exemplifies what the Antichrist will do at the End of the Age. Key words in the next three verses that prefigure the Antichrist are *peaceably* and *intrigue* in verse 21, and *deceitfully* in verse 23.

Antiochus Epiphanes picked up where his father Antiochus the Great left off. He was another king of the North (Syria) who attacked the king of the South (Egypt). Before he did that he convinced everyone he was just moving a small number of troops to the Egyptian border. He actually moved a large army, but he had to move it into Israel before getting to the Egyptian border.

> **what others say**
>
> **John F. Walvoord**
>
> Beginning with verse 21 [through verse 35], a major section of this chapter is devoted to a comparatively obscure Syrian ruler who was on the throne from 175 to 164 BC, previously alluded to as the "little horn" (Dan. 8:9–14, 23–25). He

reigned in the days of the decline of the Syrian power and the rise of Rome to the west, and only his death in 164 BC prevented his humiliation by Rome. From the standpoint of Scripture and the revelation by the angel to Daniel, this was the most important feature of the entire third empire.[9]

go to

deceit
Matthew 24:5;
2 Timothy 3:13

ten kingdoms
Daniel 7:24;
Revelation 13:1;
17:12

covenant
Daniel 11:28–29

<u>Deceit</u> can only prosper where there is ignorance. When the Rapture occurs the only true leaders and religious people left on earth will be lost. The Antichrist will rise to power in a world of biblical ignorance. His deceitful ways and sweet-sounding words of peace and prosperity will meet no resistance because people will not recognize him for what he is.

Our national leaders are diligently working to establish a world government. That government will divide into <u>ten kingdoms</u>. The Antichrist will not be given the honor of being king over one of those kingdoms, but with Satan's help he will seize the world government through intrigue.

A Powerful Military Leader with His Own High Priest

DANIEL 11:22 *With the force of a flood they shall be swept away from before him and be broken, and also the prince of the covenant.* (NKJV)

This angelic prophecy states that the contemptible king would destroy a great army. It also predicted a prince of the covenant would be destroyed.

Antiochus Epiphanes attacked Egypt and the Egyptians struck back with a large army. The casualties on both sides were high, but Antiochus Epiphanes won the battle and captured the Egyptian king Ptolemy Philometor, the son of Cleopatra (Antiochus's sister).

Antiochus Epiphanes broke so many agreements and betrayed so many people it is difficult to say who the prince of the <u>covenant</u> was. One could pick from several examples. The best guess, however, seems to be the Jewish high priest Onias III. Antiochus Epiphanes had him deposed and murdered. Then he appointed the brother of Onias III, a man named Jason, to be the high priest of Israel. With the approval of Antiochus Epiphanes, Jason persuaded many Jews to

go to

False Prophet
Revelation 16:13

truth
Daniel 8:12

great
Daniel 8:9

deceit
2 Thessalonians
2:10;
Matthew 24:11, 24

elect
Matthew 24:24

abandon their faith. The Antichrist will be a powerful military leader, and he will have his own religious spokeman called the <u>False Prophet</u>, who will cause multitudes to follow his anti-Christian beliefs.

Deceit and More Deceit

DANIEL 11:23 *And after the league is made with him he shall act deceitfully, for he shall come up and become strong with a small number of people. (NKJV)*

Here the angel was prophesying the fact that the contemptible person (Antiochus Epiphanes) would make an agreement with his captive (Ptolemy Philometer), but Antiochus Epiphanes would be deceiving him. With only a few people he would rise to power.

After Antiochus Epiphanes defeated Egypt's army and captured Ptolemy Philometor, the Egyptians quickly crowned Philometor's brother, Ptolemy Euergetes, king. Antiochus Epiphanes wanted to march against him, but he had lost too many troops when he defeated Ptolemy Philometor. He saw the crowning of Ptolemy Euergetes as an opportunity to divide the remaining Egyptian forces, to take more spoils, and perhaps to have himself crowned king of Egypt. He made an agreement to help his captured nephew Ptolemy Philometor regain the crown in exchange for Philometor's help and support against Ptolemy Euergetes. It worked. <u>Truth</u> was thrown to the ground. Ptolemy Philometor helped Antiochus Epiphanes and his support strengthened the Syrian king. But what Philometor didn't know until later was the fact that Antiochus Epiphanes was just tricking him. It was a deceitful tactic on the part of Antiochus Epiphanes to make himself exceedingly <u>great</u>.

<u>Deceit</u> will be a way of life during the Tribulation Period. The Antichrist will perform satanic miracles and deceive many. Jesus said that many false prophets will appear and deceive many people. He said, "False christs and false prophets will rise and show great signs and wonders to deceive, if possible, even the <u>elect</u> (Matthew 11:24 NKJV).

That he will "become strong with a small number of people" is a reminder that the Antichrist will begin as the "little horn" (Daniel 7:25). He will rise from obscurity to a position of world domination with the help of a small number of world leaders. Ten leaders will come on the scene first. He will rise among them. Three will obstruct him. He will deal with them and the other seven will give their power to him.

liar
John 8:44

Antiochus Epiphanes was a living example of the Antichrist, the wicked man who will gain control of the whole world during the Tribulation Period. He talked peace and planned war. The Antichrist will use sweet-sounding words to bring in a reign of terror. The following chart highlights his dishonesty:

Integrity of the Antichrist

Characteristic	Scripture
He shall cause deceit to prosper.	Daniel 8:25
He will break his covenant.	Daniel 9:27
He will be a liar.	2 Thessalonians 2:9–10
He will be a worthless shepherd.	Zechariah 11:16–17

A Wicked Robin Hood

DANIEL 11:24 *He shall enter peaceably, even into the richest places of the province; and he shall do what his fathers have not done, nor his forefathers: he shall disperse among them the plunder, spoil, and riches; and he shall devise his plans against the strongholds, but only for a time. (NKJV)*

This angelic prophecy states that Antiochus Epiphanes would invade the richest provinces of Egypt at a time when they feel secure. He would take plunder, spoil, and riches but not keep it. He would give it to his followers, and for a time, he would plot the overthrow of Egyptian strongholds.

The covenant Antiochus Epiphanes made with Ptolemy Philometor put many of the Egyptians at ease. It did not occur to them that they were dealing with a thief and a liar. At a time when they felt secure, Antiochus Epiphanes raided some of the richest provinces of Egypt. He took wealth and territory that none of his ancestors were able to take. Then, like the head of a gang of thieves, he distributed the loot among his followers. That bought the loyalty of even more men, so he planned to attack more places. But things eventually changed.

attack
Daniel 11:39

The Antichrist will do the same thing. He will attack and plunder several nations in North Africa, including Egypt, Libya, and Ethiopia (verses 42–43). He will turn back only after he hears disturbing news out of the east and north (verse 44).

The angel said Antiochus Epiphanes shall devise his plans against the strongholds, but "only for a time." God controls all things, and he had drawn a line that Antiochus could not cross. Consider the fact that God said the Jews would serve the king of Babylon seventy years. The Two Witnesses will prophesy 1,260 days. Jesus said, "Jerusalem will be trampled by Gentiles until the times of the Gentiles are fulfilled" (Luke 21:24 NKJV). Gabriel told Daniel the Messiah would appear seven weeks and sixty two weeks (173,880 days) after the command to restore and build Jerusalem. The angel was saying Antiochus will be limited and his days will be numbered. Concerning the Antichrist, it means the Tribulation Period will last seven years or 2,520 days and not one day more. We will soon see that the Antichrist will prosper until the wrath has been accomplished (verse 36). And we have already seen that the saints will be given into his hands for a time and times and half a time (Daniel 7:25).

During the Tribulation Period the Antichrist will <u>attack</u> and conquer many nations. He will use his booty and conquered territory to reward those wicked people who support him.

Treason in the South

DANIEL 11:25 *He shall stir up his power and his courage against the king of the South with a great army. And the king of the South shall be stirred up to battle with a very great and mighty army; but he shall not stand, for they shall devise plans against him. (NKJV)*

Here the angel predicted Antiochus Epiphanes would build up his forces and muster the courage to mount a great attack on Egypt. He predicted that Egypt would fight back with a powerful army, but Egypt would lose due to plots devised against it.

Antiochus Epiphanes attacked Egypt. This time the king of the South was another brother of Ptolemy Philometor named Ptolemy Physcon. He pulled together a large army and fought back, but some of his men committed treason, deserted him, and joined Antiochus Epiphanes. Their unfaithfulness caused Egypt's defeat.

The king of the <u>South</u> and his four-nation alliance will wage war against the Antichrist, but he will not be able to stand, and the Antichrist will defeat him and his army.

Daniel received this vision (the Vision of the Anointed One) two hundred years before any of these battles occurred.

South
Daniel 11:39

Feast of Passover
John 13:1

Do Not Bite the Hand That Feeds You

DANIEL 11:26 *Yes, those who eat of the portion of his delicacies shall destroy him; his army shall be swept away, and many shall fall down slain. (NKJV)*

This angelic prediction identifies some of those who would be involved in the treason as those who eat from the king's provisions. In other words, the king of the South would be betrayed by members of his own court. That betrayal would lead to a military defeat and many casualties.

Information is scarce, but it seems that most of the members of the court were related to both Ptolemy Physcon (the reigning king) and Ptolemy Philometor (the captured king). Some were more loyal to Ptolemy Philometor and believed Antiochus Epiphanes was just helping him recover his throne, so they betrayed Physcon, Egypt was defeated, and many Egyptians were killed.

Jesus celebrated the <u>Feast of Passover</u> with his disciples in the Upper Room. After they finished eating, he humbly washed their feet, but was troubled in his spirit because he knew one of those he ate with would betray him. Out of friendship and love he gave Judas Iscariot a piece of bread. Judas took a bite, quickly left, and turned his back on the one who loved him more than anyone else.

At the end of the age, Jesus said that many will betray one another and hate one another (Matthew 24:10). He said people will be betrayed even by parents and brothers, relatives and friends, and they will put some to death (Luke 21:16).

Lies, Lies, and More Lies

DANIEL 11:27 *Both these kings' hearts shall be bent on evil, and they shall speak lies at the same table; but it shall not prosper, for the end will still be at the appointed time. (NKJV)*

white horse
Revelation 6:2

peace
Daniel 8:25

covenant
Daniel 9:27

mouth
Daniel 7:8;
Revelation 13:5

covenant
Exodus 19:5;
Leviticus 24:8; 26:9

The angel told Daniel the king of the North (Syria) and the king of the South(Egypt) would sit at the same table. They would have evil in their hearts and lie to each other. But the lies would not aid either one because the end would still come at the time of God's choosing.

Antiochus Epiphanes and Ptolemy Philometor sat down to discuss the situation. They were supposedly going to settle their differences, but all they did was lie to one another.

Revelation pictures the Antichrist arriving on the scene riding a <u>white horse</u>. He will use <u>peace</u> to destroy many and a <u>covenant</u> to dupe Israel. His actions will make Antiochus Epiphanes look like an amateur, and the gullibility of Ptolemy will be exceeded only by the gullibility of our future government leaders.

The Antichrist will come forth with a <u>mouth</u> that boasts great things and utters proud words. He will be an eloquent speaker and a tremendous negotiator.

He Opposed God's Covenant

> **DANIEL 11:28** *While returning to his land with great riches, his heart shall be moved against the holy covenant; so he shall do damage and return to his own land. (NKJV)*

Here the angel prophesied that Antiochus would leave Egypt with a large amount of wealth and return to his own land, but he would oppose the <u>covenant</u> God had with Israel. He would violate that covenant before returning home.

It appeared that Antiochus Epiphanes and Ptolemy Philometor had settled their differences around the conference table. A large amount of Egypt's wealth was handed over to Antiochus Epiphanes, and he headed back to Syria with his army. The route home took him through Israel.

Things had changed in Israel since Antiochus Epiphanes had passed through on his way to Egypt. A rumor had circulated that Antiochus Epiphanes was dead, which caused many Jews to rejoice. Some of them had revolted and driven the Syrians out of Jerusalem. Antiochus Epiphanes learned of this as he neared Jerusalem and decided to make the Jews pay. God's covenant with Israel was not something he believed anyway, so he attacked and plundered the city, killed approximately forty thousand Jews, sold thousands more into slavery, looted the Temple, and let his troops rape the women.

fatal
Revelation 13:3, 12, 14

> what others say
>
> ### Stephen R. Miller
>
> Then Gabriel arrived at the real purpose of all this historical data—to set the stage for the persecution of the Jewish people.[11]

When the Antichrist comes on the scene and history approaches the Tribulation Period midpoint the Antichrist will appear to be killed by a <u>fatal</u> wound to the head. It will be a sword wound and it will be healed to the amazement of the whole world. Multitudes will follow him, and yet, he will be worse than Antiochus Epiphanes ever thought of being.

In connection with this, many prophetic writers believe Zechariah's worthless shepherd is a type of the Antichrist (Zechariah 11:17). He will be struck by a sword causing his right arm to wither and his right eye to be blinded.

A Worthless Agreement

> DANIEL 11:29 *"At the appointed time he shall return and go toward the south; but it shall not be like the former or the latter.* (NKJV)

The angel told Daniel Antiochus Epiphanes would invade Egypt one more time, but things would be different this time.

Antiochus Epiphanes was determined to conquer Egypt, so he tried again. His two nephews, Ptolemy Philometor and Ptolemy Physcon, had settled their differences and were sharing the throne. They opposed Antiochus Epiphanes and appealed to Rome for help.

They're Back

> DANIEL 11:30 *For ships from Cyprus shall come against him; therefore he shall be grieved, and return in rage against the holy covenant, and do damage. So he shall return and show regard for those who forsake the holy covenant.* (NKJV)

Satan
Revelation 12:9–13

abomination
Daniel 9:27; 12:11;
Matthew 24:15, 21

Alexandria
an Egyptian port
city on the
Mediterranean Sea
built by Alexander
the Great

Sabbath
the seventh day of
the week, Saturday

The angel predicted that Antiochus Epiphanes would be opposed by ships of the western coastlands. They would cause him to change his mind about invading Egypt again. He would turn around and vent his rage on the covenant of God one more time. But he would deal kindly with those who abandoned the covenant.

When the two Egyptian kings appealed to Rome for help the Romans responded by sending their navy. Rome's naval commander met Antiochus Epiphanes at **Alexandria** and told him to get out of Egypt and leave the nation alone. The order was by decree of the Roman Senate and if Antiochus did not obey he would be attacked by Rome. Then the commander drew a circle on the ground around the feet of Antiochus and demanded that he not step out of it until he stated his intentions. Antiochus decided to leave Egypt.

Antiochus Epiphanes headed home through Israel, but he was even more furious than before. His entire army was aware that he was afraid and running, so when he got to Jerusalem he vented his anger and plundered the city again, killing thousands of Jews and selling thousands more into slavery. He outlawed the Jewish religion and replaced it with Greek worship. He outlawed circumcision, the reading of the Scriptures, and the observance of the **Sabbath**. Those who abandoned the Jewish faith were spared, but those who did not were killed.

At the Tribulation Period midpoint <u>Satan</u> and his angels will be hurled down to the earth out of heaven. Satan will know his time is short, and he will be filled with fury. He will vent his fury on God's people and destroy whatever he can before the Second Coming of Christ.

More Contemptible Acts

> **DANIEL 11:31** *And forces shall be mustered by him, and they shall defile the sanctuary fortress; then they shall take away the daily sacrifices, and place there the abomination of desolation.* (*NKJV*)

The angel revealed that the army of Antiochus Epiphanes would desecrate the Temple (see Illustration #17). They would abolish the daily sacrifice and set up the <u>abomination</u> that would make the Temple desolate.

Antiochus Epiphanes posted some of his troops to guard the Temple with reserve troops nearby. The Sabbath came and thousands of Jews gathered at the Temple to offer sacrifices and worship God. They were ignoring Antiochus Epiphanes, so he counted them among his enemies and had his army kill them. Then he built an altar to one of his Greek gods, brought in Jews, and compelled them to sacrifice pigs on it to his heathen gods. Those who refused were killed.

He was insane and often referred to himself as the Greek god Zeus. He was a type of the Antichrist who will sit in the Temple and call himself God (2 Thessalonians 2:4). His outlawing Jewish worship and replacing it with Greek worship prefigures the Antichrist bringing an end to the sacrifices and offerings at the Temple with a demand that people worship him (Daniel 9:27; Revelation 13:15). His numbering those Jews who refused to stop their worship at the Temple among his enemies and having them killed is a forerunner of the Antichrist, who will consider those who refuse to take the mark and worship him to be his enemies and therefore to be killed (Revelation 13:15–18). Also, Antiochus Epiphanes placed an image of Zeus in the holy place at the Temple. Jesus said the Antichrist will do this and the Jews should flee into the mountains when it happens (Matthew 24:16–17).

what others say

Ed Hindson

Part of the deception perpetrated by the False Prophet will be his power to give life to the "image of the beast" (Revelation 13:15). The biblical text uses the word *eikon* ("icon") for "image." It means a representation derived from a prototype or a "perfect likeness." It looks like the real thing, but it isn't. While we cannot be certain what "image of the beast" refers to, more and more scholars are suggesting the possibility of a televised holographic image or a computer icon.[12]

Thomas Ice and Timothy Demy

He believed himself to be Zeus, and on Chislev 25 (December 16, 167 BC) he defiled the temple in Jerusalem by erecting an altar to Zeus on the altar and offered swine's flesh as a burnt offering. He then directed that similar offerings be made monthly. Such defilement or "abomination of desolation" fulfilled Daniel's prophecy and ultimately led to the Maccabean revolution.[13]

deceived
2 Thessalonians
2:9–12

lukewarm
Revelation 3:15–16

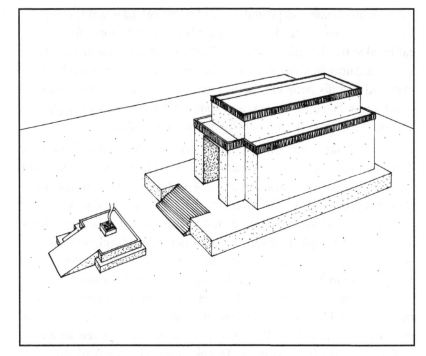

Illustration #17
The Temple in
Jerusalem—The
abomination that
causes desolation
will be set up on a
wing of the Temple.
Sacrifices made on
the outside altar will
be stopped.

Flattery from Hell

DANIEL 11:32 Those who do wickedly against the covenant he
shall corrupt with flattery; but the people who know their God
shall be strong, and carry out great exploits. (NKJV)

Daniel was informed by the angel that Antiochus Epiphanes would
corrupt some of the unfaithful Jews with flattering words, but the
faithful Jews would firmly resist him.

The Jews had their share of traitors and lukewarm believers. Some,
such as the new high priest Alcimus, were even leaders in the Jewish
religion. Antiochus Epiphanes courted them with flattering words in
order to corrupt them to his false religion and use them against the
faithful. Many who questioned the Word of God were <u>deceived</u>, but
a group of strong believers revolted.

Jesus placed church members in one of three states: cold, <u>luke-</u>
<u>warm</u>, or hot. The cold are pretenders who lack true spiritual life.
The lukewarm are indifferent or straddling the fence. The hot are
passionate about their love for him. This last group is the only one
Jesus finds acceptable.

The Maccabean Period

DANIEL 11:33 *And those of the people who understand shall instruct many; yet for many days they shall fall by sword and flame, by captivity and plundering.* (NKJV)

tribulation
Matthew 24:9

power
Revelation 13:7, 15

Here the angel predicted that a group of wise people would teach many, but for a while they would be delivered up to <u>tribulation</u> in four ways:

1. Some would be killed by the sword.

2. Some would be killed by fire.

3. Some would be captured.

4. Some would be robbed.

Hassideans
an orthodox religious sect of Jews

A large number of Jews recognized the corruption, treachery, and false teachings of Antiochus Epiphanes. They wisely tried to remain faithful to God and teach others. Some, who were called the **Hassideans**, revolted and fled into the mountains. They joined the Maccabees family and fought against Antiochus Epiphanes and the rulers who followed him. They carried on their struggle for independence for more than a hundred years. Many died in war, some were tortured and burned, while others were captured. Most had their villages and camps plundered and destroyed.

A Jewish priest named Mattathais, who wanted the Jews to remain faithful to God, killed an unfaithful Jew who was about to offer a heathen sacrifice at the Temple. Fearing for his life, Mattathais took his five sons, one of which was named Judas Maccabaeus, and fled into the hills. The family became known as the Maccabees because of their subsequent revolt against Antiochus. They were very successful in their struggle against him, and so upset him that he could no longer eat, and he eventually died in his own land of malnutrition.

For a time (the seven-year Tribulation Period) the Antichrist will be given <u>power</u> to make war against God's people and conquer them. The False Prophet will set up an image and kill those who refuse to worship it. Many of God's people will fall.

Lukewarm

go to

drunkenness
Zechariah 12:2

DANIEL 11:34 *Now when they fall, they shall be aided with a little help; but many shall join with them by intrigue.* (NKJV)

The angel predicted the fall of the wise (Maccabees). They would also receive a little help and have many insincere people join them. The courageous struggle of the Maccabees cost the family and their followers many lives. They eventually lost the struggle, but not before they won several major battles. Some of their victories were so impressive that many Jews thought the Maccabees might win. That caused a dilemma for the fence-sitting Jews. They feared the wrath of Antiochus Epiphanes if he won, but they also feared the wrath of their countrymen if the Maccabees won. They wanted to be on the winning side, so every Maccabean victory was accompanied by more Jews joining the cause. However, many of them were not true believers; they just did not want to be accused of treason if their people won.

The Time of the End

DANIEL 11:35 *And some of those of understanding shall fall, to refine them, purify them, and make them white, until the time of the end; because it is still for the appointed time.* (NKJV)

This angelic prophecy starts with those of understanding (the faithful) during the struggle of the Maccabees and skips forward to the Time of the End. The angel predicted that some of those of understanding would fall, but their misfortune would continue as a test of their zeal and faith until the Time of the End.

The Jews moved from being under the control of the Syrians to being under the control of the Romans. In AD 70 Jerusalem and the Temple were destroyed. Those who weren't killed were scattered throughout the world. Some of the faithful have been robbed, persecuted, and killed ever since. Multitudes were burned to death in Hitler's ovens. Today, they have their nation back, but they are a cup of drunkenness for the entire world. This will continue until the Second Coming of Christ at the end of the Tribulation Period.

go to

boasting
Daniel 7:8, 20

God
2 Thessalonians
2:3–4

> **what others say**
>
> **The Wycliffe Bible Commentary**
>
> They were the separatists of that day, who refused the pagan vices of their Greek lords no less than the beautiful lies of the heathen ritual and religion. They constitute the main link between the Testaments, for their spiritual descendants appear in the Gospels as the Pharisees (whose name means "separated ones"). How sad that their descendants fell from their true principles![14]

The Coming Antichrist

DANIEL 11:36 *"Then the king shall do according to his own will: he shall exalt and magnify himself above every god, shall speak blasphemies against the God of gods, and shall prosper till the wrath has been accomplished; for what has been determined shall be done. (NKJV)*

This angelic revelation lists several characteristics of the coming Antichrist:

1. "The shall shall do according to his own will" speaks of his absolute authority in the world. He will be a dictator with a massive military and worldwide support. Whatever he says will be carried out. God is One who does according to his will (Daniel 4:35). Alexander the Great and Antiochus the Great are examples of kings in this chapter who did according to their will (verses 3, 16).

2. "He shall exalt and magnify himself above every god" speaks of his <u>boasting</u>. His heart will be filled with pride. He will boast of his abilities, achievements, and greatness. An example of self-exalting people in this chapter is the Jews who aided Antiochus the Great against Egypt (verse 14). They failed miserably.

3. "[He] shall speak blasphemies against the <u>God</u> of gods" means his speeches will be filled with anti-God, anti-Christ, anti-Bible, anti-Christian, anti-Semitic, and anti-Church rhetoric. Christians and Jews will be persecuted and killed. Elsewhere Daniel said he will speak pompous words (Daniel 7:8, 11, 20). John said he will have a mouth speaking great things and blasphemies (Revelation 13:5–6).

earth
Revelation 13:8

Lake of Fire
Revelation 19:20

4. "[He] shall prosper till the wrath has been accomplished" speaks of his rapid rise to power over the <u>earth</u>, and his terrible end at the set time in the <u>Lake of Fire</u>. Antiochus Epiphanes is an example of a man in this chapter whose days were numbered (verse 24).

5. "For what has been determined shall be done" means everything that has been prophesied will be fulfilled.

The Antichrist will say unheard-of things against the God of gods.

Prince of Darkness
the Antichrist

what others say

Grant R. Jeffrey

In total contrast to Jesus who came to "do his Father's will" the Antichrist will "do according to his own will." The coming **Prince of Darkness** will be a true child of this age of assertiveness, self-promotion, and self-will. He will exalt his own sinful desires against all opposition until he is defeated by Christ.[15]

John C. Whitcomb

The shocking challenge to God's sovereignty that men will see in this depraved world ruler calls for clear reminders that evil is not only temporarily tolerated by God but is actually included in His decree (cf. Gen. 45:5, 7; 50:20). Two years earlier, Daniel had been told in similar terms that God would accomplish His purposes through this wicked one "even until a complete destruction, one that is decreed, is poured out on the one who makes desolate." Thus, a recurring theme of the book of Daniel is the absolute sovereignty of God in the midst of human and angelic rebellion (cf. Dan. 4:17, 25).[16]

More About the Antichrist

> DANIEL 11:37 *He shall regard neither the God of his fathers nor the desire of women, nor regard any god; for he shall exalt himself above them all.* (NKJV)

Here are four more things the angel revealed to Daniel about the coming Antichrist. These are gods he will not honor:

1. "He shall regard neither the God of his fathers" is unclear in that some translations read "gods" (plural) and some read God (singular). The plural form "gods" indicates that he will come from a pagan Gentile family that worships many gods, but the singular form "God" indicates that he will come from a monotheistic family, probably Jewish, that worships one God, such as Abraham, Isaac, and Jacob did. Whether he will be a Gentile or a Jew is debatable, but the text clearly indicates that he will be unlike Antiochus Epiphanes, who esteemed Zeus and built temples for the gods of his ancestors. Family religion and heritage will mean nothing to this man.

worship
Revelation 13:4

2. "Nor the desire of women" is also somewhat unclear. A few commentators say this is an indication that the Antichrist will be gay, but most say it means he will have no desire for the Messiah. It is well-known that the desire of all Jewish women was to be the mother of the Messiah. The Antichrist will not esteem the Messiah. As far as his sexual preferences are concerned, he may be gay because "forbidding to marry" and "unloving" or "without natural affection" are characteristics of his administration (1 Timothy 4:3 NKJV; 2 Timothy 3:3 KJV). So he will definitely be anti-Christ, and he may be gay.

3. "Nor regard any god" means he will be an unbeliever or an apostate, one who will not worship anyone's god because he will sit in the Temple and declare that he is God. This will account for much of the apostasy at the end of the age.

4. "He shall exalt himself above them all" is a repeat of verse 36 and verifies other statements that his ultimate goal will be to have everyone <u>worship</u> him.

The Antichrist will be involved in New Age teaching at its very worst. He will blaspheme the God of heaven and then tell people that he is God. Multitudes who will absolutely refuse to worship the Lord God Almighty will gladly worship this demon-possessed man as their god.

His Chief Love

DANIEL 11:38 *But in their place he shall honor a god of fortresses; and a god which his fathers did not know he shall honor with gold and silver, with precious stones and pleasant things.* (NKJV)

power
Revelation 13:2

Daniel 11:37 discussed gods the Antichrist will not honor. This verse identifies what god he will honor: the god of fortresses. Fortresses are a symbol of power. The Antichrist will sell his soul for <u>power</u>. He will spend great wealth to acquire it and will use it to honor his god. And who is his true god? Satan.

It is critical to remember that John pictured this Satan worshiper coming forth as a man of peace carrying a bow and no arrows, but going out conquering and to conquer (Revelation 6:2). He will receive his power from Satan and make war on God's people (Revelation 13:4–7). He will be like Antiochus Epiphanes, who acquired much of Egypt's wealth through lies at a conference table. Then he returned home through Israel and stopped long enough to let his troops plunder, kill, rape, and make war on the Jews (verses 27–28). The Antichrist will confirm a covenant of peace with Israel at the beginning of the Tribulation Period and be captured while his troops are plundering, killing, raping, and making war on the Jews at the end of the Tribulation Period (Daniel 9:24–27; Zechariah 14:2; Revelation 19:20). What else should people expect from a man whose god is a murderer and the father of lies (John 8:44)?

It is important to remember that during the Tribulation the Antichrist and his False Prophet will establish a one-world religion with demon possession and Satan worship being major characteristics (Revelation 17). Notice the following chart.

Religion of the Antichrist

Characteristic	Scripture
He will persecute the saints of the Most High.	Daniel 7:25
He will understand sinister schemes.	Daniel 8:23
He will desecrate the Jewish Temple.	Daniel 9:26
He will seize the kingdom by intrigue.	Daniel 11:21
He will speak blasphemies against the God of gods.	Daniel 11:36
He will act against the strongest fortresses with a foreign god.	Daniel 11:39
He will receive his authority from the dragon (Satan).	Revelation 13:4
He will be drawn into the Battle of Armageddon by demonic spirits.	Revelation 16:13–14

go to

given
Revelation 13:2,
4–5, 14–15

god
Daniel 11:38

world
2 Corinthians 4:4

flattery
Daniel 11:32

foreign
not the God of Israel

what others say

Grant R. Jeffrey

The closing days of this age will witness an unparalleled revival of idol worship and satanic rituals involving demons. Only two decades ago such a statement would have seemed absurd. However, the rise of open worship of Satan and a growing fascination with the occult characterize our generation.[17]

Charles H. Dyer

The Antichrist will spend his money on weapons of war. His strength will come from fortresses, not from faith in God. World events will seem to vindicate this leader's faith in bombs and bullets. Daniel describes a series of coalitions that rise against the Antichrist during the seven-year period [the Tribulation Period]. But these other alliances are no match for the power of the end-time ruler.[18]

Satanic Power

DANIEL 11:39 *Thus he shall act against the strongest fortresses with a foreign god, which he shall acknowledge, and advance its glory; and he shall cause them to rule over many, and divide the land for gain. (NKJV)*

The Antichrist will rise to power as a man of peace, but he will really be a man of war. He will seek, and be given, great power and authority. Then he will immediately use it to let the world know he is in control. He will quickly attack some of the strongest powers on earth with the help of a **foreign** god called the god of fortresses. That god is the god of the world—Satan.

The Antichrist will use flattery and bribes to procure and honor followers. He will appoint those who follow him to positions of authority over large numbers of people, and he will divide his conquered territories among those who make commitments to him.

Again, the example is Antiochus Epiphanes, who entered into a false covenant with Egypt so he could lull her asleep and plunder many of her richest provinces. Then he used the booty to buy the support of renegades who would help him continue his crime spree (verse 24). These will be some of the sinister schemes and intrigues of Satan's man. He will influence people to take the mark of the Beast, get them to worship him as god, and reward them with plunder, position, and power.

go to

end
Daniel 11:35

beast
Daniel 7:6

kingdom
Daniel 7:17

Gog
Ezekiel 38:2

chariots
possibly tanks

cavalry
possibly troops on
horseback

The Time of the End

DANIEL 11:40 *"At the time of the end the king of the South shall attack him; and the king of the North shall come against him like a whirlwind, with chariots, horsemen, and with many ships; and he shall enter the countries, overwhelm them, and pass through. (NKJV)*

"At the time of the <u>end</u>" (Daniel 11:40 NKJV) refers to the End of the Times of the Gentiles not the end of the world. These three things will take place:

1. Up to this point the king of the South has always referred to Egypt. But starting with this verse it is probably referring to a four-nation Arab coalition led by Egypt. The third <u>beast</u> in chapter 7 is such a <u>kingdom</u>. This coalition will engage the Antichrist in battle.

2. Up to this point the king of the North has always referred to Syria. But starting with this verse the king of the North is probably a coalition of northern nations including Russia, Syria, and others. This attack on the Antichrist will probably be Russia's second attempt to take control of the Middle East by force. Almost all prophetic experts expect Russia (<u>Gog</u>, of the land of Magog) to lead a coalition of nations against Israel in the latter days of this age. But a few prophetic experts including myself expect two different Russian-led invasions. The king of the North will use **chariots**, **cavalry**, and a large naval force.

3. The Antichrist will strike back with a great force and satanic power. He will defeat the kings of the North and South, invade several Middle Eastern countries, and overwhelm them.

Jesus said, "Watch," and here are three things to watch for:

1. A coalition of nations stationing troops in the Middle East.

2. A coalition of nations in Africa.

3. A coalition of nations north of Israel.

Kenneth O. Gangel

Precisely at this point too many well-meaning evangelical scholars have gone awry trying to identify these two kings in light of nations prominent and powerful at the time. Egypt and Russia seem likely choices, and proponents introduce Ezekiel 38–39 to bolster that viewpoint. But the flow of Daniel 11:36–39 seems to occur considerably later than Ezekiel 38–39. The king of the North could be the same entity, but we should not treat those passages as one event.[19]

John Hagee

This is not the first time we have seen the kings of the North and the South. This time, as before, they represent a resurgent Russian Empire conspiring with a Pan-Islamic Confederation to cleanse Jerusalem and seize control of the oil of the Middle East. Though savaged in battle when they attack Israel, these kings will draw on their vast resources of men and material to field a viable fighting force once again.[20]

A multitude of experts teach that there will be a future Russian invasion of Israel. Some merge the Scriptures in Daniel 11:40–45 with those in Ezekiel 38 and 39 and teach that there will be just one invasion. Others point to several differences between the two passages and say that it will take two invasions to resolve the problems. The first invasion would be the one described in Ezekiel 38 and 39 in which Russia's army and air force would suffer a terrible defeat. The second invasion would be the one described here in Daniel 11 in which Russia's navy would be defeated. This would explain why the nations of Persia, Gomer, and Togarmah are mentioned in Ezekiel but not in Daniel and why the Antichrist is mentioned in Daniel but not in Ezekiel. The first invasion could be to plunder and loot, while the second invasion could be to oppose the Antichrist.

Center Stage

DANIEL 11:41 *He shall also enter the Glorious Land, and many countries shall be overthrown; but these shall escape from his hand: Edom, Moab, and the prominent people of Ammon.* (NKJV)

The whole world will suffer at the hands of the Antichrist, but the Middle East will be the major hot spot. The Arabs will want to

go to

confirm
Daniel 9:27

covenant
Isaiah 28:14–22

many countries
Daniel 11:40

flee
Matthew 24:16

destroy the nation of Israel because of their ancient hatred, and because they will want to retake the Temple Mount. The Antichrist will want to occupy Israel so he can maintain a foothold in the Middle East to protect his oil supplies and be worshipped in the Temple.

Other nations will want to take Israel, so they can drive the Antichrist out and seize the oil for themselves. This area will see a lot of action during the Tribulation Period.

Three things we learn in this verse:

1. "He shall also enter the Glorious Land" (Daniel 11:41 NKJV) means the Antichrist will move his military into Israel. This is consistent with chapter 9 where we learn that he will <u>confirm</u> a <u>covenant</u> with many for seven years regarding Israel and then break it 3 1/2 years later.

2. "<u>Many countries</u> shall be overthrown" (11:41 NKJV) signifies the defeat of several nations. This includes the king of the North, the king of the South, and all their allies. They will try to drive the Antichrist out of the Middle East, but he will be too powerful for them.

3. "Edom, Moab, and the prominent people of Ammon" (11:41 NKJV) is a reference to three areas located in the nation we call Jordan (see Illustration #2) today. The capital of Jordan is Amman, a name derived from Ammon. This area will be spared during the Tribulation Period. The ancient city of Petra is located in southern Jordan and that seems to be the place where many Jews will <u>flee</u> to during the last half of the Tribulation Period, so this may explain why these three areas are spared.

what others say

Charles H. Dyer

I believe the invasion of the Beautiful Land in Daniel 11:41 is parallel to the gathering of the armies at Armageddon. The Antichrist summons an "International Task Force" to eliminate the final pockets of resistance to his domination of the world. They gather at Armageddon and move south toward Egypt and Africa.[21]

When the Antichrist gains control of the one-world government he will be praised, at first, as a savior, but things will turn sour. He will have to use force to hold his government together. Consider this example: At first the Muslims will like his world religion because he will tolerate everything except Christianity and Judaism. However, what do you think will happen when he demands they worship him instead of Allah? In conclusion, the Antichrist will gain control, be all-powerful, and do as he pleases, but the time will come when he does have some opposition. The only problem is that his opposition won't be strong enough to stop him.

Egypt's Terrible Fate

> **DANIEL 11:42** *He shall stretch out his hand against the countries, and the land of Egypt shall not escape.* (NKJV)

After establishing a military presence in the land of Israel, the Antichrist will extend his power over many countries. How many countries is not said, but this is the third time we have been told this. And it is plain that God intends for Egypt to be one of the nations dominated by the Antichrist.

Today, Egypt is a target for some of the most dangerous terrorists in the world. Muslim fanatics are desperately trying to take over the government and turn Egypt into a staging ground for attacks on Israel. If they succeed, something will have to be done to protect Israel. This is not a good sign, but it is interesting to watch Bible prophecy be fulfilled.

what others say

Mark Hitchcock

Scripture has much to say about the nation of Egypt during the Tribulation:

- Egypt's army will be destroyed by God (Isaiah 19:16; Ezekekiel 38–39).
- After Egypt's army is destroyed by God, Egypt will be easy prey for the Antichrist. He will conquer and plunder Egypt (Daniel 11:41–43).
- Egypt will become a wasteland and a wilderness (Isaiah 19:16–17; Joel 3:19).
- Many in Egypt will turn to the Lord for salvation (Isaiah 19:22).

go to

covetous
Exodus 20:17

God's future dealings with Egypt are among the most beautiful demonstrations of his grace. No nation has as long a history of rejection of divine revelation as Egypt. From the times of Abraham, Joseph, and Moses, Egypt has consistently rejected the true God. But in his infinite mercy and grace, God will make himself known to the Egyptians, will bless them, and will bring them into harmony with their neighbors.[22]

Riches and Power

DANIEL 11:43 *He shall have power over the treasures of gold and silver, and over all the precious things of Egypt; also the Libyans and Ethiopians shall follow at his heels. (NKJV)*

When Egypt falls the Antichrist will plunder the nation. It seems like a poor nation by the world's standards, but some of their ancient treasures are among the most valuable in the world. Articles of gold and silver have been displayed in many places around the world and, by anyone's standards, are priceless. The Antichrist will covet these articles.

However, he will not only be <u>covetous</u> and greedy but will be a military genius as well. He will want to secure his southern flank in the Middle East, so after he conquers Egypt he will move against the Libyans and Nubians (Sudan, Ethiopia, and possibly Djibouti). They will quickly surrender.

One might wonder why a loving God would allow this to happen, but there is a lot of wickedness in this area of the world and God often uses one wicked group to punish another (e.g., Libya has killed many of its own people, forced the Muslim religion on others, and tried to export revolution to other nations).

Armageddon

DANIEL 11:44 *But news from the east and the north shall trouble him; therefore he shall go out with great fury to destroy and annihilate many. (NKJV)*

The Antichrist will have very little time to celebrate his impressive victories in Africa. News will soon reach him that a great army is massing in the East and another is gathering in the North. Identifying the army from the East is no problem. The majority of prophecy experts agree that this is a reference to the kings of the East mentioned in Revelation. According to that prophecy, the Euphrates River will dry up and a 200-million-man army (China and her allies) will march into the Middle East. Identifying the king of the North is a problem. Russia and her allies will have suffered major defeats by this time, so we have no strong explanation other than to say this northern army will probably come from many nations around the world including remnants from Russia, Turkey, Syria, and Lebanon.

These armies will pose a major threat to the Antichrist. His anger will burn and he will go forth with plans to destroy these great armies. Can you imagine how many people will die in this battle when just one of these armies will have 200 million troops?

go to

East
Revelation 16:12–16

200 million
Revelation 9:14–16

world
Revelation 16:14

people
Revelation 19:17–21

killing one-third
Revelation 9:15

Jerusalem
1 Chronicles 11:5–8

armies
Revelation 19:11–16

---

what others say

Grant R. Jeffrey

The eastern armies will fight as they march across Asia, killing one-third of humanity in their path. The final battle will center on the Valley of Jezreel [also called the Plain of Esdralon] "to a place called in Hebrew, Armageddon."[23]

Charles R. Swindoll

No doubt, he will make his final stand on the plain of Megiddo, or Jezreel, in the center of Israel. As the hordes from the east (probably China) and the Antichrist's forces from the west descend on Israel, the stage will be set for the final conflict—the battle of Armageddon (Rev. 16:12–16).[24]

No More Antichrist

DANIEL 11:45 *And he shall plant the tents of his palace between the seas and the glorious holy mountain; yet he shall come to his end, and no one will help him." (NKJV)*

This identifies the place where the Antichrist will locate his military headquarters near the end of the Tribulation Period. "Between the seas" (Daniel 11:45 NKJV) means between the Mediterranean Sea and the Dead Sea. "The glorious holy mountain" (11:45 NKJV) means at Jerusalem (also called Mount Zion). "He shall come to his end" (11:45 NKJV) is a reference to the Second Coming of Jesus with the armies of heaven, the capture of the Antichrist, and the

go to

lake of fire
Revelation 19:20

Antichrist being thrown alive into the <u>lake of fire</u> burning with brimstone.

Today there are a lot of people who have high hopes for a New World Order. They are working day and night to organize the United Nations into a world government that can impose its will on every nation. They have charted an international criminal court to try national leaders and others who do not cooperate, have founded command-and-control centers for an international army to support their world government, and are looking for a great leader who can pull off all this together. They will find one, but their world government will eventually come crashing down.

what others say

David Jeremiah with C. C. Carlson

When the nations that are gathered together against Jerusalem see the Lord's armies in heaven coming after them, they will forget about the fact that they are at war with each other. They will all get together and decide that they are going to fight against the Lord. All the armies with their military leaders and advanced technology won't have a chance. After the Antichrist is captured, and the False Prophet too, the two of them will be thrown alive into the Lake of Fire.[25]

Chapter Wrap-Up

- During the reign of King Cyrus of Persia, a heavenly being appeared to Daniel and revealed that he had given Darius the Mede supernatural help when he came to power. He predicted that Cyrus would be followed by four more kings in Persia and the fourth would stir up the Persians against the Greeks. Then a Greek king (Alexander the Great) would rise to power and defeat Persia. At the height of the Greek king's power he would die, and his kingdom would be divided into four parts and given to those who were not his heirs. (Daniel 11:1–4)

- One of Alexander's generals acquired the territory north of Israel and another acquired the territory south of Israel. The Bible calls the northern power the king of the North and it calls the southern power the king of the South. These two groups fought with each other for many years. When the armies campaigned against one another they passed through Israel and the Jewish people often suffered. These two nations worshiped idols, deceived each other, made and broke several peace treaties, drew other armies into their struggles, persecuted the Jews, and often imposed their beliefs on the Jews. (Daniel 11:5–20)

- One king of the North was Antiochus Epiphanes, and the Bible calls him a contemptible person. He was not the rightful heir to the throne in Syria, but through deceit and cunning he managed to crown himself king. He deposed the Jewish high priest in Israel and appointed one of his own choosing, persuaded many Jews to abandon their faith, captured most of Egypt, made and broke several peace treaties, plundered Jerusalem and the Temple, enslaved and killed thousands of Jews, outlawed the Jewish religion, and desecrated the Temple. He is a forerunner of the Antichrist because that wicked man (the Antichrist) will do many of these same things but to a greater extent. (Daniel 11:21–34)

- The vision in this chapter skips forward more than two thousand years to a description of the coming Antichrist at the Time of the End (the End of the Age not the end of the world). He will have absolute authority over his empire, be filled with pride and boasting, blaspheme God, declare that he is God, defile the Temple, honor Satan, fight many wars, conquer many people, and appoint his wicked supporters to positions of power. (Daniel 11:35–39)

- This vision describes some of the wars the Antichrist will be involved in at the End of the Age. He will send troops to the Middle East. An army from the South and another from the North will try to drive him out, but he will defeat them both. He will occupy and plunder many countries including Egypt, Ethiopia, and Sudan, but not Jordan. Two other great armies will be organized to attack him: an unidentified army from the North and a great army from the East (China and her allies). Jesus will come to stop them from destroying the whole earth, and when he does they will settle their differences, join forces, and attack Jesus at the Battle of Armageddon. In the end the Antichrist will be captured and destroyed. (Daniel 11:40–45)

Study Questions

1. What does this chapter teach us about the permanence of Gentile world kingdoms?

2. What do we learn about the ambition of some leaders from the constant struggles between the kings of the North and the kings of the South?

3. Contrast the beginning of the career of the Antichrist with the end of his career.

4. Where will the Antichrist get his power, and what will it take to overcome him?

5. Will the Antichrist be a man of peace or a man of war?

DANIEL 12 Final Remarks

Chapter Highlights:
- Time of the End
- Some Good News
- Seal the Words
- Extra Days
- Go Your Way

Let's Get Started

This book begins with the fall of <u>Jerusalem</u> and Israel, and ends with the restoration of Israel and the beginning of the Millennium. The entire book spans the time between the beginning of the Times of the Gentiles and the End of the Times of the Gentiles (see Time Line #2, Appendix A). Israel is God's clock that signals the Time of the End. The Jews have suffered many things and will suffer more things in the future, but their return to the land is an indication that the end of their problems is in sight.

Jerusalem
Daniel 1:1

Chapter 12 concludes the Vision of the Anointed One that began in chapter 10. It is a vision about the latter days and refers to days yet to come (Daniel 10:14). It even reveals what will happen at the time of the end (Daniel 11:40). This is the end of the Times of the Gentiles not the end of the world. For this to happen, Israel must be back in the land. A reunited Europe and a world government must come on the scene. There must be great persecution and trouble for the Jews, especially from Syria in the North and Egypt in the South. There must be a phony peace treaty. The Jews must rebuild the Temple. The Antichrist must appear and more. Any observer of the daily news should quickly realize that this is shaping up.

The Times of the Gentiles will end with the Second Coming of Jesus. That will be the end to all of these bad things. And the saved Jews and Gentiles will have a wonderful new beginning.

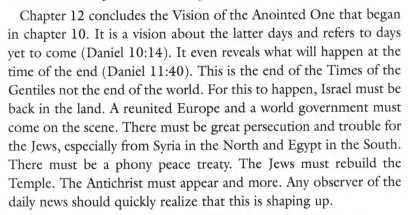

what others say

David R. Reagan

An example of an historical development is the re-establishment of the nation of Israel on May 14, 1948. The Bible is full of prophecies that the Jews will be regathered to their land in the End Times, right before the return of the Messiah (Isa. 11:10–12). For almost 2,000 years, the Jews were dispersed all over the world, with seemingly no hope of ever existing again as a nation. Because of this dispersion, the prophecies

go to

End
Daniel 11:35, 45

Michael
Daniel 10:13, 21

archangel
Jude 1:9

prince of Persia
Daniel 10:13

Michael
who is like unto God

concerning the end-time existence of Israel were not under-standable. The same was true of the prophecies (Zech. 12:1–6; Luke 21:24) regarding the Jewish reoccupation of Jerusalem [and the Temple Mount] that occurred on June 7, 1967.[1]

Thomas Ice and Timothy Demy

One of the core elements of end-time prophecy relating to the tribulation is the biblical prediction that there will be a revived form of the fourth of the four Gentile kingdoms predicted in Daniel 2 and 7. Since Rome was clearly the fourth kingdom, it follows that some form of that kingdom will be revived. What all the king's horses and all the king's men could not do, God will allow the Antichrist to accomplish for a brief period of time (in the future) . . . Developments in our own day relating to the reunification of Europe are an indication that God is preparing the world for just such a configuration as predicted thousands of years ago in the Bible.[2]

The Time of the End

> **DANIEL 12:1**
> *"At that time Michael shall stand up,*
> *The great prince who stands watch over the sons of your people;*
> *And there shall be a time of trouble,*
> *Such as never was since there was a nation,*
> *Even to that time.*
> *And at that time your people shall be delivered,*
> *Every one who is found written in the book. (NKJV)*

This verse makes several points:

1. "At that time" identifies the time we are dealing with. It takes us back to the events in the closing verses of chapter 11 where we were studying the Time of the End.

2. "Michael" is **Michael** the archangel. He is the powerful angel who helped Gabriel overcome the prince of Persia and who will help cast Satan out of heaven. His name means "who is like unto God." He may be the most powerful angel in heaven.

3. "Who stands watch over the sons of your people" identifies Michael's main responsibility. It is to protect Daniel's people (the nation of Israel). There have been many attempts to eliminate them but it is Michael's responsibility to prevent that.

4. "Shall stand up" means Michael will intercede on behalf of Israel and exercise his protective powers over the nation. He will act like a sentry and make sure nothing destroys the people of Israel. Those who do attack Israel will be challenging one of the most powerful spiritual forces in heaven.

5. "A time of trouble" is another name for the Tribulation Period. Jesus was talking about that time when he said, "There will be great tribulation, such as has not been seen since the beginning of the world until this time, no, nor ever shall be. And unless those days were shortened, no flesh would be saved; but for the elect's sake those days will be shortened" (Matthew 24:21–22 NKJV). The distress will include all the seal, trumpet, and bowl judgments prophesied in Revelation.

6. "Delivered" refers to a specific group of people who will survive the Tribulation Period. In the whole land of Israel two-thirds of the Jews will perish, but one-third will be delivered.

7. "The book" called the **Lamb's Book of Life**, contains the names of those Jews who are faithful to God. Everyone whose name is on this list will survive the Trbulation Period.

go to

judgments
Revelation 6–16

one-third
Zechariah 13:8

book
Exodus 32:33;
Revelation 3:4–5;
20:12–15; 21:27

Lamb's Book of Life
contains the names of everyone who truly accepts Jesus as their Savior

Many people have the mistaken idea that death is the end of things. The Bible clearly states, "It is appointed for men to die once, but after this the judgment" (Hebrews 9:27 NKJV). Daniel makes it clear that there is a judgment and God is in the bookkeeping business. This is good news for those who accept Jesus, but it couldn't be worse for those who do not. Notice again what he said:

1. "A fiery stream issued and came forth from before Him. A thousand thousands ministered to Him; ten thousand times ten thousand stood before Him. The court was seated, and the books were opened" (Daniel 7:10 NKJV).

2. "But I will tell you what is noted in the Scripture of Truth" (Daniel 10:21).

3. "Your people shall be delivered, every one who is found written in the book" (Daniel 12:1 NKJV).

Stephen R. Miller

Although many saints will suffer—some will even die (cf. Revelation 7:14; 20:4)—during the tribulation, the Lord will appear and rescue the faithful. Even martyred saints will be "delivered" eternally from the "second death" (Revelation 21:8). The context is clear that this deliverance will take place at the end of the tribulation; Scripture elsewhere relates that believers in Israel will be rescued at this time (e.g. Joel 2:32). The tribulation will be dreadful, but one purpose of it will be to bring the Jewish people to an attitude where they will receive Jesus as their Messiah. This it will accomplish (cf. Zechariah 12:10; Romans 11:25–27). Of course, multitudes of people throughout the earth also will see their need for Christ and turn to him for salvation during this period (cf. Revelation 7:9–17).[3]

Sinclair B. Ferguson

Scripture promises us that the last days (that is, the period between Pentecost and the return of Christ [Acts 2:16–17]) will be punctuated by times of special stress and danger (2 Timothy 3:1). This will reach a climax at "the time of the end": "there shall be a time of trouble, such as never was since there was a nation, even to that time" (v. 1). Daniel, however, must not allow himself to be overwhelmed with despair because God will provide His people with protection, specifically in the work of Michael.[4]

John C. Whitcomb

Christ will rescue His people "at that time" through various means at His disposal. The two witnesses whom Antichrist kills will be resurrected and will visibly ascend to heaven (Revelation 11:11–12); their 144,000 disciples will be sealed (Revelation 7:3–8); the bulk of the nation will be "nourished" 1260 days (Revelation 12:6), whereas Satan's pursuing armies are swallowed up by the earth (12:15–16); those few believers who physically survive the Great Tribulation will be honored (Matthew 25:31–40); and those beheaded for their testimony will be raised from the dead to reign with Him (Revelation 20:4).[5]

The names of the Tribulation Period reveal clues about the terrible events to come. A few of them are found in the following chart.

The Tribulation Period

Description	Scripture
The indignation	Isaiah 26:20
The day of the Lord's vengeance	Isaiah 34:8
The time of Jacob's trouble	Jeremiah 30:7
The seventieth week	Daniel 9:24–27
A day of	Zephaniah 1:14–16
wrath	
trouble and distress	
devastation and desolation	
darkness and gloominess	
clouds and thick darkness	
trumpet and alarm	

thousand
Revelation 20:4–6

Old Testament Saints
Matthew 27:52–53

Crucifixion
Matthew 27:32–50

Old Testament Saints
true believers in God who lived before the death of Christ

Crucifixion
the execution of Jesus Christ on the cross

Some Good News

DANIEL 12:2
And many of those who sleep in the dust of the earth shall awake,
Some to everlasting life,
Some to shame and everlasting contempt. (NKJV)

Most of what we have read about the Time of the End has been bad news, but there is also a lot of good news. One promising event will be the resurrection of the dead. A study of the subject reveals that there will be two resurrections (see Time Line #4, Appendix A). Jesus said, "Do not marvel at this; for the hour is coming in which all who are in the graves will hear His voice and come forth—those who have done good, to the resurrection of life, and those who have done evil, to the resurrection of condemnation" (John 5:28–29 NKJV). The first resurrection is called the Resurrection of Life; the second is called the Resurrection of Condemnation. The first is a resurrection of believers; the second is a resurrection of unbelievers. Revelation teaches that the Millennium, a <u>thousand</u>-year period, will be between the two. Also, Scripture reveals that the first resurrection will have four phases while the second resurrection will have just one.

First Resurrection (Resurrection of Life)

Phase 1—Resurrection of Jesus and some **Old Testament Saints** three days after the **Crucifixion**.

go to

Two Witnesses
Revelation 11:3–12

raised
Matthew 27:52–53

Great White Throne Judgmen
Revelation 20:11–15

Two Witnesses
two powerful men of God who will preach during the Tribulation Period

everlasting life
eternal or unending life

Great White Throne Judgment
the judgment of the unsaved

judgment seat
the throne God will sit on when he judges unbelievers

Phase 2—Resurrection of the Church at the Rapture before the Tribulation Period

Phase 3—Resurrection of the **Two Witnesses** near the Tribulation Period midpoint

Phase 4—Resurrection of the Tribulation Saints and the remainder of the Old Testament Saints at the end of the Tribulation Period

Second Resurrection (Resurrection of Condemnation)

Phase 1—Resurrection of all unbelievers at the end of the Millennium

In this verse the angel is discussing the resurrection of the Jews. The resurrection of the Gentiles is not being considered. A few of the Jewish believers were <u>raised</u> to **everlasting life** when Jesus was raised. The other Jewish believers will be raised to everlasting life when the Tribulation Period is over. All unbelieving Jews will be raised a thousand years later in the Second Resurrection.

"Some to shame and everlasting contempt" is a reference to the **Great White Throne Judgment**. The names of the unbelievers (those who did not accept Jesus as the Messiah) have not been placed in the Lamb's Book of Life. When they are raised they will stand before the **judgment seat** of God and be cast into the Lake of Fire where they will suffer everlasting punishment. Will the Jews be resurrected?

Messianic Jews (those who accept Christ) are Christians that will be resurrected in *Phase 2*. The Old Testament Saints are believing Israel in the Old Testament and some were resurrected in Phase 1 along with Christ. Other Old Testament Saints will be resurrected with the Tribulation Saints—both Jews and Gentiles who accept Christ after the Rapture. Some believing Jews will flee to Petra during the Tribulation Period and will not be killed, but instead will live on earth into the Millenium.

what others say

N. W. Hutchings

The resurrection of the Church is not in view here because the Rapture of the Church will have already occurred. There is no evidence that the Church will go through the Tribulation. Every saved person of the **dispensation of grace** will be resurrected before the Tribulation begins. Daniel was not concerned about the gentiles; he was concerned only about his people. The resurrection described by the Lord in this scripture relates only to Israel.[6]

go to

wisdom
James 1:5

despise
Proverbs 1:7

death
Matthew 24:9

testimony
Revelation 6:9

saved
Ephesians 2:8–10

those in need
Matthew 25:31–40

A Promise to Soul Winners

DANIEL 12:3
Those who are wise shall shine
Like the brightness of the firmament,
And those who turn many to righteousness
Like the stars forever and ever. (NKJV)

Wisdom comes from God. Fools despise it, but the wise seek it. Those who are wise in this verse are those who lead people to Christ during the Time of the End. This is true for the Church today, but it will be especially true of those who witness during the difficult days of the Tribulation Period. During the Tribulation, many believers will be put to death because of the Word of God and the testimony they maintain. They will accept Christ, be saved, and lead others to Christ. They will help those in need at the cost of their lives.

These wise believers are going to shine with a brightness like the brightness of the heavens, and the believers who lead others to Christ will shine like the stars.

dispensation of grace
the time the true Church is on earth before the Rapture (the Church Age)

what others say

David Jeremiah with C. C. Carlson

God says that during that time of awful trouble on the Jewish nation, he is going to raise up some who are going to be teachers of righteousness. Can you imagine what it will cost a person to stand up in the Tribulation Period with a Bible in hand and declare the righteousness of God? Those people know that when they teach the truth of God, their heads could roll at any moment. There is a special place in God's kingdom for those who accurately teach God's Holy Book.[7]

Seal the Book Until . . .

DANIEL 12:4 *"But you, Daniel, shut up the words, and seal the book until the time of the end; many shall run to and fro, and knowledge shall increase."* (NKJV)

go to

pass away
Matthew 5:18

expositions
explanations

Daniel was told to close and seal the book of Daniel until the Time of the End, which probably means to preserve the book and its prophecies until the End of the Age. And since Daniel couldn't do that himself it means this book's messages are divinely protected by God. Not one word will <u>pass away</u> until everything is fulfilled. It also means that some of these things cannot be understood until then, but the word *until* implies that the time will come when these things can be understood.

Some experts say "run to and fro" refers to rapid travel, and "knowledge shall increase" refers to an explosion of knowledge. They cite how man has progressed from traveling 30 mph by horse in Daniel's day to traveling several hundred mph by airplane today. And how it took about seventeen hundred years for knowledge to double after the death of Christ, but now with computers, the Internet, etc., it doubles in under two years. But while knowledge and speed of travel have increased many people still will be perplexed by what is happening at the Time of the End, and they will be searching for answers. Fortunately, many will search in the Word of God and knowledge of Bible prophecy will greatly increase.

what others say

Jack Van Impe

Isn't it strange that **expositions** of this book were not attempted until recent times? No expositor made any published attempt to explain Daniel, verse by verse, until the twentieth century.[8]

Charles H. Dyer

As the "Time of the End" draws closer, we should expect to see our understanding of Bible prophecy increase. World events will finally begin to line up more precisely with events predicted in the Bible. When the morning newspaper and the evening news start sounding more like the words of Daniel, Jesus, or the Apostle John, our "prophetic blinders" will be removed. God does predict the future, and his prophecies will all begin to make sense to us when world events parallel the predictions found in the Bible.[10]

Two Heavenly Beings

DANIEL 12:5 *Then I, Daniel, looked; and there stood two others, one on this riverbank and the other on that riverbank. (NKJV)*

At the beginning of this vision we learned that Daniel was standing on the bank of the <u>Tigris</u> River (see Illustration #2). Now we learn that he saw two "others"—one on each side of the river. It is not said, but in all likelihood they were angels.

A Question for Jesus

DANIEL 12:6 *And one said to the man clothed in linen, who was above the waters of the river, "How long shall the fulfillment of these wonders be?" (NKJV)*

When this vision began we learned that Daniel saw someone dressed in <u>linen</u>. From Daniel's description and other Scriptures we concluded that Daniel saw Jesus. Then <u>two</u> others appeared and asked Jesus a question that many want answered: How long will it be before these astonishing things are **fulfilled**?

Care must be taken to fully understand what exactly was asked. The question is not "How long will it be until the Time of the End?" but "How long will it take for these things to be fulfilled at the Time of the End?" Israel will not be delivered until they decide to stop trusting in themselves and start trusting in their Messiah, the Lord Jesus Christ.

> ### what others say
>
> **Stephen R. Miller**
>
> The angel's question indicates that he was curious about these future events. It is interesting to observe there are things that even angels do not know but desire to learn (cf. 1 Peter 1:12). Certainly interest in future things is natural on the part of human beings.[10]

Jesus Takes an Oath

DANIEL 12:7 *Then I heard the man clothed in linen, who was above the waters of the river, when he held up his right hand and his left hand to heaven, and swore by Him who lives forever, that it shall be for a time, times, and half a time; and when the*

go to

Tigris
Daniel 10:4

linen
Daniel 10:5

two
Daniel 12:5

fulfilled
take place or happen

forever
Revelation 10:5–6

time
Daniel 7:25

42 months
Revelation 13:5

Jerusalem
Zechariah 14:2–3

the books
Daniel 9:2

power of the holy people has been completely shattered, all these things shall be finished. (NKJV)

A person usually raises one hand to take an oath, but Jesus raised both hands. Raising one hand in a court of law symbolizes the veracity and significance of a witness's words, but here Jesus raised both hands as if to say, "My answer is doubly significant." It was a way of stressing the certainty of his words. He then took an oath and, because he could swear by none higher, swore by God, who lives <u>forever</u>.

His answer, "A <u>time</u>, times, and half a time" (Daniel 12:7 NKJV), is explained in Daniel 4:16 to be three and one-half years. Specifically, it is the last three and one-half years (<u>42 months</u> or 1,260 days) of the Tribulation Period. During that time <u>Jerusalem</u> will be turned over to the Antichrist, the Temple will be desolate, the Jewish people will turn to Jesus as their Messiah, and all of the prophecies will be fulfilled.

> ### what others say
>
> **Sinclair B. Ferguson**
>
> It conveys a sense of extended periods of time, but it also conveys something of God's sovereign control over all events. By His own power He is able to cut short apparently inevitable historical developments. All these things will be finished, adds the heavenly figure, "when the power of the holy people has been completely shattered" (v. 7). When the powers of darkness have done their worst against the kingdom of God, and the truth of God has been set at a final devaluation, God will act.[11]

I Just Don't Get It

DANIEL 12:8 *Although I heard, I did not understand. Then I said, "My lord, what shall be the end of these things?" (NKJV)*

Daniel was a highly educated man who studied <u>the books</u> of Scripture. He even admitted that he heard what Jesus said. But he confessed that he did not understand it, so he asked Jesus to tell him more.

Don't Worry About It

DANIEL 12:9 *And he said, "Go your way, Daniel, for the words are closed up and sealed till the time of the end." (NKJV)*

Daniel asked for more information, but Jesus did not provide it. Jesus could have explained the vision but gently told Daniel to go about his business because the words of the vision are closed up and <u>sealed</u>. People may understand some of it as the Time of the End approaches, but not everything will be fully understood until the last three and one-half years of the Tribulation Period arrive.

go to

sealed
Daniel 12:4

refined
Zechariah 13:8–9

Word
Revelation 6:9–11

144,000
Revelation 7:4–14

Two Witnesses
Revelation 11:3

angel
Revelation 14:6

grow worse and worse
2 Timothy 3:13

deceive
2 Thessalonians 2:9–10

blind
2 Corinthians 4:4

possible
Matthew 24:24

what others say

King James Bible Commentary

Daniel, even though the recipient of this revelation, did not fully comprehend it. From our perspective, 2500 years later with several Old Testament books Daniel did not have (Zechariah, for example), and the New Testament as well, we have a much better idea of what these prophecies mean and how they will transpire.[12]

A Great Separation

DANIEL 12:10 *Many shall be purified, made white, and refined, but the wicked shall do wickedly; and none of the wicked shall understand, but the wise shall understand.* (NKJV)

Jesus told Daniel that many will be **purified** and **refined** at the Time of the End. One-third of the Jews and multitudes of Gentiles will believe the <u>Word</u> of God and accept Jesus as their Messiah. The world can expect some great revivals during the Tribulation Period; the <u>144,000</u> Jewish **evangelists**, the <u>Two Witnesses</u>, and God's <u>angel</u> will reach multitudes for Christ.

However, the wicked will continue in their sin. The apostle Paul even said they will <u>grow worse and worse</u>. This verse indicates a great separation with multitudes being saved and living holy lives, while the remainder of society becomes more immoral and violent. Satan will <u>deceive</u> the wicked, so that none of them will understand what is going on. They will be <u>blind</u> to the realization that it is the Time of the End. But it will not be <u>possible</u> to deceive the wise. They will understand and put their faith in Jesus.

purified
to receive eternal life and the forgiveness of sins

refined
their ways will be made perfect

evangelist
one who declares the true Word of God

what others say

Oliver B. Greene

Those whose "eyes of understanding" have been opened by the Holy Spirit see the End of this Age approaching; but the

go to

held up
Daniel 12:7

Abomination
Daniel 9:27

Lake
Revelation 19:20

sealed
Daniel 12:4, 9

elect
Mark 13:26–27

Utopian millennium
perfect society for
1,000 years

elect
Jews who follow
God; his chosen
people

wicked who are blinded by "the God of this Age" [Satan] see nothing about which to be alarmed. They live as though they plan to stay here forever. They have no time for God, and no desire to prepare to meet him. Things will continually grow worse as the end approaches.[13]

M. R. De Haan

What it really means is that the wicked shall do more wicked[ness], because they do not understand. They do not know the program, they do not know what God is doing, they do not believe that the end is near; somehow they feel that they are going to pull themselves up by their bootstraps, that everything is going to come out all right, that finally man will learn his lesson and bring in the man-made **Utopian millennium** of peace. They are deluded by Satan who has blinded their eyes. . . .[14]

An Extra 30 Days

> DANIEL 12:11 *And from the time that the daily sacrifice is taken away, and the abomination of desolation is set up, there shall be one thousand two hundred and ninety days. (NKJV)*

We recall that Jesus held up his hands and took an oath that the last half of the Tribulation Period would last three and one-half years or 1,260 days. We also remember that the angel Gabriel told Daniel that the last half of the Tribulation Period would begin when the Abomination of Desolation is set up on the wing of the Temple. From this we can calculate that there will be 1,260 days from the Tribulation Period midpoint to the Second Coming of Jesus. The Antichrist will rule during those years and then be cast into the Lake of Fire. But the Abomination of Desolation (Image of the Beast) will remain for an extra 30 days (1,260 days + 30 days = 1,290) before being destroyed. Why it will be permitted to exist for those 30 days is not said. It seems to be one of those sealed things, but here are three possibilities:

1. It will take time to rid the earth of the Antichrist's impact.

2. It will take time to gather the **elect** and assemble them in Israel.

3. There will be a period of grace before judgment (see next verse).

nations
Matthew 25:31–46

what others say

Alvin M. Shifflett

What exactly does the phrase "abomination of desolation" mean? First, it involves the temple area. Most scholars agree that in 165 BC, Antiochus Epiphanes created an abominable act when he sacrificed a pig on the temple altar, and forced some of the Jews to eat pork. That has become known as a "type" of the abomination to come. Apparently it will be either an idol on the temple grounds or some unclean abominable sacrifice. It occurs after the abolition of sacrifices . . . "at a time when the daily sacrifice is abolished . . ." There is absolutely no reason to assume that the Lord is giving Daniel instructions about some abolition of sacrifices to come in the Christian era. Christ ended the need for all such sacrifices![15]

Jimmy DeYoung

The most exciting, documented evidence that the Lord's return could be close at hand is the activity surrounding preparations for the rebuilding of the temple on the Temple Mount in Jerusalem. There are Jewish men who now believe they are qualified to serve as "priests." Their priestly garments are made and in storage; all the implements to be used for the sacrifices and worship at the temple are ready; biblical harps are being handmade for the Levite orchestra; and a "red heifer" is even available for the "purification" of everything for the temple.[16]

45 More Days

DANIEL 12:12 *Blessed is he who waits, and comes to the one thousand three hundred and thirty-five days. (NKJV)*

Here a period of forty-five days is mentioned and again Jesus did not explain. Most experts realize that the reason is sealed, but a few speculate on the matter because people want to know. Just remember that any answer is conjecture.

However, the verse does add to what we know. Something will happen at the end of the forty-five-days that will be a blessing to everyone who reaches the end of it. This implies that not everyone will make it. It is my opinion that this forty-five-day period is when Jesus will judge the <u>nations</u>. Some will be blessed with the privilege of entering the Millennium, while others will be cursed and sent to eternal punishment.

go to

Go your way
Daniel 12:9

die
Hebrews 9:27

awake
Daniel 12:2

Messianic Kingdom
the Millennial kingdom when Christ will reign on earth

Marriage Supper of the Lamb
a feast on earth attended by Jesus

> **what others say**
>
> **David Hocking**
>
> This may be the setting up of the **Messianic Kingdom** with Jesus Christ ruling in Jerusalem. There are many topographical changes that will take place. A Millennial Temple will be established even though it won't take the Lord any time at all to build it. The Dead Sea will be changed so that fish will live in it. . . . Revelation 19 talks about the "Marriage **Supper of the Lamb**." It's possible that the blessing "on he who waits" is the Marriage Supper of the Lamb which could easily last 45 days or longer.[17]

Some Final Advice for Daniel

DANIEL 12:13 *But you, go your way till the end; for you shall rest, and will arise to your inheritance at the end of the days." (NKJV)*

Jesus ended the vision without answering Daniel's question, but these closing remarks are very important. Here are five points:

1. *"Go your way"* means continue on with your life. Don't worry about these things; trust Jesus and be faithful.

2. *"You shall rest"* probably refers to Daniel's death. Unless a person leaves in the Rapture that person is destined to <u>die</u>.

3. *"At the end of the days"* can mean several things: at the end of the Tribulation Period, at the end of the 1,290 days, or at the end of the 1,335 days. It probably means the 1,335 days.

4. *"Will arise"* refers to the time when multitudes will <u>awake</u> or arise from the dead. This multitude here includes the Old Testament Saints and the Tribulation Saints (Resurrection of Life).

5. *"To your inheritance"* means to take possession of your rewards. Daniel, no doubt, will receive many rewards.

Leon J. Wood

If Daniel is to be resurrected at this time, it follows that other Old Testament saints will be resurrected then as well, thus giving evidence that the likely time of resurrection for all Old Testament saints will be at the close of the Tribulation.[18]

Rodney Stortz

The message to Daniel is a message to us. Go your way. When you die you will rest from your labors. But one day after you have rested, you will rise again.[19]

Chapter Wrap-Up

- Chapter 12 concerns what will happen to Israel at the Time of the End or the End of the Times of the Gentiles, not the end of the world. Michael the archangel is assigned to protect Israel and he will be careful to intercede for Israel against her enemies. The Tribulation Period will be a time of great trouble; a time worse than anything that has happened before, but the saved of Israel will be delivered. (Daniel 12:1)

- Much of the Tribulation Period is bad news, but there is also good news. One good thing is the resurrection of the Jewish believers. The unbelievers, however, will be raised to shame and everlasting contempt in the Resurrection of Condemnation, while the believers will be raised to everlasting life in the fourth phase of the Resurrection of Life. Those who led others to Christ during the Tribulation Period will shine with the brightness or glory of Christ. (Daniel 12:2–3)

- Daniel was twice told to close up and seal the words of this prophecy until the Time of the End. These prophecies will be divinely preserved and protected until then, and some prophecies will not be understood until then. When the Time of the End arrives two things will take place: a) people will be perplexed by world events, and b) many will study Bible prophecy causing an explosion in prophetic knowledge. (Daniel 12:4, 9)

- Jesus appeared and took an oath that the last half of the Tribulation Period would last for three and one-half years or 1,260 days. During that terrible time the wicked will be confused and grow worse, but multitudes will understand the Tribulation events and be saved. After the Tribulation Period there will be two brief periods of time, one of 30 days and another of 45 days. The purpose is not revealed, but it probably concerns the judgment of the nations and preparations for the Millennium. (Daniel 12:5–7; 10–12)

- Daniel was told to go his way twice in this chapter, which was a way of telling him to be at peace, trust Christ, and continue his course. He was also told he would die but would be raised to receive an inheritance at the Time of the End. (Daniel 12:9, 13)

Study Questions

1. What are some of the good things that will happen at the Time of the End?

2. What are some of the bad things that will happen at the Time of the End?

3. What indication do we have that heaven and hell actually exist?

4. What are the three time periods mentioned in this chapter? When will the Tribulation Period end and when will the Millennium begin?

5. What did Jesus say would happen to Daniel?

Time Line #1—The Life of Daniel

	Daniel's birth	Daniel taken to Babylon	Nebuchadnezzar's first dream (statue of five kingdoms)	Shadrach, Meshach & Abed-Nego in the fiery furnace	Nebuchadnezzar's second dream (tree in the middle & testimony)	Visions of the four beasts	Visions of the ram and the goat	Handwriting on the wall Medes & Persians victorious	Daniel in the lions' den Visions of the seventy weeks	Vision of the Anointed One
Chapter		1	2	3	4	7	8	5	6 9	10 11 12
Age		13–14 yrs. old	17–18 yrs. old	Early 30s	57–58 yrs. old			80 yrs. old		Mid 80s
	620–618 BC	605 BC	603 BC	585 BC	562 BC	544 BC		539 BC	537 BC	534 BC

Nabopolassar — Nebuchadnezzar — Various Kings — Belshazzar, Co-Regent Nabonidus, King — Darius — Cyrus

BABYLONIAN — MEDO-PERSIAN

Time Line #2—The Times of the Gentiles*

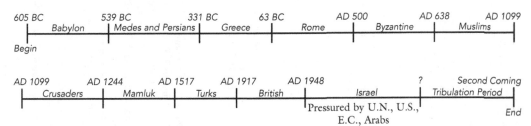

605 BC | 539 BC | 331 BC | 63 BC | AD 500 | AD 638 | AD 1099
Babylon | Medes and Persians | Greece | Rome | Byzantine | Muslims
Begin

AD 1099 | AD 1244 | AD 1517 | AD 1917 | AD 1948 | ? | Second Coming
Crusaders | Mamluk | Turks | British | Israel | Tribulation Period
Pressured by U.N., U.S., E.C., Arabs
End

* Gentiles exercise either partial or total control over Jerusalem.

Time Line #3—Daniel's Seventy Weeks/Seventy Sevens

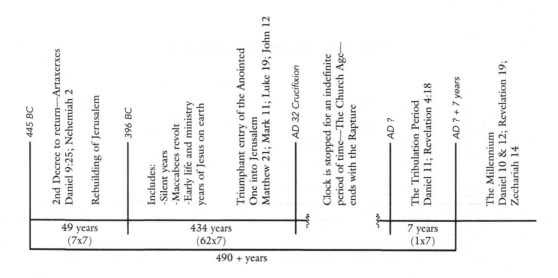

445 BC

2nd Decree to return—Artaxerxes
Daniel 9:25; Nehemiah 2

Rebuilding of Jerusalem

396 BC

Includes:
-Silent years
-Maccabees revolt
-Early life and ministry
years of Jesus on earth

Triumphant entry of the Anointed
One into Jerusalem
Matthew 21; Mark 11; Luke 19; John 12

AD 32 Crucifixion

Clock is stopped for an indefinite
period of time—The Church Age—
ends with the Rapture

AD ?

The Tribulation Period
Daniel 11; Revelation 4:18

AD ? + 7 years

The Millennium
Daniel 10 & 12; Revelation 19;
Zechariah 14

49 years (7x7)   434 years (62x7)   7 years (1x7)

490 + years

Time Line #4—The Two Resurrections

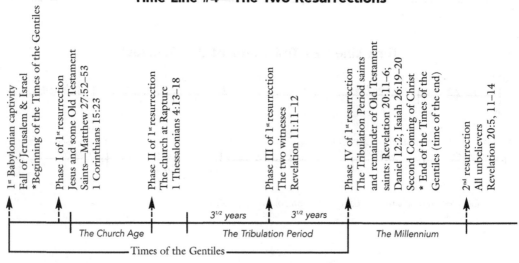

1st Babylonian captivity
Fall of Jerusalem & Israel
*Beginning of the Times of the Gentiles

Phase I of 1st resurrection
Jesus and some Old Testament
Saints—Matthew 27:52–53
1 Corinthians 15:23

Phase II of 1st resurrection
The church at Rapture
1 Thessalonians 4:13–18

Phase III of 1st resurrection
The two witnesses
Revelation 11:11–12

Phase IV of 1st resurrection
The Tribulation Period saints
and remainder of Old Testament
saints: Revelation 20:11–6;
Daniel 12:2; Isaiah 26:19–20
Second Coming of Christ
* End of the Times of the
Gentiles (time of the end)

2nd resurrection
All unbelievers
Revelation 20:5, 11–14

The Church Age   3½ years   The Tribulation Period   3½ years   The Millennium

——— Times of the Gentiles ———

Appendix B - The Answers

CHAPTER ONE

1. God delivered Jerusalem into the hands of her enemy. He used a pagan king, Nebuchadnezzar, to defeat the Jews. (Daniel 1:1–2)

2. He changed Daniel's country, name, status, residence, language, and school, but he could not change Daniel's allegiance to his God. (Daniel 1:8)

3. Ashpenaz was afraid of Nebuchadnezzar, so he thought the king might kill him for disobedience if Daniel was unhealthy. (Daniel 1:10)

4. His request for a ten-day test shows that he was willing to trust the outcome to God. (Daniel 1:12)

5. They were healthier, better nourished, wiser, and more intelligent than anyone else in Babylon. (Daniel 1:15, 20)

CHAPTER TWO

1. He suspected they were guilty of conspiracy and lying. (Daniel 2:9)

2. Instead of depending upon God, they were depending on man's ability to get messages from the stars, moon, and spirits, which, of course, failed them. (Daniel 2:10)

3. The six steps were to ask for permission to speak, request for time, tell his friends, ask them to pray with him, pray, and praise God. (Daniel 2:16–19)

4. The God of heaven. He is the God of gods and the Lord of kings. (Daniel 2:44, 47)

5. Each person will have to decide. But most commentators say "no" because he called Daniel's God "your God" not "my God." (Daniel 2:47)

CHAPTER THREE

1. Probably anti-Semitism. It is bad because people should not be persecuted for refusing the religion of those in power. We should oppose those who want to force people to worship their way. (Daniel 3:8, 12)

2. He said to worship the image or be cast into a blazing furnace. Multitudes will have to make this choice during the Tribulation Period. Revelation teaches that those who do not worship the image will be killed and those who do will be cast into the Lake of Fire. (Daniel 3:11)

3. No. They were not sure they would be rescued. But just like Daniel did earlier, they had resolved not to defile themselves. Our commitments to God should be kept no matter what. (Daniel 3:18)

4. He saw four men walking around in the fire. They were unharmed. One of them appeared out of nowhere and was like a son of the gods. He asked the three Jews to come out. (Daniel 3:25–26)

5. No one could say anything against the God of Shadrach, Meshach, and Abed-Nego. If they did they would be cut to pieces and their houses would be destroyed. Free speech and freedom of worship were not allowed by this one-world leader. (Daniel 3:29)

CHAPTER FOUR

1. Daniel had the spirit of God in him. (Daniel 4:9, also see Daniel 1:17, 20)

2. A messenger who was one of the holy ones, probably angels, from heaven. Mercifully, he left the stump, preserved it, and limited Nebuchadnezzar's affliction to seven years. (Daniel 4:14–16)

3. That the Most High is sovereign over the kingdoms of men, gives kingdoms to anyone he wishes, and sets over them the lowliest of men. Those who do not know this do not know God. (Daniel 4:17)

4. No. When Nebuchadnezzar did not repent he was driven from his beautiful palace and stricken with a mental illness. (Daniel 4:29–33)

5. He is able to humble the proud. No—everything he does is right, and all his ways are just.

Humbling Nebuchadnezzar was an important factor in his repentance. (Daniel 4:37)

CHAPTER FIVE

1. He would be clothed in purple, have a gold chain placed around his neck, and made the third highest ruler in Babylon. He responded, keep your gifts and give your rewards to someone else. The king gave him the rewards anyway. (Daniel 5:16, 17, 29)

2. No. He refused the king's gifts and rewards, and he issued a scathing reprimand to the king for his sin. (Daniel 5:18–23)

3. No. The walls, guards, weapons, and troops did not keep the hand of God out or stop him from causing the fall of Babylon. (Daniel 5:5, 30)

4. Yes. Because of sin God judged Belshazzar and Babylon. He decreed their fall. (Daniel 5:26–28)

5. He turned pale, was very scared, his knees knocked, and his legs gave way. But he did not repent. (Daniel 5:6)

CHAPTER SIX

1. He was an honest government official. (Daniel 6:4–5)

2. Those in charge may try to force everyone to worship someone other than the true God. (Daniel 6:7, 12)

3. Both are important, but man's laws are sometimes wrong and they can change. God's law is always right and is eternal. (Daniel 6:9, 14, 26)

4. He was innocent in God's sight and trusted God. (Daniel 6:21, 23)

5. Yes. And Darius told the whole world. (Daniel 6:27)

CHAPTER SEVEN

1. The Antichrist. He will boast, overthrow three of the ten kings, take over the fourth kingdom (the one-world government), wage war on the saints, and change times and laws. (Daniel 7:8, 20–21, 24–25)

2. God: the Ancient of Days and the Most High; Jesus: Son of Man. (Daniel 7:9, 13, 18, 22, 24–25)

3. God will take his power away. It will happen at the Second Coming of Jesus. (Daniel 7:13–14, 26)

4. No. He was troubled in his spirit (his thoughts disturbed him), he turned pale, and he kept quiet about it. (Daniel 7:15 and 28)

5. The four beasts symbolize four kingdoms or groups of nations. From a moral perspective

nations act more like beasts than God. The history of nations is mostly unchristian and vicious. (Daniel 7:17)

CHAPTER EIGHT

1. Because of rebellion. Rebellion causes people to reject Christ and disobey God. Some of the forms of rebellion include these acts: establishing a world religion and world government, promoting things contrary to the will of God like abortion and homosexuality, the killing of Christians and Jews, trading land for peace in Israel, trying to rebuild the Temple to restart animal sacrifice, and because of rebellion, God will permit the Antichrist to rise to power. But no matter what we do, we are accountable to God for our actions. (Daniel 8:12)

2. The only reliable source is the Bible itself. Without Gabriel's explanations we could not understand this vision. (Daniel 8:19–26)

3. Bible prophecy is history written before it happens. Daniel's prophetic Vision of the Ram and the Goat was literally fulfilled by history. (Daniel 8:20–21)

4. No. It will have deceit, corruption, devastation, and violent religious persecution. (Daniel 8:24–25)

5. His power will be satanic. He will rule the world, but God will destroy him. (Daniel 8:24–25)

CHAPTER NINE

1. He was reading the book of Jeremiah, knew God keeps his covenants, knew what was in the Law of Moses, and knew God brought Israel out of Egypt. (Daniel 9:2, 4, 11, 13, 15)

2. Forgiveness requires humility, sincere prayer, and confession. Daniel fasted, prayed, wore sackcloth, and sat in ashes. He confessed his sins over and over again. (Daniel 9:3–16)

3. He is righteous, merciful, forgiving, mighty, and can be angered. (Daniel 9:7, 9, 15–16)

4. To obtain forgiveness for Israel and Judah, to turn away God's anger, to show concern for God's name, and to enlist God's help. (Daniel 9:16–19)

5. It will begin when a world leader signs a seven-year covenant. He will break the covenant, stop the animal sacrifices, and desecrate the Temple. (Daniel 9:27)

CHAPTER TEN

1. Yes. Daniel said the message is true and the heavenly being said it is written in the Book of Truth. (Daniel 10:1, 21)

2. God hears prayer. Evil spirits can hinder answers to prayer, and the answer may have a dramatic effect on us. (Daniel 10:2, 8–10, 13, 15–17)

3. No. He became sick, was helpless and afraid, went into a deep sleep, couldn't talk, and had trouble breathing. (Daniel 10:8–10; 15–17)

4. Some are good and others are bad; some serve God while others serve Satan. Angels deliver messages, fight wars, and assist God's people. (Daniel 10:10–13, 18–19)

5. They are real, powerful, can hinder prayer, rule over nations, and oppose the angels of God. (Daniel 10:13)

CHAPTER ELEVEN

1. All of them will fall. Persia was defeated by Greece. Greece was divided into four kingdoms. The Antichrist's kingdom will also fall. (Daniel 11:3–4, 45)

2. Some leaders are never satisfied with the glory, power, and wealth they have. They covet what others have and are willing to seize it by force. (Daniel 11:8, 18, 21, 24, 28, 39, 42–43)

3. When he begins he will do as he pleases, exalt himself, and attack mighty fortresses. When he comes to his end no one will help him. (Daniel 11:36–45)

4. He will get his power from the god of fortresses (Satan), and he will not be overcome until Jesus returns to capture him. (Daniel 11:38, 45)

5. He will present himself as a man of peace, but his short career will be marred by several wars. (Daniel 11:39–40, 41, 43–45)

CHAPTER TWELVE

1. Israel will be delivered. The Old Testament and Tribulation Saints will be raised, and multitudes will be saved. (Daniel 12:1, 2, 10)

2. It will be a time of great trouble. The wicked will continue in their sin and not understand what is going on. They will be destined for everlasting shame and contempt. (Daniel 12:1, 2, 10)

3. Multitudes who sleep in the dust of the earth will awake: some to everlasting life, others to shame and everlasting contempt. (Daniel 12:2)

4. 1,260 days, 1,290 days, and 1,335 days. The Tribulation Period will end 1,260 days after the Abomination of Desolation is set up. The Millennium will begin 75 days after the Tribulation Period ends. (Daniel 12:7, 11)

5. He would die, be raised from the dead, and receive a reward. (Daniel 12:13)

Endnotes

Chapter 1

1. Jack W. Hayford, *Until the End of Time*, The Spirit-Filled Life Bible Study Guides, B13 (Nashville: Thomas Nelson, 1994), 22.

2. Uriah Smith, *Daniel and the Revelation* (Nashville: Southern Publishing Association, 1907), 24.

3. Kay Arthur, *God's Blueprint for Bible Prophecy* (Eugene, OR: Harvest House, Precept Ministries International, 1995), 30.

4. Merrill F. Unger, *Unger's Commentary on the Old Testament* (Chattanooga, TN: AMG Publishers, Tyndale Theological Seminary, 2002), 1609.

5. Hal Lindsey, *Daniel* (Palos Verdes, CA: Hal Lindsey Ministries), taped message 352.

6. Peter and Paul Lalonde, *301 Startling Proofs and Prophecies* (Niagara Falls, Ontario: Prophecy Partners, 1996), 204.

7. David Jeremiah with C. C. Carlson, *The Handwriting on the Wall* (Dallas: Word Publishing, 1992), 29.

8. *The World Book Encyclopedia*, vol. H (Chicago: World Book, Inc., 1990), 254.

9. Grant R. Jeffrey, *Final Warning* (Toronto, Ontario: Frontier Research Publications, 1995), 19.

10. Jack Van Impe, *2001: On the Edge of Eternity* (Dallas: Word Publishing, 1996), 168.

11. John Hagee, *Day of Deception* (Nashville: Thomas Nelson, 1997), 214.

12. J. Vernon McGee, *Thru the Bible with J. Vernon Mcgee*, vol. 3, Proverbs–Malachi (Pasadena, CA: Thru The Bible Radio, 1982), 529.

13. Arno Froese, *Daniel's Prophecy Made Easy* (Columbia, SC: The Olive Press, Midnight Call Ministries, 2004), 26–27.

14. Jay Alan Sekulow, *Case Notes*, vol. 2, no. 5, The American Center for Law and Justice.

15. John Phillips, *Exploring the Book of Daniel* (Grand Rapids, MI: Kregel Publications, 2004), 36.

16. Theodore H. Epp, *Christ Reflected in Bible Characters* (Lincoln, NE: Back to the Bible, Good News Broadcasting Association, 1959), 67–68.

17. John R. Rice, *5 Great Decisions for God* (Murfreesboro, TN: Sword of the Lord Publishers, 1978), 7.

18. Charles Stanley, *The Glorious Journey* (Nashville: Thomas Nelson, 1996), 359.

19. Stephen R. Miller, *Daniel*, The New American Commentary, vol. 18 (Nashville: Broadman & Holman, 1994), 69.

20. Charles Halff, *Significance of Bible Numbers*, Message of the Christian Jew (San Antonio, TX: The Christian Jew Foundation), 6.

21. Tremper Longman III, *Daniel*, The NIV Application Commentary (Grand Rapids, MI: Zondervan, 1999), 54.

22. Alexander Maclaren, *Anxious Care*, Classic Sermons on Faith and Doubt compiled by Warren W. Wiersbe (Grand Rapids, MI: Kregel Publications, 1991), 21.

23. Rick Joyner, *The Final Quest* (Charlotte, NC: Morning Star Publications, 1996), 10.

Chapter 2

1. Tim LaHaye, *Tim Lahaye Prophecy Study Bible* (Chattanooga, TN: AMG Publishers, 2001), 993.

2. Tremper Longman III, *Daniel*, The NIV Application Commentary (Grand Rapids, MI: Zondervan, 1999), 76–77.

3. John Phillips, *Exploring the Book of Daniel* (Grand Rapids, MI: Kregel Publications, 2004), 45.

4. Rodney Stortz, *Daniel: The Triumph of God's*

Kingdom (Wheaton, IL: Crossway Books, 2004), 29.

5. *The Nelson Study Bible* (Nashville: Thomas Nelson, 1997), 1419.

6. *The Pulpit Commentary*, Daniel, Hosea & Joel, vol. 13 (Grand Rapids, MI: Wm. B. Eerdmans, 1978), Daniel, 51.

7. Leon J. Wood, *A Commentary on Daniel* (Eugene, OR: Wipf and Stock Publishers, 1973), 55.

8. John C. Whitcomb, *Daniel* (Chicago: Moody Press, The Moody Bible Institute of Chicago, 1985), 42–43.

9. Theodore H. Epp, *Christ Reflected in Bible Characters* (Lincoln, NE: Back to the Bible, Good News Broadcasting Association, 1959), 68–69.

10. Oliver B. Greene, *Daniel* (Greenville, SC: The Gospel Hour, 1964), 69.

11. C. I. Scofield, *The New Scofield Study Bible* (New York: Oxford University Press, 1967), 898.

12. J. Vernon McGee, *Thru the Bible with J. Vernon Mcgee*, vol. 3, Proverbs–Malachi (Pasadena, CA: Thru The Bible Radio, 1982), 538.

13. Grant R. Jeffrey, *Final Warning* (Toronto, Ontario: Frontier Research Publications, 1995), 31.

14. John Hagee, *Beginning of the End* (Nashville: Thomas Nelson, 1996), 37.

15. Scofield, *The New Scofield Study Bible*, 1368.

16. Mark Hitchcock, *The Complete Book of Bible Prophecy* (Wheaton, IL: Tyndale, 1999), 25.

17. Dave Breese, *Raging into Apocalypse*, William T. James, gen. ed. (Green Forest, AR: New Leaf Press, 1996), 91.

18. Peter and Paul Lalonde, *301 Startling Proofs and Prophecies*, 243.

19. David Reagan, *The Master Plan* (Eugene, OR: Harvest House, Lamb & Lion Ministries, 1993), 79.

20. Charles H. Dyer, *World News and Bible Prophecy* (Wheaton, IL: Tyndale, 1993), 205.

21. Grant R. Jeffrey, *Prince of Darkness* (New York: Bantam Books, 1994), 81.

22. Richard Booker, *Blow the Trumpet in Zion* (Shippensburg, PA: Destiny Image Publishers, Sound of the Trumpet, Inc., 1985), 113.

23. Scofield, *The New Scofield Study Bible*, 900.

Chapter 3

1. Hal Lindsey, *Daniel* (Palos Verdes, CA: Hal Lindsey Ministries), taped message 355.

2. H. A. Ironside, *Daniel* (Grand Rapids, MI: Kregel Publications, 2005), 33.

3. A. Edwin Wilson, *Selected Writings of A. Edwin Wilson* (Hayesville, NC: Schoettle Publishing Co., Inc., 1996), 24.

4. Kenneth O. Gangel, *Holman Old Testament Commentary on Daniel*, Max Anders, gen. ed., vol. 18 (Nashville: Broadman & Holman, 2001), 75.

5. Arno Froese, *Daniel's Prophecy Made Easy* (Columbia, SC: The Olive Press, Midnight Call Ministries, 2004), 72.

6. *The Pulpit Commentary*, Daniel, Hosea & Joel, vol. 13 (Grand Rapids, MI: Wm. B. Eerdmans, 1978), Daniel, 125.

7. John C. Whitcomb, *Daniel* (Chicago: Moody Press, The Moody Bible Institute of Chicago, 1985), 56.

8. David Jeremiah with C. C. Carlson, *The Handwriting on the Wall* (Dallas: Word Publishing, 1992), 75.

9. Dave Breese, *Destiny Bulletin/Newsletter* (Hillsboro, KS: Christian Destiny, October 1997), 4.

10. Henry M. Morris, *The Revelation Record* (Wheaton, IL: Tyndale, 1983), 333.

11. Kay Arthur, *God's Blueprint for Bible Prophecy*, 36.

12. *King James Bible Commentary* (Nashville: Thomas Nelson, 1999), 964.

13. John F. Walvoord, *Daniel: the Key to Prophetic Revelation* (Chicago: Moody Press, The Moody Bible Institute, 1989), 88.

14. Jeremiah and Carlson, *The Handwriting on the Wall*, 77–78.

15. John Phillips, *Exploring the Book of Daniel* (Grand Rapids, MI: Kregel Publications, 2004), 65.

16. John Wesley, *Anxious Care*, Classic Sermons on Faith & Doubt Compiled by Warren W. Wiersbe (Grand Rapids, MI: Kregel Publications, 1991), 147–48.

17. Whitcomb, *Daniel*, 59.

18. Charles R. Swindoll, *Daniel: God's Pattern for the Future* (Anaheim, CA: Insight for Living, 1996), 42.

19. *King James Bible Commentary*, 965.

Chapter 4

1. *Harper's Bible Dictionary* (New York: Harper & Row, 1973), 56–57.

2. Kenneth O. Gangel, *Holman Old Testament*

Commentary on Daniel, Max Anders, gen. ed., vol. 18 (Nashville: Broadman & Holman, 2001), 93.

3. H. A. Ironside, *Daniel* (Grand Rapids, MI: Kregel Publications, 2005), 33.

4. Rick Joyner, *The Final Quest* (Charlotte, NC: Morning Star Publications, 1996), 11.

5. Ron Carlson and Ed Decker, *Fast Facts on False Teachings* (Eugene, OR: Harvest House, 1994), 183.

6. *The Wycliffe Bible Commentary* (Chicago: Moody Press, The Moody Bible Institute, 1962), 783.

7. Frank Ramirez, *Daniel* (Elgin, IL: Brethren Press, FaithQuest, 1998), 25.

8. Billy Graham, *Angels* (Waco, TX: Word Books, 1986), 10.

9. Sinclair B. Ferguson, *The Communicator's Commentary, Daniel*, vol. 19 (Waco, TX: Word Books, 1988), 93.

10. M. R. De Haan, *Daniel the Prophet* (Grand Rapids, MI: Kregel Publications, 1995), 133–34.

11. Tim LaHaye and Ed Hindson, *The Popular Encyclopedia of Bible Prophecy* (Eugene, Or: Harvest House, 2004), 22.

12. *The Wycliffe Bible Commentary*, 784.

13. Ramirez, *Daniel*, 26.

14. Donald E. Gowan, *Abingdon Old Testament Commentaries, Daniel* (Nashville: Abingdon Press, 2001), 81.

15. John Phillips, *Exploring the Book of Daniel* (Grand Rapids, MI: Kregel Publications, 2004), 81.

Chapter 5

1. Henry M. Morris, *God and the Nations* (Green Forest, AR: Master Books, Inc, 2002), 67–68.

2. Union Gospel Press Publication, *Bible Expositor and Illuminator* (Cleveland OH: Incorporated Trustees of the Gospel Worker Society, October 19, 1997), 90.

3. Ibid., 92.

4. Merrill F. Unger, *Unger's Commentary on the Old Testament*, 1631.

5. H. A. Ironside, *Daniel* (Grand Rapids, MI: Kregel Publications, 2005), 55.

6. Kenneth O. Gangel, *Holman Old Testament Commentary on Daniel*, Max Anders, gen. ed., vol. 18 (Nashville: Broadman & Holman, 2001), 137.

7. Charles R. Swindoll, *Daniel: God's Pattern for the Futureo* (Anaheim, CA: Insight for Living, 1996), 58.

8. Arno Froese, *Daniel's Prophecy Made Easy* (Columbia, SC: The Olive Press, Midnight Call Ministries, 2004), 96–97.

9. Ralph Vincent Reynolds, *Truth Shall Triumph* (Hazelwood, MO: Pentecostal Publishing House, 1965), 105–6.

10. F. B. Huey Jr., *The New American Commentary, Jeremiah, Lamentations*, vol. 16, (Nashville: Broadman Press, 1993), 253–54.

11. Paul Benware, in Tim LaHaye and Ed Hindson, *The Popular Encyclopedia of Bible Prophecy* (Eugene, OR: Harvest House, 2004), 176.

12. J. G. Hall, *Prophecy Marches On* (Springfield, MO: Gospel Publishing House, 1963), 34.

Chapter 6

1. John C. Whitcomb, *Daniel* (Chicago: Moody Press, The Moody Bible Institute of Chicago, 1985), 82.

2. Union Gospel Press Publication, *Bible Expositor and Illuminator* (Cleveland, OH: Incorporated Trustees of the Gospel Worker Society, January 1978), 104.

3. Sinclair B. Ferguson, *The Communicator's Commentary, Daniel*, vol. 19 (Waco, TX: Word Books, 1988), 128.

4. Jack W. Hayford, *Hayford's Bible Handbook* (Nashville: Thomas Nelson, 1995), 694.

5. Frank Ramirez, *Daniel* (Elgin, IL: Brethren Press, FaithQuest, 1998), 42.

6. Dave Breese, *Destiny Bulletin/Newsletter* (Hillsboro, KS: Christian Destiny, November 1997), 3.

7. Theodore H. Epp, *Christ Reflected in Bible Characters* (Lincoln, NE: Back to the Bible, Good News Broadcasting Association, 1959), 72.

8. Faith McDonnell and Steve Beard, *Faith Under Fire*, Good News, (Wilmore, KY: Forum for Scriptural Christianity, Inc., November/December 1997), 12.

9. Kenneth O. Gangel, *Holman Old Testament Commentary on Daniel*, Max Anders, gen. ed., vol. 18 (Nashville: Broadman & Holman, 2001), 168–69.

10. Leon J. Wood, *A Commentary on Daniel* (Eugene, OR: Wipf and Stock Publishers, 1973), 167.

11. Merrill F. Unger, *Unger's Commentary on the Old Testament*, 1637.

12. Kay Arthur, *God's Blueprint for Bible Prophecy*, 50.

13. Billy Graham, *Angels* (Waco, TX: Word Books, Publisher, 1986), 24.

14. Henry H. Halley, *Halley's Bible Handbook* (Grand Rapids, MI: Zondervan Publishing House, 1965), 345–46.

15. Donald E. Gowan, *Abingdon Old Testament Commentaries, Daniel* (Nashville: Abingdon Press, 2001), 100.

16. Uriah Smith, *Daniel and the Revelation*, 135.

17. John F. Walvoord, *Daniel: the Key to Prophetic Revelation* (Chicago: Moody Press, The Moody Bible Institute, 1989), 144.

Chapter 7

1. David Hocking, *Dare to Be a Daniel*, vol. 2 (Orange, CA: Promise Publishing, 1991), 9.

2. Wallace Emerson, *Unlocking the Mysteries of Daniel* (Orange, CA: Promise Publishing, 1988), 25.

3. N. W. Hutchings, *Exploring the Book of Daniel* (Oklahoma City, OK: Hearthstone Publishing, 1989), 150.

4. Dave Breese, *The Book of Daniel*, taped message, DB 99 (Colton, CA: World Prophetic Ministry).

5. Emerson, *Unlocking the Mysteries of Daniel*, 117.

6. J. Vernon McGee, *Thru the Bible with J. Vernon Mcgee, Proverbs–Malachi*, vol. 3 (Pasadena, CA: Thru The Bible Radio, 1982), 568.

7. Hal Lindsey, *Daniel* (Palos Verdes, CA: Hal Lindsey Ministries), taped message 359.

8. Edward Tracy, *The Covenant of Death* (Pine Grove, CA: Convale Publications, 1971), 30.

9. Hutchings, *Exploring the Book of Daniel*, 151–52.

10. David Hocking, *Dare to Be a Daniel*, vol. 2 (Orange, CA: Promise Publishing, 1991), 6.

11. Wallace Emerson, *Unlocking the Mysteries of Daniel* (Orange, CA: Promise Publishing, 1988), 127–28.

12. Edward Tracy, *The Covenant of Death* (Pine Grove, CA: Convale Publications, 1971), 35.

13. Lindsey, *Daniel*, taped message 359.

14. Emerson, *Unlocking the Mysteries of Daniel*, 129.

15. Hutchings, *Exploring the Book of Daniel*, 157–58.

16. Hocking, *Dare to Be a Daniel*, 10–11.

17. Grant R. Jeffrey, *Final Warning* (Toronto, Ontario: Frontier Research Publications, 1995), 51.

18. John Hagee, *Beginning of the End* (Nashville: Thomas Nelson, 1996), 117–18.

19. Jack Van Impe, *2001: On the Edge of Eternity* (Dallas: Word Publishing, 1996), 70.

20. Breese, *The Book of Daniel*, taped message, DB 99.

21. Stephen R. Miller, *Daniel, The New American Commentary*, vol. 18 (Nashville: Broadman & Holman, 1994), 204.

22. Henry M. Morris, *The Revelation Record* (Wheaton, IL: Tyndale, 1983), 398.

23. Hutchings, *Exploring the Book of Daniel*, 171–72.

24. Renald E. Showers, *The Most High God* (Bellmawr, NJ: The Friends of Israel Gospel Ministry Inc., 1982), 81.

25. Charles H. Dyer, *World News and Bible Prophecy* (Wheaton, IL: Tyndale, 1993), 194.

26. Uriah Smith, *Daniel and the Revelation*, 17–18.

27. Leon J. Wood, *A Commentary on Daniel* (Eugene, OR: Wipf and Stock Publishers, 1973), 196.

28. Henry M. Morris, *God and the Nations* (Green Forest, AR: Master Books, 2002), 149.

29. Ed Hindson, *Is the Antichrist Alive and Well* (Eugene, OR: Harvest House, 1998), 11.

30. Thomas Ice and Timothy Demy, *Fast Facts on Bible Prophecy* (Eugene, OR: Harvest House, Pre-Trib Research Center, 1997), 14.

31. Jeffrey, *Final Warning*, 86.

32. Irvin Baxter Jr., *Endtime Magazine* (Richmond, IN: Endtime, Inc., July/August 1997), 7.

33. J. R. Church, *Raging into Apocalypse*, William T. James, gen. ed. (Green Forest, AR: New Leaf Press, 1996), 198–99.

34. Hagee, *Beginning of the End*, 123–24.

Chapter 8

1. Tim LaHaye, *Tim LaHaye Prophecy Study Bible* (Chattanooga, TN: AMG Publishers, 2001), 1006–7.

2. C. I. Scofield, *The New Scofield Study Bible* (New York: Oxford University Press, 1967), 910.

3. Kenneth O. Gangel, *Holman Old Testament Commentary on Daniel*, Max Anders, Gen. Ed., vol. 18 (Nashville: Broadman & Holman, 2001), 224.

4. Uriah Smith, *Daniel and the Revelation*, 191.

5. *The Nelson Study Bible* (Nashville: Thomas Nelson, 1997), 1434.

6. N. W. Hutchings, *Exploring the Book of Daniel* (Oklahoma City, OK: Hearthstone Publishing, 1989), 185.

7. Leon J. Wood, *A Commentary on Daniel* (Eugene, OR: Wipf and Stock Publishers, Leon J. Wood, 1973), 210.

8. Kay Arthur, *God's Blueprint for Bible Prophecy*, 69.

9. Rodney Stortz, *Daniel: the Triumph of God's Kingdom* (Wheaton, IL: Crossway Books, 2004), 134.

10. John F. Walvoord, *Daniel: the Key to Prophetic Revelation* (Chicago: Moody Press, The Moody Bible Institute, 1989), 88.

11. *The Wycliffe Bible Commentary* (Chicago: Moody Press, The Moody Bible Institute, 1962), 792.

12 John Phillips, *Exploring the Book of Daniel* (Grand Rapids, MI: Kregel Publications, 2004), 138.

13. Billy Graham, *Angels* (Waco, TX: Word Books, Publisher, Billy Graham, 1986), 121–22.

14. William E. Biederwolf, *The Prophecy Handbook* (World Publishing, 1991), 215.

15. H. A. Ironside, *Daniel* (Grand Rapids, MI: Kregel Publications, 2005), 84.

Chapter 9

1. Renald E. Showers, *The Most High God* (Bellmawr, NJ: The Friends of Israel Gospel Ministry, Inc., 1982), 111.

2. Theodore H. Epp, *Christ Reflected in Bible Characters* (Lincoln, NE: Back to the Bible, Good News Broadcasting Association, 1959), 74.

3 Sinclair B. Ferguson, *The Communicator's Commentary, Daniel*, vol. 19 (Waco, TX: Word Books, Publisher, Word, Inc., 1988), 191.

4. John White, *Decision Magazine*, October 1994 (Minneapolis, MN: Billy Graham Evangelistic Association), 14.

5. Uriah Smith, *Daniel and the Revelation*, 236.

6. Randall Price, *Jerusalem in Prophecy* (Eugene, OR: Harvest House, World of the Bible Ministries, Inc., 1998), pp. 101–2.

7. Jim Combs, *Mysteries of the Book of Daniel* (Springfield, MO: Tribune Publishers, 1994), 102.

8. M. R. De Haan, *Daniel the Prophet* (Grand Rapids, MI: Kregel Publications, 1995), 250.

9. Uriah Smith, *Daniel and the Revelation*, 242.

10. *King James Bible Commentary* (Nashville: Thomas Nelson, 1999), 973.

11. Randall Price and Thomas Ice, in Tim LaHaye and Ed Hindson, *The Popular Encyclopedia of Bible Prophecy* (Eugene, OR: Harvest House, 2004), 359.

12. Grant R. Jeffrey, *Triumphant Return* (Toronto, Ontario: Frontier Research Publications, 2001), 237.

13. Grant R. Jeffrey, *Final Warning* (Toronto, Ontario: Frontier Research Publications, 1995), 65.

14. *The Wycliffe Bible Commentary* (Chicago: Moody Press, The Moody Bible Institute, 1962), 795.

15. John R. Rice, *The Second Coming of Christ in Daniel* (Murfreesboro, TN: Sword of the Lord Publishers), 31.

16. Jeffrey, *Triumphant Return*, 66.

Chapter 10

1. William L. Owens, *The Reality of Evil Spirits* (Fayetteville, NC: World for Christ Evangelistic Association, Inc., 1970), 107.

2. Charles Stanley, *The Glorious Journey* (Nashville: Thomas Nelson, 1996), 470.

3. Arno Froese, *Daniel's Prophecy Made Easy* (Columbia, SC: The Olive Press, Midnight Call Ministries, 2004), 172.

4. Tim LaHaye, *Tim LaHaye Prophecy Study Bible* (Chattanooga, TN: AMG Publishers, 2001), 1012.

5. M. R. De Haan, *Daniel the Prophet* (Grand Rapids, MI: Kregel Publications, 1995), 264.

6. Henry H. Halley, *Halley's Bible Handbook* (Grand Rapids, MI: Zondervan Publishing House, 1965), 345–46.

7. Owens, *The Reality of Evil Spirits*, 106.

8. Billy Graham, *Angels* (Waco, TX: Word Books, Publisher, Billy Graham, 1986), 124.

9. *The Nelson Study Bible* (Nashville: Thomas Nelson, 1997), 1438.

10. De Haan, *Daniel the Prophet*, 271–72.

11. Oliver B. Greene, *Daniel* (Greenville, SC: The Gospel Hour, 1964), 407.

Chapter 11

1. *The Wycliffe Bible Commentary* (Chicago: Moody Press, The Moody Bible Institute, 1962), 797.

2. Billy Graham, *Angels* (Waco, TX: Word Books, 1986), 110.

3. *King James Bible Commentary* (Nashville: Thomas Nelson, 1999), 975–76.

4. Stephen R. Miller, *Daniel*, The New American Commentary, vol. 18 (Nashville: Broadman & Holman, 1994), 295.

5. Tremper Longman III, *Daniel*, The NIV Application Commentary (Grand Rapids, MI: Zondervan, 1999), 275.

6. Rodney Stortz, *Daniel: The Triumph of God's Kingdom* (Wheaton, IL: Crossway Books, 2004), 198.

7. Merrill F. Unger, *Unger's Commentary on the Old Testament*, 1681.

8. Oliver B. Greene, *Daniel* (Greenville, SC: The Gospel Hour, 1964), 426.

9. John F. Walvoord, *Daniel: the Key to Prophetic Revelation* (Chicago: Moody Press, 1989), 264.

10. Renald E. Showers, *The Most High God* (Bellmawr, NJ: The Friends of Israel Gospel Ministry, 1982), 158.

11. Miller, *Daniel*, 300.

12. Ed Hindson, *Is the Antichrist Alive and Well?* (Eugene, OR: Harvest House, 1998), 38.

13. Thomas Ice and Timothy Demy, *Fast Facts on Bible Prophecy* (Eugene, OR: Harvest House, Pre-Trib Research Center, 1997), 7.

14. *The Wycliffe Bible Commentary*, 797.

15. Grant R. Jeffrey, *Prince of Darkness* (New York: Bantam Books, 1994), 31.

16. John C. Whitcomb, *Daniel* (Chicago: Moody Press, 1985), 154.

17. Jeffrey, *Prince of Darkness*, 288.

18. Charles H. Dyer, *World News and Bible Prophecy* (Wheaton, IL Tyndale House Publishers, 1993), 215.

19. Kenneth O. Gangel, *Holman Old Testament Commentary on Daniel*, Max Anders, gen. ed., vol. 18 (Nashville: Broadman & Holman, 2001), 307.

20. John Hagee, *Beginning of the End* (Nashville: Thomas Nelson, 1996), 175.

21. Dyer, *World News and Bible Prophecy*, 233.

22. Mark Hitchcock, *The Complete Book of Bible Prophecy* (Wheaton, IL: Tyndale, 1999), 102–3.

23. Jeffrey, *Prince of Darkness*, 257.

24. Charles R. Swindoll, *Daniel: God's Pattern for the Future* (Anaheim, CA: Insight for Living, 1996), 135.

25. David Jeremiah with C. C. Carlson, *The Handwriting on the Wall* (Dallas: Word Publishing, 1992), 232–33.

Chapter 12

1. David R. Reagan, *Tim LaHaye Prophecy Study Bible* (Chattanooga, TN: AMG Publishers, 2001), 1016.

2. Thomas Ice and Timothy Demy, *Fast Facts on Bible Prophecy* (Eugene, OR: Harvest House, Pre-Trib Research Center, 1997), 172–73.

3. Stephen R. Miller, *Daniel*, The New American Commentary, vol. 18 (Nashville: Broadman & Holman, 1994), 315.

4. Sinclair B. Ferguson, *The Communicator's Commentary, Daniel*, vol. 19 (Waco, TX: Word Books, 1988), 242.

5. John C. Whitcomb, *Daniel* (Chicago: Moody Press, The Moody Bible Institute of Chicago, 1985), 162.

6. N. W. Hutchings, *Exploring the Book of Daniel* (Oklahoma City, OK: Hearthstone Publishing, 1989), 321.

7. David Jeremiah with C. C. Carlson, *The Handwriting on the Wall* (Dallas: Word Publishing, 1992), 322.

8. Jack Van Impe, *2001: On the Edge of Eternity* (Dallas: Word Publishing, 1996), 116.

9. Charles H. Dyer, *World News and Bible Prophecy* (Wheaton, IL Tyndale House Publishers, 1993), 267.

10. Miller, *Daniel*, 323.

11. Sinclair B. Ferguson, *The Communicator's Commentary, Daniel*, vol. 19 (Waco, TX: Word Books, 1988), 247.

12. *King James Bible Commentary* (Nashville: Thomas Nelson, 1999), 978.

13. Oliver B. Greene, *Daniel* (Greenville, SC: The Gospel Hour, 1964), 484.

14. M. R. De Haan, *Daniel the Prophet* (Grand Rapids, MI: Kregel Publications, 1995), 313–14.

15. Alvin M. Shifflett, *The Beast of the East* (Lancaster, PA: Starburst Publishers, 1992), 47–48.

16. Jimmy DeYoung, *Tim LaHaye Prophecy Study Bible* (Chattanooga, TN: AMG Publishers, 2001), 1080.

17. David Hocking, *Dare to Be a Daniel*, vol. 2 (Orange, CA: Promise Publishing, 1991), 206–7.

18. Leon J. Wood, *A Commentary on Daniel* (Eugene, OR: Wipf and Stock Publishers, 1973), 329.

19. Rodney Stortz, *Daniel: the Triumph of God's Kingdom* (Wheaton, IL: Crossway Books, 2004), 233.

Excerpts from the following are used by permission with all rights reserved:

The Book of Daniel (tapes) by Dave Breese. Christian Destiny, Hillsboro, KS.

Daniel the Prophet by M. R. DeHaan. Kregel Publications, Grand Rapids, MI.

On the Brink by Daymond R. Duck. Starburst Publishers, lancaster, PA.

The Book of Revelation—The Smart Guide to the Bible by Daymond R. Duck. Thomas Nelson Publishers, Nashville, TN.

Unlocking the Mysteries of Daniel by Wallace Emerson. Promise Publishing, Orange, CA.

Angels by Billy Graham. Word Publishers, Nashville, TN.

Daniel by Oliver B. Greene. The Gospel Hour, Greenville, SC.

Day of Deception and Beginning of the End by John Hagee. Thomas Nelson Publishers, Nashville, TN.

Dare to Be a Daniel by David Hocking. Promise Publishing, Orange, CA..

Exploring the Book of Daniel by N. W. Hutchings. Hearthstone Publishing, Oklahoma City, OK.

Prince of Darkness and *Final Warning* by Grant R. Jeffrey. Frontier Research Publications, Mississauga, ON, Canada.

Handwriting on the Wall by David Jeremiah. Word Publishers, Nashville, TN.

301 Startling Proofs & Prophecies by Peter and Paul LaLonde. Prophecy Partners, Niagara Falls, ON, Canada.

Daniel (tapes) and *International Intelligence Briefing* by Hal Lindsey. Hal Lindsey Ministries, Palos Verdes, CA.

Thru the Bible with J. Vernon McGee by J. Vernon McGee. Thomas Nelson Publishers, Nashville, TN.

The Beast of the East by Alvin Shifflett. Starburst Publishers, Lancaster, PA.

On the Edge of Eternity by Jack Van Impe. Word Publishers, Nashville, TN.

Index

A

Abed-Nego, 13, 32, 34, 48, 58, 63, 72–75
  allegations against, 74
  Azariah, 33
  Babylonian meaning, 13
  character of, 75
  Daniel's prayer partner, 48
  faith of, 81
  God who delivered, 155
  represents Israel in the Tribulation, 63
  setting a trap for, 73
  what God did for, 88
Abimelech, 20
abomination of desolation, 6, 66, 175, 251, 262, 304–5, 334–35
  antichrist will set up, 262
  definition, 6
  likened to Nebuchadnezzar's statue, 66
  set up on the wing of the Temple, 334
Abraham, 25, 231, 248, 271
  friend of God, 271
  God made a covenant, 25
abyss, 104
adoration, 40, 72
  definition, 72
adulation, 164
  definition, 164
advisers, 26, 28–34, 83, 119, 125, 154–55
alcohol, 95, 130, 282
Alexander the Great, 6, 50, 184–85, 210–15, 224, 279, 282, 309
  death of, 224
  definition, 6
Alexandria, 93, 304
  definition, 304
Americans, 152, 158, 242, 293
Ammon, 316
ancient city of Babylon, 6, 128, 176

illustration, 128
Ancient of Days
  definition, 188
  Jesus will approach the, 192
  Times of the Gentiles, 176
  will take his seat, 188
ancient of instruments, 68–70
  illustration, 70
ancient wisdom, 108
  definition, 108
angel(s)
  active during the Tribulation period, 102–3
  council of, 101, 106, 112
  definition, 69
  fallen, 56, 265, 281
  guardian, 86
  guide, comfort, and provide for the people of God, 107
  messengers of God, 112
  seven, 101
animals, 48, 102, 104, 105, 113, 118, 196, 218, 261
  sacrifice of, 218, 261
anoint, 252, 267
  definition, 252
anointed, 253
Anointed One, 259, 265, 267, 279, 290, 294, 301, 323
  definition, 290
anointing, 253
antichrist, 47, 49, 54–57, 65–66, 82–83, 111–14, 186–91, 196–99, 214–17, 260–63
  abomination of desolation, 66
  allegiance to the, 70
  beast, 82
  definition, 57
  empire, 56
  leadership of the, 111
  likened to Nebuchadnezzar, 63, 68, 80, 111
  one-world religion, 75
  Satan worship, 56
  will rule the world, 57
Antiochus the Great, 214–17,

219–20, 284–85, 288–89, 290–91, 292–24, 300–310
anti-Christian, 208, 298
anti-God, 57, 67, 75, 129, 130, 201, 214, 309
anti-Nazi, 11
anti-Semitic, 201, 214, 309
anti-Semitism, 34, 71, 152, 159
  definition, 71
apostle, 97, 112, 269, 330
  definition, 97
Arab, 25, 183–85, 196, 293, 314
Arabs, 293
Aramaic language, 29, 30, 67, 111, 129, 208, 215
archangel, 101, 103, 278, 324, 337
  definition, 103
  Gabriel, 101
  Michael, 103, 278, 324, 337
Arioch, 34, 35, 40, 41
  takes Daniel to, 40, 41
  Nebuchadnezzar, 34, 35
Armageddon, 25, 177, 191, 237, 258, 272, 276, 316, 318–19, 321
Artaxerxes, 254–55
Arthur, Kay
  on God, 9–10, 73, 164, 212
Ashpenaz, 10–13, 15–18, 21
Assyria, 4, 7, 25, 99, 239
astrologers
  ask for dream, 29
  denounce Jews, 153
  failure of, 132
  God warns against, 74, 95
  Nebuchadnezzar summons, 27–28
  occultic practice, 29
  offer to interpret first dream, 29
  were not Jews, 30
astrology, 11, 29, 98, 224
  characteristic of the new age movement, 98
  definition, 11

atonement, 253
Azariah, 12, 13, 16, 21, 33, 36
  Hebrew meaning, 13

B

Baal, 9
Babylon, 3, 5, 8, 68, 126
  city of Satan, 68
  illustration, 8
  Judah would be destroyed by, 3
  mother of harlots, 5
  rulers of, 126
Babylonian captivity, 8, 10, 49,
  64, 234
Babylonian Empire, 18
Babylonian ziggurat, 5
  illustration, 5
Battle of Armageddon, 177,
  237, 258, 276, 312, 319, 321
Baxter, Irvin, Jr., 200
beast(s)
  bear, 174, 181
  in Daniel, 19
  definition, 57
  leopard, 174, 175, 176, 183,
  184
  lion, 174, 180, 183, 196
  ten-horned, 184–85, 186,
  196, 199, 200
beautiful land, 316
Bel, 4, 9, 13
  definition, 4
believing Israel, 195, 218, 226, 328
  definition, 195
Belshazzar, King, 7, 22, 125,
  127, 128, 129, 133, 134, 135
  feast of, 128–29
  Nebuchadnezzar's
  grandson, 125, 129
  queen of, 133, 134, 135
Belteshazzar, 4, 13, 107, 108, 265
  Daniel is named, 4, 13, 107,
  108, 265
  under Nebuchadnezzar's god,
  97
Benware, Paul, 143
Bernice, 285–86
Biederwolf, William E., 220
bird, 48, 49, 100, 102, 105,
  110, 118, 119
black magic, 11, 28
  definition, 11
blaspheme, 201, 216, 245,
  311, 321

blaspheme, 129
blasphemer, 72, 128, 152, 199
  definition, 128
blitzkrieg, 289
  definition, 289
boasting, 309, 321
Booker, Richard, 57
books, 190
bottomless pit, 103, 199, 225,
  226
  definition, 103
Breese, David
  on the antichrist, 70
  on Daniel's scenario of history,
  52
  on human destiny, 188
  on reality, 157
  on understanding God, 177

C

Callinicus, Seleucus, 284, 287
  sons of, 287
Calneh
  city of, 4
captives, 12, 16, 21, 22, 41, 146
captives of Judah, 41
  definition, 41
Carlson, C. C.
  on cultic music, 69
  on end times, 320
  on mind control, 11
  on spiritual warfare, 76
  on Tribulation Period, 329
Carlson, Ron, 98
Ceraunus, Seleucus, 284, 287
chaff, 47
  definition, 47
Chaldeans, 6, 41, 71–75, 108
chariots, 144, 192, 314
  definition, 314
chasten, 222
  definition, 222
cherubim, 274
  definition, 274
China, 144, 156, 319, 321
Christ Jesus, 14, 43, 97, 201,
  236, 269, 275, 327, 331, 336
church
  definition, 195
church age, 329, 342
Church, J. R., 202
city of God, 4, 247
claws, 118, 119, 196
cleansed, 219, 261, 315

definition, 219
Cleopatra, 292, 293, 296–97
club of Rome, 57
Combs, Jim, 247
concubines, 26, 128, 133, 285
  definition, 128, 285
confession, 235, 236
  to admit one's guilt, 236
confession of faith, 59
  definition, 59
confirm, 260, 312
  definition, 260
consummation of history, 52
  definition, 52
convictions, 5
co-regent, 125, 126, 145, 177,
  283, 341
  definition, 125
council on foreign relations, 57
counterculture, 11
  definition, 11
covenant
  definition, 3, 260
  of God, 304
crucifixion, 259, 327
  definition, 327
cudgels, 46
  definition, 46
cults, 33, 155
cuneiform, 7
  definition, 7
curses, 241
  definition, 241
Cush, 4
Cyrus, King, 22
  as horn, 209
  parents of, 127, 146

D

darkness, 39, 76, 101, 103, 152,
  178, 327
daughter of king of south, 284
David, 25, 26
Day of Jacob's Trouble, 117
Dead Sea Scrolls, 6, 7, 207
  definition, 6
Decker, Ed, 98
defilement, 175, 220, 305
  definition, 220
De Haan, M. R.
  on angels, 275
  on the end of age, 110
  on Gabriel's visitation, 248,
  270–71

on the utopian millennium of
  peace, 334
delivered, 21, 22, 122, 243,
  307, 325, 326
  definition, 9
demon possession, 312
demonic spirits, 265, 312
  definition, 265
demons, 265, 270, 272, 281
Demy, Timothy
  on the Antichrist, 199
  on Antiochus Epiphanes, 305
  on an end-time prophecy, 324
  on prophetic goals of the
    seventy weeks, 252—53
desecrating, 140
  definition, 140
despotic, 125
  definition, 125
Deuteronomy, 241, 242
dew, 104, 111, 113, 139
DeYoung, Jimmy, 335
discernment, 39
  definition, 39
dispatches, 72
  definition, 72
dispensation of grace, 329
  definition, 329
divided nature, 27
divine qualities, 37
divinely, 3, 330, 337
dominion, 36, 48, 92, 113, 168,
  193
  definition, 92, 193
Duair, 65
Dura, plain of, 64, 65, 67
Dyer, Charles H.
  on the Antichrist, 313, 316
  on Daniel's visions, 194
  on factionalism, 56
  on Time of the End, 330
dynasties, 284
  definition, 284

E

eagle, 105, 118, 180, 196
  wings like, 180
earthly kingdoms, 47, 168, 198
earthly life of Jesus, 110, 258
earthly minded, 136
  definition, 36
ecumenical, 70
Edom, 316
education

of Nebuchadnezzar's royal
  captives, 12
Egypt
  Antichrist overtakes, 318
  king of, 292
  pyramids of, 93
Elam, 209
elect, the, 92, 96, 298, 325, 334
  definition, 96, 334
emasculate, 122, 236
  definition, 236
Emerson, Wallace
  on Daniel's first vision, 176
  on great sea, 178
  on leopard, 184
  on Russia, 182
enchanters, 27, 28, 132
End of the Age, 42, 56, 96,
  112, 156, 191, 307, 311
  demonic activity, 56
  Gabriel talks about, 296
  Paul writes about, 152
enlightenment, 39, 98
  definition, 39
Epiphanes, Antiochus, 175, 214,
  220, 296, 303
Epiphanes, Antiochus Theos,
  284, 285
Epiphanes, Ptolemy, 284, 288,
  289, 292, 293
Epp, Theodore H.
  on Daniel's courage, 15
  on Daniel's prayer life, 38
  on the Holy Spirit of God, 235
  on a prayer life, 157
Erech
  city of, 4
esteemed, 276, 311
Euergetes, Ptolemy, 284, 285,
  286, 298
eunuchs, 10, 137
  definition, 10
Euphrates River, 4, 103, 144,
  145, 319
  definition, 103
Europe, 25, 53, 56, 200, 260
European Union, 200, 259, 260
evangelists, 333
  definition, 333
everlasting contempt, 327, 328
everlasting dominion, 113, 119,
  122, 193
everlasting kingdom, 92, 122,
  203
everlasting life, 327, 328

definition, 328
everlasting righteousness, 250,
  252–53
evidence, 81, 92, 243
evil spirits, 28, 272, 276
evince, 246
  definition, 246
exalts, 116
execution, 34, 152, 156
exile, 117, 151, 156
exiles from Judah, 159, 160
expositions, 330
  definition, 330
Ezekiel, 6, 251
  definition, 6

F

factionalism
  definition, 56
faith, 81
fallen angels, 56, 103, 265, 272,
  281
  definition, 265
False Prophet, 63, 71, 92, 298,
  307, 312
  definition, 70
false prophet(s), 3, 92, 96, 112,
  298
  definition, 3
  during the Tribulation Period,
    92
  in End of the Age, 96, 112
fasting, 162, 234, 235, 246,
  272, 273
  definition, 162
  demonstrates, 162
  deny himself, 234, 235
fear, 120, 168, 221
  definition, 168
Feast of Passover, 301
Ferguson, Sinclair B.
  on God's words, 237
  on the last days, 326
  on Nebuchadnezzar's demise,
    107
  on the perpetual conflict of
    the King of Darkness and
    King of Light, 152
  on the Tribulation Period,
    332
fierce features, 224, 249
  definition, 224
fiery furnace
  four men in, 84

illustration of, 80
Nebuchadnezzar threatens
with, 69, 73
ordered seven times hotter,
79, 80
Shadrach, Meshach, and
Abed-Nego come out of, 85
Shadrach, Meshach, and
Abed-Nego inside, 82, 83
final seven years, 260
fire, 189
flute, 68, 87, 153
definition, 68
food, 12, 15–18
Daniel declines the king's,
15–18
foreign, 312, 313
definition, 313
foreign god, 312, 313
foreordained, 146
definition, 146
foreshadows, 129, 166, 185,
279
definition, 166
forgiveness, 139, 141, 163, 239,
240, 247
definition, 239
fortresses, 287, 312–313
fortune-telling, 97, 98
four horns, 224, 279
four horsemen of the
Apocalypse, 102
definition, 102
fragments, 192
definition, 192
frauds, 30, 136
definition, 30
friends, Daniel's, 13, 15, 16, 18,
28, 36–37, 63, 71, 75
Froese, Arno
on Daniel's vision, 268
on the Gentile world, 139
on the mystery Babylon, 68
on the Lord Jesus Christ, 14
fruit, 99, 100, 102
fulfilled, 259, 277, 291, 331
definition, 331

G

Gabriel, angel, 101, 217, 221,
222
visits Daniel, 101, 217, 221,
222
Gangel, Kenneth O.

on Daniel's friends, 159
on Daniel's vision, 209
on Egypt and Russia, 315
on the foolishness and
wickedness of a pagan king,
137
on the warrior king, 94
on the writing of the book of
Daniel, 67
Garden of Eden, 4
Gaza, 287, 288
antichrist in, 287
definition, 287
Gentile kingdoms, 54, 60, 187,
214, 324
Gentile world government, 43,
45–47, 50, 53–56, 58, 60,
120, 193
gifts, 136, 145
given up, 284
definition, 284
global cooperation, 55, 201
global ethic, 55
global identification, 55
global management, 55
global religion, 70, 77
global rules, 55
global society, 12
global sovereignty, 55
global standards, 55
global trade, 55, 226, 227
globalism, 55, 225
meaning of, 55
glorious holy mountain, 292,
319
glorious land, 214, 291, 292, 316
definition, 214
goat, 207
attacks ram, 213
Gabriel explains, 221, 223
horns of, 210–11
God
anger of, 240, 244, 252
attributes of, 37, 38
blessing of, 4, 15
characteristics of, 13, 239, 243
control of, 38–39
Daniel praises, 38–39
Daniel's faith in, 4, 15–16, 35,
161
dominion and power from, 48
judgment and grace of,
110–11
justice of, 57, 121, 122
makes covenants, 236

name of, 112, 118, 201, 247
Nebuchadnezzar's
understanding of, 108, 113
sovereignty of, 9, 138, 310
wisdom and power of, 37, 40
Word of, 83, 87, 164, 177, 185,
191, 202, 212, 233–34, 237,
274, 277, 306, 329
God-fearing, 59
definition, 59
God of heaven, 36, 37, 48, 96,
97, 110, 118, 311
definition, 36
gods, 33, 74, 86
God's calendar, 202–3
God's standard of punishment,
232
God's statue, 7, 44, 45, 60, 125,
149, 173, 175, 183, 208
body parts of, 44, 60
illustration #5, 45
Gog and Magog
definition, 182
gold, statue's, 49, 64
gold chain, 145
golden lampstand, 130, 189
definition, 130
illustration #15, 131
Gowan, Donald E.
on Darius's letter, 167
on the fulfillment of
Nebuchadnezzar's dream,
120
grace, 19, 115, 122
definition, 149
grace of God, 14, 19, 78, 111,
115
definition, 78
Graham, Billy
on angels, 107, 165, 279
on Armageddon, 272
on spiritual warfare, 281
Great Tribulation, 117, 325,
326
Great White Throne Judgment,
328
definition, 328
greater, 19, 121, 175, 196, 321
definition, 196
Greece, 50, 57, 93, 174–75,
185, 210–11
as goat, 211, 276
prince of, 276
Greek Empire, 51, 213, 214,
224, 225, 282–83

illustration #8, 51
Greek word, 3, 67
Greek worship, 304, 305
Greene, Oliver B.
  on Daniel's weakness, 275
  on God's power, 39
  on Time of the End, 333–34
  on the wages of sin, 295
guardian angels, 86
  definition, 86

H

Hagee, John
  on American education, 12
  on the Antichrist, 187
  on Christians, 202
  on military weaponry, 46
  on Russia, 315
Halff, Charles,
  on the number ten, 17
Hall, J. G.
  on Darius, 146
Halley, Henry H.
  on angels, 271
  on the Babylonian captivity,
    166
Ham, 4
Hananiah, 12, 13, 16, 21, 33,
    36
  Hebrew meaning, 13
hand, 130, 131, 141, 270
handed over, 203, 204, 285, 302
harp, 68, 69, 87, 153
  definition, 68
Harper's Bible Dictionary, 93
Hassideans, 307
  definition, 307
Hayford, Jack W.
  on Daniel in Babylon, 5
  on living out biblical
    principles, 153
health, 17, 235
Hebrew names, 12–14, 36
Hebrew word, 3, 215, 250
hedge of protection, 104, 164
hell, 86, 94, 242
  definition, 94
herald, 68–69
  definition, 68
herald, Nebuchadnezzar's, 68
high priest, 268, 297, 298, 321
  Alcimus, 306
  Caiaphas, 91
  definition, 268

Hindson, Ed
  on angels as watchers, 111
  on the "image of the beast,"
    305
  on the unholy trinity, 198
Hinduism, 98
  definition, 98
historical, 7, 63, 91, 119, 173,
    176, 222, 243, 279, 280,
    323, 332
  definition, 173
historical errors, 10
history, world, 126
Hitchcock, Mark
  on the nation of Egypt, 317
  on world empires, 52
Hitler, 11, 182, 199, 276, 308
Hocking, David
  on leopard, 184–85
  on lion, 181
  on Messianic kingdom, 336
  on Time of the End, 176
holiness, 163
  definition, 15
holy, 244
  definition, 244
Holy God, 107, 130, 150–51
holy people, 226, 249, 332
holy place, 251, 305
Holy Spirit, 19, 59, 64, 81, 84,
    97, 98, 108, 196, 197, 198,
    235, 333
  definition, 97
  omniscient vision of, 197
  was working through Daniel,
    108, 151
hope, 44, 81, 117, 323
horn(s)
  Antichrist, 191, 299
  definition, 68
  fourth kingdom, 196
  little, 186, 187, 191, 196,
    214, 215, 216, 296, 299
  ten, 184, 185, 186, 196, 199, 200
horoscope(s), 28, 30, 36
  definition, 30
  occultic practice, 30
house of David, 43
  definition, 43
Huey, F. B., Jr., 143
humanistic, 70
humanity, 96, 178, 319
humility, 40, 141, 162, 235
Hussein, Saddam, 94, 185
Hutchings, Noah

on America, 181
on the beasts of chapter 7 of
  Daniel, 211
on the last generation, 177
on leopard, 184
on millennium, 192
Hutchings, N. W., 328–29

I

Ice, Thomas
  on the Antichrist, 199
  on Antiochus Epiphanes, 305
  on an end-time prophecy, 324
  on prophetic goals of the
    seventy weeks, 252—53
ideology, 180
  definition, 180
idolatry, 114, 129, 140, 166,
    232
image of the Antichrist, 86, 286
image of the Beast, 6, 70, 214,
    305, 334
  definition, 6
images, 95, 98, 286
indoctrinating, 11
  definition, 11
iniquities, 244
  definition, 244
iniquity, committed, 236
iniquity, reconciliation, 250, 252
inner self, 12
  definition, 12
insight, 22, 38, 135, 187, 248,
    268
inspired by God, 3, 207
instruments, musical, 67, 68,
    69, 70, 261
intelligence, 135
intercession, 235
International Court of Justice,
    55
International Criminal Court,
    55, 320
International Monetary Fund,
    55
International Political Entity,
    199
International Task Force, 316
interpretation, Daniel's, 52,
    108, 114, 119, 142
intrigue, 180, 296
Iran, 183
Iraq, 6, 183, 184
iron, 44–47, 50–55, 174

Ironside, H. A.
  on the days to come, 228
  on Nebuchadnezzar's dream, 94
  on the Time of the End, 66
  on a warning to the unsaved, 135
Ishtar, 244
Ishtar Gate, 93, 94
  definition, 94
  illustration #13, 94
Islam, 75, 156, 293
Isle of Patmos, 177, 268
  definition, 177
Israel
  angel talks about, 291–92
  captivity of, 41, 146
  in control of Jerusalem, 247
  divided into two kingdoms, 6, 27
  establishment of Northern Kingdom, 25, 231
  people of, 4, 243, 325
  twelve tribes of, 25, 27
  UFOs in, 100, 281

J

Jacob, 20, 25, 40, 231, 311
Jacob's Trouble, Time of, 117, 327
Jason, 297
Jeffrey, Grant R.
  on the Antichrist, 57, 310
  on archaeological discovery, 12
  on Armageddon, 319
  on first day of Nisan, 257
  on the prophecies of Daniel, 263
  on satanism, 313
  on a special anointing, 253
  on ten kingdoms, 200
  on the Times of the Gentiles, 186
  on world gentile rule, 46
Jehoiakim, King, 7, 10, 12, 21
Jehovah, followers of, 36
Jehovah God, 36, 40, 59
Jeremiah, 7
Jeremiah, David
  on cultic music, 69
  on end times, 320
  on mind control, 11
  on spiritual warfare, 76
  on Tribulation Period, 329
Jeroboam, 26, 27

Jerome, 286
  definition, 286
Jerusalem,
  capital of Palestinian people, 27, 49
  Daniel was born in, 4
  Nebuchadnezzar besieges, 7
  rebuilding, 25, 253, 254, 255, 261, 262, 335
Jewish kingdoms
  illustration #4, 26
Joseph, 20, 161
Josephus, 6
Joyner, Rick
  on trances, 95
  on visions, 20
Judah
  desolation of, 246, 252
  faults of, 239
  God's displeasure with, 9
  Jehoiakim is king of, 7, 9
  people of, 3, 4, 231, 237
  Southern Kingdom of Israel, 6, 8, 25
judgment seat, 79, 328
  definition, 328

K

King James Bible Commentary
  on the courage of Shadrach, Meshach, and Abed-Nego, 74, 86
  on God's honor, 249
  on the sons of Seleucus II, 287
  on understanding Daniel's prophecies, 333
Kingdom of Everlasting Righteousness, 252, 253
  definition, 252
kingdom theology, 203, 253
Kuwait, 6

L

LaHaye, Tim
  on angels as watchers, 111
  on Nebuchadnezzar's vision, 26
  on prophecies of the End Times, 269
  on the writing of the book of Daniel, 207
Lalonde, Peter and Paul
  on the formative stages of one

empire, 54
  on scattering of Jews, 10
Lamb
  definition, 186
Lamb's Book of Life, 325, 328
  definition, 325
language, 30, 67, 129
Laodice, 285–86
last days, 29, 42, 72, 74, 182, 197, 326
  definition, 74
latter days, 42, 271, 274, 314, 323
  definition, 271
law, 241
  definition, 241
Law of God, 15
  definition, 15
Law of the Medes and Persians, 152, 154, 155, 158, 167
Law of Moses, 238, 240–42
  definition, 240
leopard, 175, 176, 183, 184, 185, 196, 202, 206
Libyans, 318
light, 39, 134, 153
  definition, 134
Lindsey, Hal
  on God's protection, 64
  on hostage taking, 10
  on war, 179, 182
lion, 175, 176, 180, 181, 183, 203
lions, den of, 149, 158, 161, 160, 162–63, 165, 166–67
  Daniel in, 149–69
  illustration #16, 162
literature, 4, 11, 18, 39
Living God, 87, 139, 164, 167, 168
  definition, 164
Longman, Tremper, III
  on Antiochus III, 288
  on God's giving, 19
  on Nebuchadnezzar's advisers, 27
longsuffering, 128, 129
love, 40, 68, 100, 129, 235
Luther, Martin, 107
lyre, 68, 87, 153
  definition, 68

M

Maccabean Period, 305, 307, 308

Maccabees, 214, 217, 220, 307, 308
Maclaren, Alexander, 19
magicians, 27, 28, 95
marduk, 9, 93
  illustration #3, 9
mark of the Beast, 77, 82, 114, 202
  definition, 82, 202
marriage supper, 336
marriage supper of the Lamb
  definition, 336
McGee, J. Vernon
  on Daniel, Hananiah, Mishael, and Azariah's captivity, 13
  on the last kingdom, 179
  on scepter of universe, 43
Medes and Persians, 50, 125, 127, 144–45
  kingdom of, 50
Medo-Persian captivity, 64
Medo-Persian Empire, 51, 173, 212, 274
  illustration, 51
  as ram, 229
men of God, 3
Mene, 142
mercy
  definition, 239
Merodach, 9, 126
Meshach, 13, 32, 34, 48, 58, 63, 72–75
  allegations against, 74
  Babylonian meaning, 13
  character of, 75
  Daniel's prayer partner, 48
  the faith of, 81
  what God did for, 88
  the God who delivered, 155
  Mishael, 33
  represents Israel in the Tribulation, 63
  setting a trap for, 73
messiah
  definition, 57
messianic Jews, 328
messianic kingdom
  definition, 336
metaphysics, 98
Michael, 103, 221, 273, 277, 324–25
  definition, 324
Middle East, 130, 180, 181, 185, 200, 314
military juggernaut

definition, 56
millennium, God's, 42, 192, 252, 323, 327, 328, 334–35
  definition, 192, 252
Miller, Stephen R.
  on angels and future events, 331
  on Daniel's diet, 17
  on Daniel's vision, 189
  on the persecution of the Jewish people, 303
  on Ptolemy IV Philometor, 288
  on the Tribulation, 326
millstone
  definition, 103
mind control, 11, 69
miracles, 92, 208, 243, 298
Mishael, 12, 13, 16, 21, 33, 36
  Hebrew meaning, 13
misrule
  definition, 195
Moab, 315–16
monotheism
  definition, 14
monotheistic family, 310–31
moral, 3
Morris, Henry M.
  on Christianity and persecution, 72
  on the end of the antichrist, 191
  on the fulfillment of prophecies, 197
  on Nebuchadnezzar's dream, 126
Moses, 84, 231, 240–41
Most High God, 84, 85, 86, 92, 122, 137, 164
  definition, 85
mother of Harlots, 5, 130
Mount of Transfiguration
  definition, 84
mountain, rock as big as, 47
music, 68–71, 87, 153, 261
Muslims, 245, 317
myriads, 275
Mystery Babylon, 68
mystery(ies), 43, 98, 133, 134, 173
  revealer of, 42, 43

N

Nabonidus, 125–27, 132–33, 145, 177

nabonidus cylinder
  definition, 6
Nabopolassar, 6, 126
NATO, 183
Nazi beliefs, 11
Nazi government, 11
Nelson Study Bible, The
  on Alexander's conquest, 211
  on Nebuchadnezzar's dreams, 32
  on the Prince of the Kingdom of Persia, 273
new age beliefs, 33
new age cults, 155
new age movement, 33, 98
  characteristics, 98
new age teaching, 311
new agers
  definition, 33
new world empire, 127
new world government, 200
new world order, 53, 54, 55, 57, 202
Nimrod, 4, 5, 67, 68
Noah, 4, 67, 243
nondescript, 209
North, 283–87, 294, 296, 302
North Atlantic Treaty Organization (NATO), 183
northern kingdom, 6, 8, 25, 26, 27, 231, 238
Nubians, 318

O

oblation
  definition, 12
occult, 5, 281, 313
occultic, 28, 30
occultism, 33, 98
occultists, 133
offering and incense
  definition, 58
Old Roman Empire, 52, 53, 55, 173, 174, 184, 187, 214, 294
  definition, 53
  illustration #9, 52
Old Testament Saints, 327, 328, 337
  definition, 327
omens
  definition, 11, 19
omnipotent, 37, 38, 87
  definition, 37

omniscient, 37, 143, 197
definition, 37, 197
one hundred years, 263, 293
one-world government, 55, 56, 86, 200, 205, 214, 317
Onias III, 297, 298
Oppert, 65
ordained
definition, 268
Owens, William L.
on Satan and evil, 265, 272

P

pagan king, 9, 15, 77, 84, 91, 110, 137, 167
definition, 9
pagan religions, 5, 122
paganism, 75, 87, 133
parable
definition, 17
parade of two world powers, 5
parallel, 316, 330
Patmos, Isle of, 177, 268
Paul, 20, 40, 72, 95, 112, 152, 266, 333
Pentecost, 29, 84, 326
definition, 84
Peres, 143
persecution, 17, 72, 107, 111, 157, 201, 218–20, 303, 323
Persia, 7, 126, 127, 143, 209, 211, 224, 273, 276, 277
four kings in, 272, 320
prince of, 273, 276, 327
Persian Empire, 209, 211
Persian Gulf, 6
personification
definition, 272
Peter, 29, 84, 95, 157, 223, 266
petition, 159
Petra, 106, 166, 218, 316, 328
definition, 166, 218
pharaoh, 20, 120, 121
Philadelphus, Ptolemy, 284–85
Phillips, John
on God-breathed text, 215
on Nebuchadnezzar's contempt toward Daniel, 77
on Nebuchadnezzar's psychics, 28
on the temptation for food, 15
on terror stalking the earth, 120
Philometor, Ptolemy, 297–98, 300–303

Philopator, Demetrius, 296
Philopator, Ptolemy, 284, 288–89
Philopator, Seleucus, 284, 295, 296
Pilate's wife, 20
plain of Dura, 64, 65, 67
plaster
definition, 130
Polybius, 288
polygamist
definition, 128
polytheism
definition, 14
postincarnate, 266
praise, 37, 40, 86, 121, 129, 235
prayer
changes things, 37
Daniel's need of, 37, 40, 156, 232
deliberate, humble, and sincere, 235
more than talking to God, 235
of praise and thanksgiving, 37
in private, 156, 267
Satan hates men of, 157
seven biblical reasons for unanswered, 239
precursor
definition, 296
prefects, 154
prefigures the Antichrist, 175, 296
preincarnate
definition, 84
preparation day
definition, 161
Pre-Tribulation, 60, 175, 197
Price, Randall, 246, 252–53
pride, 114, 116, 121, 138, 141, 288
characteristics, 116
prince of Bel, 4, 13
prince of the covenant, 297, 298
Prince of Darkness
definition, 310
Prince of the host
definition, 217
Prince of Persia, 273, 276, 324
Prince of Princes, 226, 227, 249
Procession Street, 93
prophetic, 176, 203, 226, 256
definition, 173
psaltery, 68, 73, 76, 87, 153
definition, 68

psychics, 28, 39, 97
Ptolemy I, 284
Pulpit Commentary, The
on the power of a higher God, 33
on true religion, 68
purified
definition, 333
purple, 94, 132, 136, 145
definition, 145

Q

Queen Mother of Belshazzar, 134–35, 151

R

Ramirez, Frank
on martyrdom, 157
on an offer of hope, 117
on rulers' responsibilities, 105
rapacious
definition, 182
Raphia, 288
rapture, 60, 114, 115, 117
before Tribulation Period, 175, 197
Reagan, David
on Daniel's dreams and visions, 56
on Jews regathering to their land, 323
rebellion, 5, 95, 237, 289, 290
reconsecrated, 219
refined, 189, 333
definition, 333
Rehoboam, 26
reincarnation, 98
repent, 3, 115, 118, 119, 132, 231, 232, 241, 242
repentance, 115, 118, 162, 232, 238
repented
definition, 118
resurrection of condemnation, 327, 337
resurrection of life, 327, 336, 337
revenge, 282, 285, 286
reverence, 37, 168
revival, 203, 313, 333
Reynolds, Ralph Vincent, 140
Rice, John R.
on the blessing of God, 15

on the destruction of the
temple, 259
rich man, 94
rock
supernaturally cut, 46
symbol of Jesus, 47
Roman Empire, Old, 53, 55,
60, 173, 174, 185, 214,
294
definition, 53
royal delicacies, 14, 18
royal family, 4, 10, 12, 125
royal occasion
definition, 81
royal palace, 115
rulers of Babylon, 126
rulers of darkness, 101
Russia, 182–84, 196, 314,
315, 319

S

Sabbath, 161, 216, 231, 232,
251, 304
definition, 304
sackcloth, 163, 234–35
definition, 234
sacred, 101, 128, 129, 141
definition, 128
sacred vessels, 129, 141
sacrilege, 128, 140, 220
definition, 128
Saladin
definition, 293
sanctuary, 217, 219, 246, 259,
304
definition, 219
Sanhedrin, 101, 261
definition, 101
satanic, 5, 70, 73, 75, 98, 199,
328, 329
definition, 73
satanism, 14
satrap, 66, 149, 150, 151, 153,
154, 160, 161
definition, 66, 149
Saudi Arabia, 156
saved, 91, 190, 328, 329
definition, 91
scenario
definition, 52
scepter
definition, 43
Scipio, 94
Scofield, C. I.

on the date the book of
Daniel was written, 208
on the millennial kingdom, 57
on the times of the Gentiles,
43, 49
Scopas, 290–91
sea, the great, 178, 179, 183
seal of God, 168
seal of the Living God
definition, 102
sealed up, 207, 215
definition, 215
seers, 3
Second Coming of Christ, 25,
42, 44, 57, 186–87, 217,
259, 294, 304
Sekulow, Jay A., 14
Seleucus I, 284
self-exaltation, 116, 226, 237
definition, 116
separation, 14, 15, 333
definition, 15
Septuagint, 6, 63, 82
definition, 6
seraphim
definition, 274
Seventieth Week of Daniel, 260,
327
seventy years, 143, 231, 233,
234, 244, 247, 250, 252
Daniel reads, 244
Gabriel announces, 250, 252
Jeremiah warns, 231
seven wonders of the ancient
world, 93, 144
Shadrach, 13, 32, 34, 48, 58,
63, 72–75
allegations against, 74
Babylonian meaning, 13
character of, 75
Daniel's prayer partner, 48
faith of, 81
God who delivered, 155
Hananiah, 33
represents Israel in the
Tribulation, 63
setting a trap for, 73
what God did for, 88
Shamanism
definition, 98
shame, 238, 239, 251, 328
Shifflett, Alvin M., 335
shining shores of eternity
definition, 157
Showers, Renald E.

on the Babylonian captives,
234
on God's sovereignty, 193
on Onias, 298
sickle
definition, 103
Sidon, city of, 291
signet ring
definition, 161
signs, 92, 96, 130, 179
definition, 92
sin, 79, 86, 139, 142, 190, 225,
231–32, 239–40, 243,
245, 247, 252, 260, 273
definition, 252
sinister schemes, 224, 296,
312–13
definition, 224
sins of commission
definition, 237
sins of omission
definition, 237
Smith, Uriah
on being esteemed, 249
on dating Jerusalem's
captivity, 7
on loving God, 245–46
on Medo-Persian rule, 210
on saints' rule, 195
on seal of God, 168
Smith's Bible Dictionary, 65
Smiting Stone, 58
soldiers, Nebuchadnezzar's, 81,
82, 85, 93, 163
Solomon, King, 20, 25, 26
death of, 25, 26
failures of, 26
son of man, 189, 192, 193,
195, 221
definition, 221
soothsayers, 33, 41, 95, 97,
131, 134
sorcerers, 27, 28, 39
south, 27, 183, 283–85, 296
in Bible, 283–85, 296
sovereign, 9, 85, 139, 291, 332
sovereignty, 55, 120, 138, 140,
182, 193, 262, 310
spirit world, 265, 266, 267,
274, 281
definition, 265
Stanley, Charles
on values, 16–17
on what should remain
private, 267

stern-faced, 224
Stortz, Rodney
  on Alexander's rise to power,
    212
  on fulfilled prophecy, 291–92
  on a message to us, 337
  on weak wise men of Babylon,
    31
subdues
  definition, 199
subjugation, 7, 199
  definition, 7
substance, 81, 177
  definition, 177
subtle, 35, 153
  definition, 153
subversive
  definition, 152
subvert
  definition, 11
subverted, 11
Sudan, 318, 321
supernaturally
  definition, 46
supplications, 234, 245–46,
  249
  definition, 234
sustaining
  definition,149
sustaining grace, 149
Swindoll, Charles R.
  on the battle of Armageddon,
    319
  on crowns of authority, 139
  on God's sovereign plan, 85

T

talent, 286
talking to God, 235, 247
Talmud, 101, 119, 257, 263
  definition, 101
taxation, 295
tekel, 142, 143
  "weigh," 143
Temple
  definition, 9
  illustration of, 306
Temple in Jerusalem, 280, 305
  illustration #17, 306
Temple Mount, 245, 261, 262,
  316, 324
  definition, 262
temple treasures
  definition, 9

Ten Commandments, 241, 245
ten-day test, 17, 107
ten thousand times ten
  thousand, 189, 190, 325
  definition, 190
testimony, 83, 91, 92, 115, 125,
  326, 329
theophany
  definition, 84
thermonuclear devices
  definition, 46
thoughts, 42, 95, 117, 194,
  205, 243, 245
  definition, 95
threshing floor
  definition, 47
throne, God's, 188, 190, 191,
  194
Tigris River, 267, 331
Time of the Indignation, 217,
  331
  definition, 222
Time of Jacob's Trouble, 116, 327
Time of the End, 220, 222,
  226, 308, 314, 324, 327,
  333
Time of Great Trouble, 337
Times of the Gentiles
  definition, 25
  end of, 42, 192, 222, 314,
    322
Titles of the Antichrist, 225,
  260
Tracy, Edward
  on ideology, 180
  on Russia, 182
traditional, 176, 182, 184, 208,
  213, 263
  definition, 176
trample and crush, 198, 199
  definition, 199
trance, 95, 222
  definition, 95
transgression
  definition, 218, 252
transported, 209, 266
treason, 32, 300, 300, 308
tree in Nebuchadnezzar's
  dream, 100–120
  cut down, 104
Tribulation Period, 49, 57, 60,
  63, 70, 71, 82, 83, 86, 102
Tribulation Saints, 195, 197,
  218, 328, 336
  definition, 195

Trilateral Commission, 57
Trinity, 59, 108, 192, 198
  definition, 59
true prophet, 3, 96, 206
  definition, 96
turbans
  definition, 81
two witnesses, 99, 300, 326,
  328, 333
  definition, 328

U

UFO, 100, 281
Ulai Canal, 209, 221
unanswered prayers, 79
understanding
  definition, 134
Unger, Merrill F.
  on Antiochus, 293
  on Daniel's death, 160
  on historical errors, 10
  on visitation of God, 133
Union Gospel Press, 128
  on Belshazzar, 128
  on Daniel's honesty, 151
  on third ruler, 132
United Nations , 49, 53, 54, 55,
  60, 187, 214, 262, 320
United Religions, 201
United States of America
  (USA), 200
usurpation
  definition, 195
utopian millennium
  definition, 334

V

Van Impe, Jack
  on culture war against
    Christians, 12
  on expositions of Daniel, 330
  on global convergence, 187
vegetables
  Daniel and his friends receive,
    18, 19
  Daniel asks for, 16
vessels, 128, 129, 130, 139,
  140, 141, 142, 233, 294, 296
vision of the Anointed One,
  267, 301, 323
vision of the antichrist, 188, 219
vision of the future, 209, 211,
  212, 213

visions
  definition, 95
  of the four beasts, 19
  of my head, 95, 99, 100, 193, 194, 205
  of ram and goat, 19, 207, 221, 248, 249, 290
visions and dreams, 18, 19, 20, 95
  definition, 19

W

wall, writing on, 141, 146, 149, 150, 173
Walvoord, John F.
  on Alexander, 213
  on Nebuchadnezzar, 76
  on the Second Coming, 169
  on Syria, 296–97
war against Christ, 82, 205, 272
war against the saints, 197, 204, 307
war between God and Satan, 272
war between South and North, 285
war on God's people, 312
war on the Jews, 312
warlike
  definition, 182
water, Daniel asks for, 16
web of control
  definition, 11
week of years, 202, 251
Wesley, John, 78
Whitcomb, John C.
  on Babylonian music, 69
  on Daniel, 151, 310

on Daniel and his fellow captives, 35
  on the great tribulation, 326
  on Meshach, Shadrach, and Abed-Nego, 83
White, John, 242–43
whole earth
  definition, 198
wickedness, 3, 137, 216, 224, 243, 318
Wilson, A. Edwin, 66
winds, four, 178, 79, 183, 213, 282
winds of the earth
  definition, 102
winds of heaven, 178–79, 183, 213, 282
wine
  Belshezzar's, 127, 128, 146
  Daniel declines, 137, 267
wings, four, 183, 184
wisdom
  definition, 134
wise men, 4, 12, 22, 28, 34, 40, 41, 96–98, 107–9, 113, 114, 132, 133, 134
witchcraft, 33, 98, 265
Wood, Leon
  on fury and strength, 211
  on plotting to kill Daniel, 160
  on the resurrection of the saints, 337
  on saints, 195
  on the wise men, 34
wonders
  definition, 92
  signs and, 92, 96, 122, 168–69

Word of God, 83, 87, 164, 177–85, 191, 202, 212, 233–34, 237, 274, 277, 306, 329
World Book Encyclopedia, 11
World Gentile Rule, 46
world government, 45
world history, 126
world kingdoms, 50, 57, 64, 125, 173, 208
writing on wall, 141, 146, 149, 150, 173
Wycliffe Bible Commentary
  on the Anointed One, 259
  on the antichrist, 215
  on circumstances at court, 99
  on Egypt, 280
  on Nebuchadnezzar's vision, 111
  on the separated ones, 309

X

Xerxes, 281, 282

Y

years, 250–63
  definition, 250
yoga
  definition, 98

Z

Zeus, 93, 105, 217, 305, 311
zither, 68
zodiac, 29, 30, 224
  definition, 29